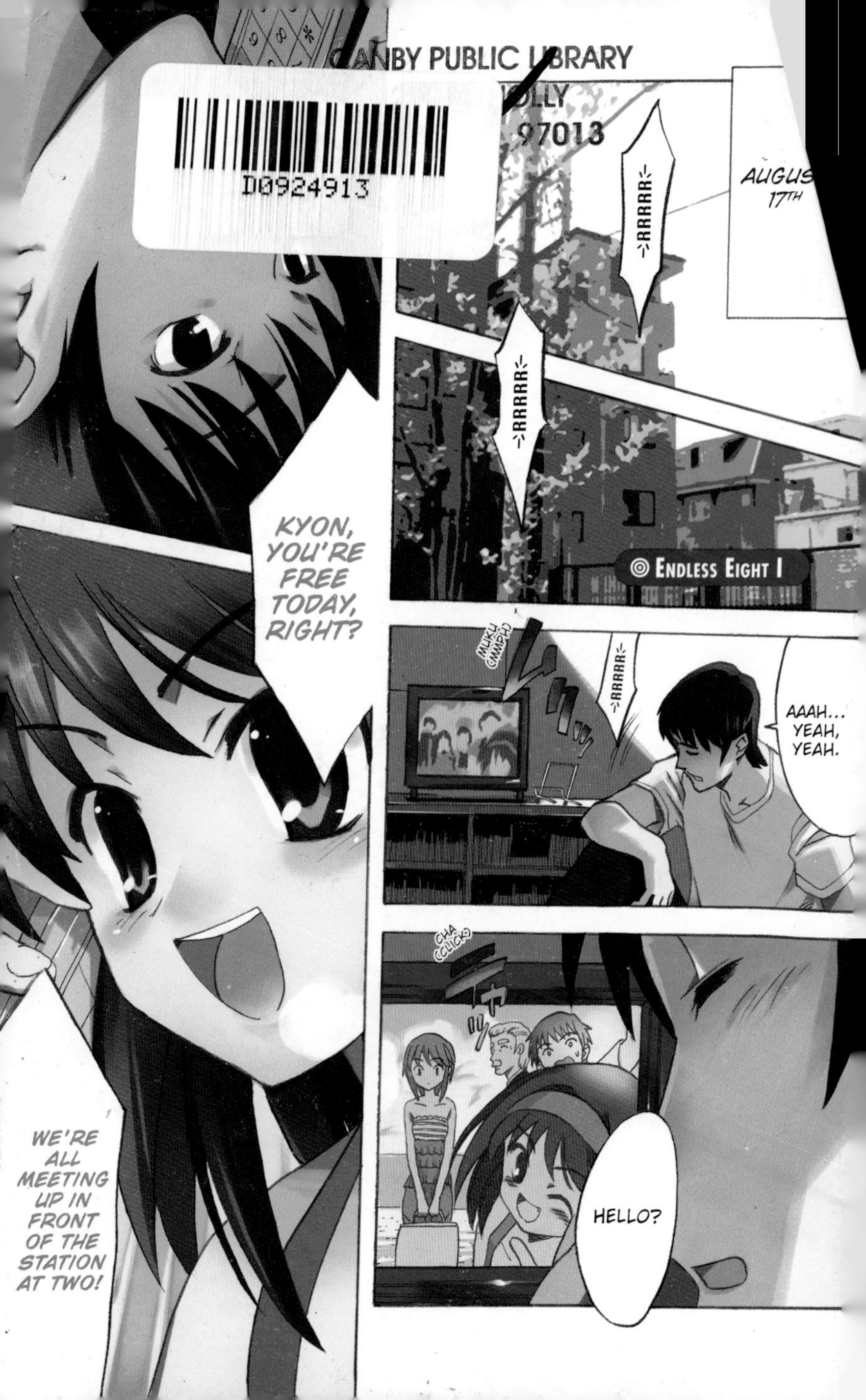
AUGUS 17TH
-RRRRR-
-RRRRR-
◎ ENDLESS EIGHT I
-RRRRR-
MUKU (MMPH)
AAAH... YEAH, YEAH.
CHA (CLICK)
HELLO?
KYON, YOU'RE FREE TODAY, RIGHT?
WE'RE ALL MEETING UP IN FRONT OF THE STATION AT TWO!

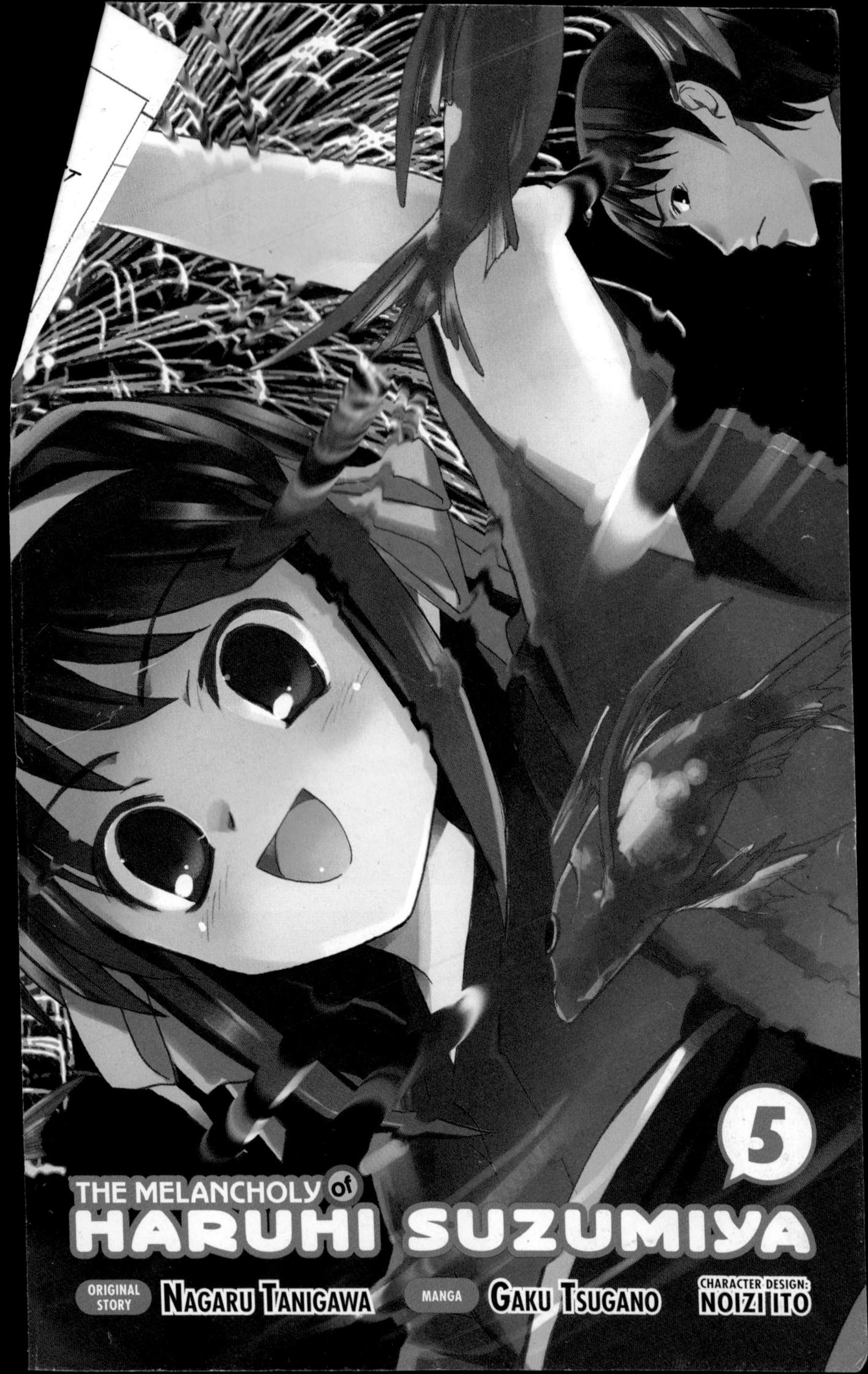
5
THE MELANCHOLY of
HARUHI SUZUMIYA
ORIGINAL STORY
NAGARU TANIGAWA
MANGA
GAKU TSUGANO
CHARACTER DESIGN:
NOIZI ITO

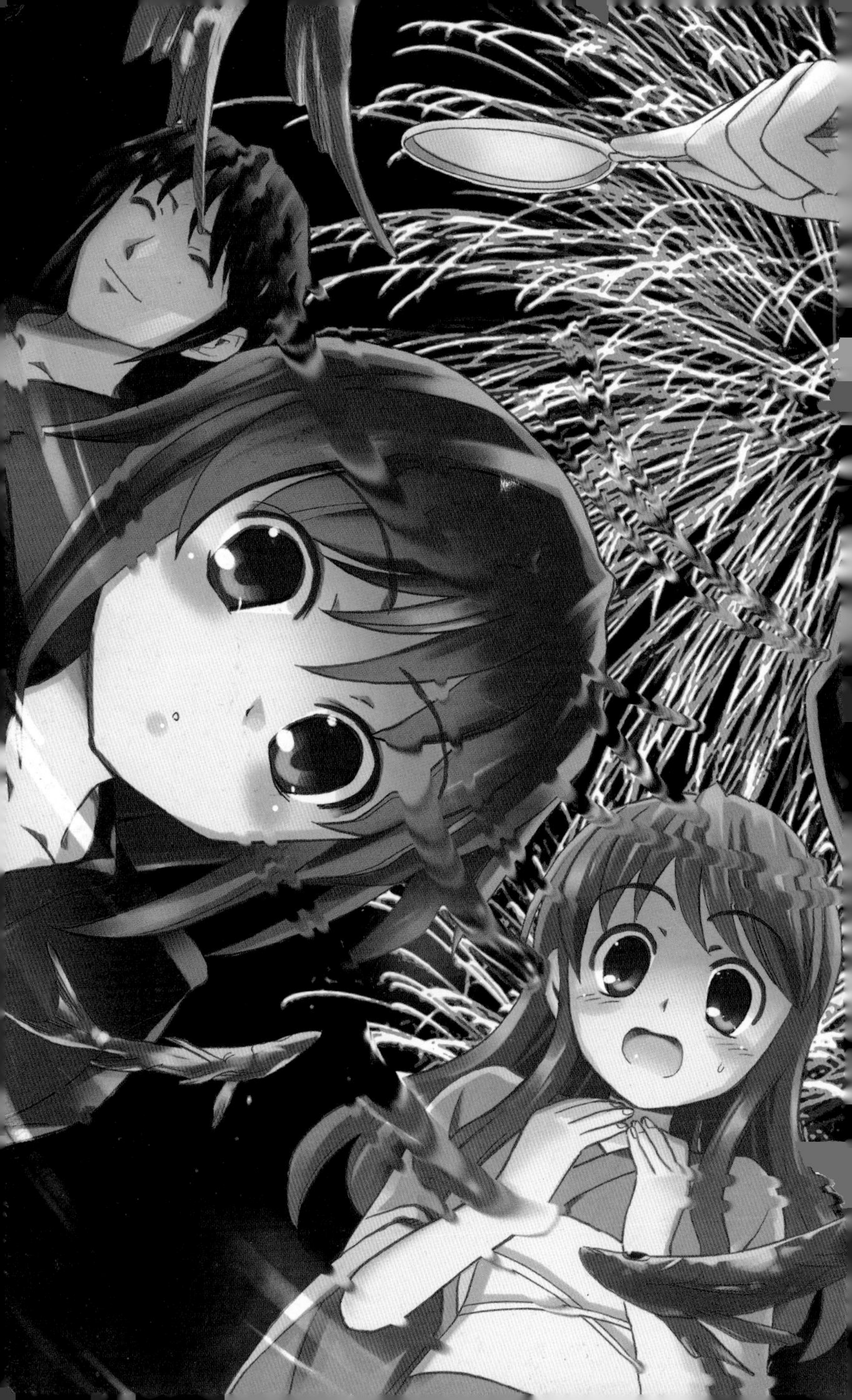

CONTENTS

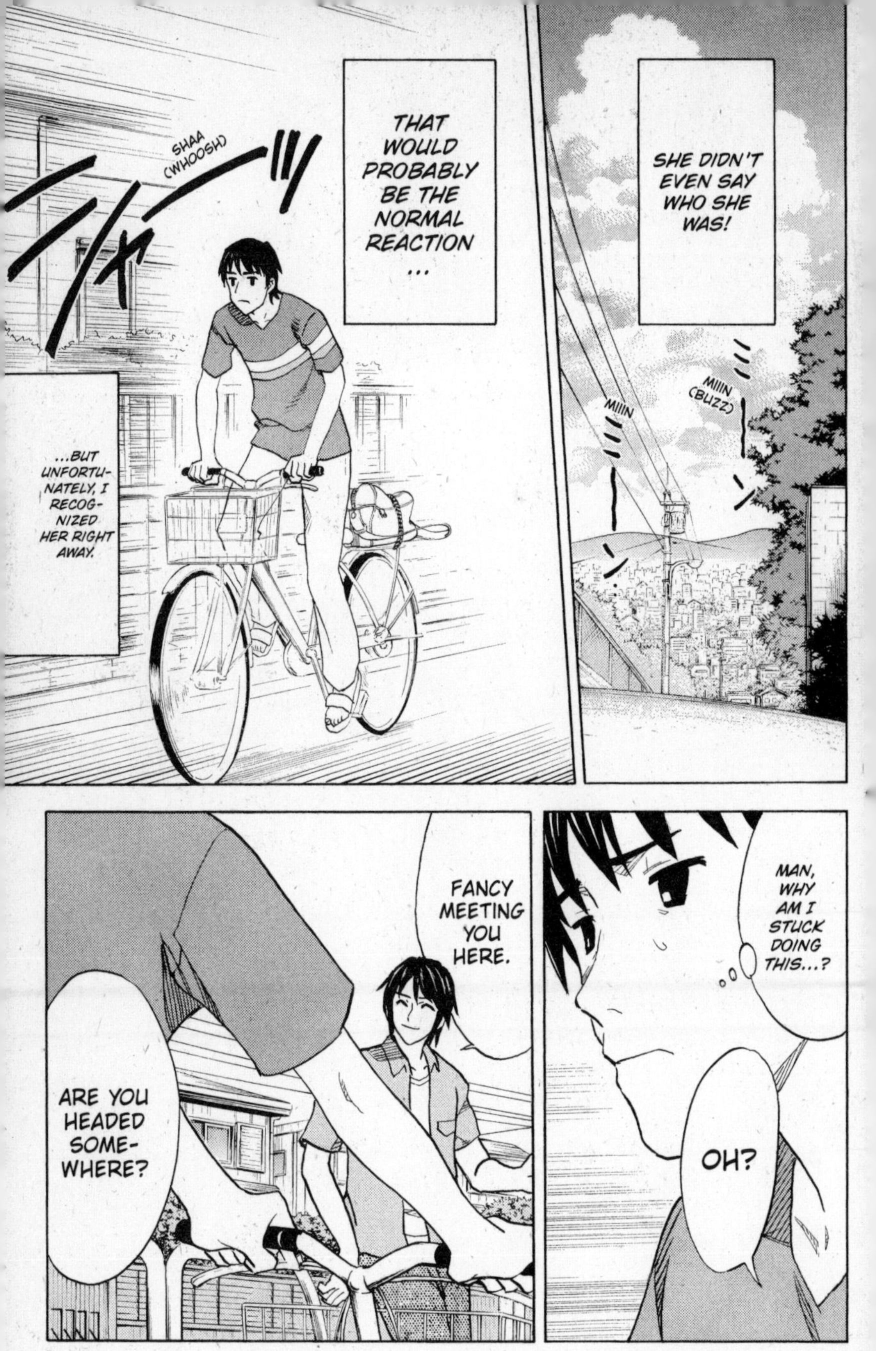
SHE DIDN'T EVEN SAY WHO SHE WAS!
MIIIN (BUZZ)
MIIIN
THAT WOULD PROBABLY BE THE NORMAL REACTION...
SHAA (WHOOSH)
...BUT UNFORTUNATELY, I RECOGNIZED HER RIGHT AWAY.
MAN, WHY AM I STUCK DOING THIS...?
OH?
FANCY MEETING YOU HERE.
ARE YOU HEADED SOMEWHERE?

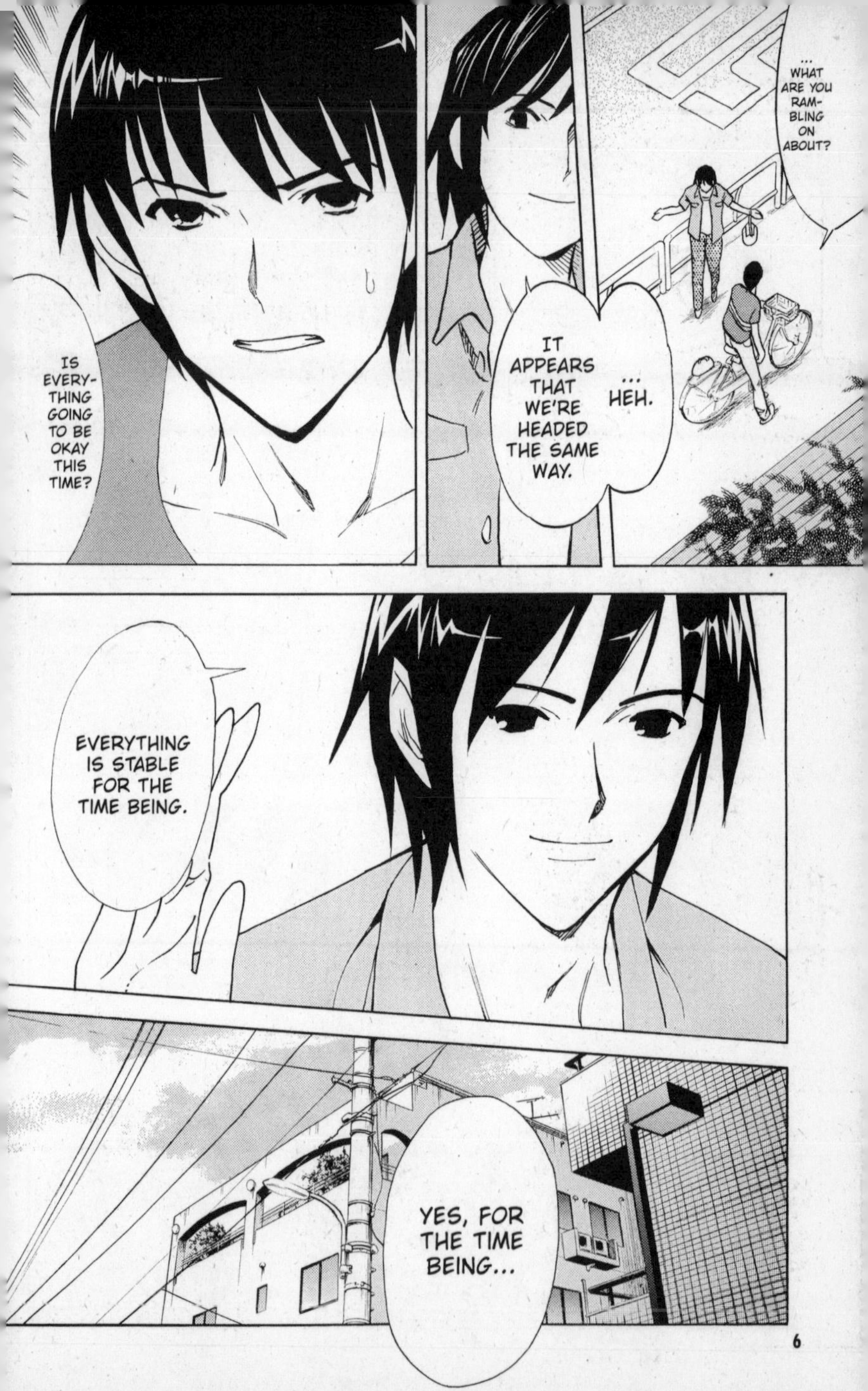
... WHAT ARE YOU RAMBLING ON ABOUT?
... HEH.
IT APPEARS THAT WE'RE HEADED THE SAME WAY.
IS EVERYTHING GOING TO BE OKAY THIS TIME?
EVERYTHING IS STABLE FOR THE TIME BEING.
YES, FOR THE TIME BEING...

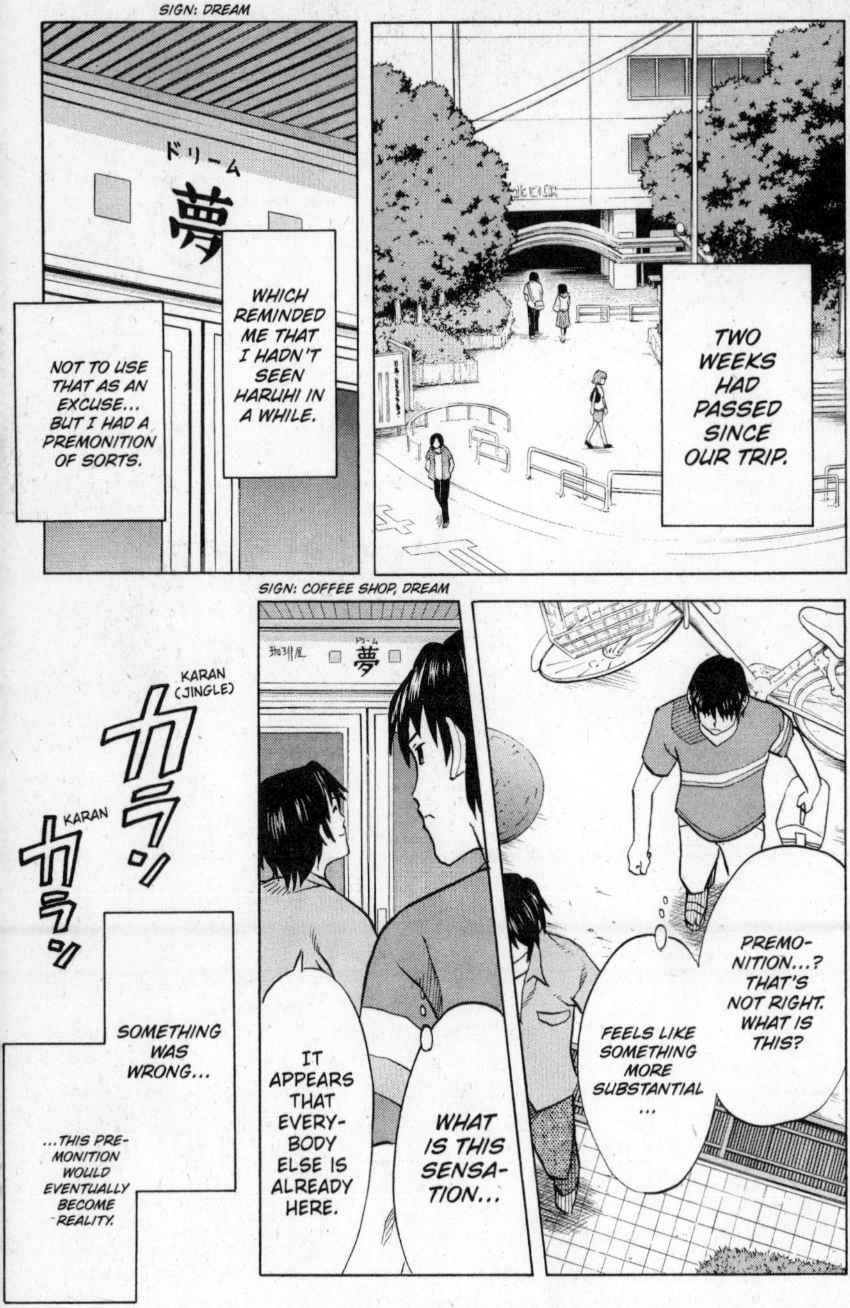
TWO WEEKS HAD PASSED SINCE OUR TRIP.
SIGN: DREAM
WHICH REMINDED ME THAT I HADN'T SEEN HARUHI IN A WHILE.
NOT TO USE THAT AS AN EXCUSE... BUT I HAD A PREMONITION OF SORTS.
PREMONITION...? THAT'S NOT RIGHT. WHAT IS THIS?
FEELS LIKE SOMETHING MORE SUBSTANTIAL...
SIGN: COFFEE SHOP, DREAM
WHAT IS THIS SENSATION...
IT APPEARS THAT EVERYBODY ELSE IS ALREADY HERE.
KARAN (JINGLE)
KARAN
SOMETHING WAS WRONG...
...THIS PREMONITION WOULD EVENTUALLY BECOME REALITY.

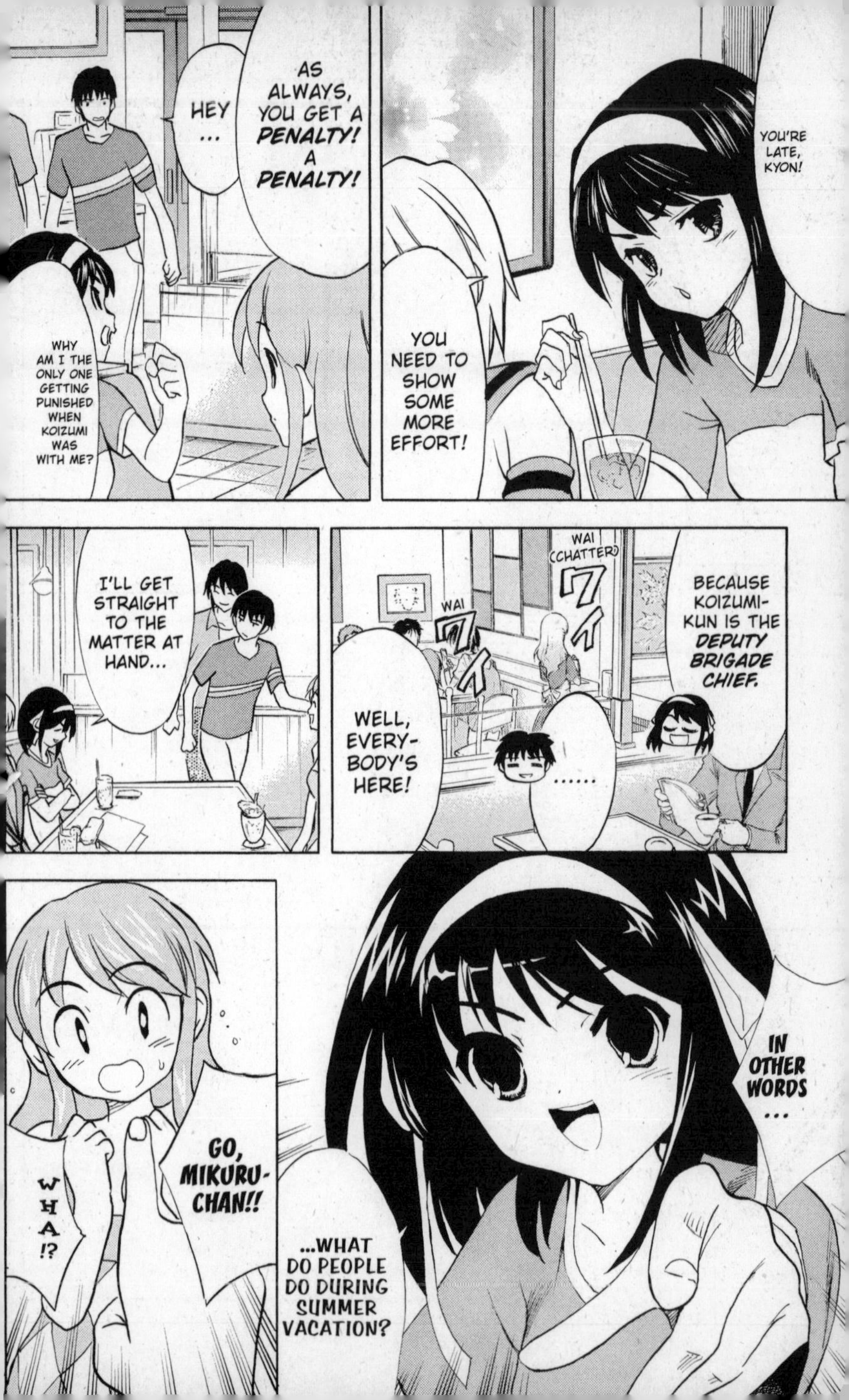
YOU'RE LATE, KYON!
YOU NEED TO SHOW SOME MORE EFFORT!
AS ALWAYS, YOU GET A *PENALTY!* A *PENALTY!*
HEY ...
WHY AM I THE ONLY ONE GETTING PUNISHED WHEN KOIZUMI WAS WITH ME?
BECAUSE KOIZUMI-KUN IS THE *DEPUTY BRIGADE CHIEF.*
WAI (CHATTER)
WAI
......
WELL, EVERY-BODY'S HERE!
I'LL GET STRAIGHT TO THE MATTER AT HAND...
IN OTHER WORDS ...
...WHAT DO PEOPLE DO DURING SUMMER VACATION?
GO, MIKURU-CHAN!!
WHA!?

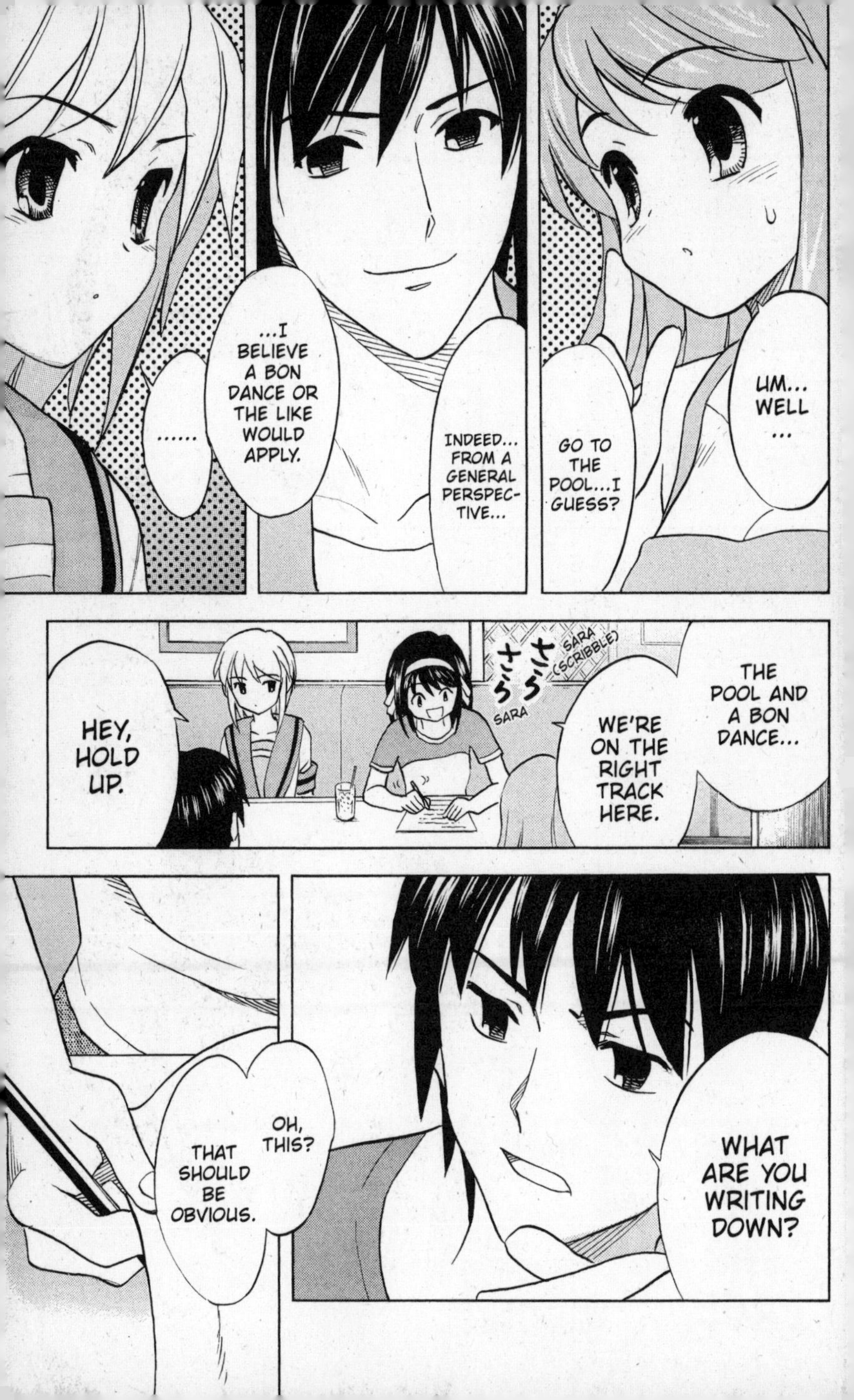
UM... WELL ...
GO TO THE POOL...I GUESS?
INDEED... FROM A GENERAL PERSPEC-TIVE...
...I BELIEVE A BON DANCE OR THE LIKE WOULD APPLY.
......
THE POOL AND A BON DANCE...
WE'RE ON THE RIGHT TRACK HERE.
さらさら
SARA SARA (SCRIBBLE)
HEY, HOLD UP.
WHAT ARE YOU WRITING DOWN?
OH, THIS?
THAT SHOULD BE OBVIOUS.

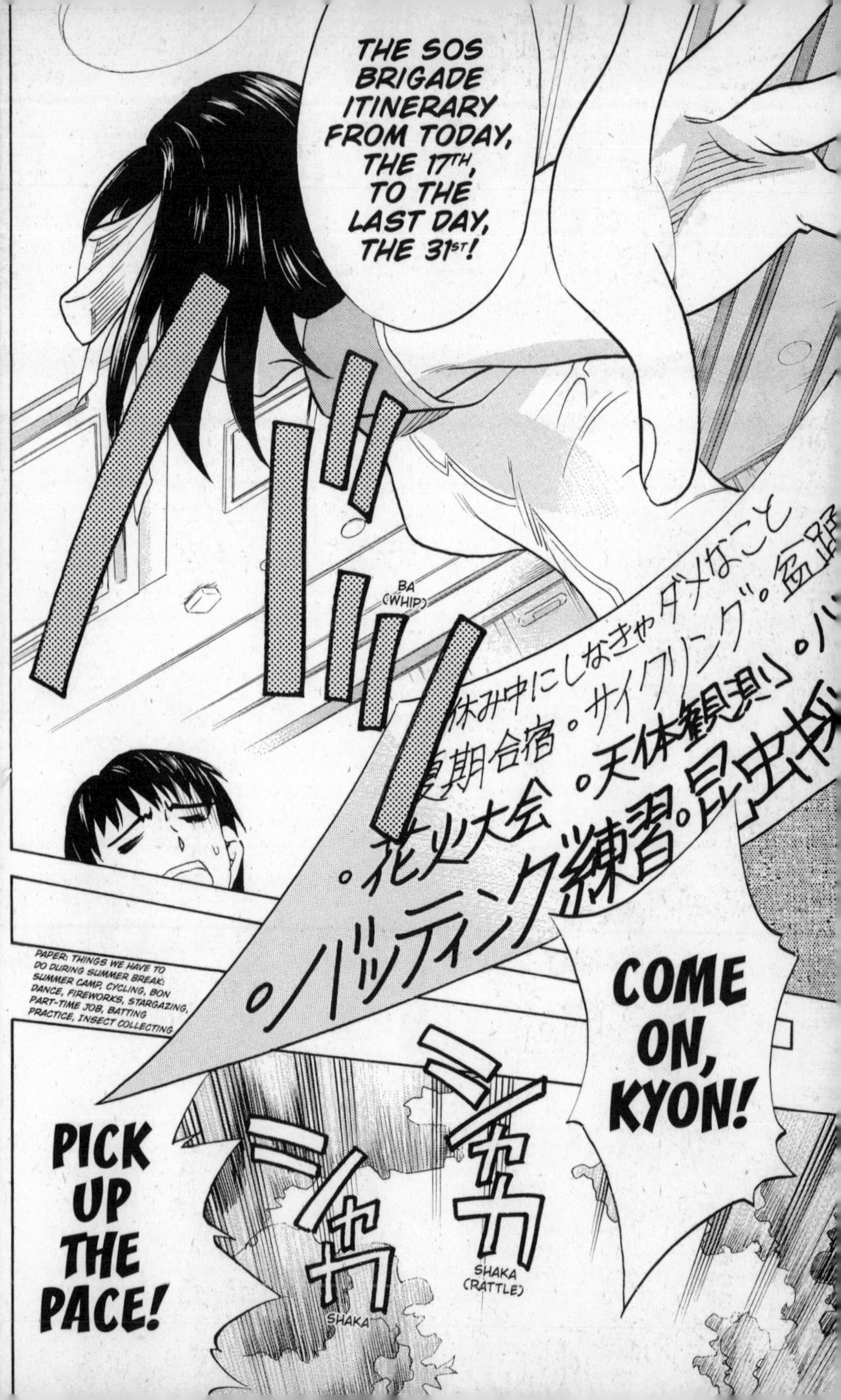
THE SOS BRIGADE ITINERARY FROM TODAY, THE 17TH, TO THE LAST DAY, THE 31ST!
BA (WHIP)
休み中にしなきゃダメなこと
期合宿。サイクリング。盆
花火大会。天体観測。バ
。バッティング練習。昆虫
PAPER: THINGS WE HAVE TO DO DURING SUMMER BREAK: SUMMER CAMP, CYCLING, BON DANCE, FIREWORKS, STARGAZING, PART-TIME JOB, BATTING PRACTICE, INSECT COLLECTING
COME ON, KYON!
SHAKA (RATTLE)
SHAKA
PICK UP THE PACE!

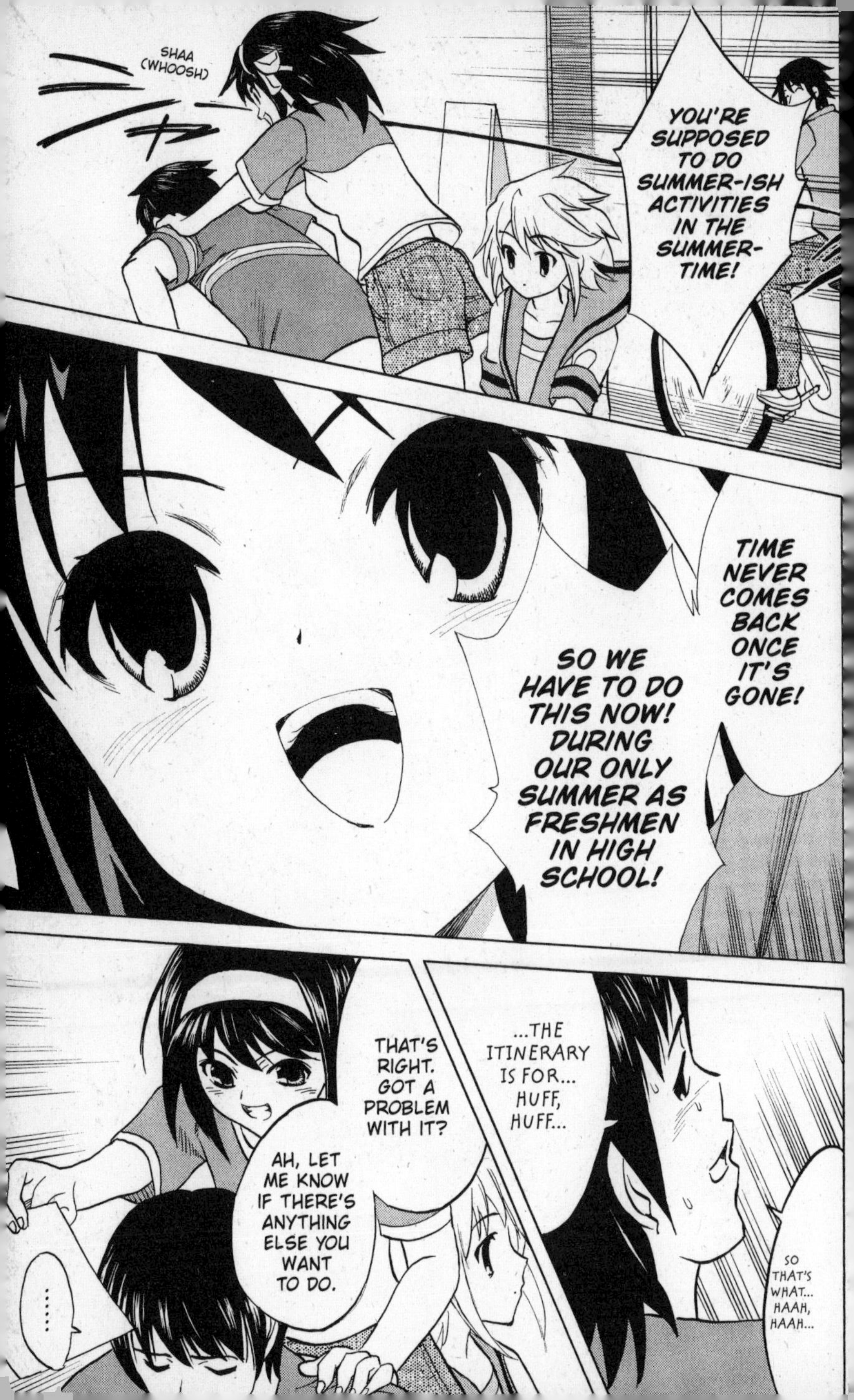
YOU'RE SUPPOSED TO DO SUMMER-ISH ACTIVITIES IN THE SUMMER-TIME!
SHAA (WHOOSH)
TIME NEVER COMES BACK ONCE IT'S GONE!
SO WE HAVE TO DO THIS NOW! DURING OUR ONLY SUMMER AS FRESHMEN IN HIGH SCHOOL!
...THE ITINERARY IS FOR... HUFF, HUFF...
SO THAT'S WHAT... HAAH, HAAH...
THAT'S RIGHT. GOT A PROBLEM WITH IT?
AH, LET ME KNOW IF THERE'S ANYTHING ELSE YOU WANT TO DO.
......

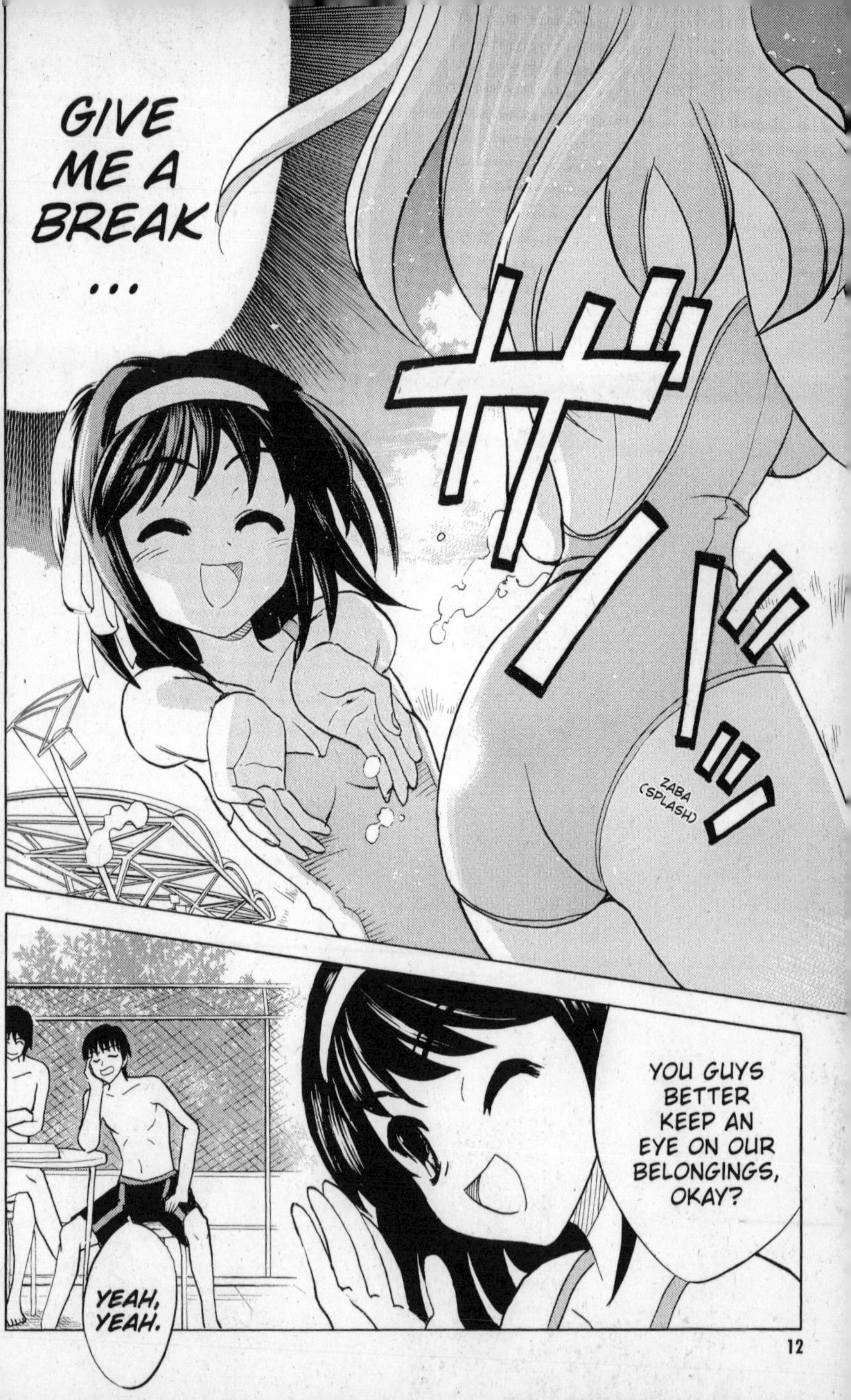
GIVE ME A BREAK...
ZABA (SPLASH)
YOU GUYS BETTER KEEP AN EYE ON OUR BELONGINGS, OKAY?
YEAH, YEAH.

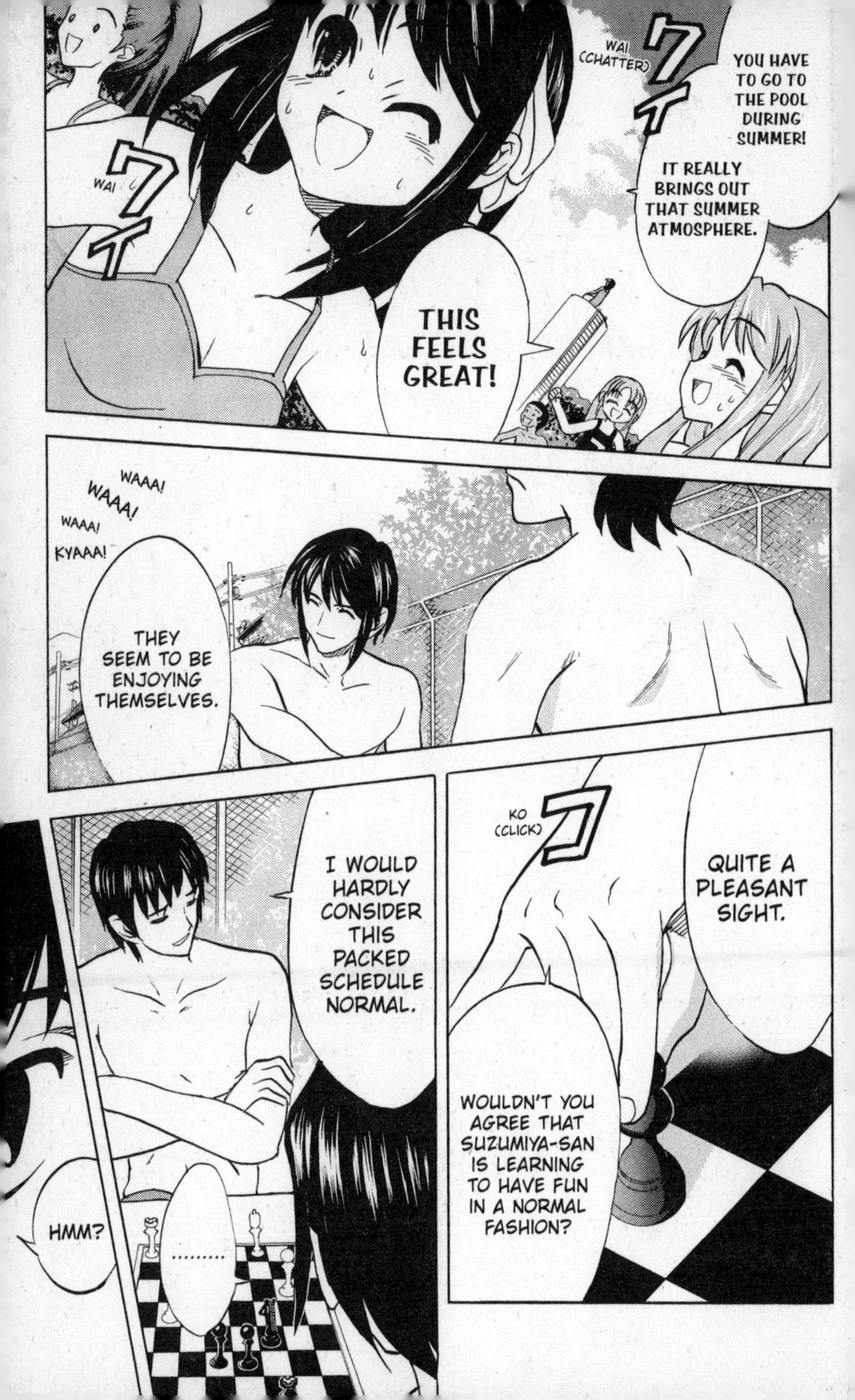
WAI (CHATTER)
YOU HAVE TO GO TO THE POOL DURING SUMMER!
IT REALLY BRINGS OUT THAT SUMMER ATMOSPHERE.
THIS FEELS GREAT!
WAI
WAAA!
WAAA!
WAAA!
KYAAA!
THEY SEEM TO BE ENJOYING THEMSELVES.
QUITE A PLEASANT SIGHT.
KO (CLICK)
WOULDN'T YOU AGREE THAT SUZUMIYA-SAN IS LEARNING TO HAVE FUN IN A NORMAL FASHION?
I WOULD HARDLY CONSIDER THIS PACKED SCHEDULE NORMAL.
....
HMM?

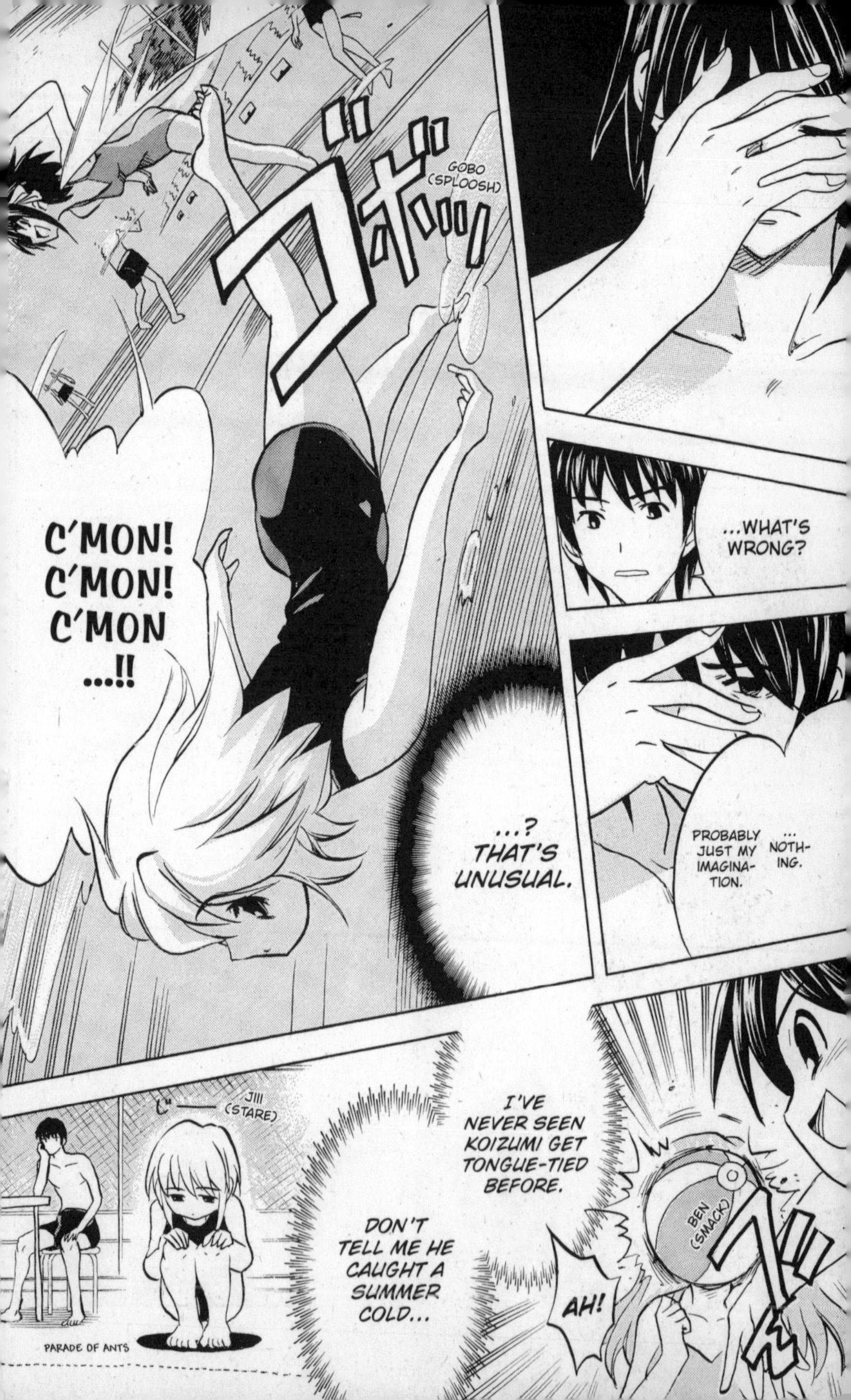
...WHAT'S WRONG?
... NOTHING.
PROBABLY JUST MY IMAGINATION.
GOBO (SPLOOSH)
C'MON! C'MON! C'MON ...!!
...? THAT'S UNUSUAL.
I'VE NEVER SEEN KOIZUMI GET TONGUE-TIED BEFORE.
BEN (SMACK)
DON'T TELL ME HE CAUGHT A SUMMER COLD...
AH!
JIII (STARE)
PARADE OF ANTS

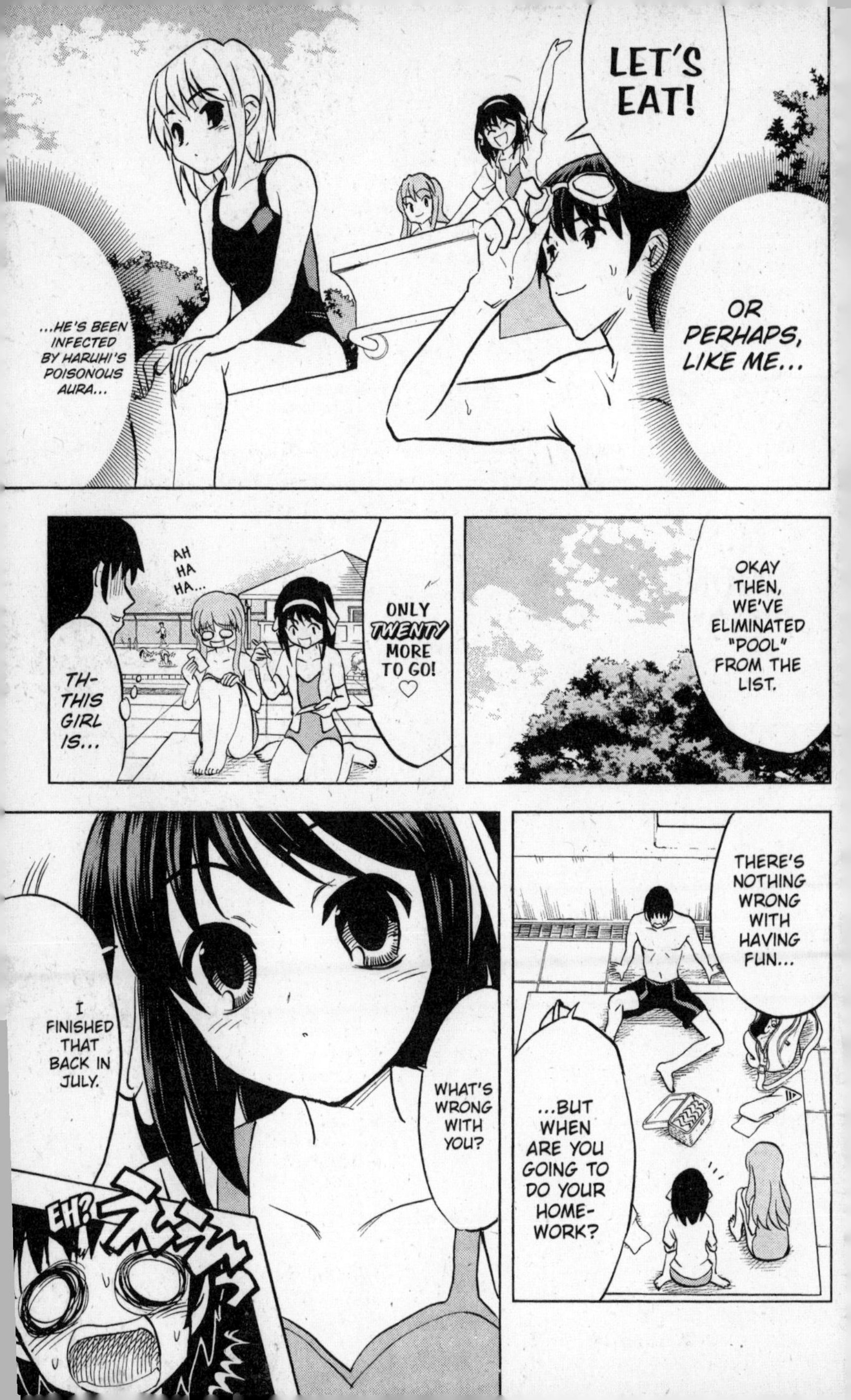
LET'S EAT!
OR PERHAPS, LIKE ME...
...HE'S BEEN INFECTED BY HARUHI'S POISONOUS AURA...
OKAY THEN, WE'VE ELIMINATED "POOL" FROM THE LIST.
ONLY TWENTY MORE TO GO! ♡
AH HA HA...
TH-THIS GIRL IS...
THERE'S NOTHING WRONG WITH HAVING FUN...
...BUT WHEN ARE YOU GOING TO DO YOUR HOME-WORK?
WHAT'S WRONG WITH YOU?
I FINISHED THAT BACK IN JULY.
EH?!

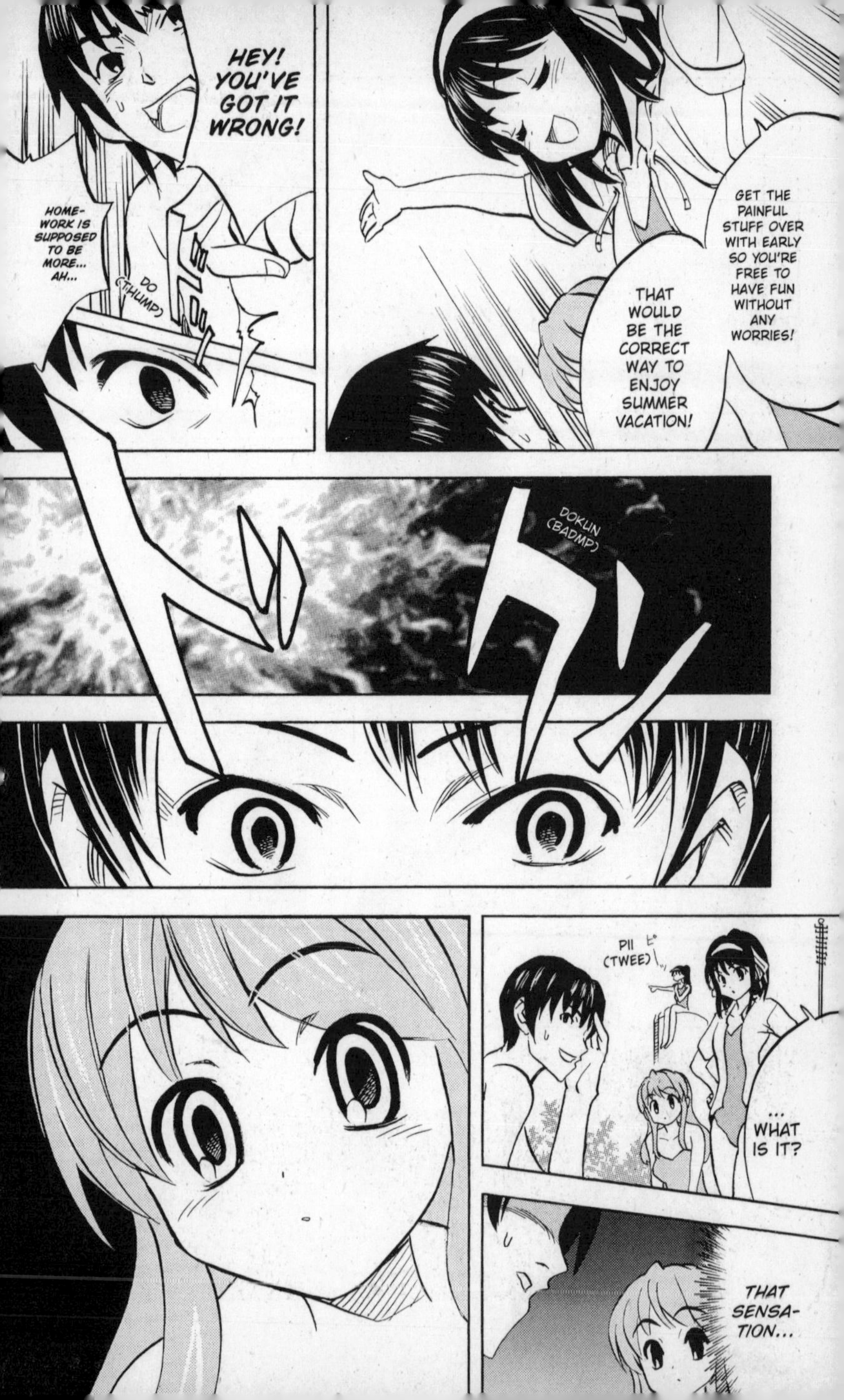
GET THE PAINFUL STUFF OVER WITH EARLY SO YOU'RE FREE TO HAVE FUN WITHOUT ANY WORRIES!
THAT WOULD BE THE CORRECT WAY TO ENJOY SUMMER VACATION!
HEY! YOU'VE GOT IT WRONG!
HOME-WORK IS SUPPOSED TO BE MORE... AH...
DO (THUMP)
DOKUN (BADMP)
PII (TWEE)
... WHAT IS IT?
THAT SENSA-TION...

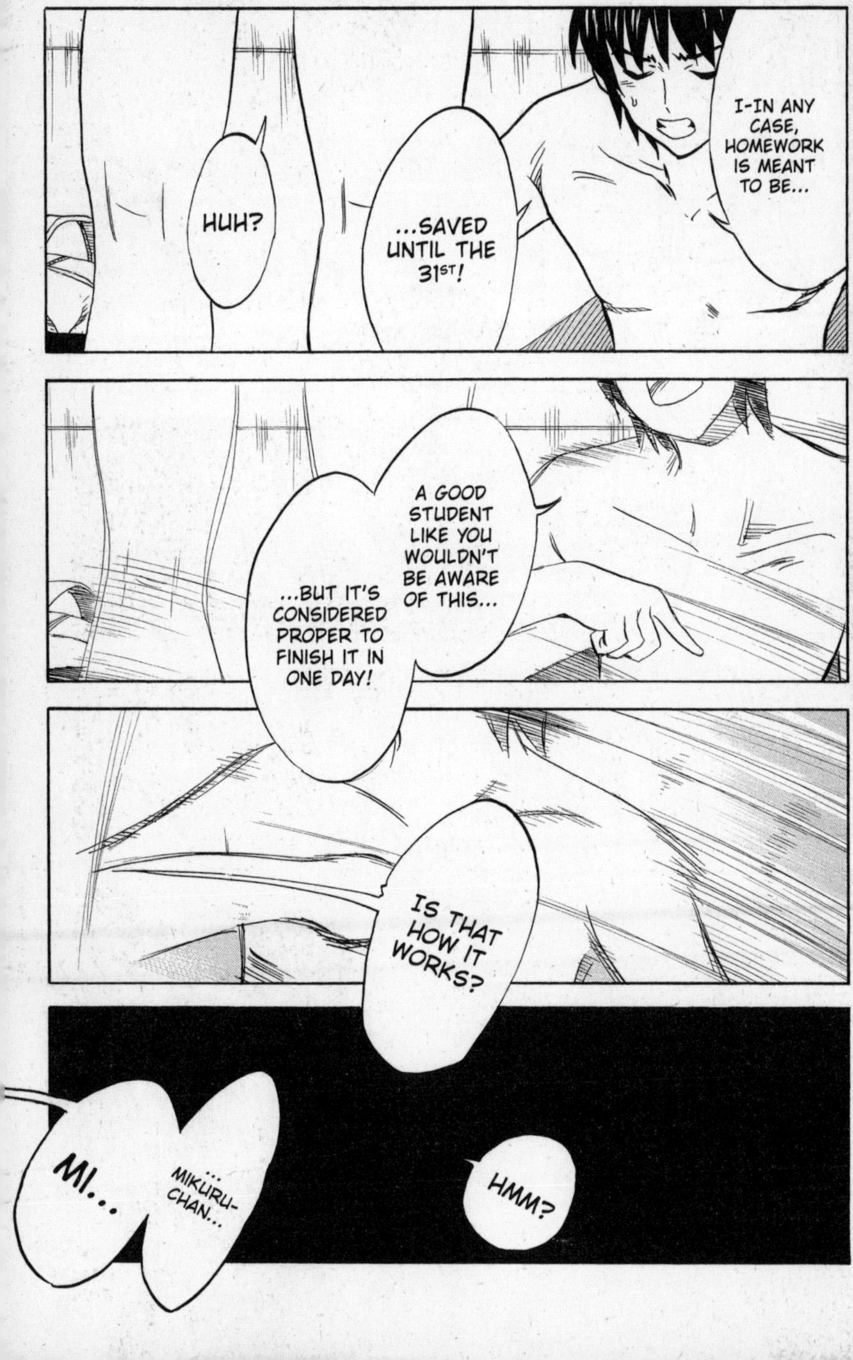
I-IN ANY CASE, HOMEWORK IS MEANT TO BE...
...SAVED UNTIL THE 31ST!
HUH?
A GOOD STUDENT LIKE YOU WOULDN'T BE AWARE OF THIS...
...BUT IT'S CONSIDERED PROPER TO FINISH IT IN ONE DAY!
IS THAT HOW IT WORKS?
HMM?
MI...
...MIKURU-CHAN...

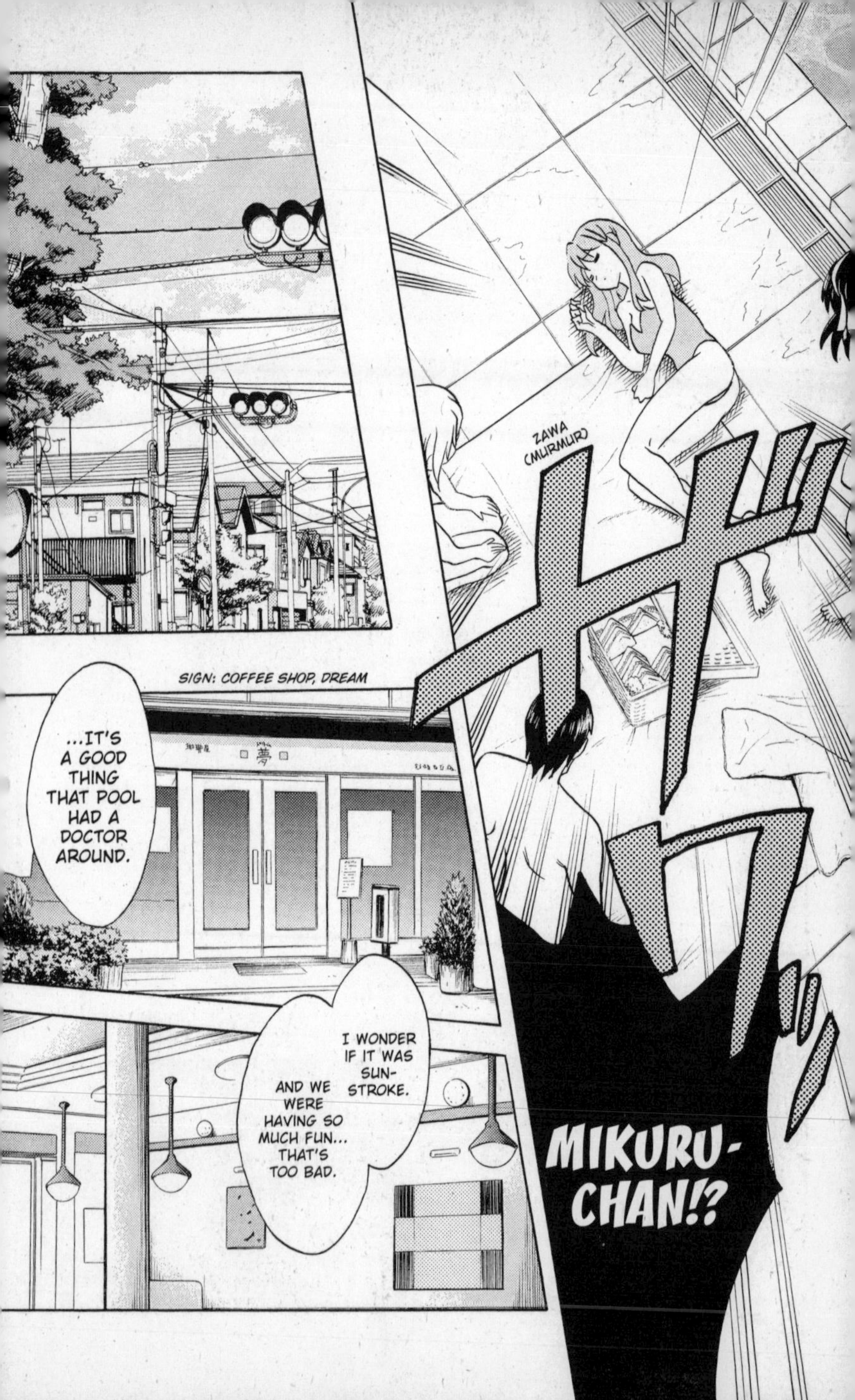
ZAWA (MURMUR)
MIKURU-CHAN!?
SIGN: COFFEE SHOP, DREAM
...IT'S A GOOD THING THAT POOL HAD A DOCTOR AROUND.
I WONDER IF IT WAS SUN-STROKE.
AND WE WERE HAVING SO MUCH FUN... THAT'S TOO BAD.

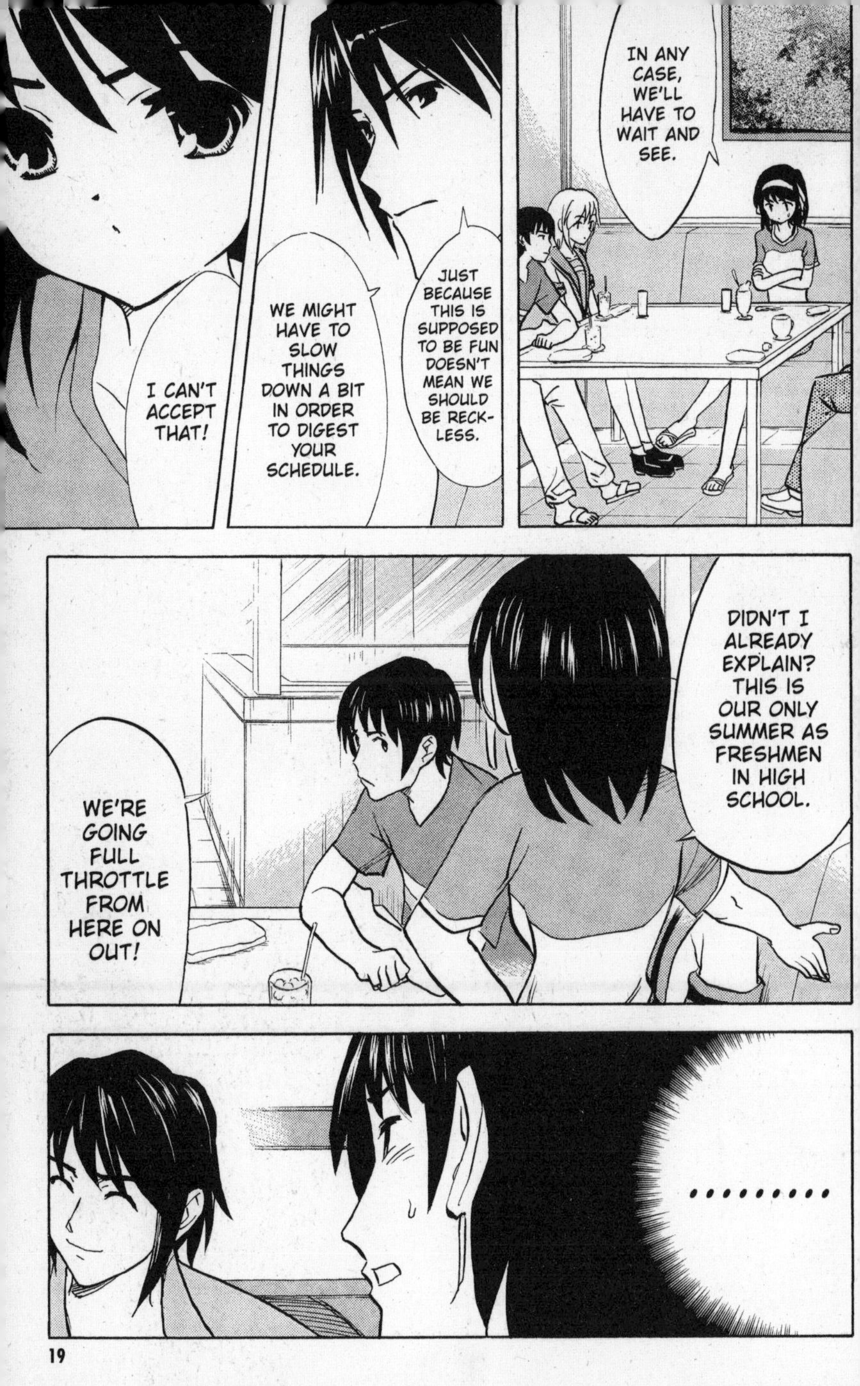

IN ANY CASE, WE'LL HAVE TO WAIT AND SEE.
JUST BECAUSE THIS IS SUPPOSED TO BE FUN DOESN'T MEAN WE SHOULD BE RECK-LESS.
WE MIGHT HAVE TO SLOW THINGS DOWN A BIT IN ORDER TO DIGEST YOUR SCHEDULE.
I CAN'T ACCEPT THAT!
DIDN'T I ALREADY EXPLAIN? THIS IS OUR ONLY SUMMER AS FRESHMEN IN HIGH SCHOOL.
WE'RE GOING FULL THROTTLE FROM HERE ON OUT!
....

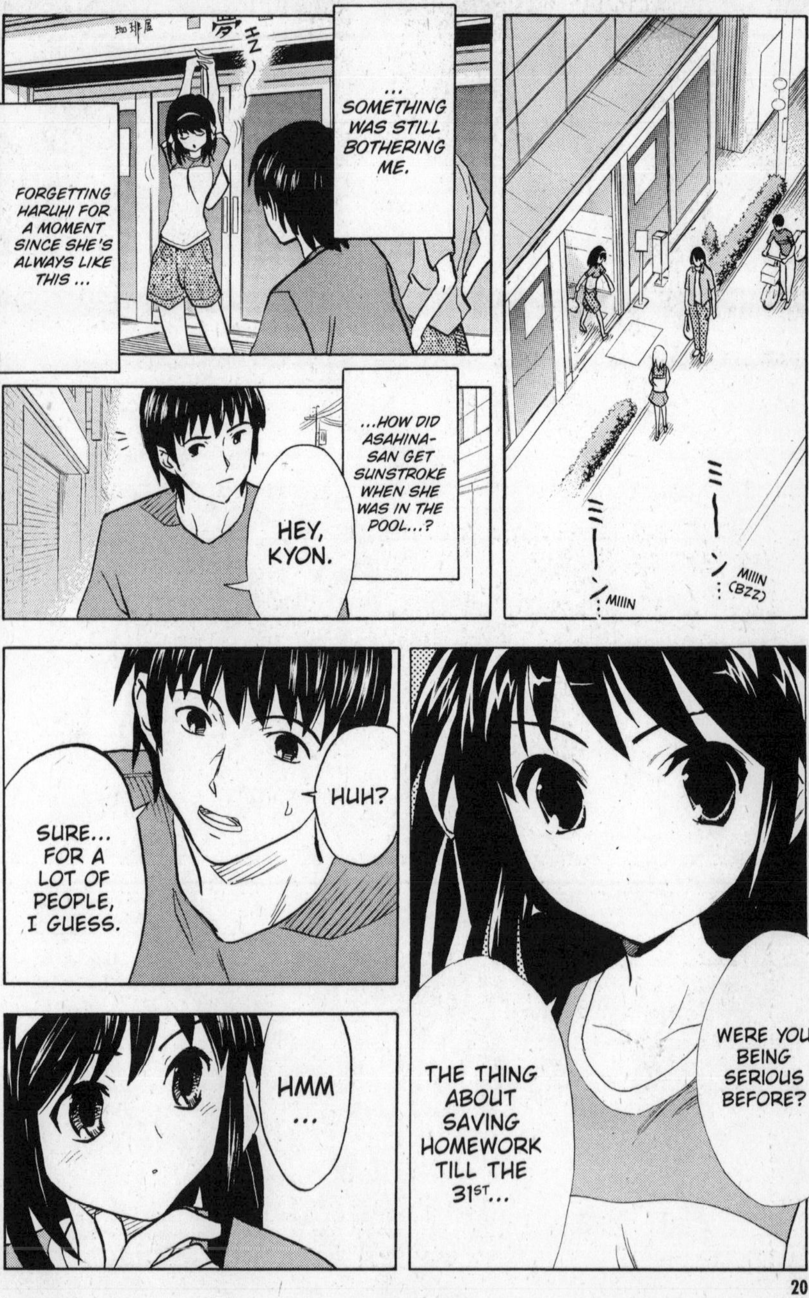
MIIIN (BZZ)
MIIIN
... SOMETHING WAS STILL BOTHERING ME.
FORGETTING HARUHI FOR A MOMENT SINCE SHE'S ALWAYS LIKE THIS ...
...HOW DID ASAHINA-SAN GET SUNSTROKE WHEN SHE WAS IN THE POOL...?
HEY, KYON.
WERE YOU BEING SERIOUS BEFORE?
THE THING ABOUT SAVING HOMEWORK TILL THE 31ST...
HUH?
SURE... FOR A LOT OF PEOPLE, I GUESS.
HMM ...

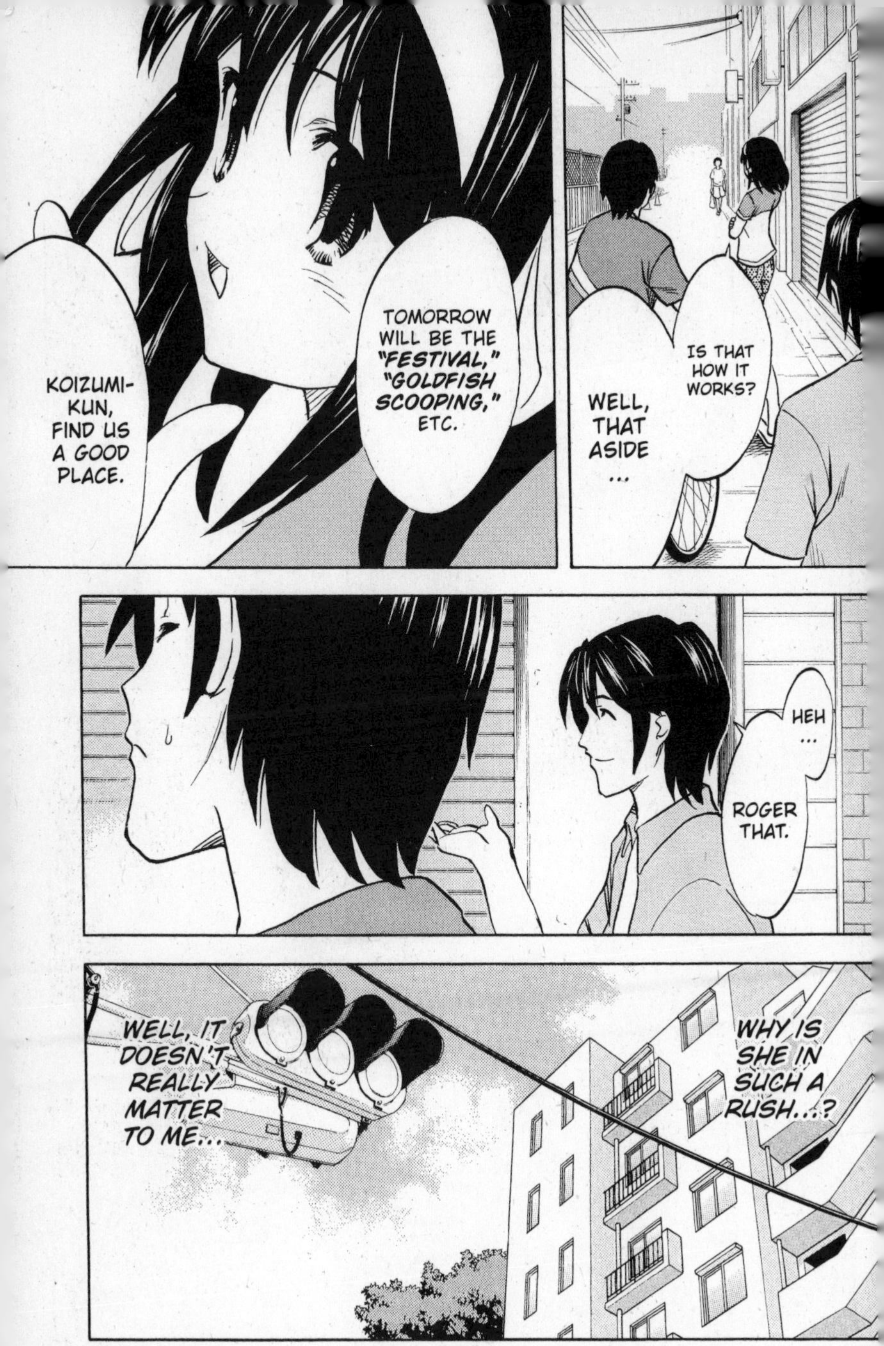
IS THAT HOW IT WORKS?
WELL, THAT ASIDE ...
TOMORROW WILL BE THE "FESTIVAL," "GOLDFISH SCOOPING," ETC.
KOIZUMI-KUN, FIND US A GOOD PLACE.
HEH ...
ROGER THAT.
WHY IS SHE IN SUCH A RUSH...?
WELL, IT DOESN'T REALLY MATTER TO ME...

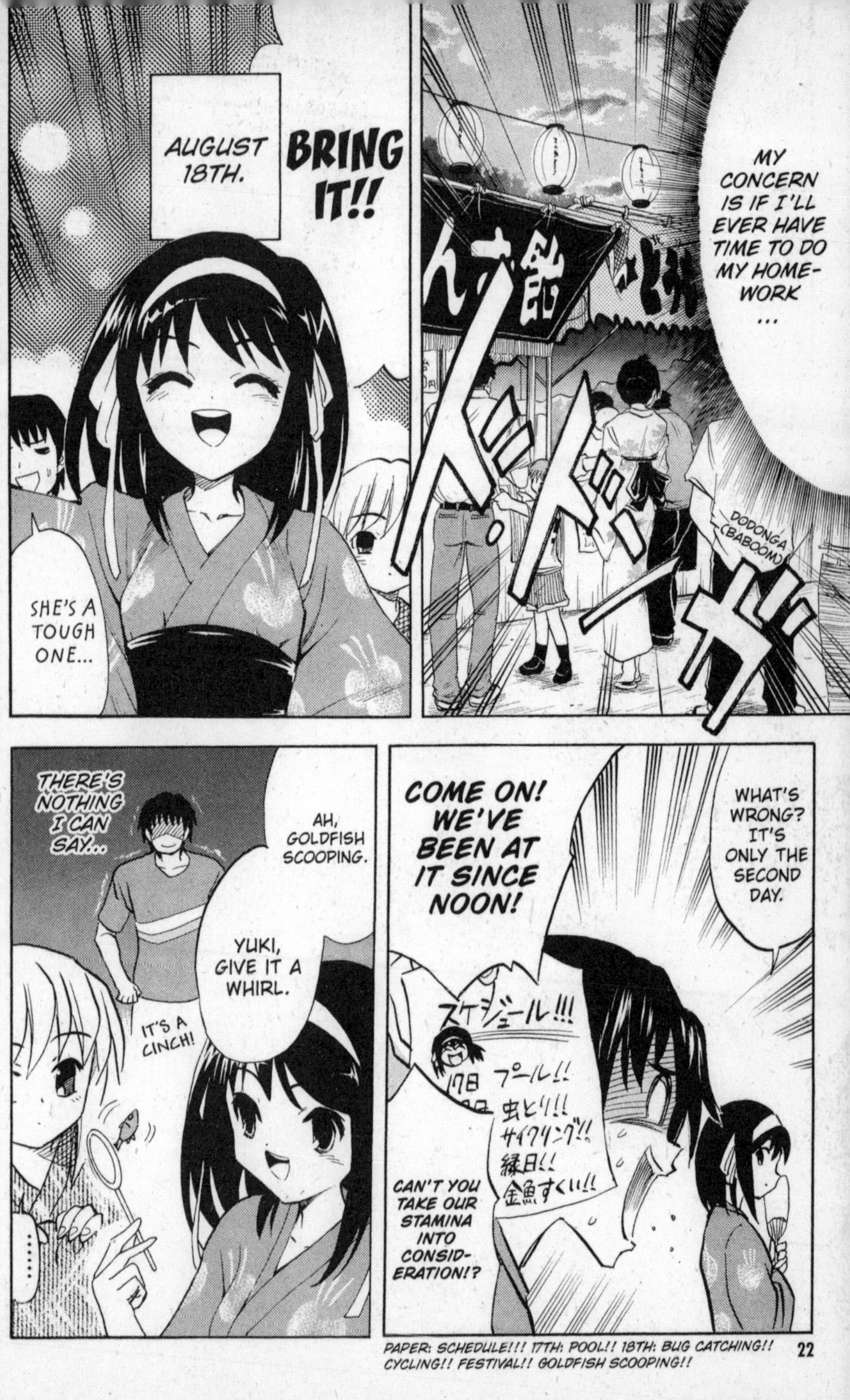
MY CONCERN IS IF I'LL EVER HAVE TIME TO DO MY HOME-WORK ...
DODONGA (BABOOM)
AUGUST 18TH.
BRING IT!!
SHE'S A TOUGH ONE...
WHAT'S WRONG? IT'S ONLY THE SECOND DAY.
COME ON! WE'VE BEEN AT IT SINCE NOON!
スケジュール!!!
17日 プール!!
虫とり!!!
サイクリング!!
縁日!!
金魚すくい!!
CAN'T YOU TAKE OUR STAMINA INTO CONSID-ERATION!?
AH, GOLDFISH SCOOPING.
THERE'S NOTHING I CAN SAY...
YUKI, GIVE IT A WHIRL.
IT'S A CINCH!
......

PAPER: SCHEDULE!!! 17TH: POOL!! 18TH: BUG CATCHING!! CYCLING!! FESTIVAL!! GOLDFISH SCOOPING!!

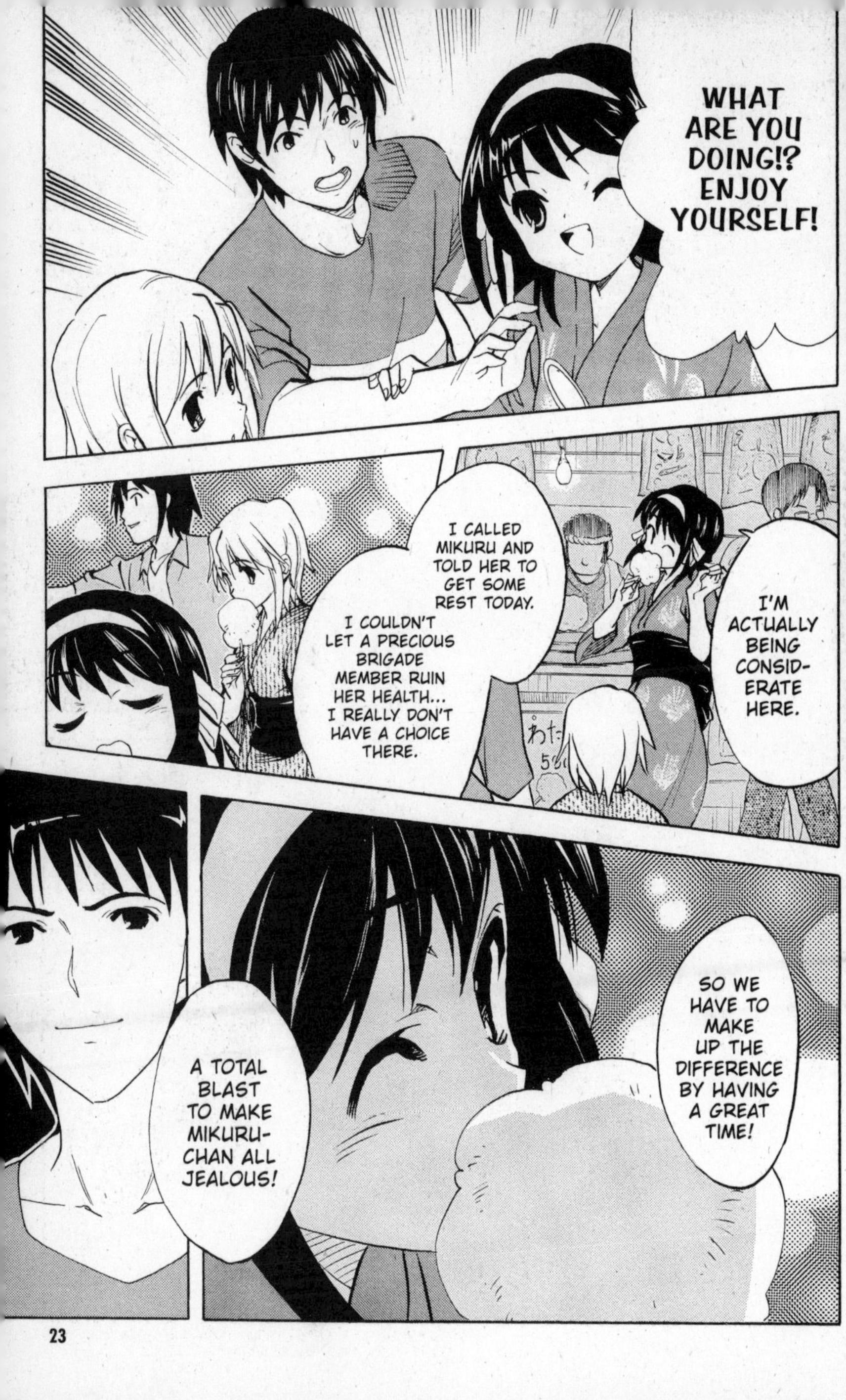
WHAT ARE YOU DOING!? ENJOY YOURSELF!
I'M ACTUALLY BEING CONSID-ERATE HERE.
I CALLED MIKURU AND TOLD HER TO GET SOME REST TODAY.
I COULDN'T LET A PRECIOUS BRIGADE MEMBER RUIN HER HEALTH... I REALLY DON'T HAVE A CHOICE THERE.
SO WE HAVE TO MAKE UP THE DIFFERENCE BY HAVING A GREAT TIME!
A TOTAL BLAST TO MAKE MIKURU-CHAN ALL JEALOUS!

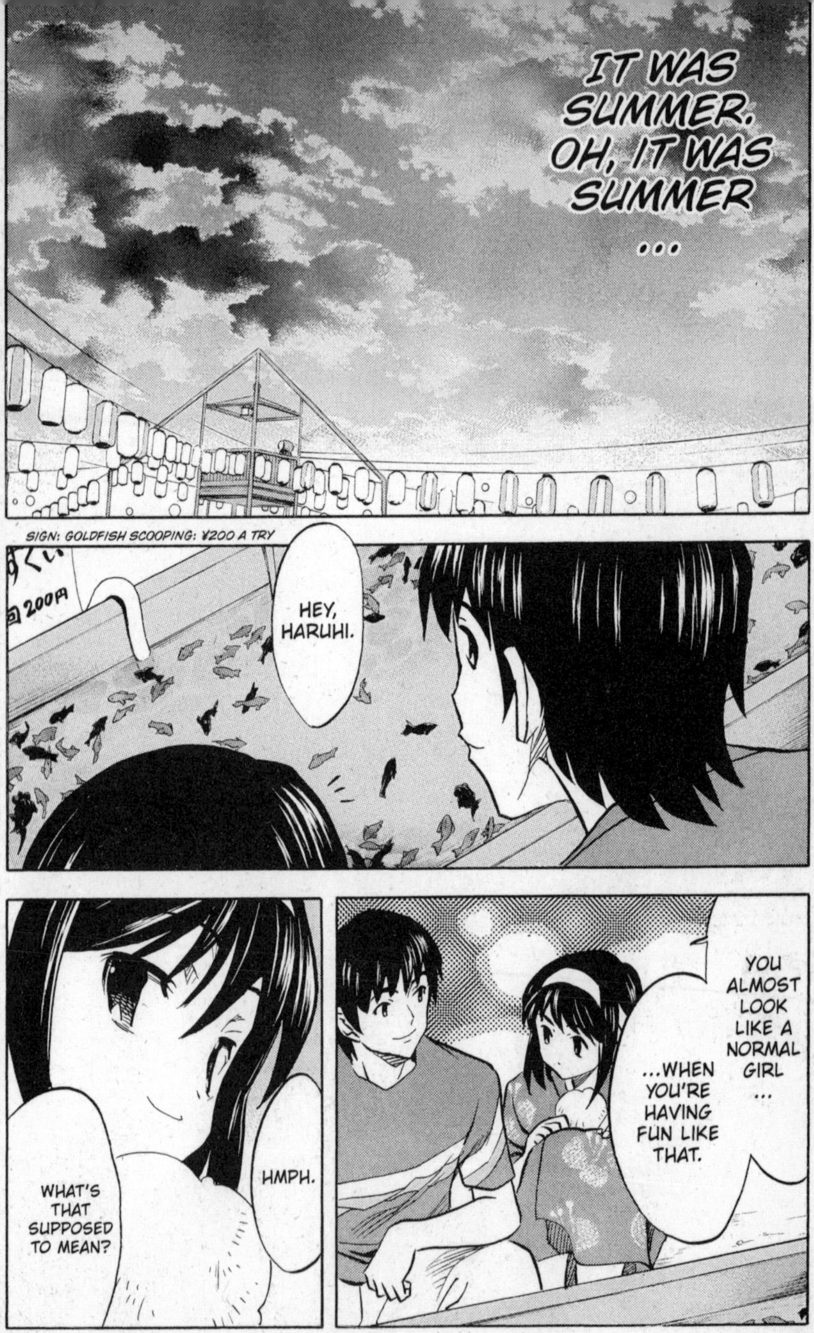
IT WAS SUMMER. OH, IT WAS SUMMER ...
SIGN: GOLDFISH SCOOPING: ¥200 A TRY
HEY, HARUHI.
YOU ALMOST LOOK LIKE A NORMAL GIRL ...
...WHEN YOU'RE HAVING FUN LIKE THAT.
HMPH.
WHAT'S THAT SUPPOSED TO MEAN?

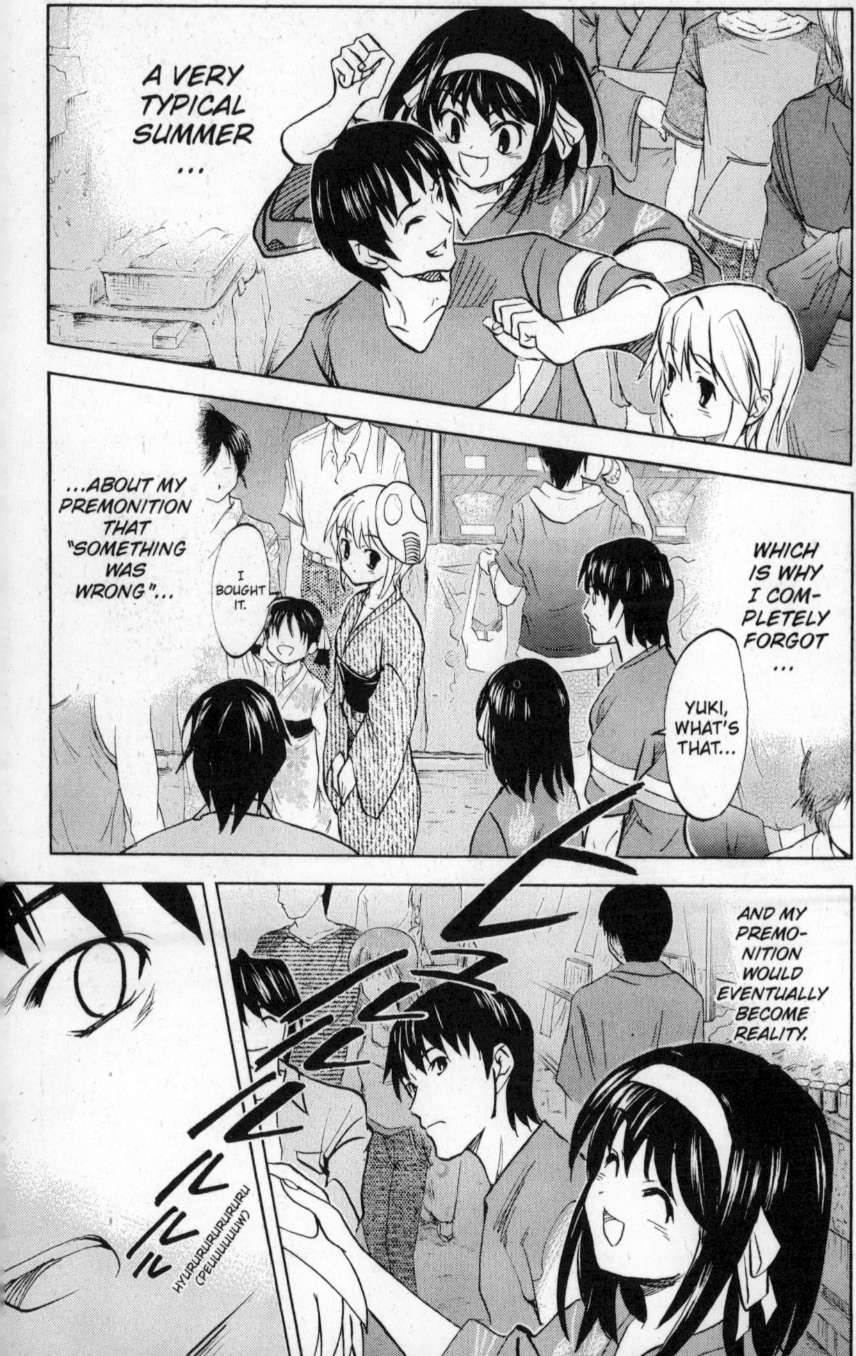
A VERY TYPICAL SUMMER ...
WHICH IS WHY I COMPLETELY FORGOT ...
YUKI, WHAT'S THAT...
I BOUGHT IT.
...ABOUT MY PREMONITION THAT "SOMETHING WAS WRONG"...
AND MY PREMONITION WOULD EVENTUALLY BECOME REALITY.
HYURURURURURURU (PEUUUUUUUW)

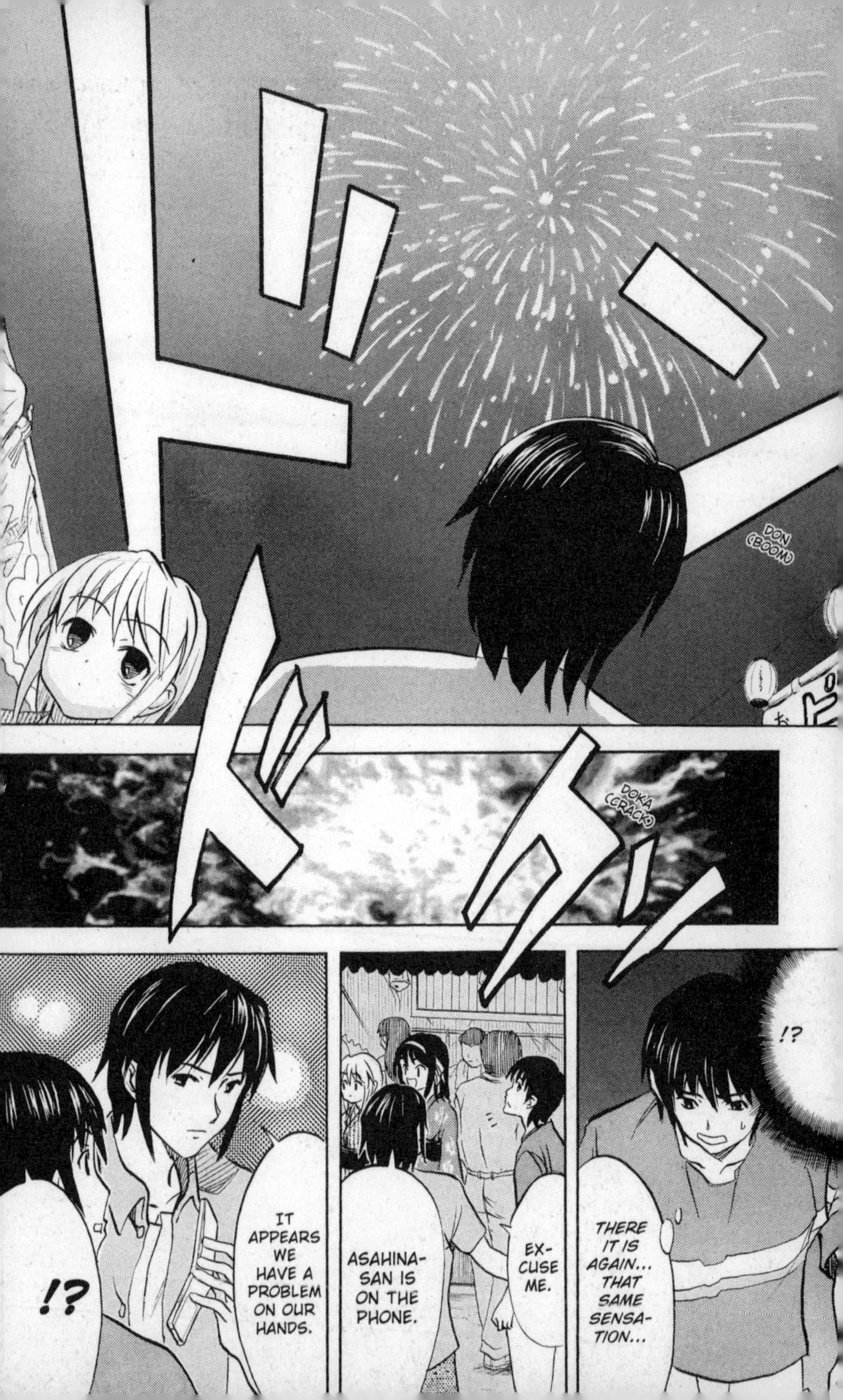
DON (BOOM)
DOKA (CRACK)
!?
THERE IT IS AGAIN... THAT SAME SENSATION...
EX-CUSE ME.
ASAHINA-SAN IS ON THE PHONE.
IT APPEARS WE HAVE A PROBLEM ON OUR HANDS.
!?

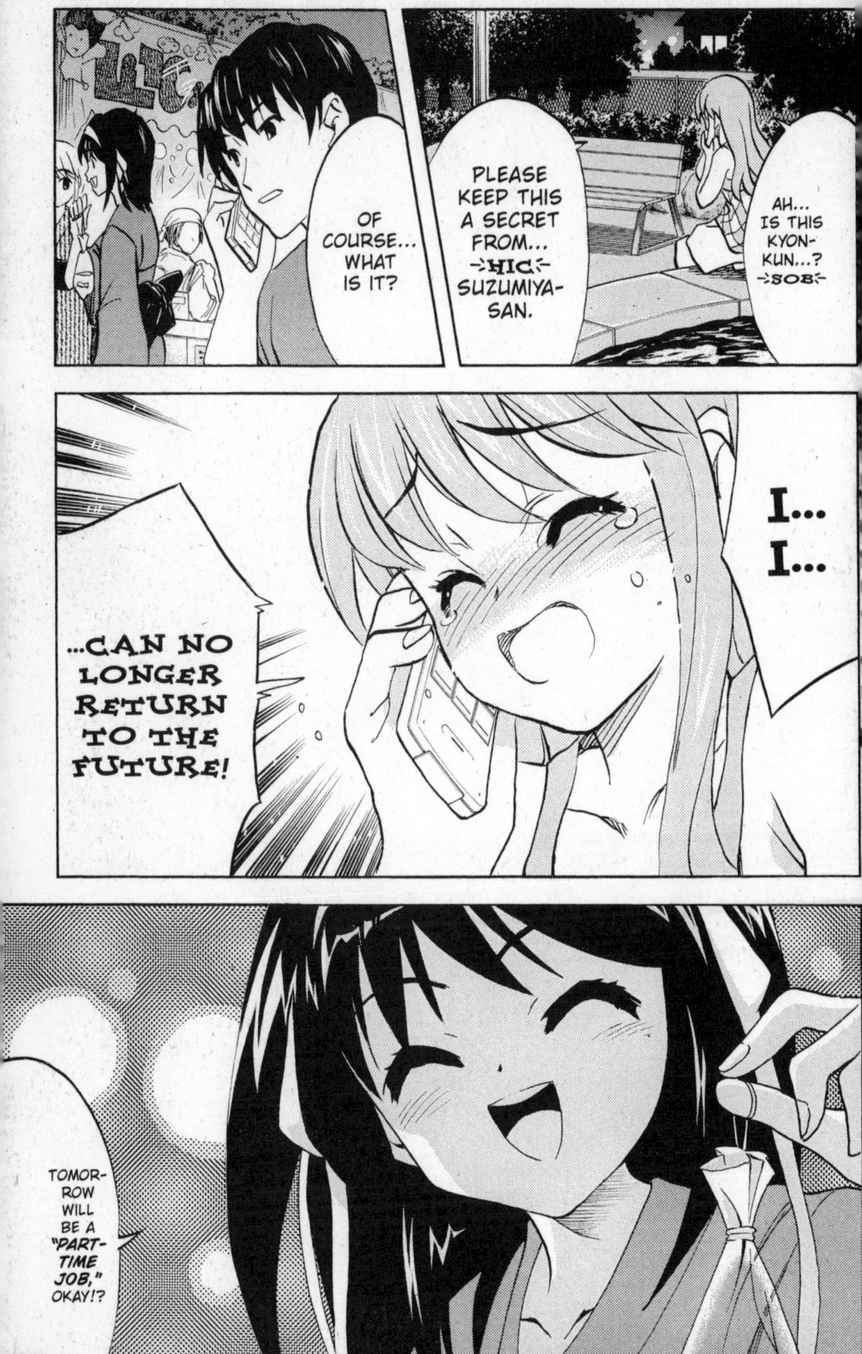
AH... IS THIS KYON-KUN...? -SOB-
PLEASE KEEP THIS A SECRET FROM... -HIC- SUZUMIYA-SAN.
OF COURSE... WHAT IS IT?
I... I...
...CAN NO LONGER RETURN TO THE FUTURE!
TOMORROW WILL BE A "PART-TIME JOB," OKAY!?

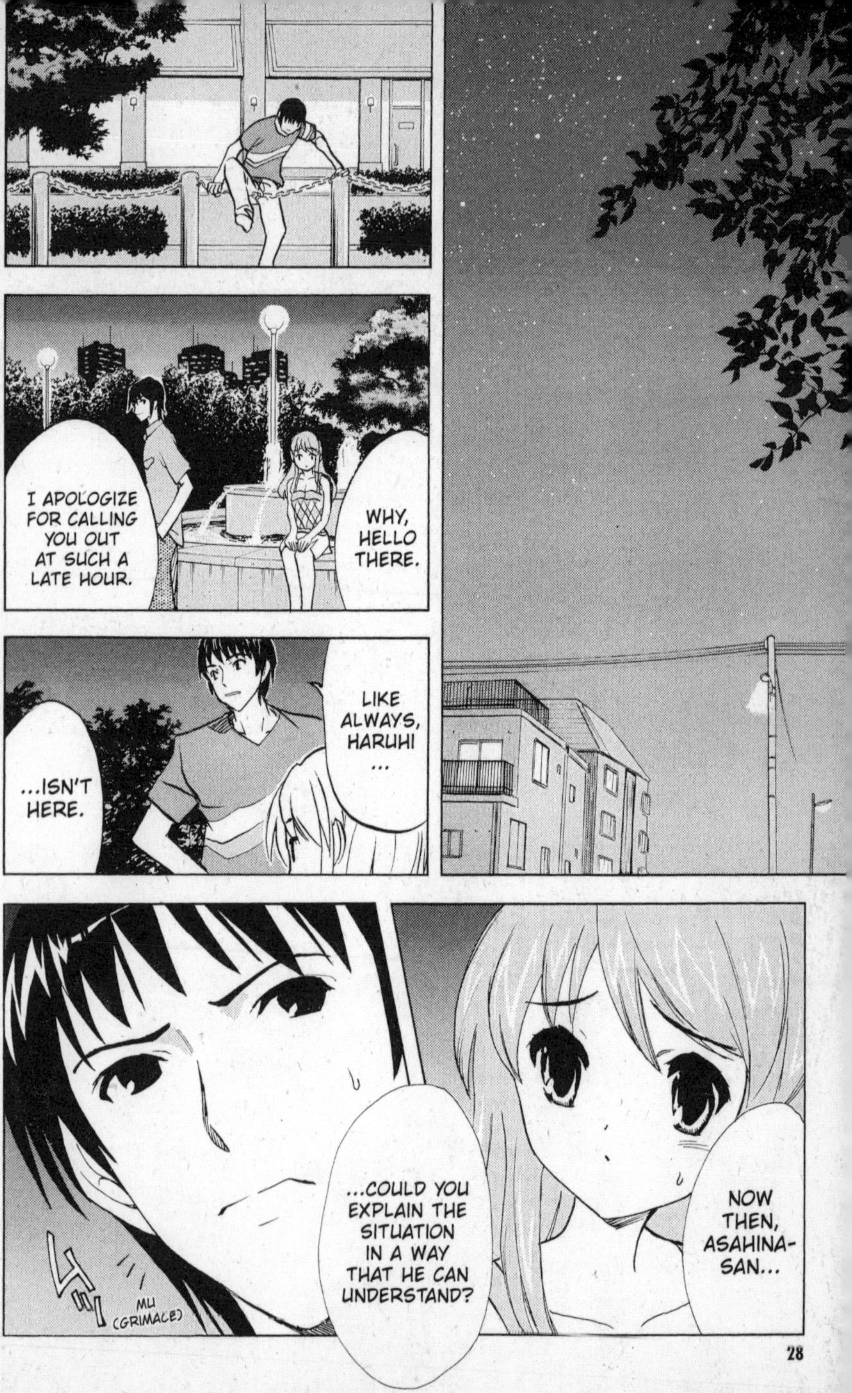
WHY, HELLO THERE.
I APOLOGIZE FOR CALLING YOU OUT AT SUCH A LATE HOUR.
LIKE ALWAYS, HARUHI ...
...ISN'T HERE.
NOW THEN, ASAHINA-SAN...
...COULD YOU EXPLAIN THE SITUATION IN A WAY THAT HE CAN UNDERSTAND?
MU (GRIMACE)

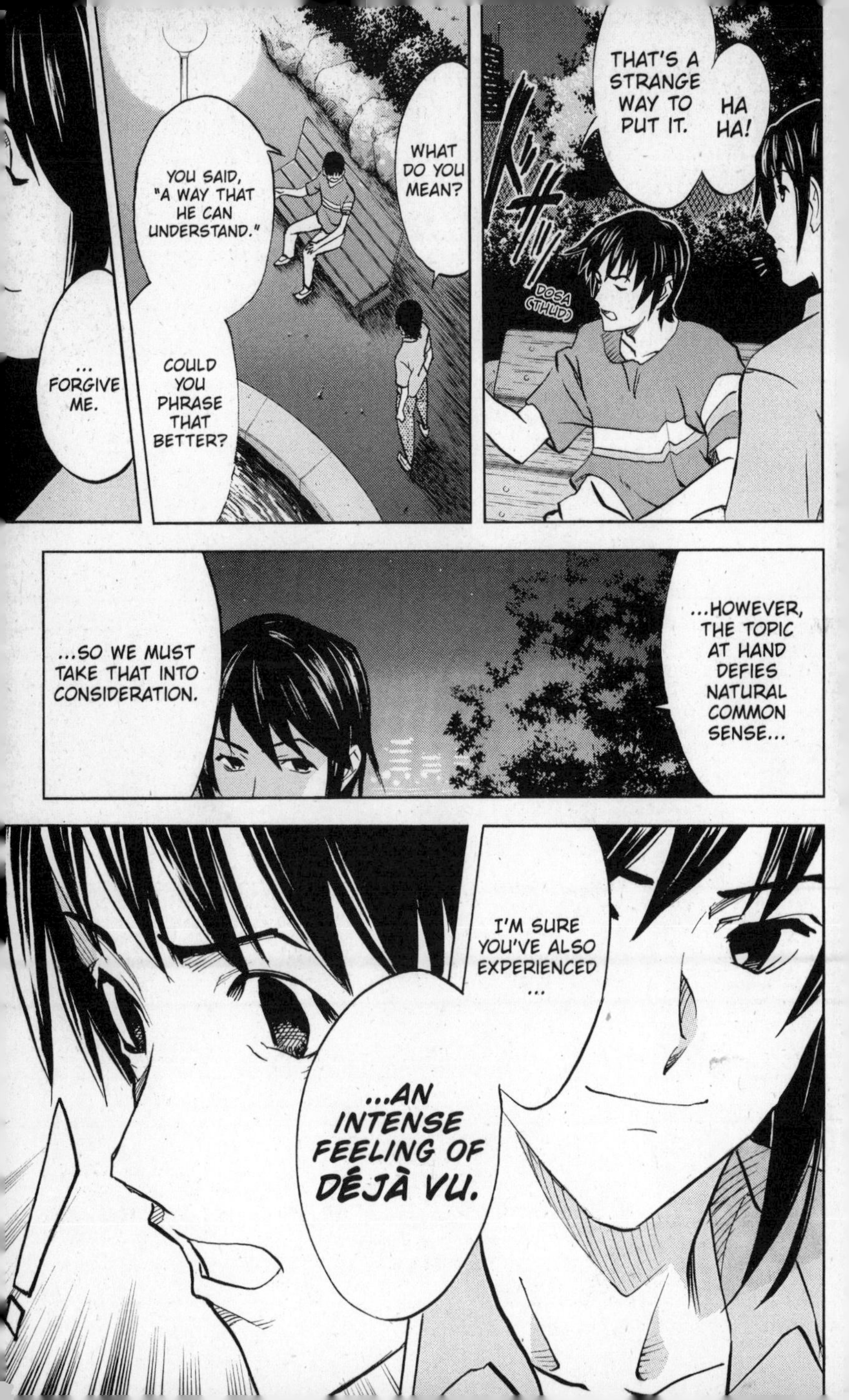
THAT'S A STRANGE WAY TO PUT IT.
HA HA!
DOSA (THUD)
WHAT DO YOU MEAN?
YOU SAID, "A WAY THAT HE CAN UNDERSTAND."
COULD YOU PHRASE THAT BETTER?
... FORGIVE ME.
...HOWEVER, THE TOPIC AT HAND DEFIES NATURAL COMMON SENSE...
...SO WE MUST TAKE THAT INTO CONSIDERATION.
I'M SURE YOU'VE ALSO EXPERIENCED ...
...AN INTENSE FEELING OF DÉJÀ VU.

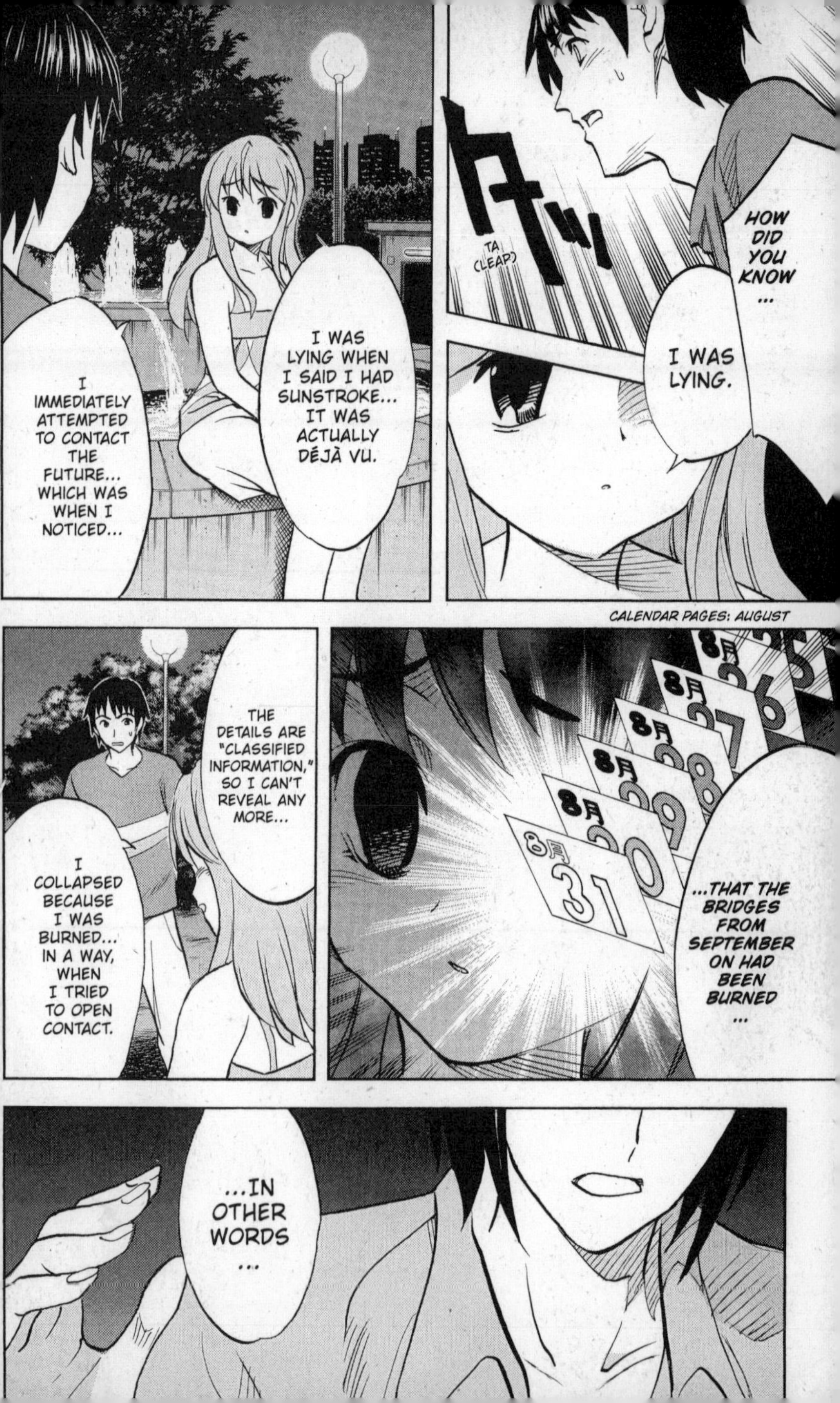
TA (LEAP)
HOW DID YOU KNOW...
I WAS LYING.
I WAS LYING WHEN I SAID I HAD SUNSTROKE... IT WAS ACTUALLY DÉJÀ VU.
I IMMEDIATELY ATTEMPTED TO CONTACT THE FUTURE... WHICH WAS WHEN I NOTICED...
CALENDAR PAGES: AUGUST
...THAT THE BRIDGES FROM SEPTEMBER ON HAD BEEN BURNED...
THE DETAILS ARE "CLASSIFIED INFORMATION," SO I CAN'T REVEAL ANY MORE...
I COLLAPSED BECAUSE I WAS BURNED... IN A WAY, WHEN I TRIED TO OPEN CONTACT.
...IN OTHER WORDS...

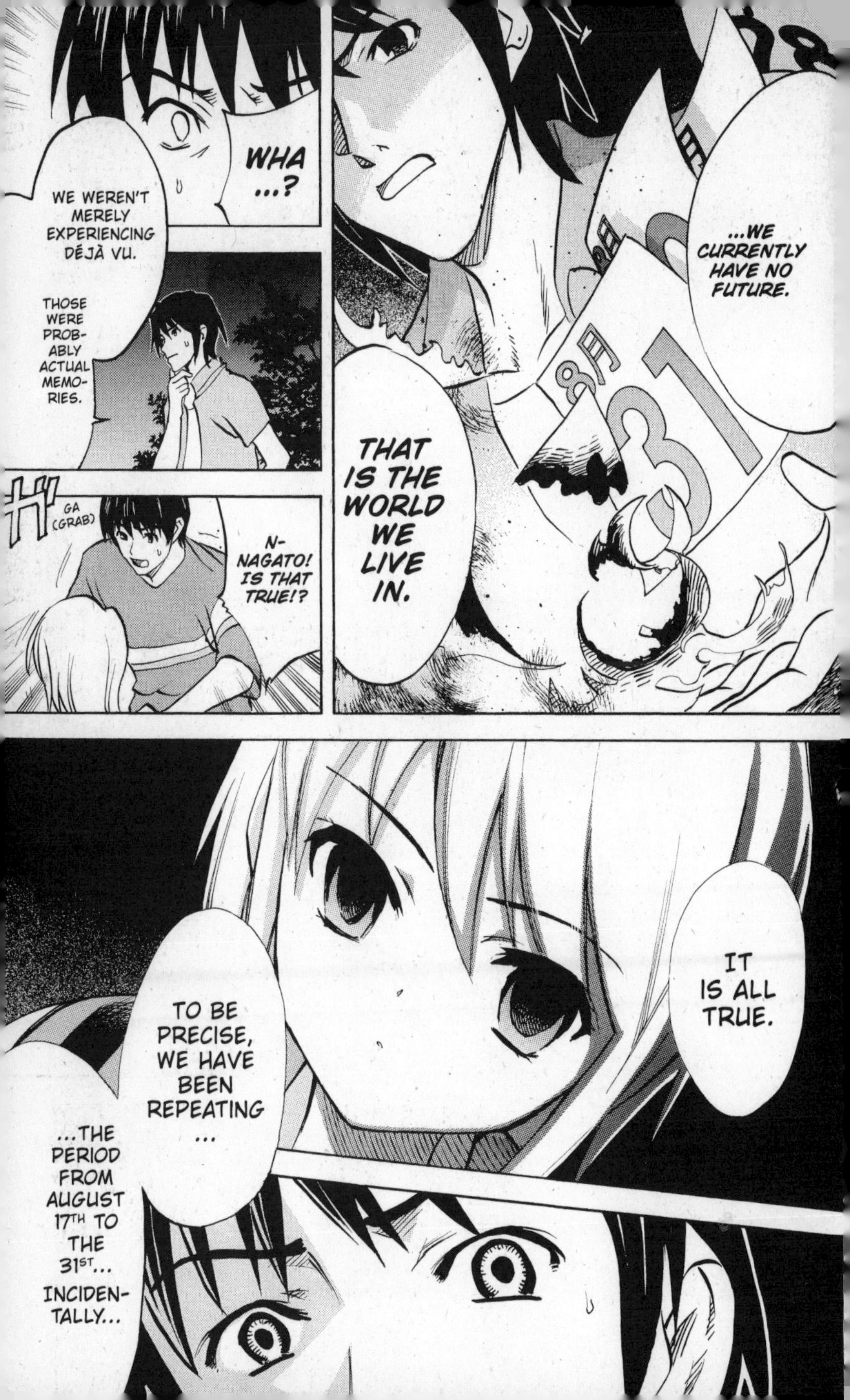
...WE CURRENTLY HAVE NO FUTURE.
THAT IS THE WORLD WE LIVE IN.
WHA ...?
WE WEREN'T MERELY EXPERIENCING DÉJÀ VU.
THOSE WERE PROBABLY ACTUAL MEMORIES.
GA (GRAB)
N-NAGATO! IS THAT TRUE!?
IT IS ALL TRUE.
TO BE PRECISE, WE HAVE BEEN REPEATING ...
...THE PERIOD FROM AUGUST 17TH TO THE 31ST... INCIDENTALLY...

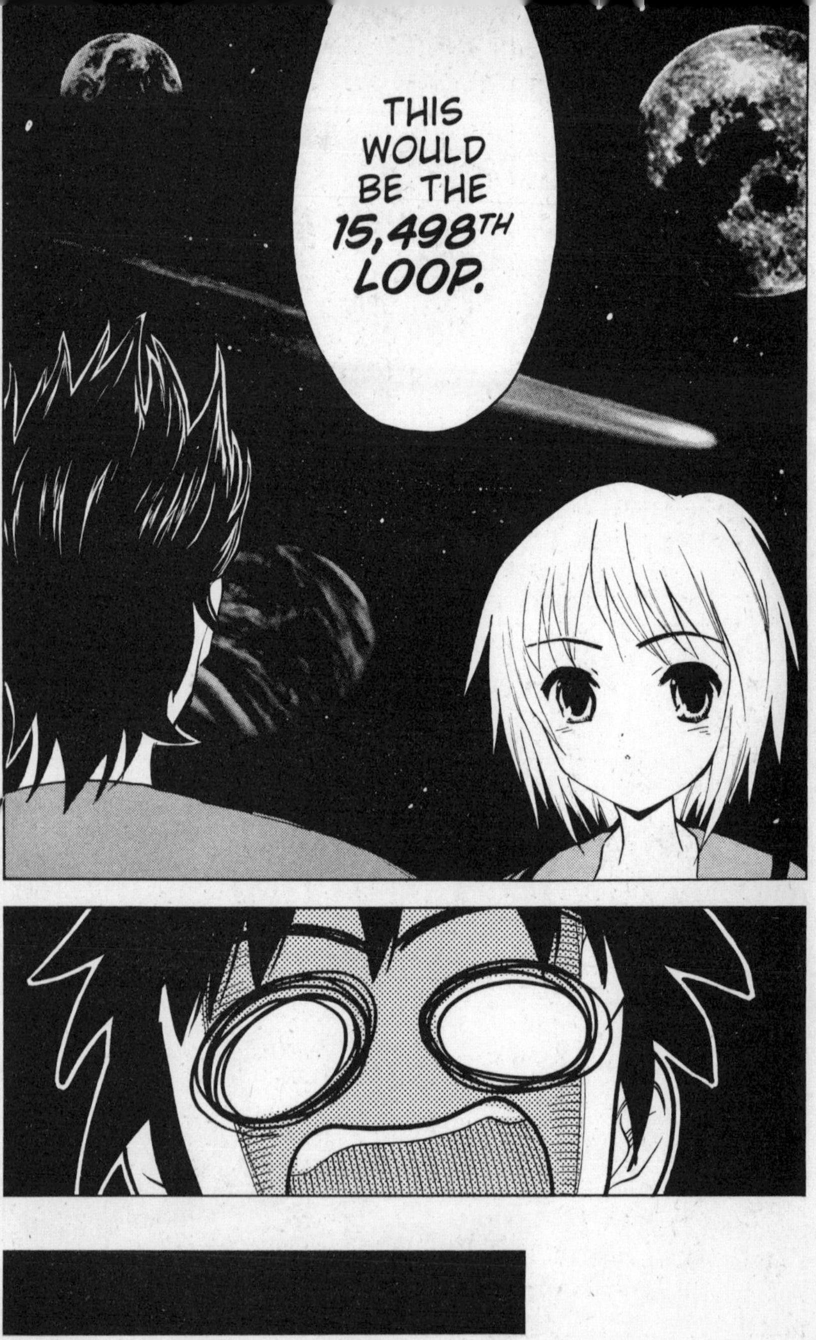
THIS WOULD BE THE 15,498TH LOOP.

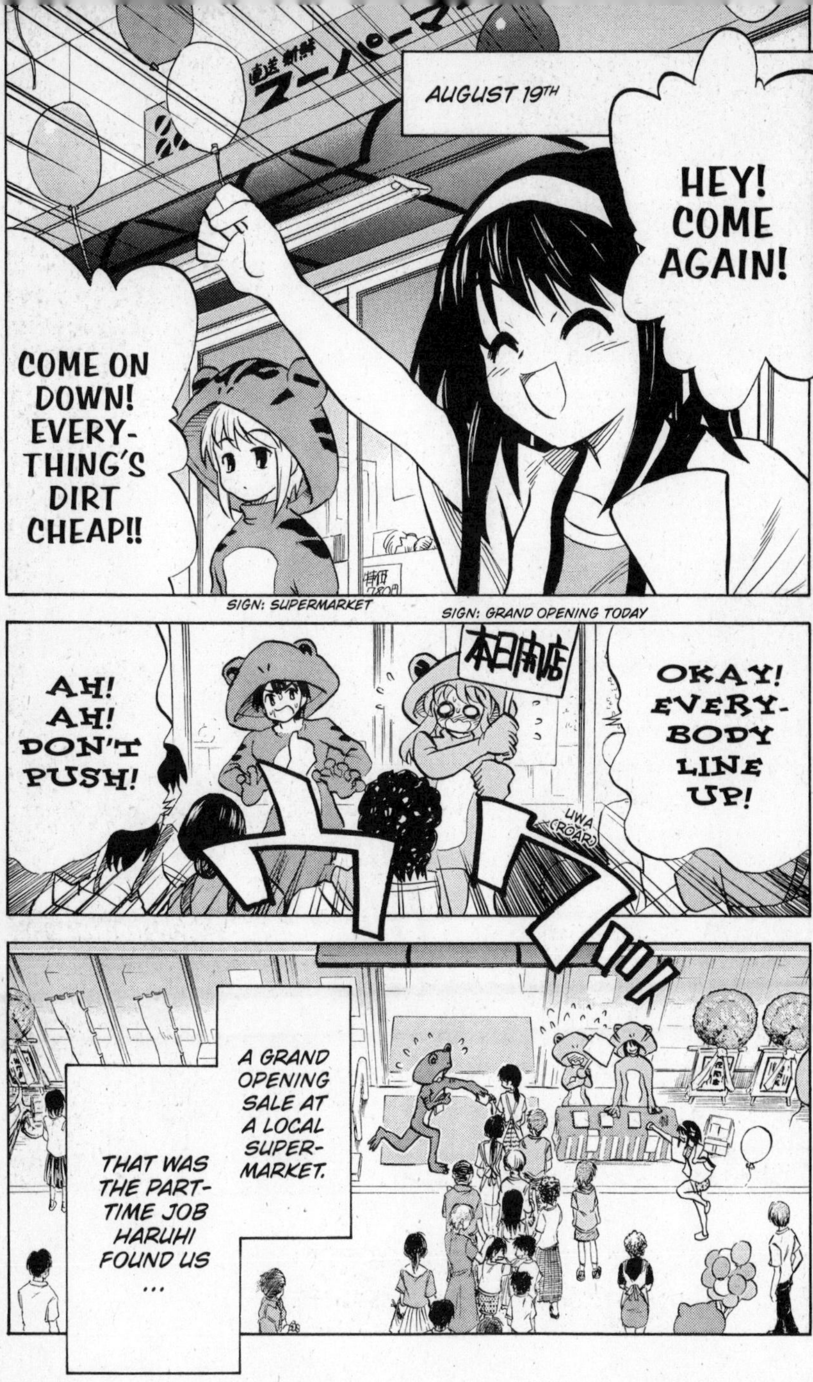
AUGUST 19TH
HEY! COME AGAIN!
COME ON DOWN! EVERY-THING'S DIRT CHEAP!!
SIGN: SUPERMARKET
SIGN: GRAND OPENING TODAY
OKAY! EVERY-BODY LINE UP!
UWA (ROAR)
AH! AH! DON'T PUSH!
A GRAND OPENING SALE AT A LOCAL SUPER-MARKET.
THAT WAS THE PART-TIME JOB HARUHI FOUND US ...

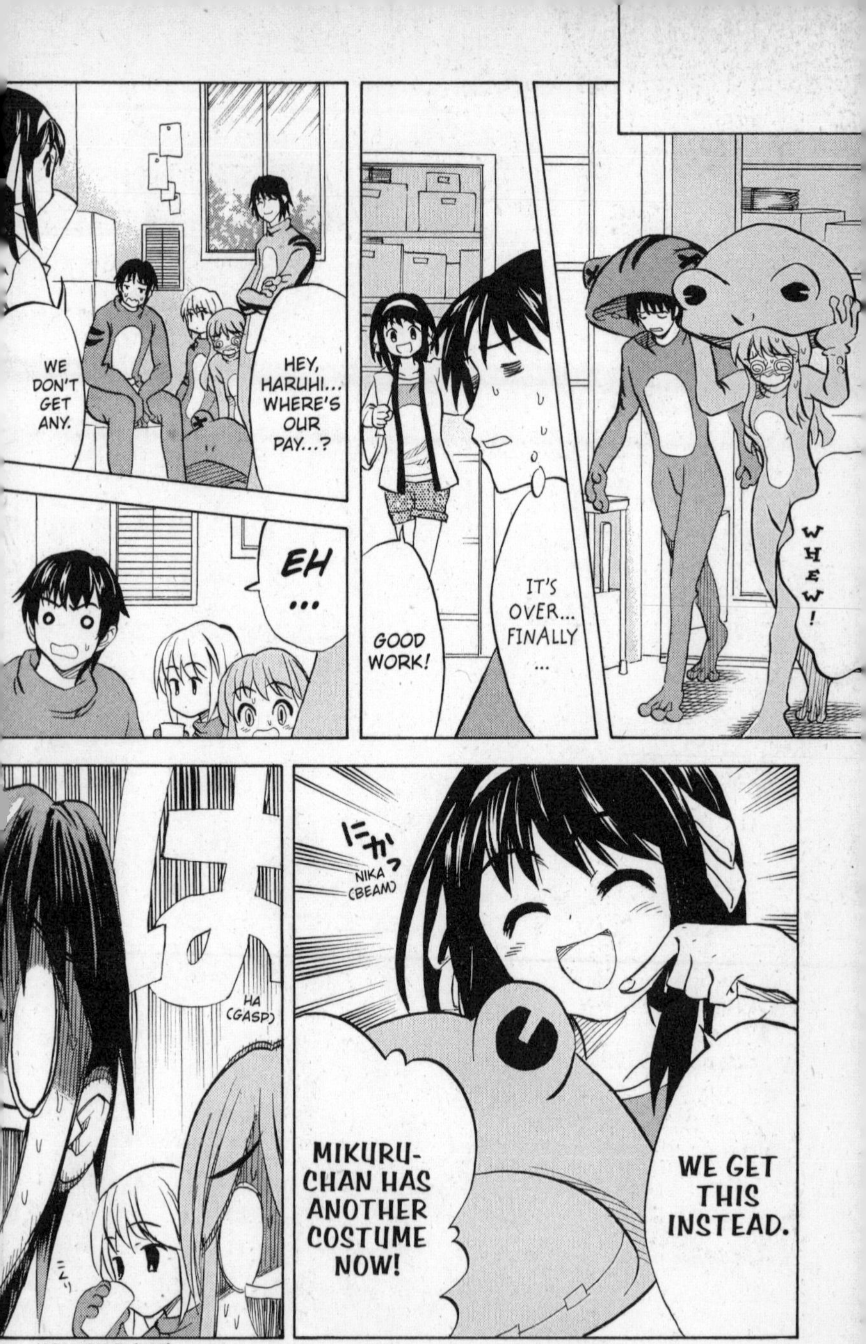
WHEW!
IT'S OVER... FINALLY...
GOOD WORK!
HEY, HARUHI... WHERE'S OUR PAY...?
WE DON'T GET ANY.
EH...
にかっ
NIKA (BEAM)
WE GET THIS INSTEAD.
MIKURU-CHAN HAS ANOTHER COSTUME NOW!
HA (GASP)
こくり

SFX: KOKURI (NOD)

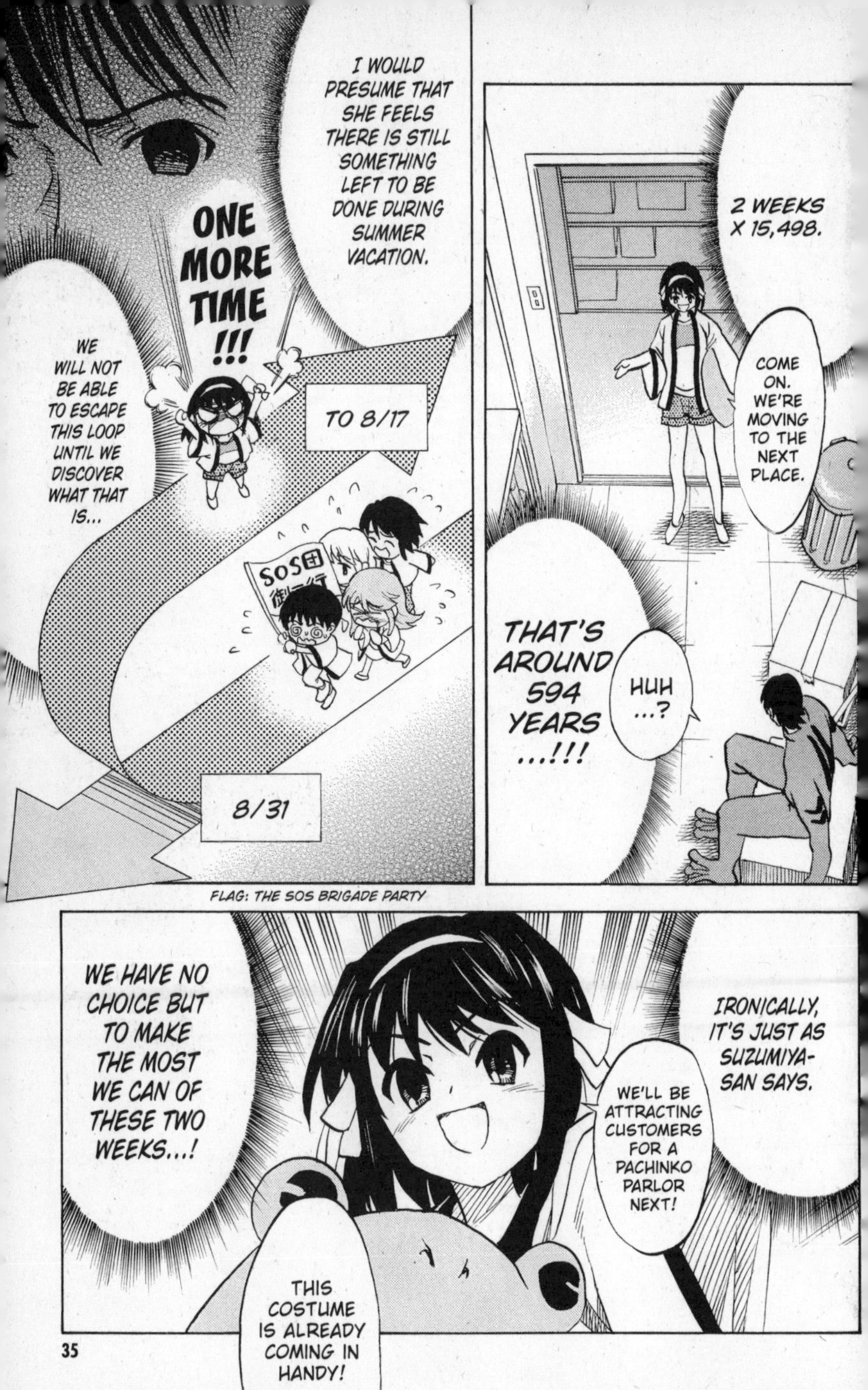
2 WEEKS X 15,498.
COME ON. WE'RE MOVING TO THE NEXT PLACE.
HUH ...?
THAT'S AROUND 594 YEARS ...!!!
I WOULD PRESUME THAT SHE FEELS THERE IS STILL SOMETHING LEFT TO BE DONE DURING SUMMER VACATION.
ONE MORE TIME !!!
TO 8/17
WE WILL NOT BE ABLE TO ESCAPE THIS LOOP UNTIL WE DISCOVER WHAT THAT IS...
8/31
FLAG: THE SOS BRIGADE PARTY
IRONICALLY, IT'S JUST AS SUZUMIYA-SAN SAYS.
WE'LL BE ATTRACTING CUSTOMERS FOR A PACHINKO PARLOR NEXT!
WE HAVE NO CHOICE BUT TO MAKE THE MOST WE CAN OF THESE TWO WEEKS...!
THIS COSTUME IS ALREADY COMING IN HANDY!

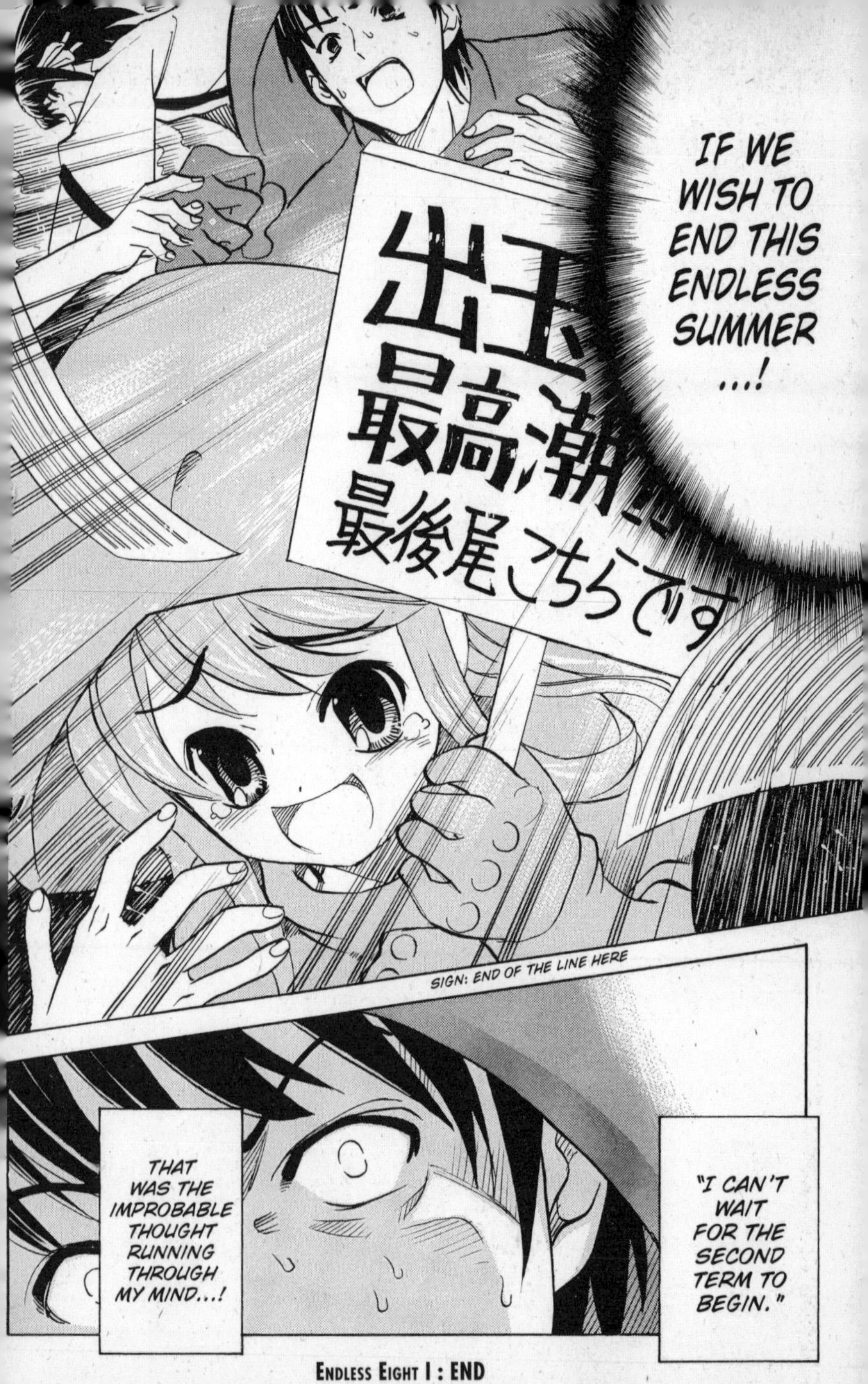
出玉、最高潮!!
最後尾こちらです
IF WE WISH TO END THIS ENDLESS SUMMER ...!
SIGN: END OF THE LINE HERE
"I CAN'T WAIT FOR THE SECOND TERM TO BEGIN."
THAT WAS THE IMPROBABLE THOUGHT RUNNING THROUGH MY MIND...!

Endless Eight I : END

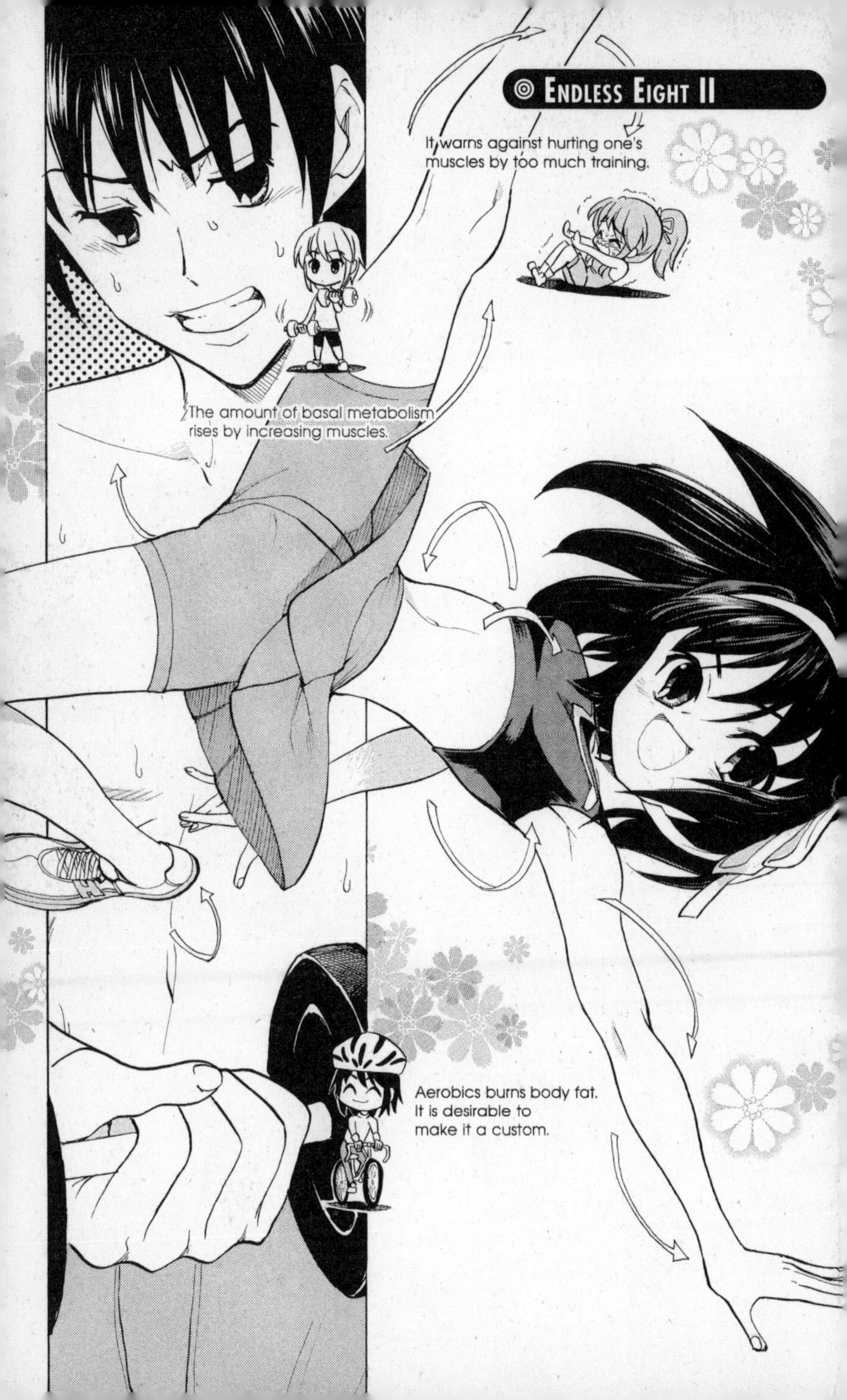
◎ ENDLESS EIGHT II
It warns against hurting one's muscles by too much training.
The amount of basal metabolism rises by increasing muscles.
Aerobics burns body fat. It is desirable to make it a custom.

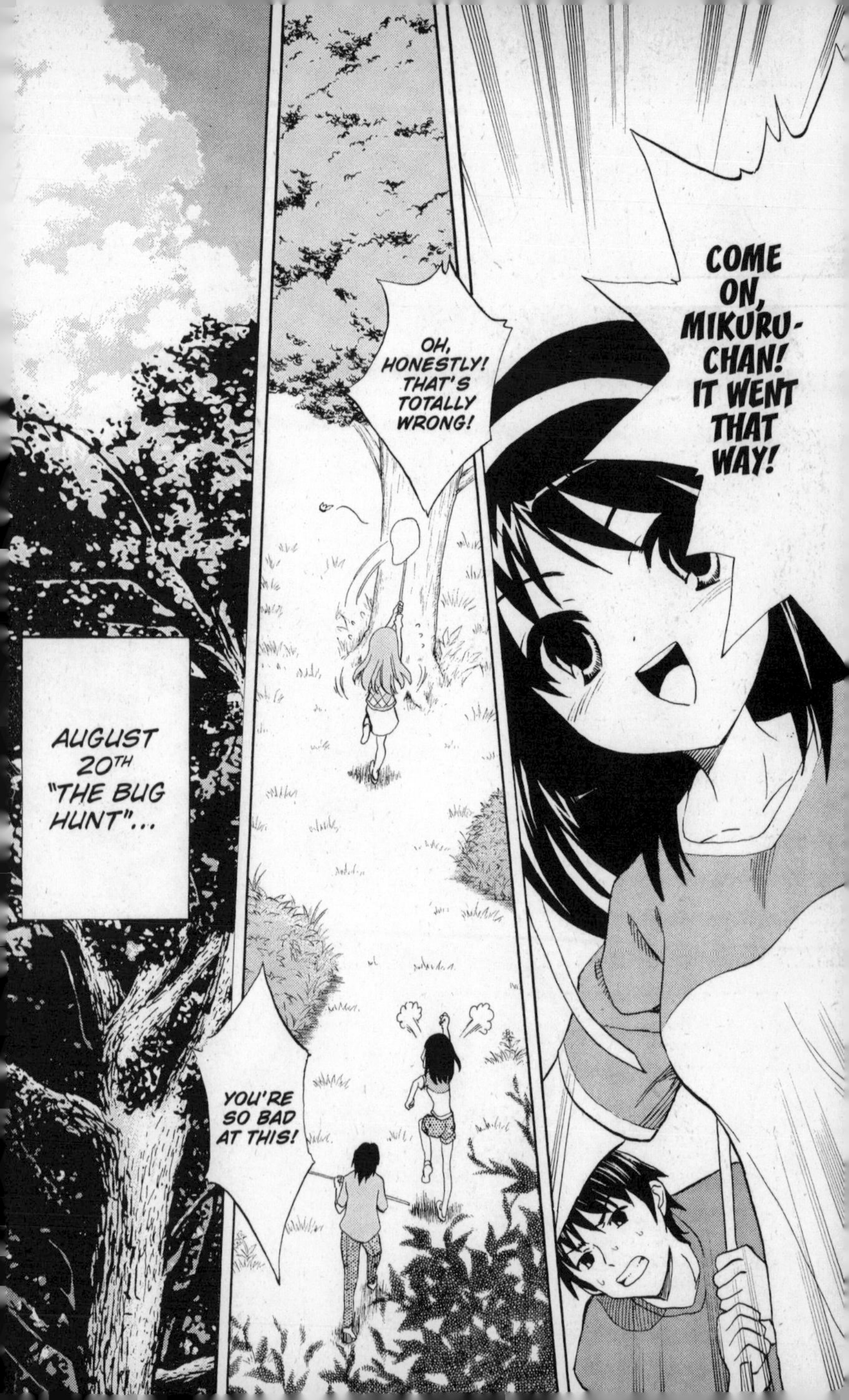
COME ON, MIKURU-CHAN! IT WENT THAT WAY!
OH, HONESTLY! THAT'S TOTALLY WRONG!
YOU'RE SO BAD AT THIS!
AUGUST 20TH "THE BUG HUNT"...

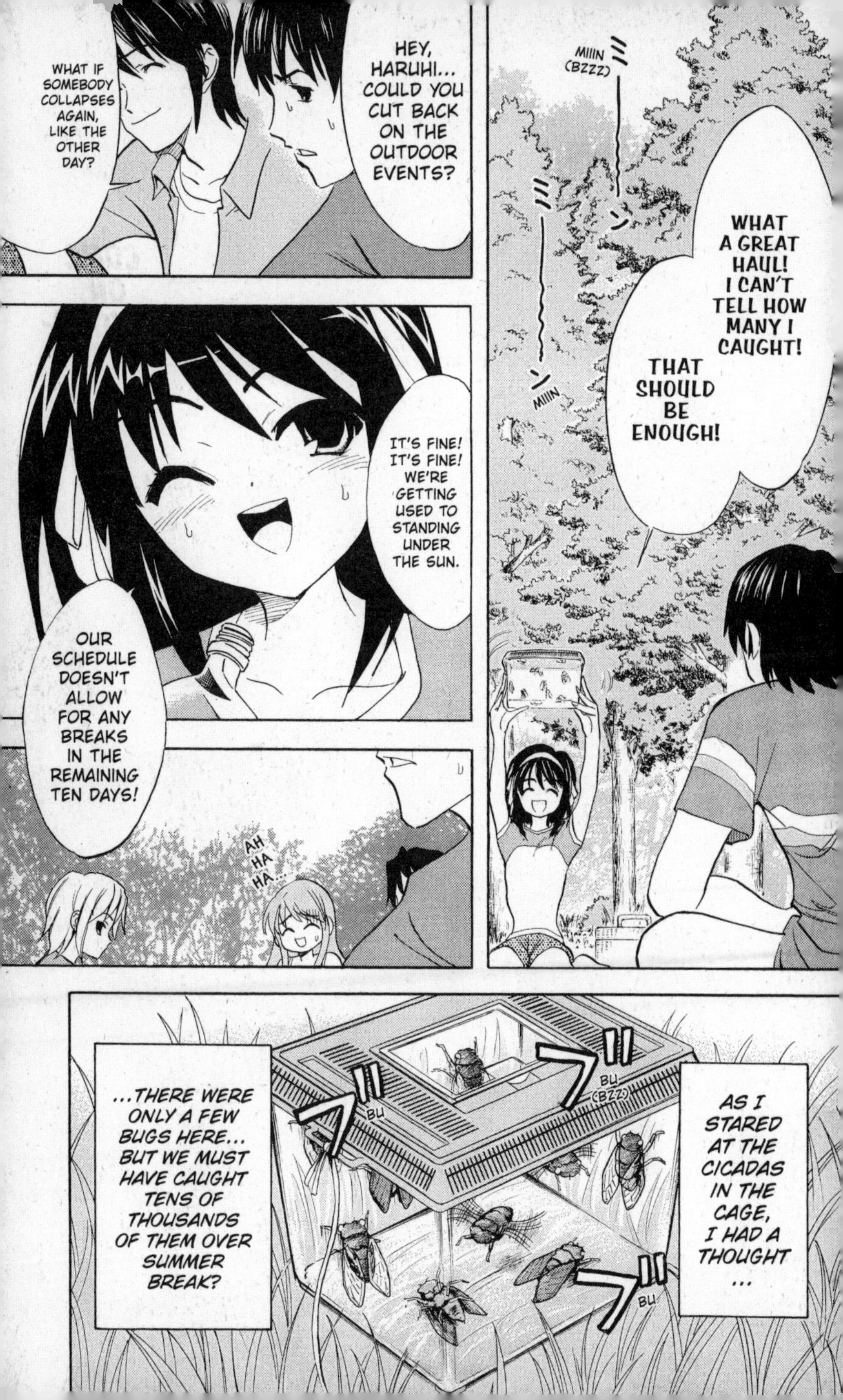
MIIN (BZZZ)
MIIN
WHAT A GREAT HAUL! I CAN'T TELL HOW MANY I CAUGHT!
THAT SHOULD BE ENOUGH!
HEY, HARUHI... COULD YOU CUT BACK ON THE OUTDOOR EVENTS?
WHAT IF SOMEBODY COLLAPSES AGAIN, LIKE THE OTHER DAY?
IT'S FINE! IT'S FINE! WE'RE GETTING USED TO STANDING UNDER THE SUN.
OUR SCHEDULE DOESN'T ALLOW FOR ANY BREAKS IN THE REMAINING TEN DAYS!
AH HA HA...
AS I STARED AT THE CICADAS IN THE CAGE, I HAD A THOUGHT...
BU (BZZ)
BU
...THERE WERE ONLY A FEW BUGS HERE... BUT WE MUST HAVE CAUGHT TENS OF THOUSANDS OF THEM OVER SUMMER BREAK?
BU

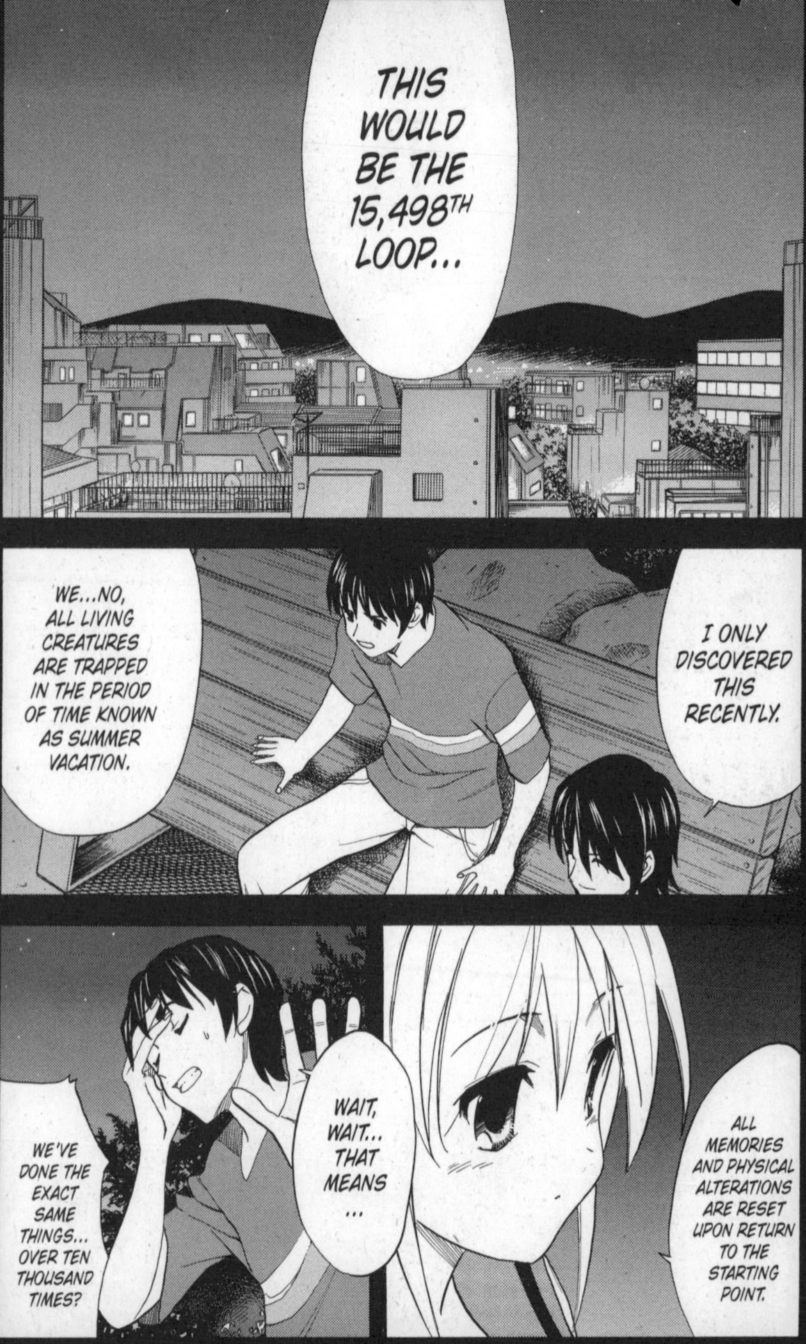
THIS WOULD BE THE 15,498TH LOOP...
I ONLY DISCOVERED THIS RECENTLY.
WE...NO, ALL LIVING CREATURES ARE TRAPPED IN THE PERIOD OF TIME KNOWN AS SUMMER VACATION.
ALL MEMORIES AND PHYSICAL ALTERATIONS ARE RESET UPON RETURN TO THE STARTING POINT.
WAIT, WAIT... THAT MEANS ...
WE'VE DONE THE EXACT SAME THINGS... OVER TEN THOUSAND TIMES?

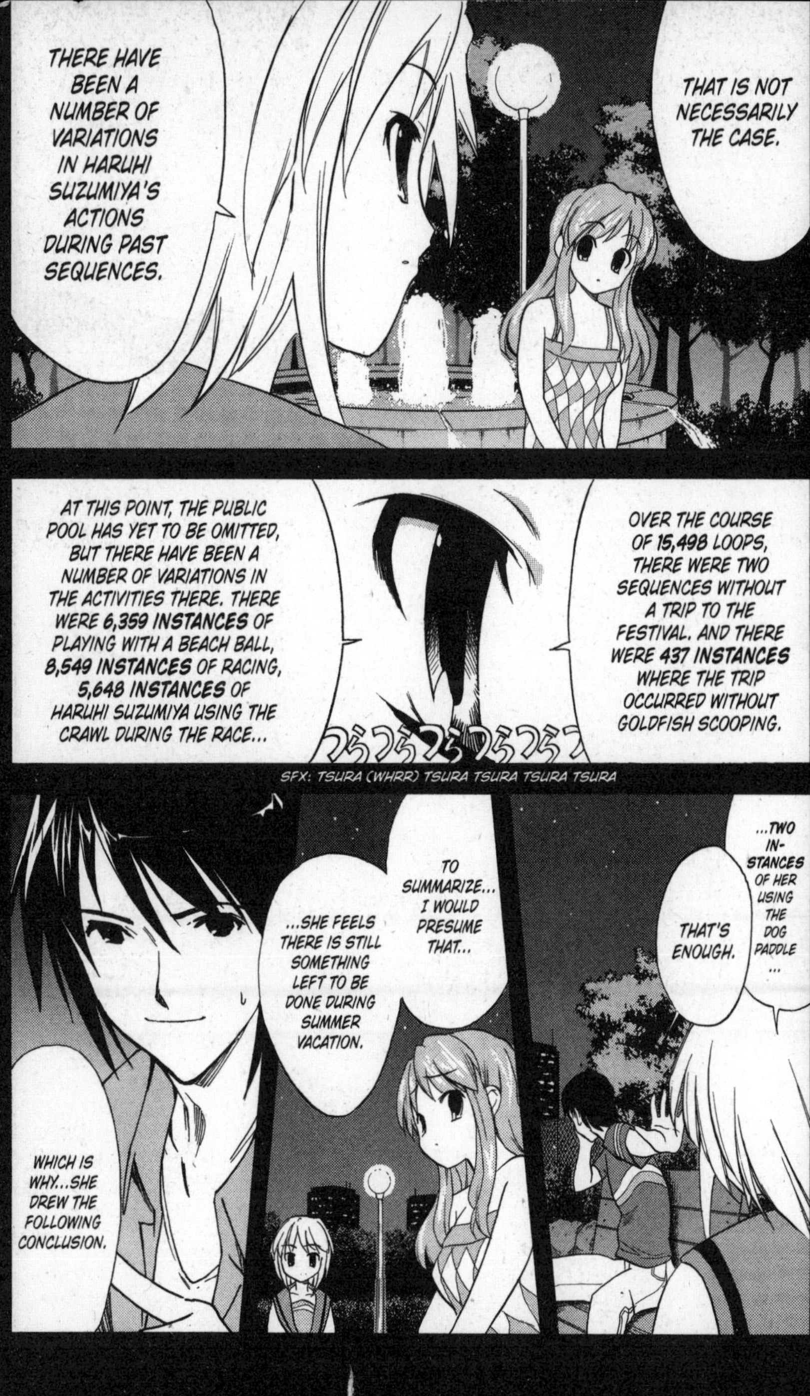
THAT IS NOT NECESSARILY THE CASE.
THERE HAVE BEEN A NUMBER OF VARIATIONS IN HARUHI SUZUMIYA'S ACTIONS DURING PAST SEQUENCES.
OVER THE COURSE OF 15,498 LOOPS, THERE WERE TWO SEQUENCES WITHOUT A TRIP TO THE FESTIVAL. AND THERE WERE 437 INSTANCES WHERE THE TRIP OCCURRED WITHOUT GOLDFISH SCOOPING.
AT THIS POINT, THE PUBLIC POOL HAS YET TO BE OMITTED, BUT THERE HAVE BEEN A NUMBER OF VARIATIONS IN THE ACTIVITIES THERE. THERE WERE 6,359 INSTANCES OF PLAYING WITH A BEACH BALL, 8,549 INSTANCES OF RACING, 5,648 INSTANCES OF HARUHI SUZUMIYA USING THE CRAWL DURING THE RACE...
SFX: TSURA (WHRR) TSURA TSURA TSURA TSURA
...TWO IN-STANCES OF HER USING THE DOG PADDLE ...
THAT'S ENOUGH.
TO SUMMARIZE... I WOULD PRESUME THAT...
...SHE FEELS THERE IS STILL SOMETHING LEFT TO BE DONE DURING SUMMER VACATION.
WHICH IS WHY...SHE DREW THE FOLLOWING CONCLUSION.

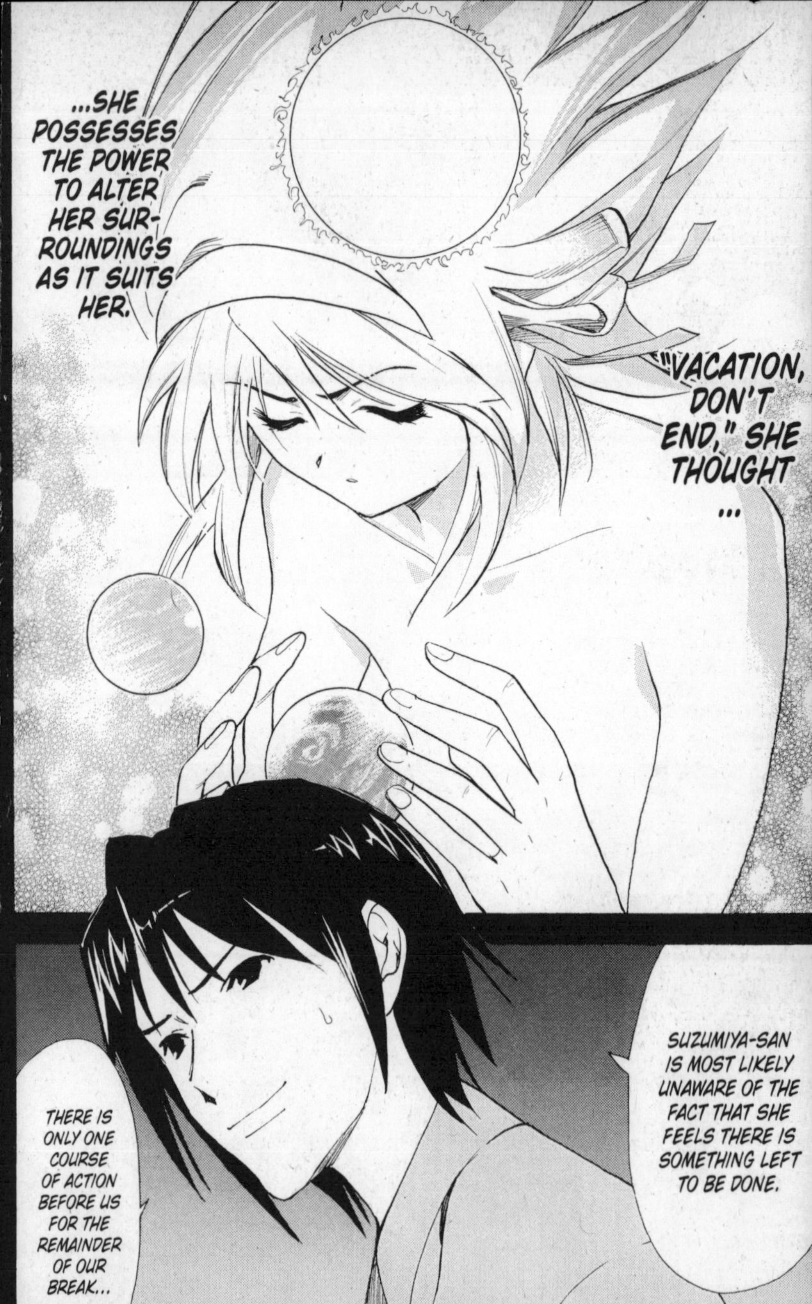
...SHE POSSESSES THE POWER TO ALTER HER SURROUNDINGS AS IT SUITS HER.
"VACATION, DON'T END," SHE THOUGHT ...
SUZUMIYA-SAN IS MOST LIKELY UNAWARE OF THE FACT THAT SHE FEELS THERE IS SOMETHING LEFT TO BE DONE.
THERE IS ONLY ONE COURSE OF ACTION BEFORE US FOR THE REMAINDER OF OUR BREAK...

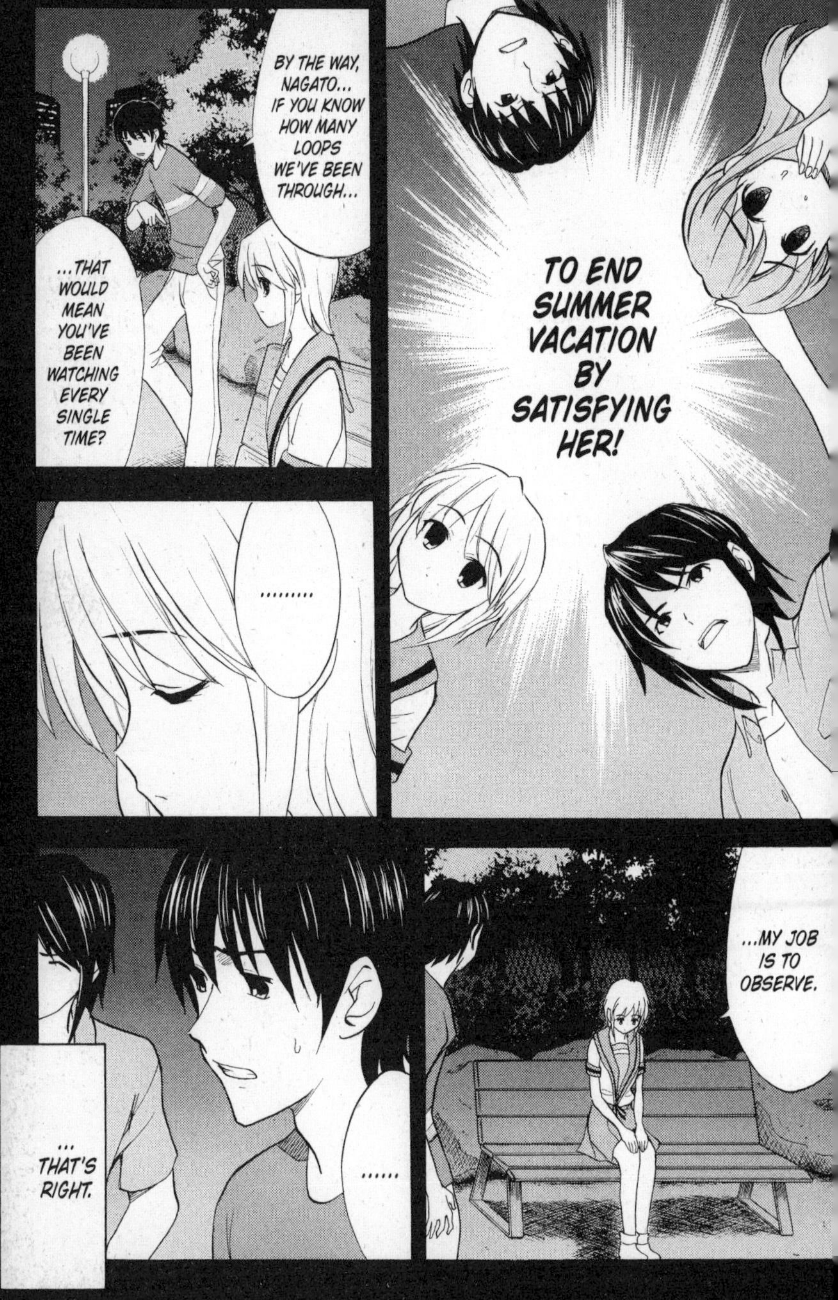
TO END SUMMER VACATION BY SATISFYING HER!
BY THE WAY, NAGATO... IF YOU KNOW HOW MANY LOOPS WE'VE BEEN THROUGH...
...THAT WOULD MEAN YOU'VE BEEN WATCHING EVERY SINGLE TIME?
....
...MY JOB IS TO OBSERVE.
......
... THAT'S RIGHT.

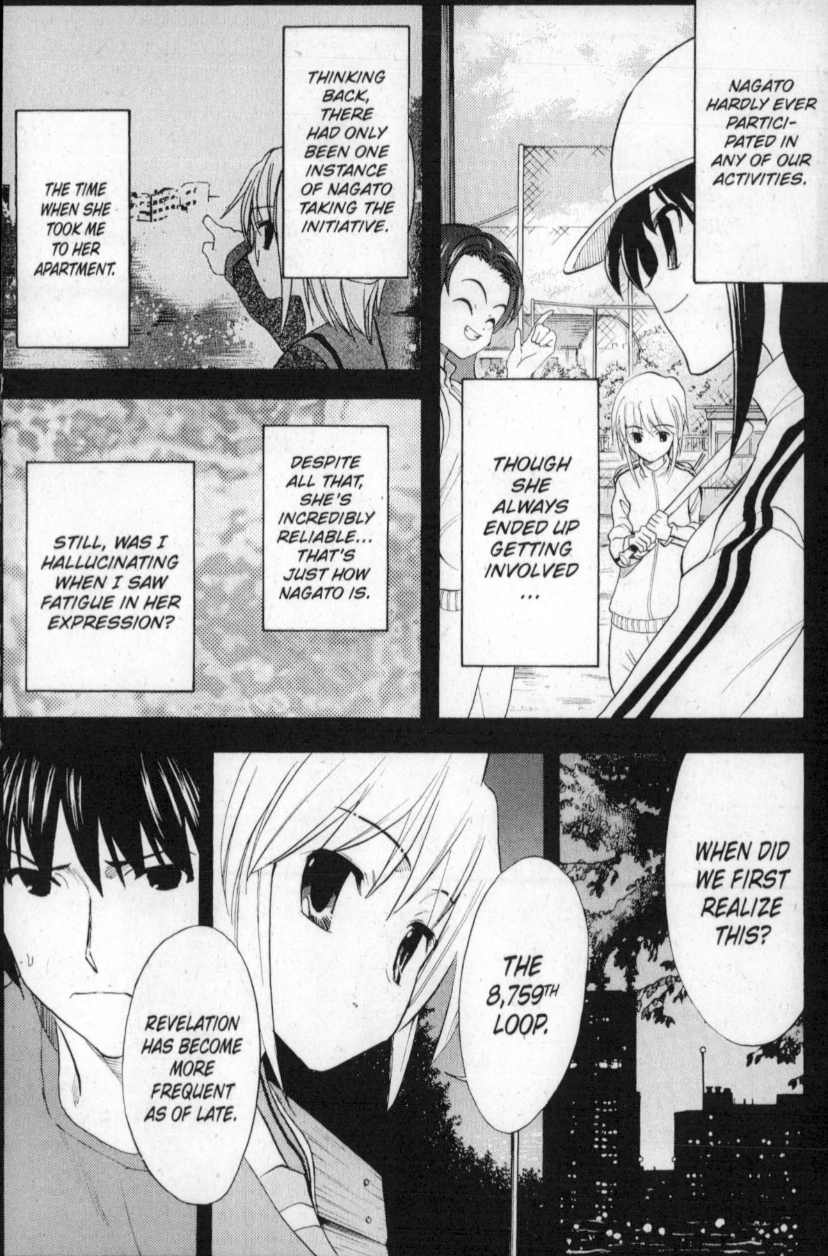
NAGATO HARDLY EVER PARTICIPATED IN ANY OF OUR ACTIVITIES.
THOUGH SHE ALWAYS ENDED UP GETTING INVOLVED...
THINKING BACK, THERE HAD ONLY BEEN ONE INSTANCE OF NAGATO TAKING THE INITIATIVE.
THE TIME WHEN SHE TOOK ME TO HER APARTMENT.
DESPITE ALL THAT, SHE'S INCREDIBLY RELIABLE... THAT'S JUST HOW NAGATO IS.
STILL, WAS I HALLUCINATING WHEN I SAW FATIGUE IN HER EXPRESSION?
WHEN DID WE FIRST REALIZE THIS?
THE 8,759TH LOOP.
REVELATION HAS BECOME MORE FREQUENT AS OF LATE.

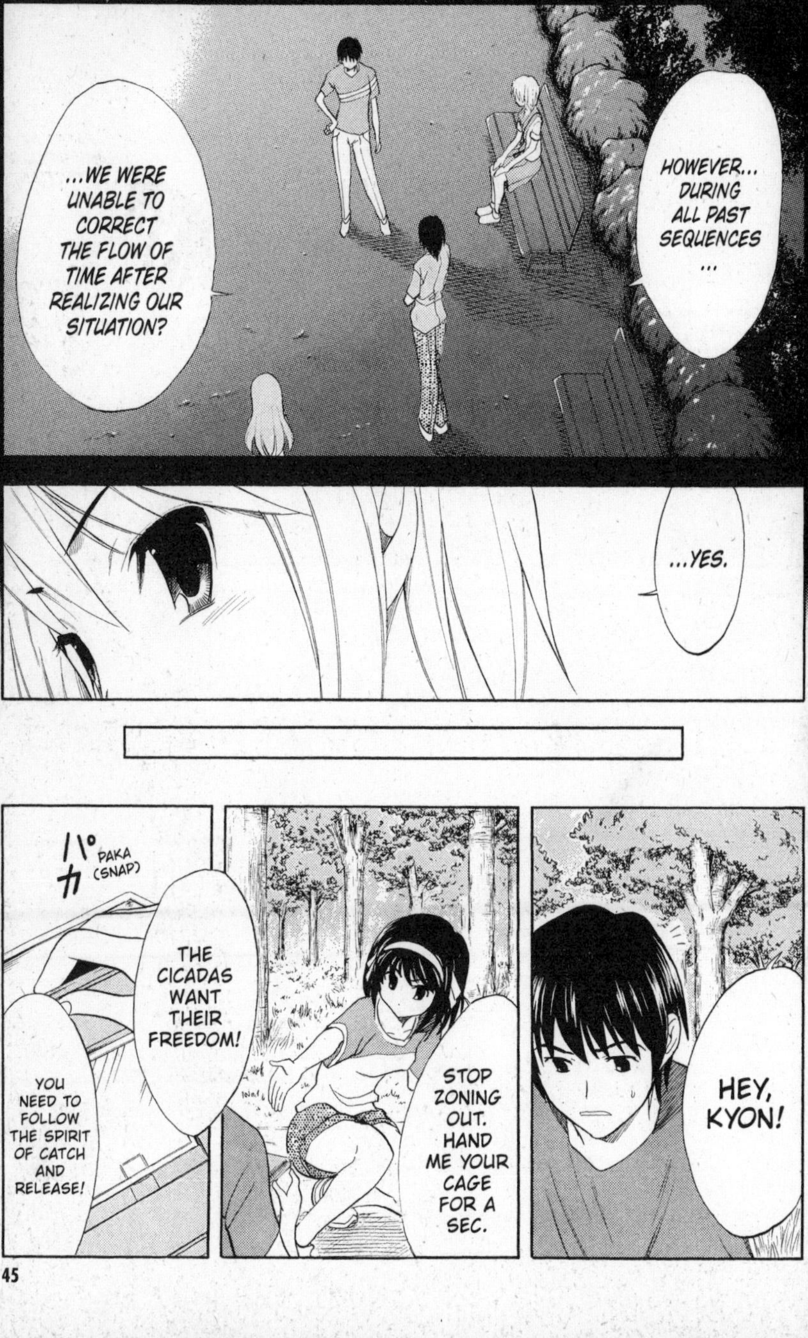
HOWEVER... DURING ALL PAST SEQUENCES ...
...WE WERE UNABLE TO CORRECT THE FLOW OF TIME AFTER REALIZING OUR SITUATION?
...YES.
HEY, KYON!
STOP ZONING OUT. HAND ME YOUR CAGE FOR A SEC.
パカ PAKA (SNAP)
THE CICADAS WANT THEIR FREEDOM!
YOU NEED TO FOLLOW THE SPIRIT OF CATCH AND RELEASE!

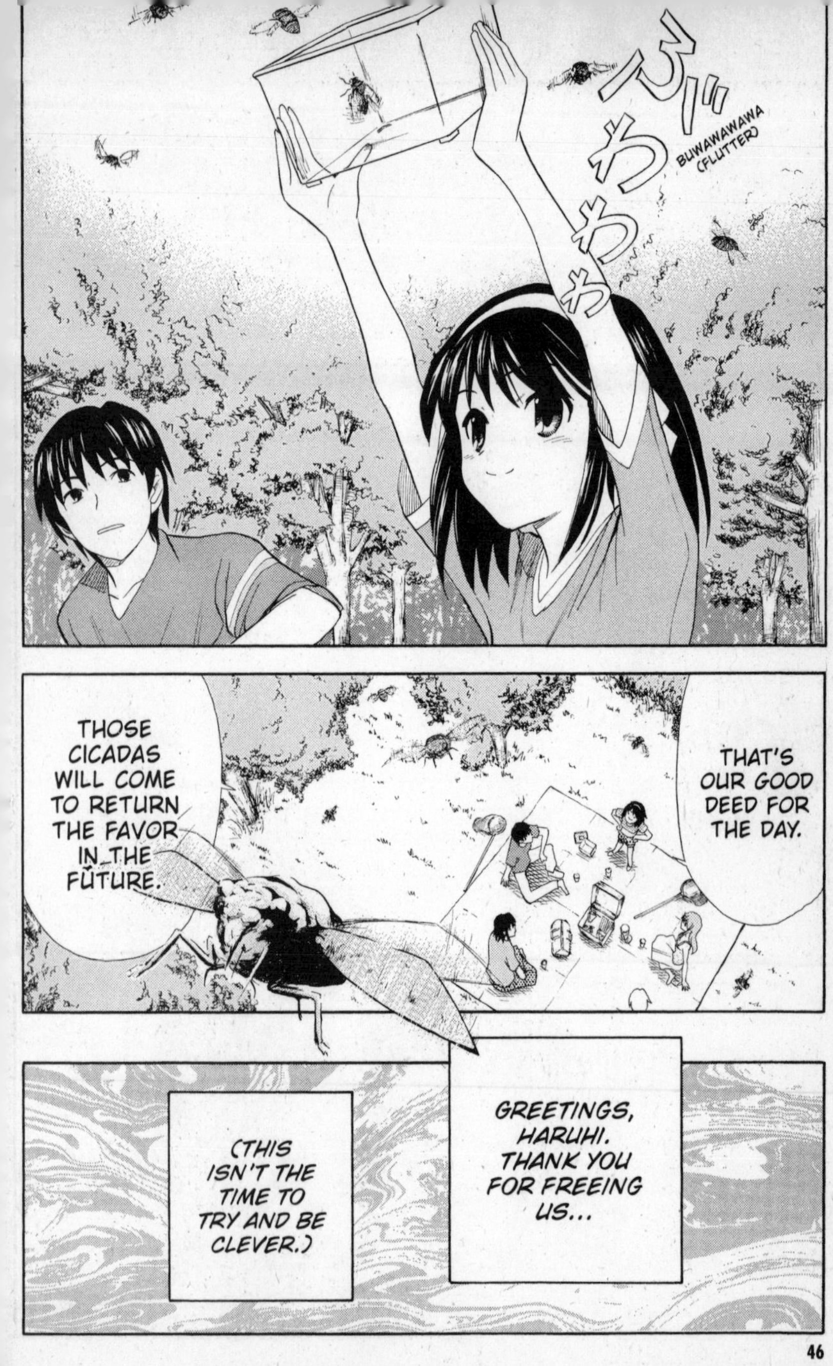
ぶわわゎ
BUWAWAWAWA (FLUTTER)
THAT'S OUR GOOD DEED FOR THE DAY.
THOSE CICADAS WILL COME TO RETURN THE FAVOR IN THE FUTURE.
GREETINGS, HARUHI. THANK YOU FOR FREEING US...
(THIS ISN'T THE TIME TO TRY AND BE CLEVER.)

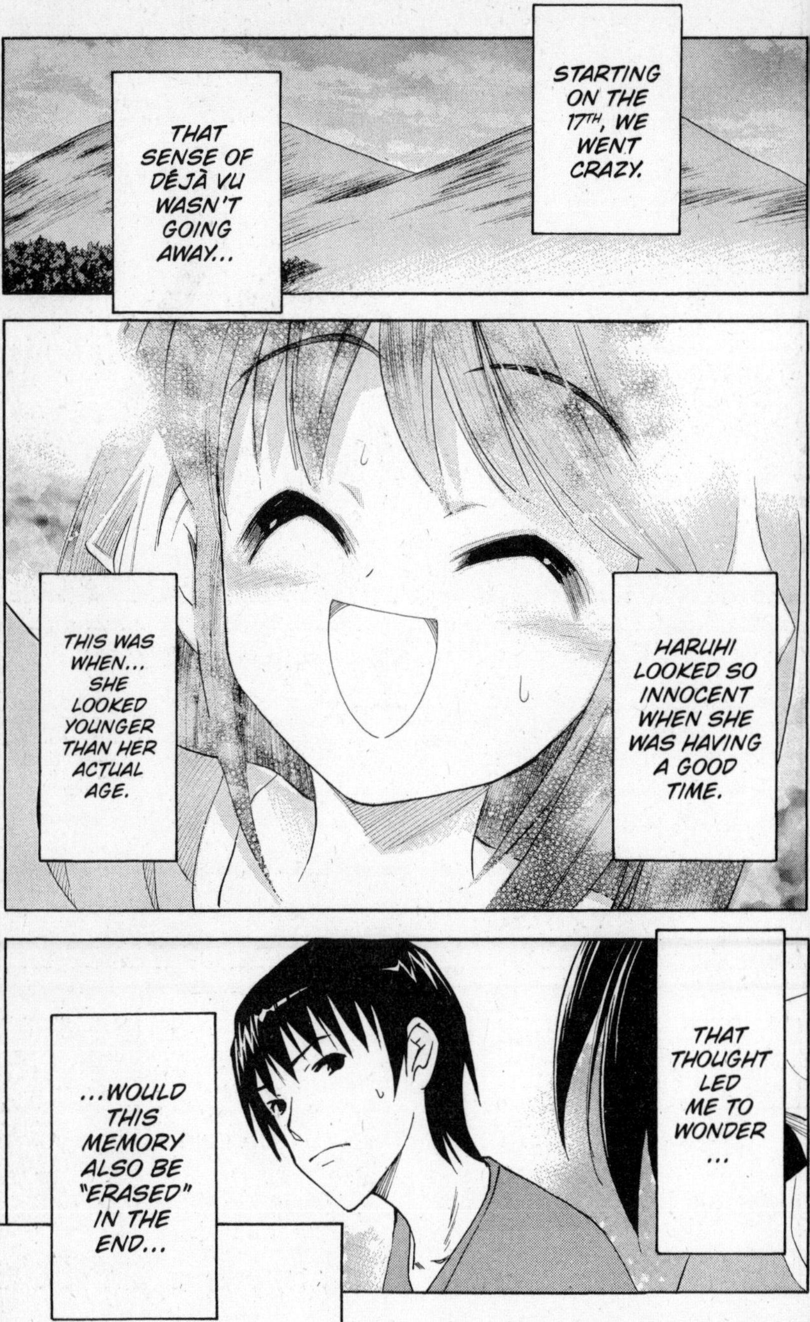
STARTING ON THE 17TH, WE WENT CRAZY.
THAT SENSE OF DÉJÀ VU WASN'T GOING AWAY...
HARUHI LOOKED SO INNOCENT WHEN SHE WAS HAVING A GOOD TIME.
THIS WAS WHEN... SHE LOOKED YOUNGER THAN HER ACTUAL AGE.
THAT THOUGHT LED ME TO WONDER ...
...WOULD THIS MEMORY ALSO BE "ERASED" IN THE END...

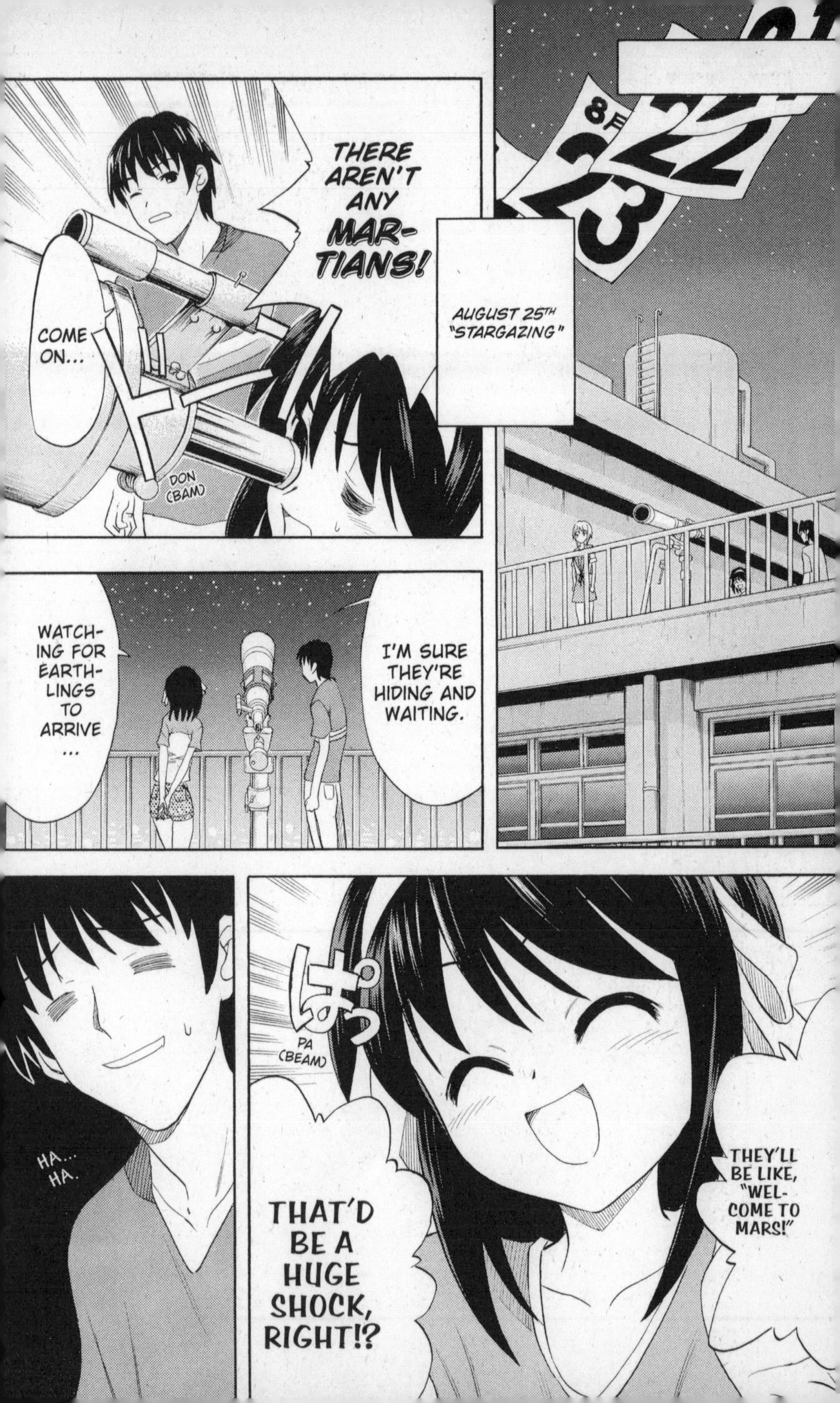
AUGUST 25TH "STARGAZING"
THERE AREN'T ANY MAR-TIANS!
COME ON...
DON (BAM)
I'M SURE THEY'RE HIDING AND WAITING.
WATCHING FOR EARTH-LINGS TO ARRIVE...
ぱっ
PA (BEAM)
THEY'LL BE LIKE, "WEL-COME TO MARS!"
THAT'D BE A HUGE SHOCK, RIGHT!?
HA... HA.

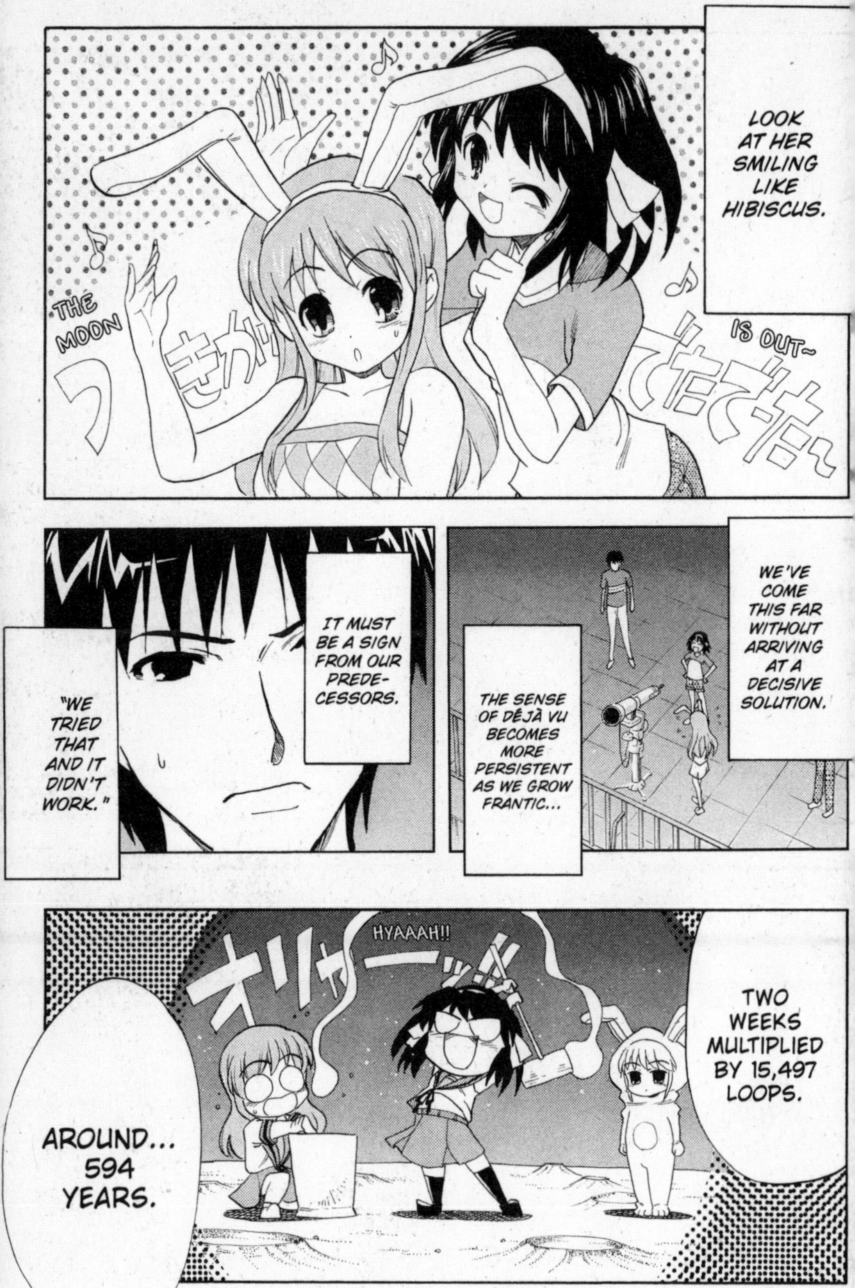
LOOK AT HER SMILING LIKE HIBISCUS.
THE MOON IS OUT~
WE'VE COME THIS FAR WITHOUT ARRIVING AT A DECISIVE SOLUTION.
THE SENSE OF DÉJÀ VU BECOMES MORE PERSISTENT AS WE GROW FRANTIC...
IT MUST BE A SIGN FROM OUR PREDE-CESSORS.
"WE TRIED THAT AND IT DIDN'T WORK."
TWO WEEKS MULTIPLIED BY 15,497 LOOPS.
HYAAAH!!
オリャーッ
AROUND... 594 YEARS.

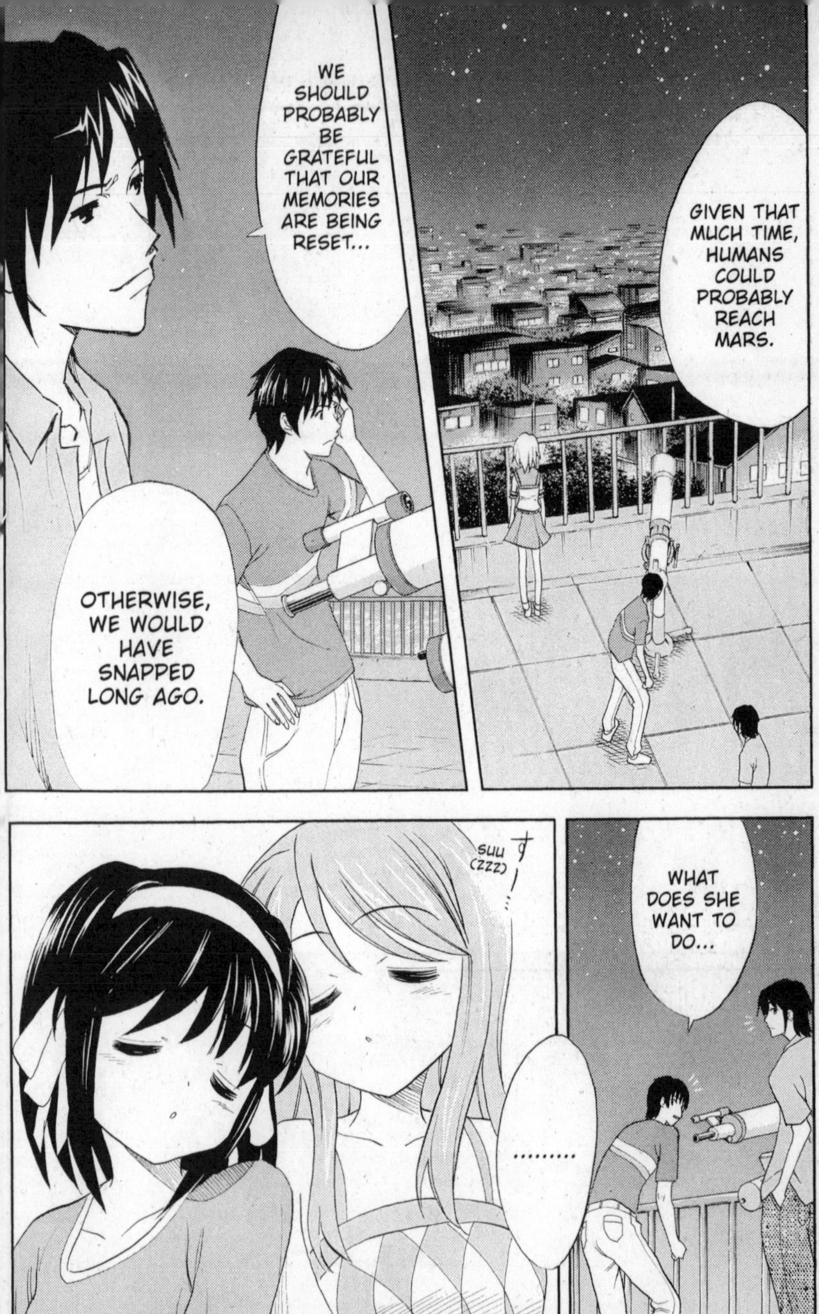
GIVEN THAT MUCH TIME, HUMANS COULD PROBABLY REACH MARS.
WE SHOULD PROBABLY BE GRATEFUL THAT OUR MEMORIES ARE BEING RESET...
OTHERWISE, WE WOULD HAVE SNAPPED LONG AGO.
WHAT DOES SHE WANT TO DO...
suu (zzz)
....

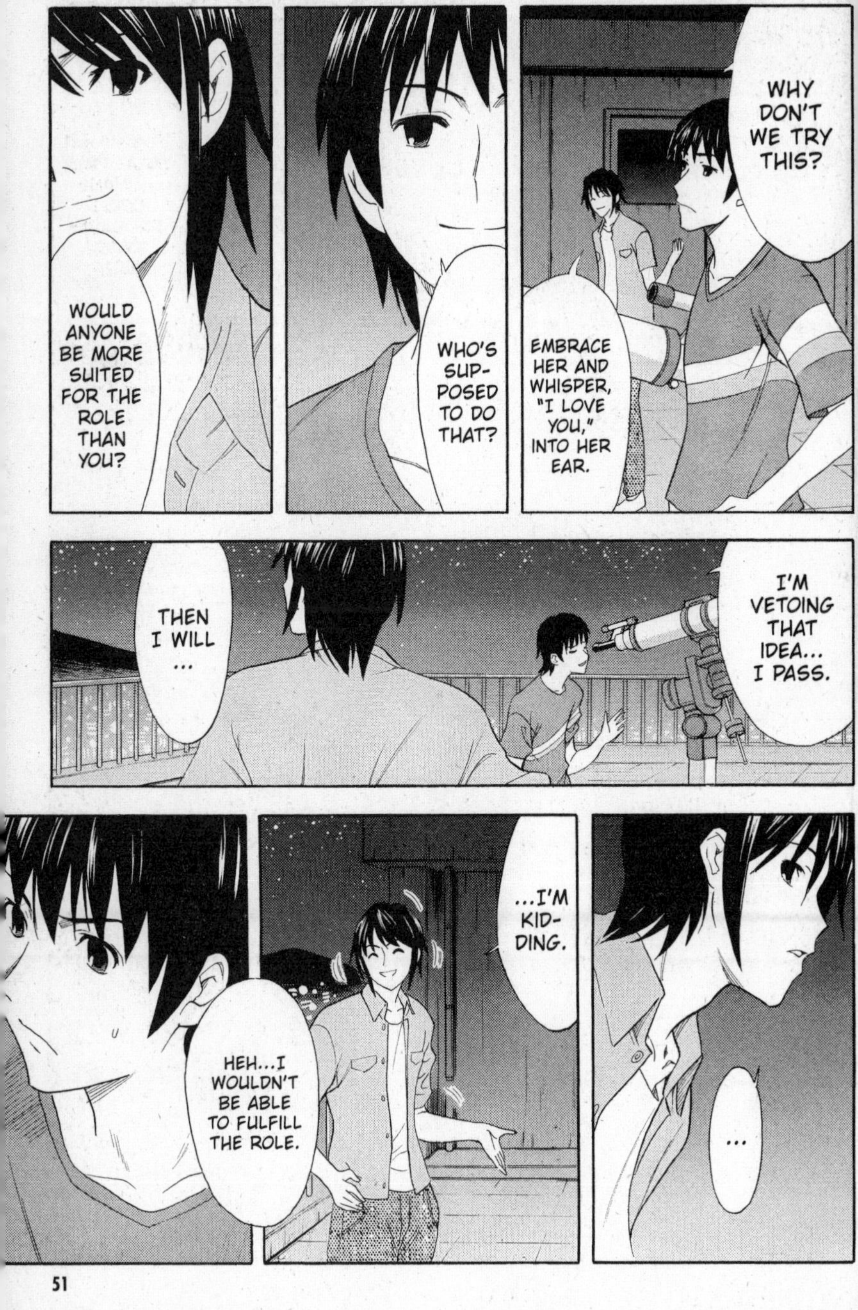
WHY DON'T WE TRY THIS?
EMBRACE HER AND WHISPER, "I LOVE YOU," INTO HER EAR.
WHO'S SUP-POSED TO DO THAT?
WOULD ANYONE BE MORE SUITED FOR THE ROLE THAN YOU?
I'M VETOING THAT IDEA... I PASS.
THEN I WILL ...
...
...I'M KID-DING.
HEH...I WOULDN'T BE ABLE TO FULFILL THE ROLE.

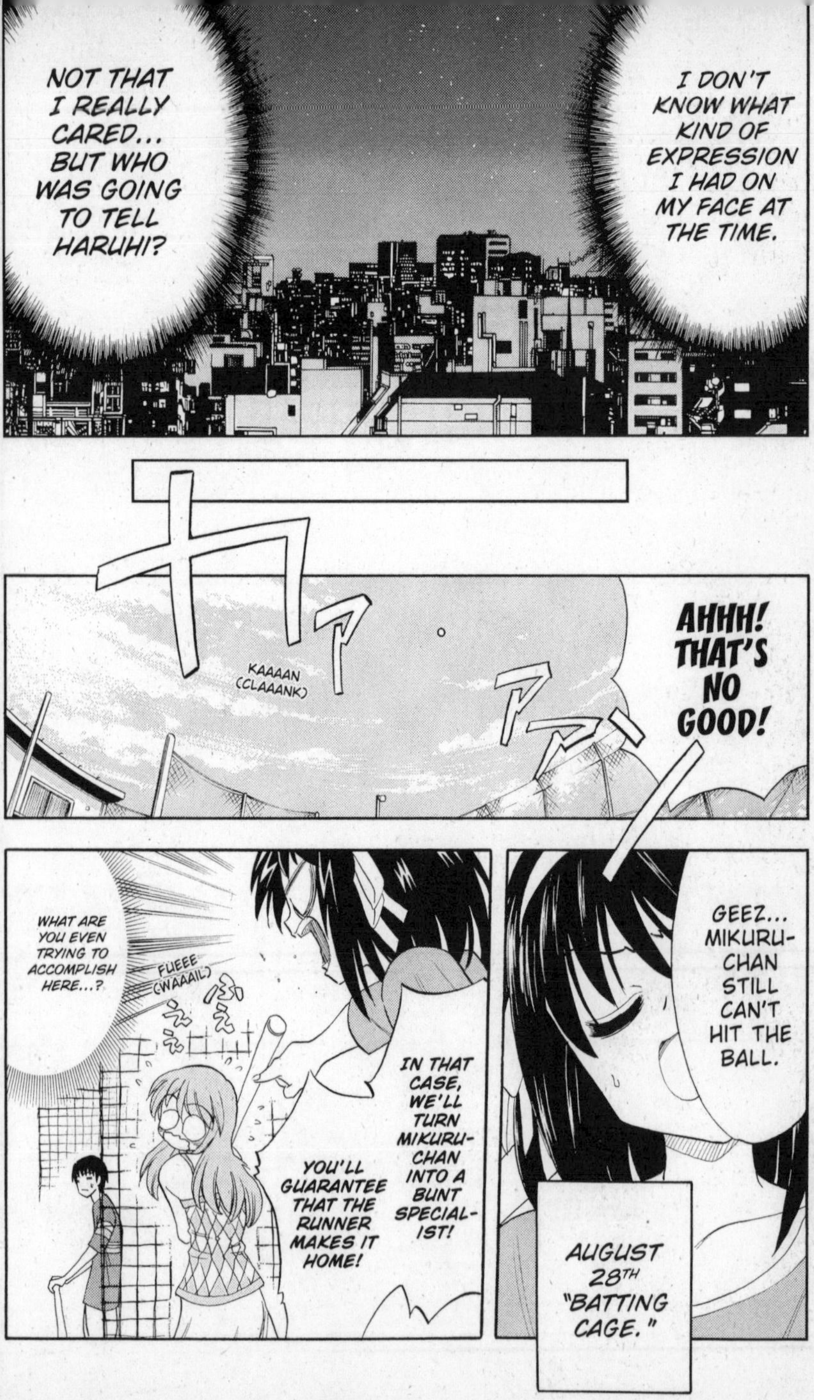
I DON'T KNOW WHAT KIND OF EXPRESSION I HAD ON MY FACE AT THE TIME.
NOT THAT I REALLY CARED... BUT WHO WAS GOING TO TELL HARUHI?
AHHH! THAT'S NO GOOD!
カァァーン
KAAAAN (CLAAANK)
GEEZ... MIKURU-CHAN STILL CAN'T HIT THE BALL.
AUGUST 28TH "BATTING CAGE."
IN THAT CASE, WE'LL TURN MIKURU-CHAN INTO A BUNT SPECIAL-IST!
YOU'LL GUARANTEE THAT THE RUNNER MAKES IT HOME!
ふぇぇ
FUEEE (WAAAIL)
WHAT ARE YOU EVEN TRYING TO ACCOMPLISH HERE...?

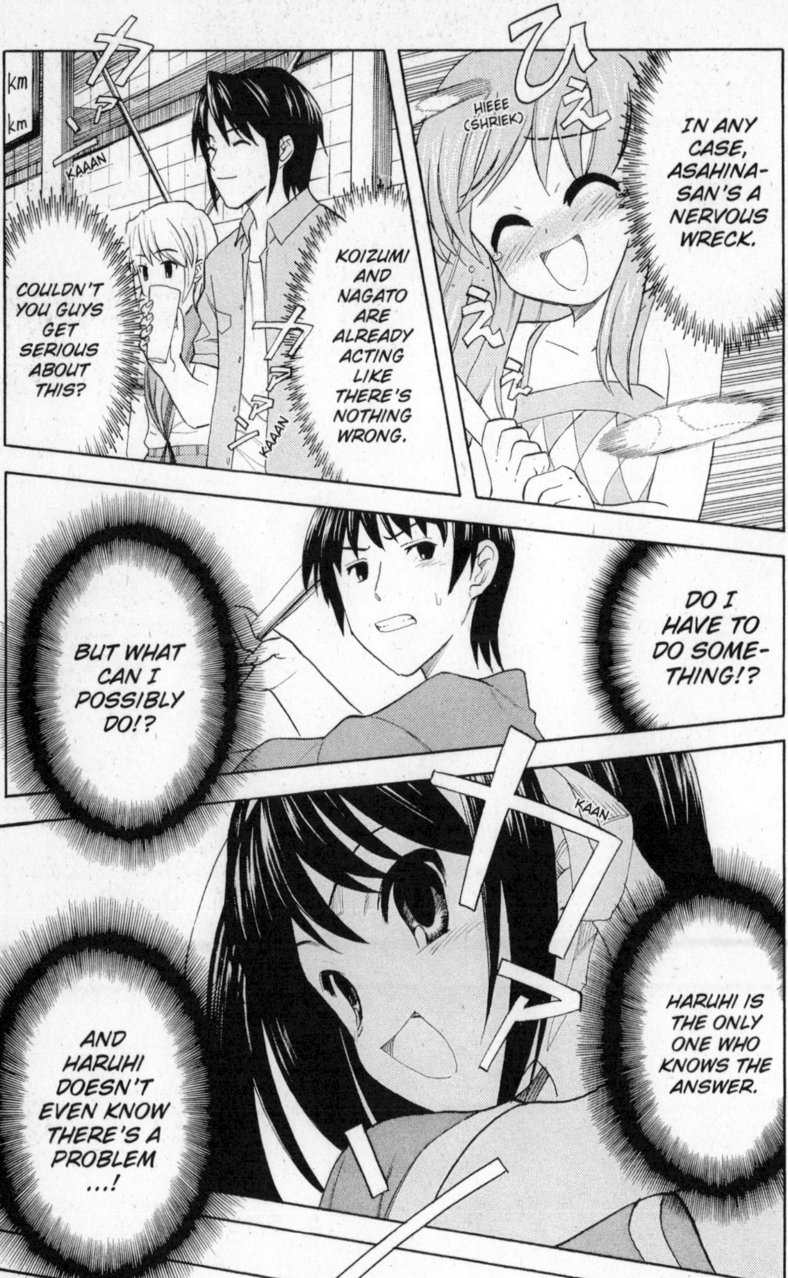
HIEEE (SHRIEK)
IN ANY CASE, ASAHINA-SAN'S A NERVOUS WRECK.
KAAAN
KOIZUMI AND NAGATO ARE ALREADY ACTING LIKE THERE'S NOTHING WRONG.
KAAAN
km
km
COULDN'T YOU GUYS GET SERIOUS ABOUT THIS?
DO I HAVE TO DO SOME-THING!?
BUT WHAT CAN I POSSIBLY DO!?
KAAN
HARUHI IS THE ONLY ONE WHO KNOWS THE ANSWER.
AND HARUHI DOESN'T EVEN KNOW THERE'S A PROBLEM ...!

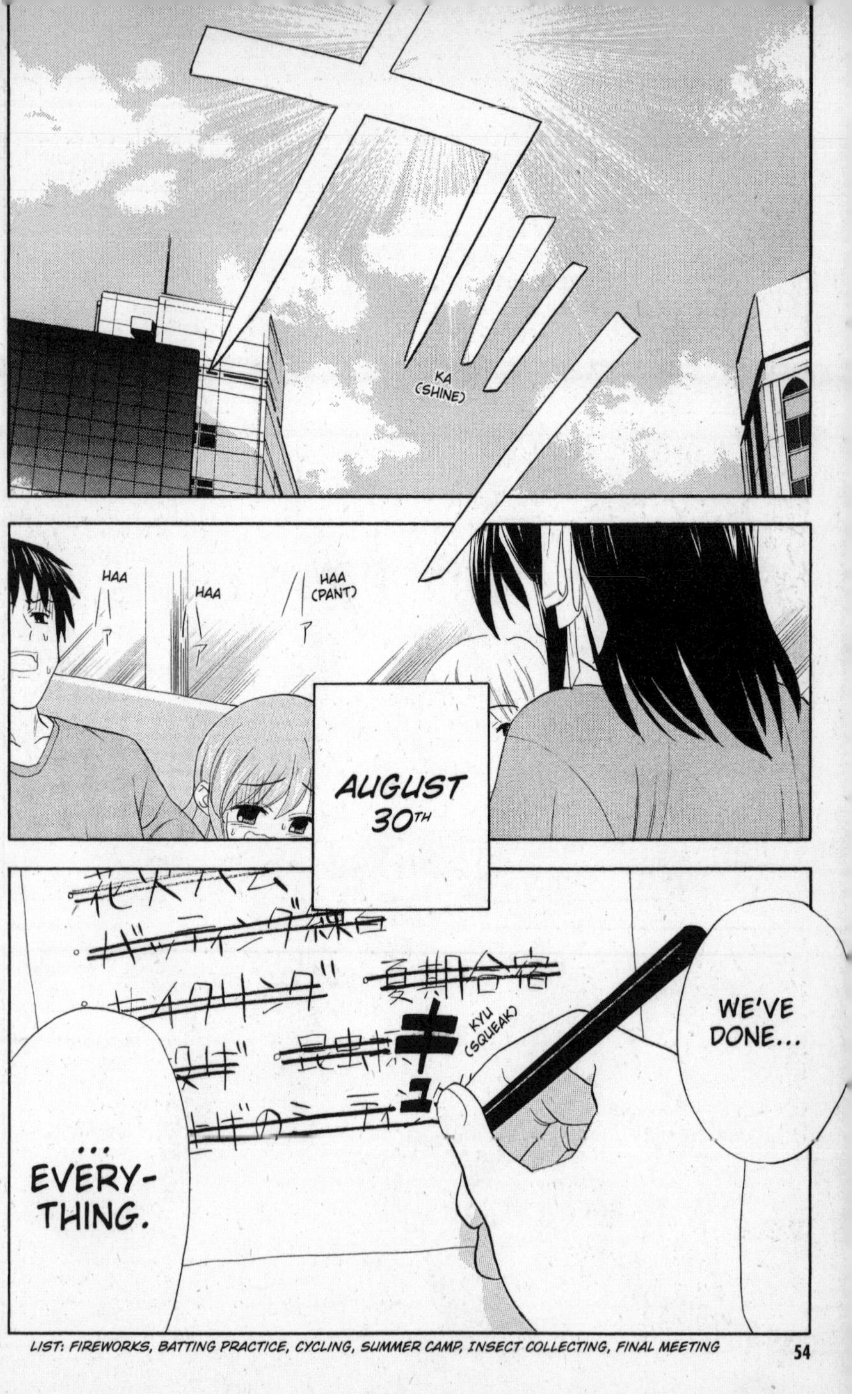
KA (SHINE)
HAA (PANT)
HAA
HAA
AUGUST 30TH
WE'VE DONE...
KYU (SQUEAK)
...EVERYTHING.

LIST: FIREWORKS, BATTING PRACTICE, CYCLING, SUMMER CAMP, INSECT COLLECTING, FINAL MEETING

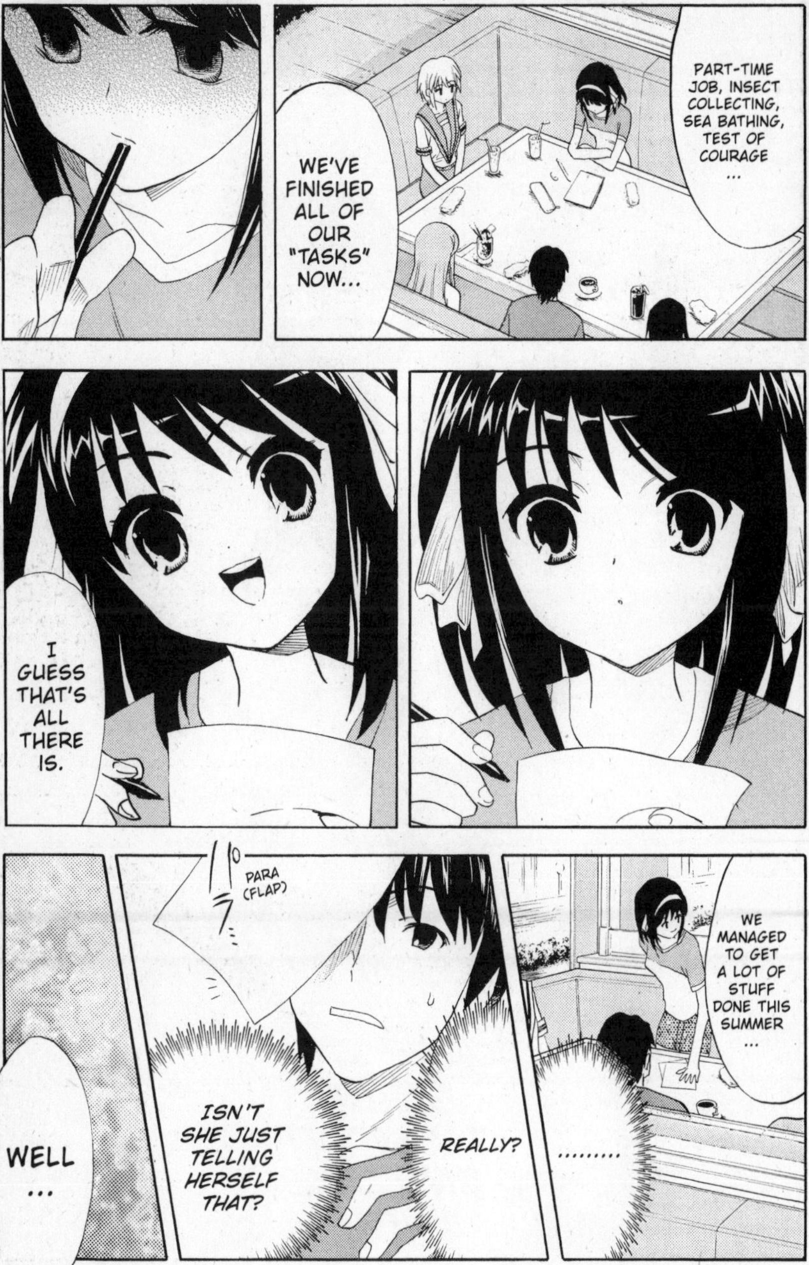
PART-TIME JOB, INSECT COLLECTING, SEA BATHING, TEST OF COURAGE ...
WE'VE FINISHED ALL OF OUR "TASKS" NOW...
I GUESS THAT'S ALL THERE IS.
WE MANAGED TO GET A LOT OF STUFF DONE THIS SUMMER ...
....
PARA (FLAP)
REALLY?
ISN'T SHE JUST TELLING HERSELF THAT?
WELL ...

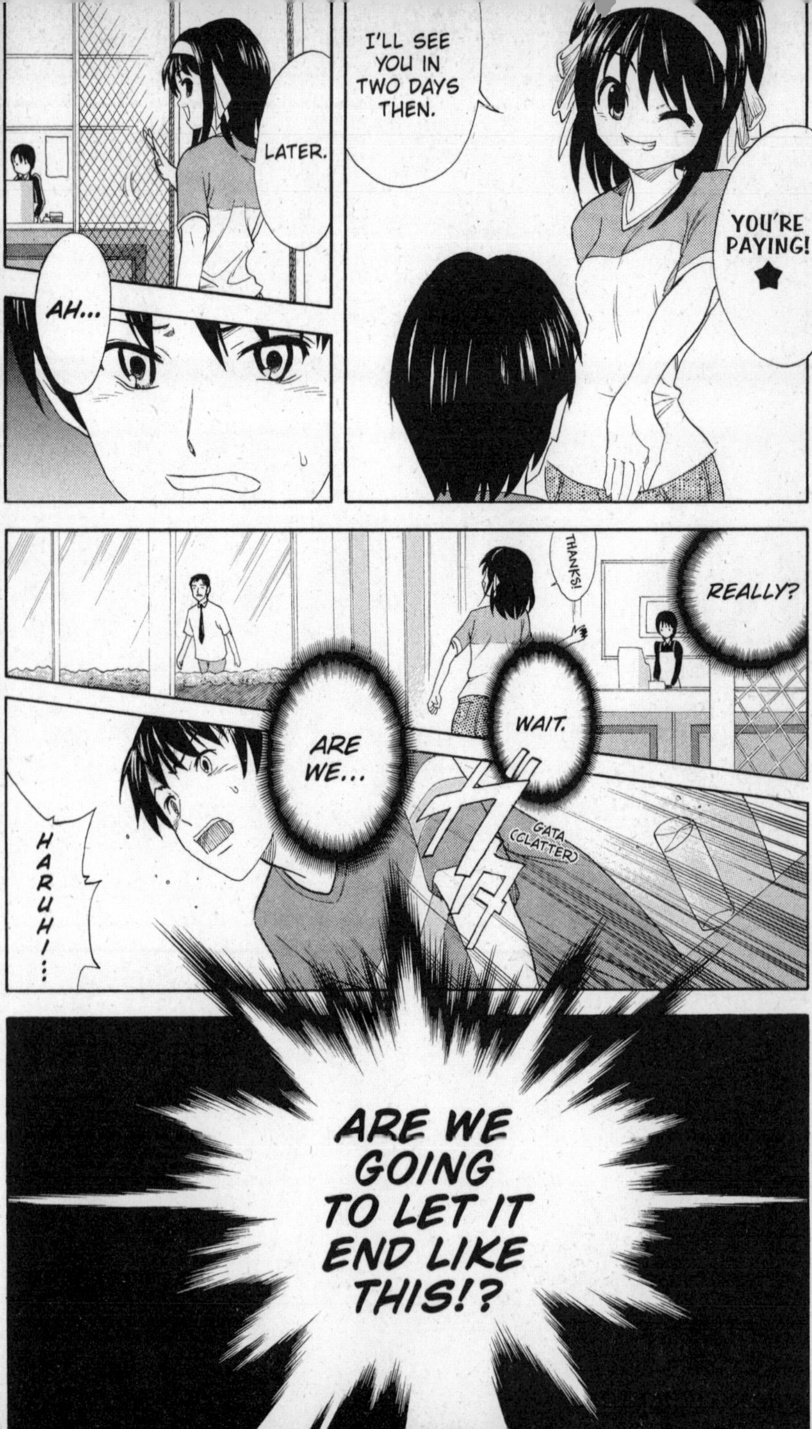
I'LL SEE YOU IN TWO DAYS THEN.
YOU'RE PAYING! ★
LATER.
AH...
THANKS!
REALLY?
WAIT.
ARE WE...
GATA (CLATTER)
HARUHI...
ARE WE GOING TO LET IT END LIKE THIS!?

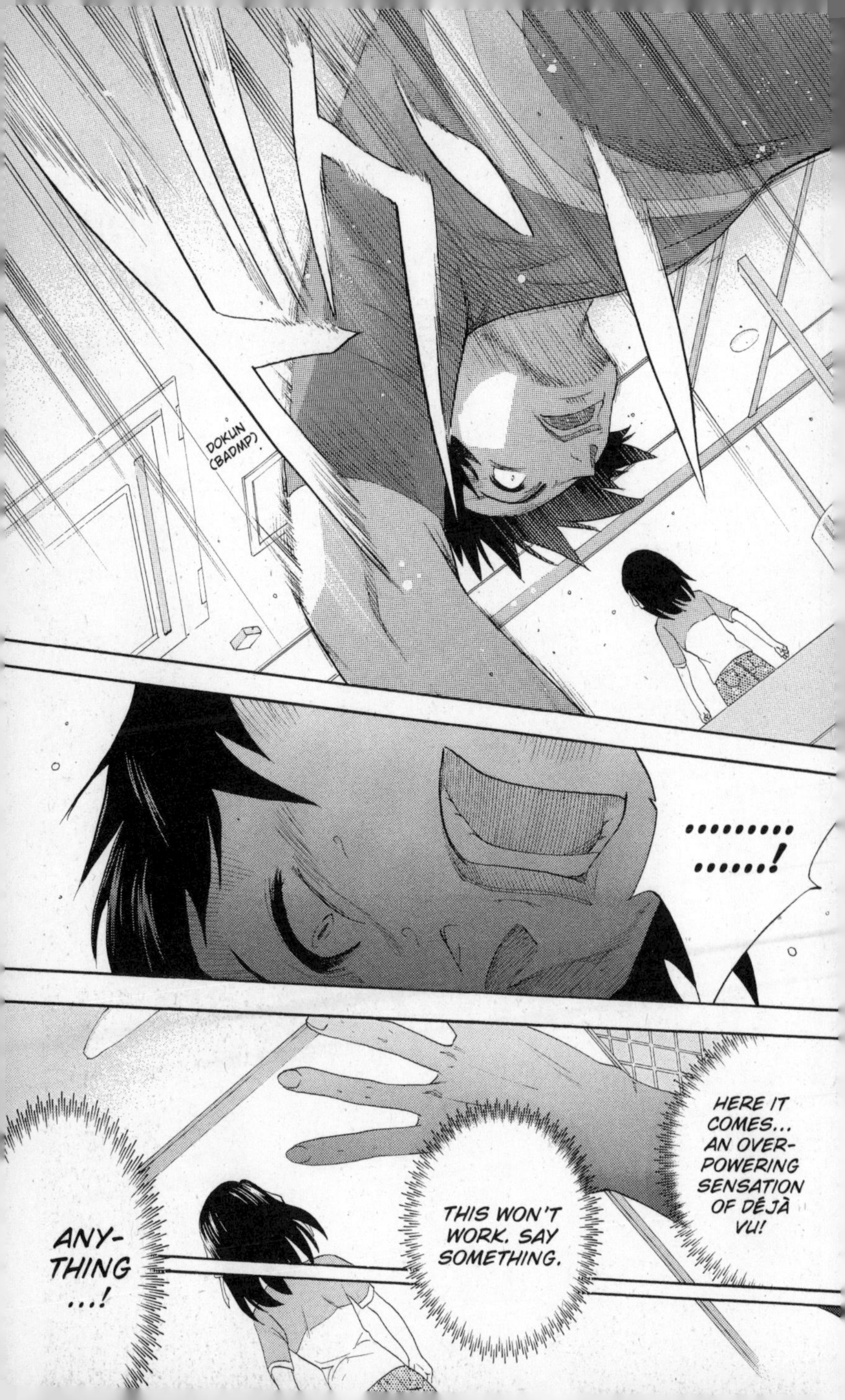
DOKUN (BADMP)
....
.......!
HERE IT COMES... AN OVER-POWERING SENSATION OF DÉJÀ VU!
THIS WON'T WORK. SAY SOMETHING.
ANY-THING ...!

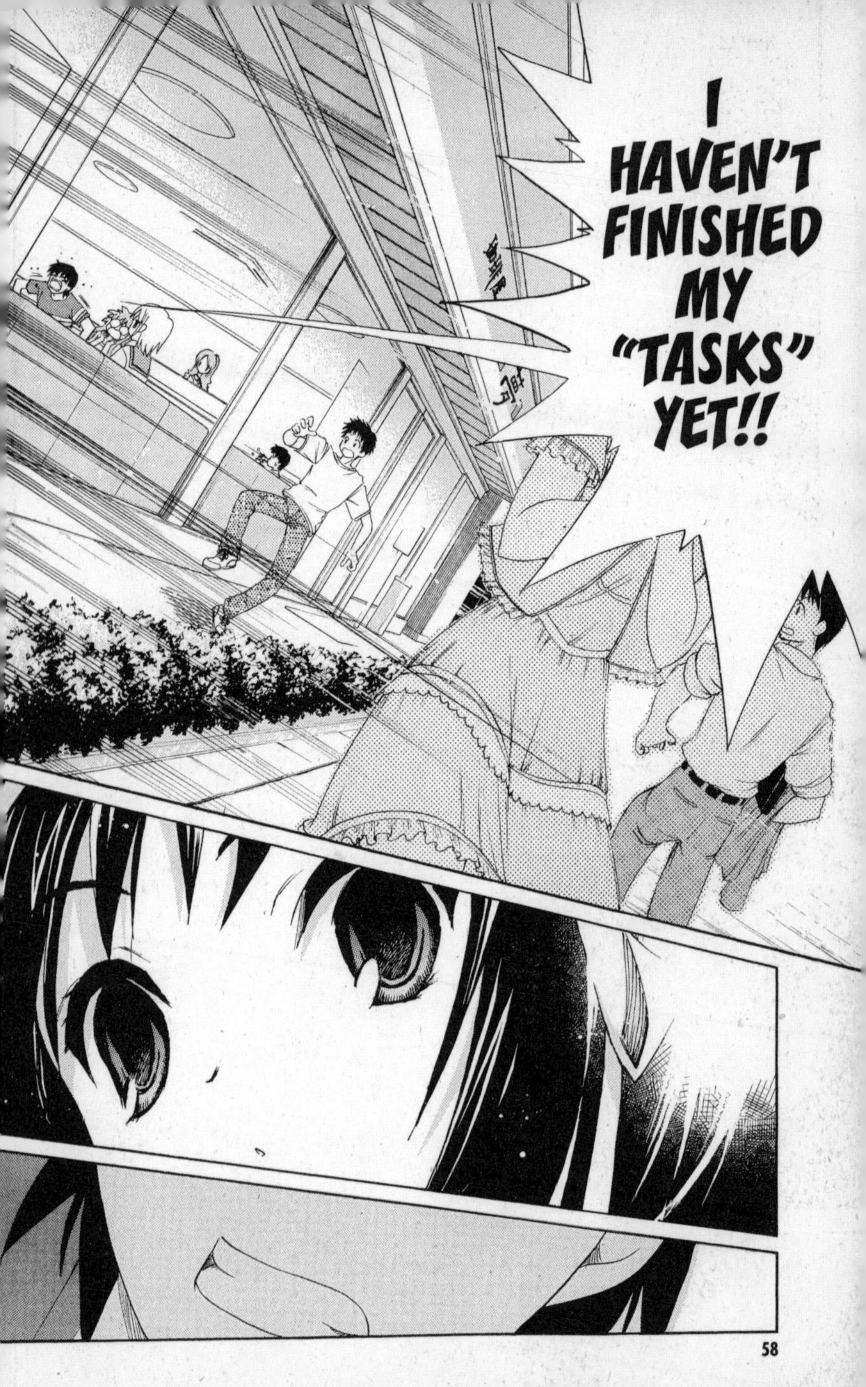
I HAVEN'T FINISHED MY "TASKS" YET!!

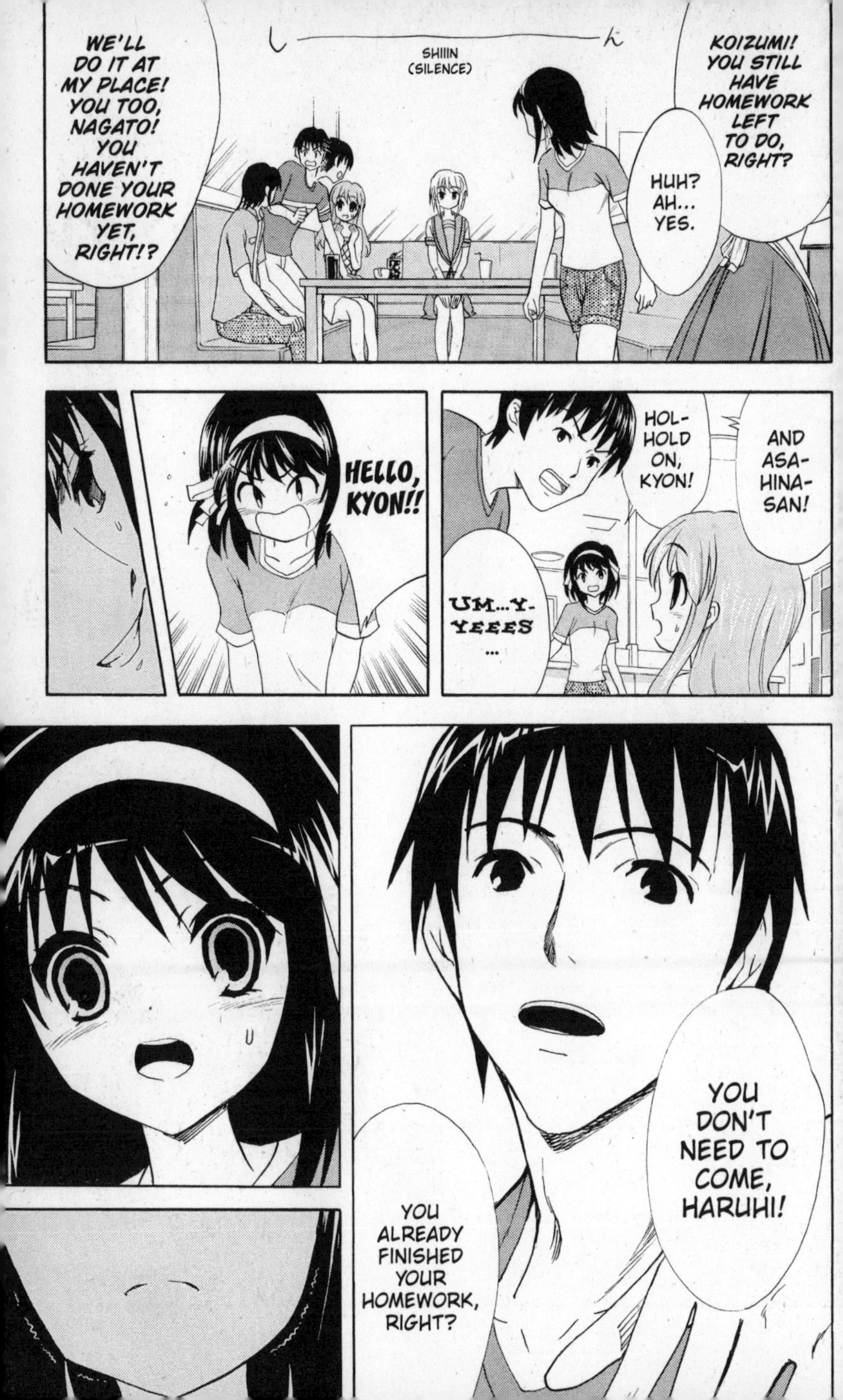
KOIZUMI! YOU STILL HAVE HOMEWORK LEFT TO DO, RIGHT?
HUH? AH... YES.
しーーん
SHIIIN (SILENCE)
WE'LL DO IT AT MY PLACE! YOU TOO, NAGATO! YOU HAVEN'T DONE YOUR HOMEWORK YET, RIGHT!?
AND ASAHINA-SAN!
HOL-HOLD ON, KYON!
UM...Y-YEEES ...
HELLO, KYON!!
YOU DON'T NEED TO COME, HARUHI!
YOU ALREADY FINISHED YOUR HOMEWORK, RIGHT?

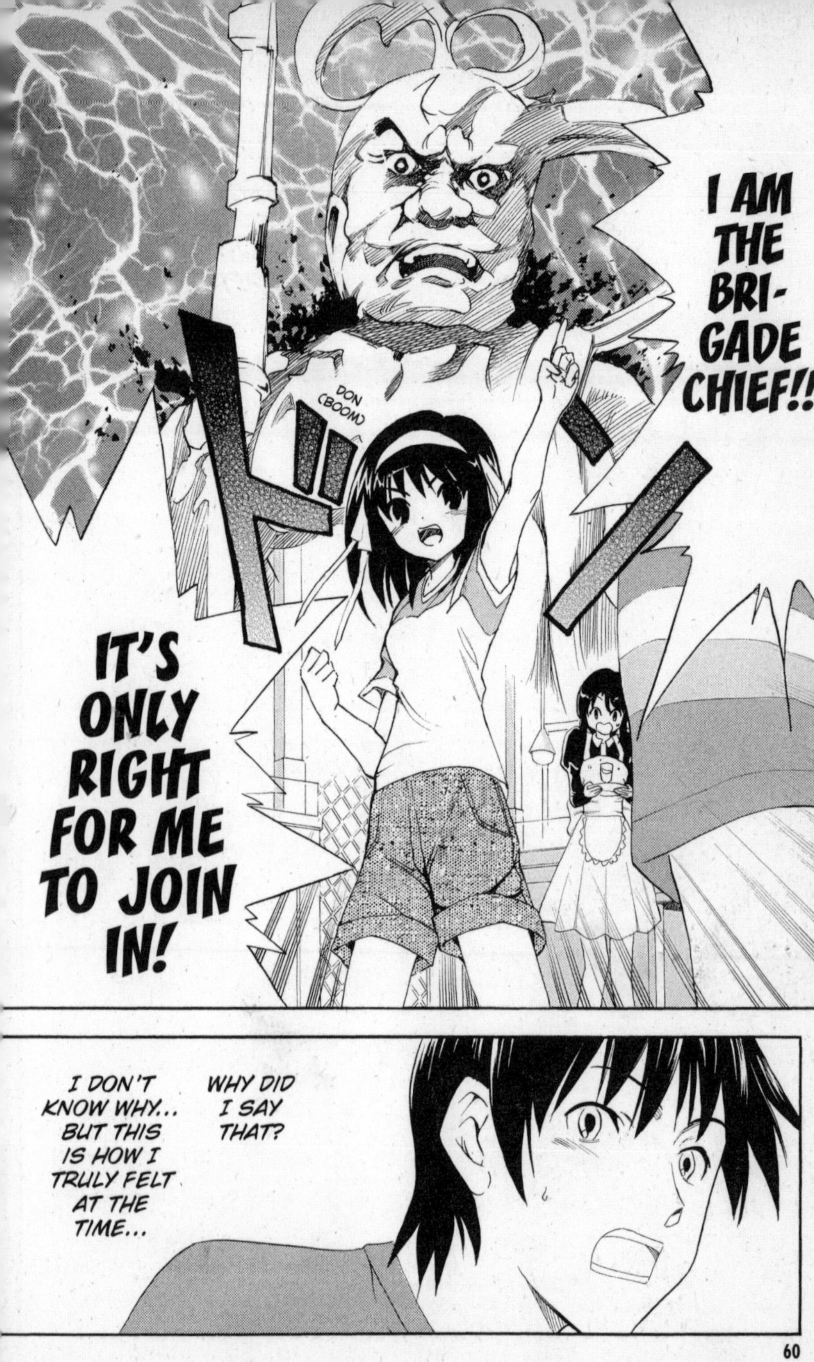
I AM THE BRI-GADE CHIEF!!
DON (BOOM)
IT'S ONLY RIGHT FOR ME TO JOIN IN!
WHY DID I SAY THAT?
I DON'T KNOW WHY... BUT THIS IS HOW I TRULY FELT AT THE TIME...

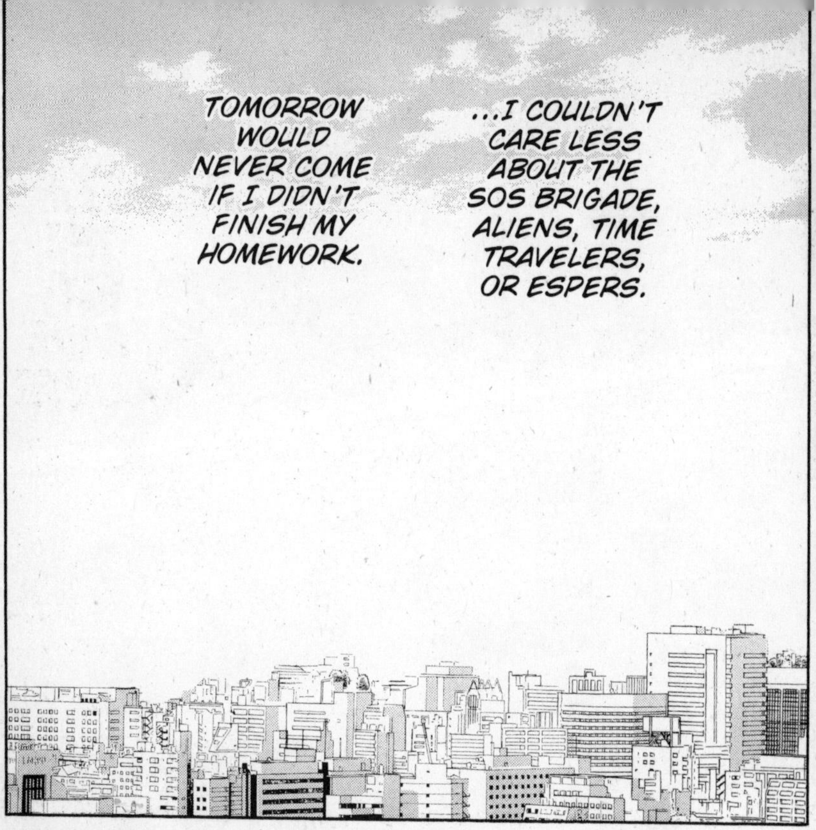
...I COULDN'T CARE LESS ABOUT THE SOS BRIGADE, ALIENS, TIME TRAVELERS, OR ESPERS.
TOMORROW WOULD NEVER COME IF I DIDN'T FINISH MY HOMEWORK.

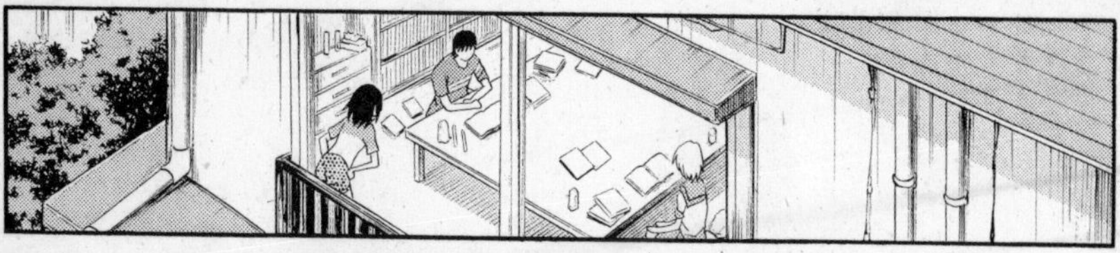

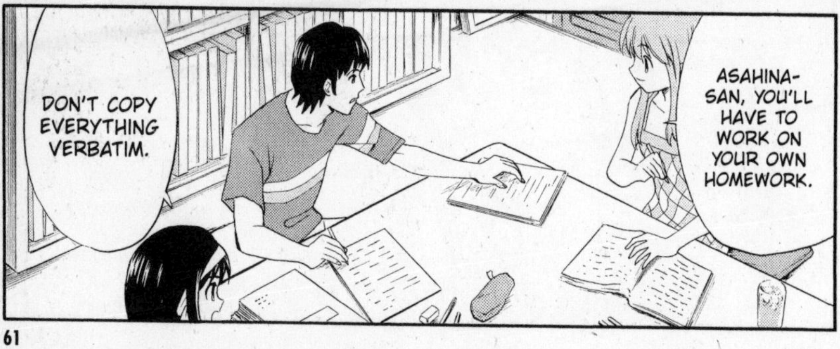
ASAHINA-SAN, YOU'LL HAVE TO WORK ON YOUR OWN HOMEWORK.
DON'T COPY EVERYTHING VERBATIM.

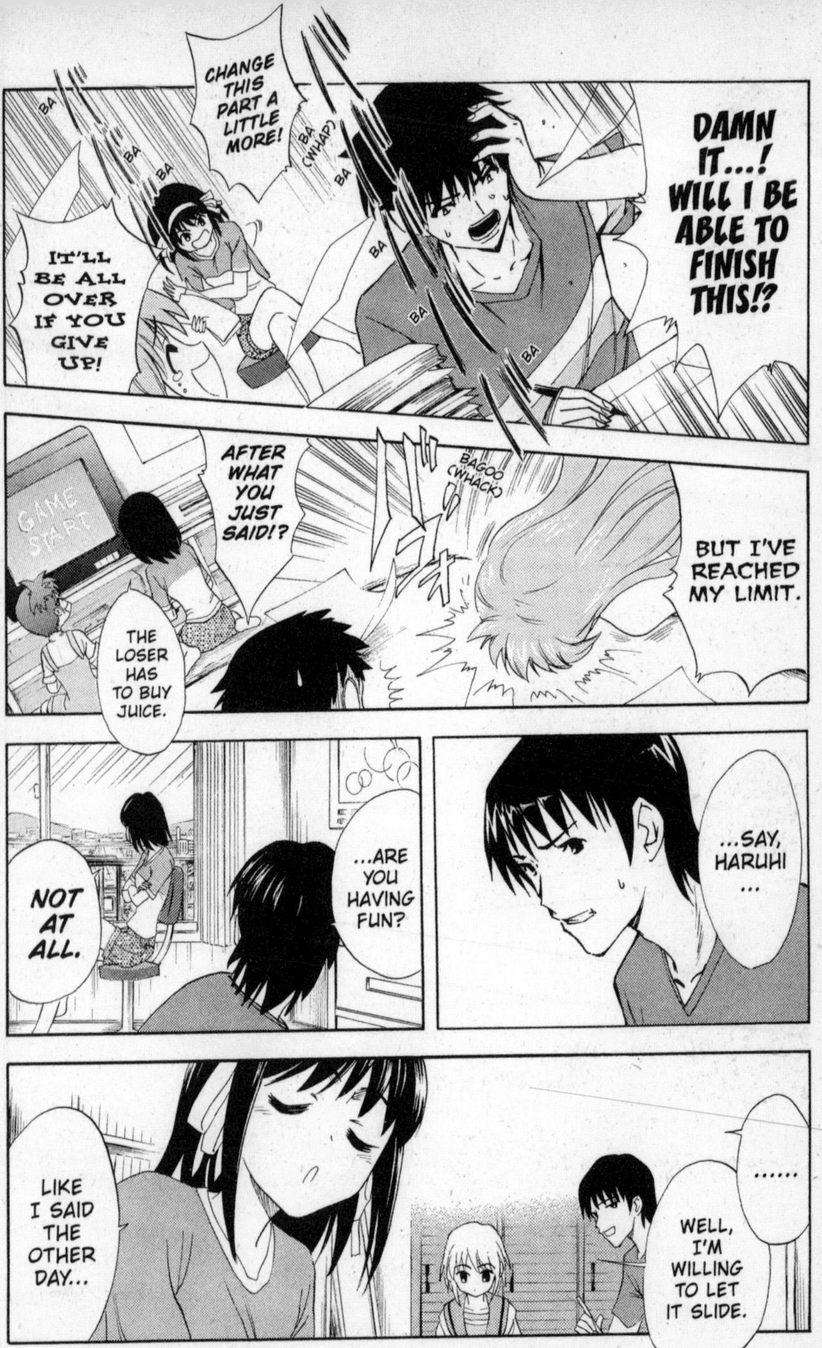
DAMN IT...! WILL I BE ABLE TO FINISH THIS!?
BA
BA (WHAP)
CHANGE THIS PART A LITTLE MORE!
BA BA BA
IT'LL BE ALL OVER IF YOU GIVE UP!
BUT I'VE REACHED MY LIMIT.
BAGOO (WHACK)
AFTER WHAT YOU JUST SAID!?
THE LOSER HAS TO BUY JUICE.
GAME START
...SAY, HARUHI ...
...ARE YOU HAVING FUN?
NOT AT ALL.
......
WELL, I'M WILLING TO LET IT SLIDE.
LIKE I SAID THE OTHER DAY...

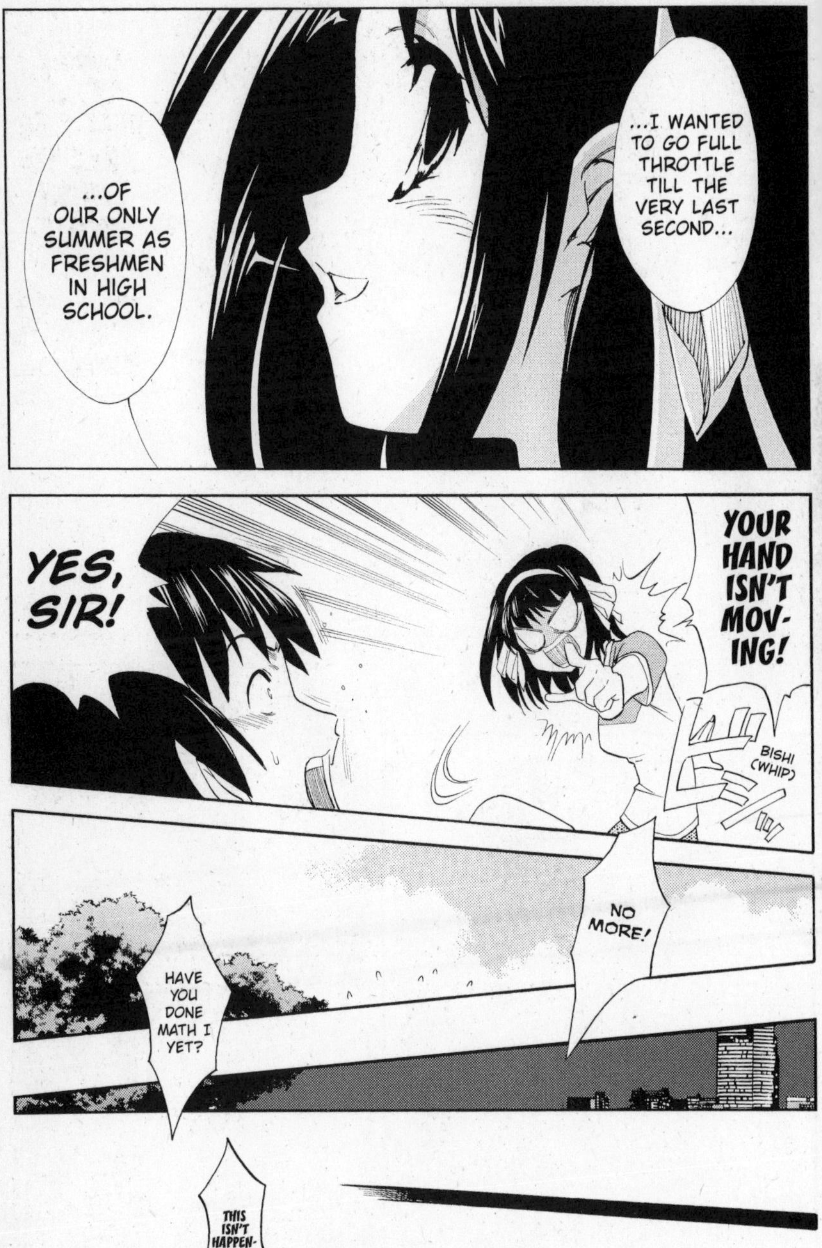
...I WANTED TO GO FULL THROTTLE TILL THE VERY LAST SECOND...
...OF OUR ONLY SUMMER AS FRESHMEN IN HIGH SCHOOL.
YOUR HAND ISN'T MOV-ING!
BISHI (WHIP)
YES, SIR!
NO MORE!
HAVE YOU DONE MATH I YET?
THIS ISN'T HAPPEN-ING!

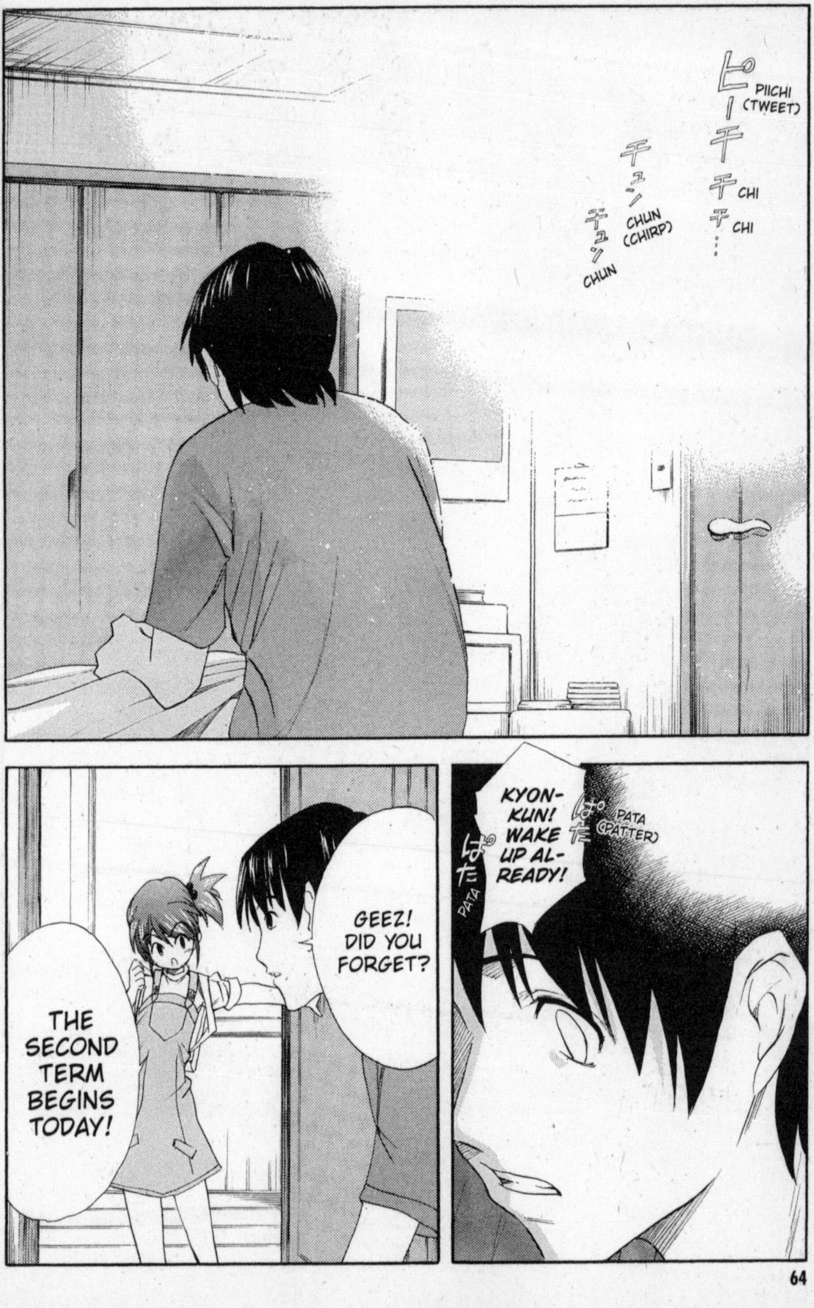
ピーチチチ…
PIICHI (TWEET)
CHI
CHI
チュンチュン
CHUN (CHIRP)
CHUN
KYON-KUN! WAKE UP AL-READY!
ぱた
PATA (PATTER)
ぱた
PATA
GEEZ! DID YOU FORGET?
THE SECOND TERM BEGINS TODAY!

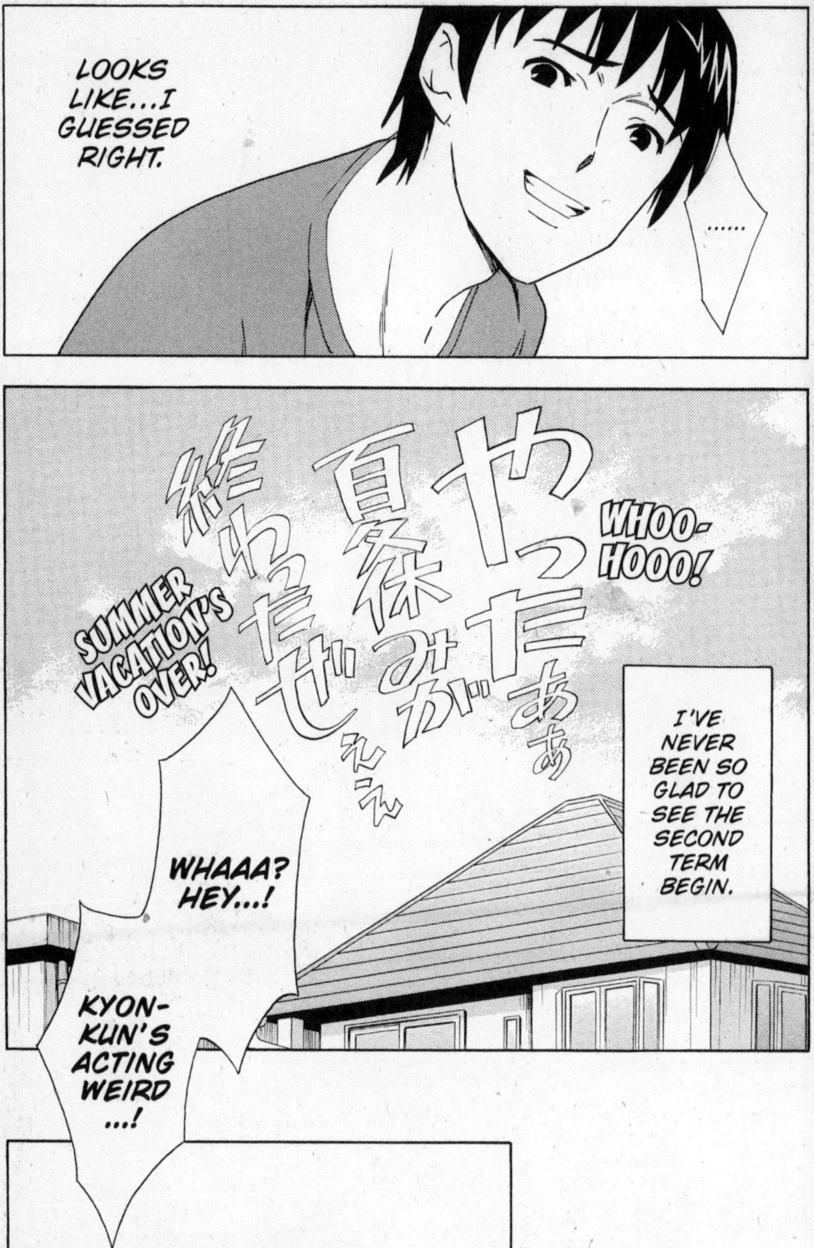
LOOKS LIKE...I GUESSED RIGHT.
......
やったああ
夏休みが
終わったぜええ
WHOO-HOOO!
SUMMER VACATION'S OVER!
I'VE NEVER BEEN SO GLAD TO SEE THE SECOND TERM BEGIN.
WHAAA? HEY...!
KYON-KUN'S ACTING WEIRD...!

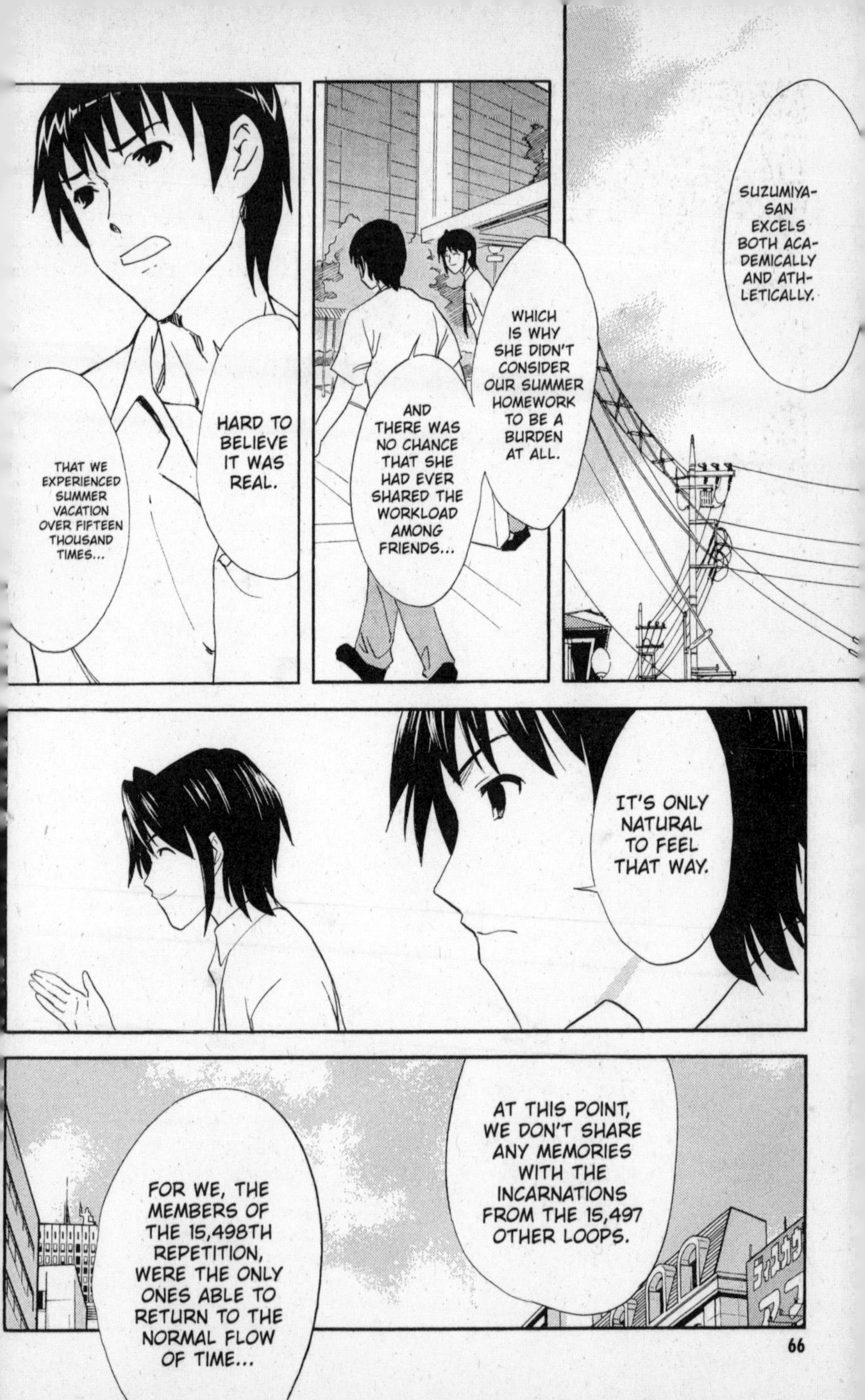
SUZUMIYA-SAN EXCELS BOTH ACADEMICALLY AND ATHLETICALLY.
WHICH IS WHY SHE DIDN'T CONSIDER OUR SUMMER HOMEWORK TO BE A BURDEN AT ALL.
AND THERE WAS NO CHANCE THAT SHE HAD EVER SHARED THE WORKLOAD AMONG FRIENDS...
HARD TO BELIEVE IT WAS REAL.
THAT WE EXPERIENCED SUMMER VACATION OVER FIFTEEN THOUSAND TIMES...
IT'S ONLY NATURAL TO FEEL THAT WAY.
AT THIS POINT, WE DON'T SHARE ANY MEMORIES WITH THE INCARNATIONS FROM THE 15,497 OTHER LOOPS.
FOR WE, THE MEMBERS OF THE 15,498TH REPETITION, WERE THE ONLY ONES ABLE TO RETURN TO THE NORMAL FLOW OF TIME...

SIGN: SOS BRIGADE

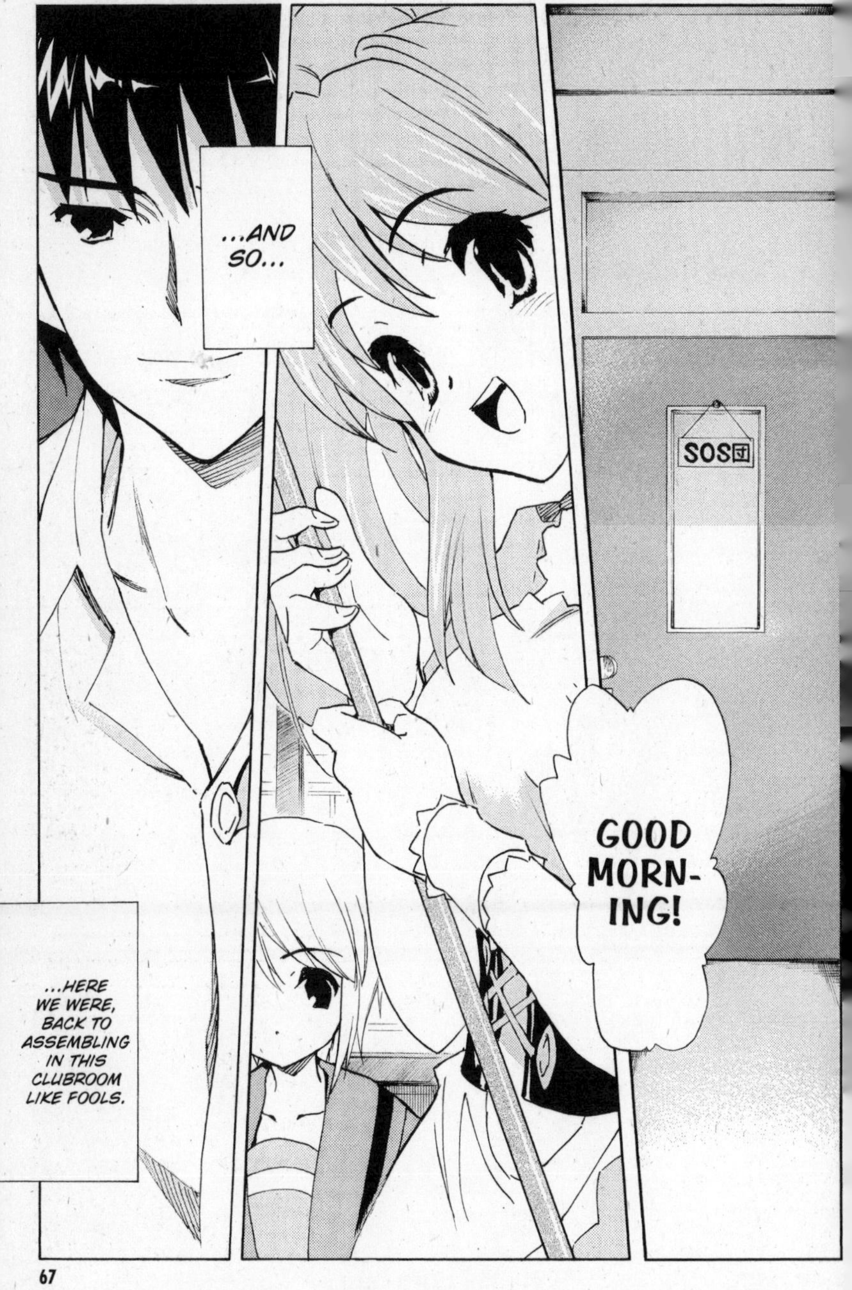
SOS団
GOOD MORNING!
...AND SO...
...HERE WE WERE, BACK TO ASSEMBLING IN THIS CLUBROOM LIKE FOOLS.

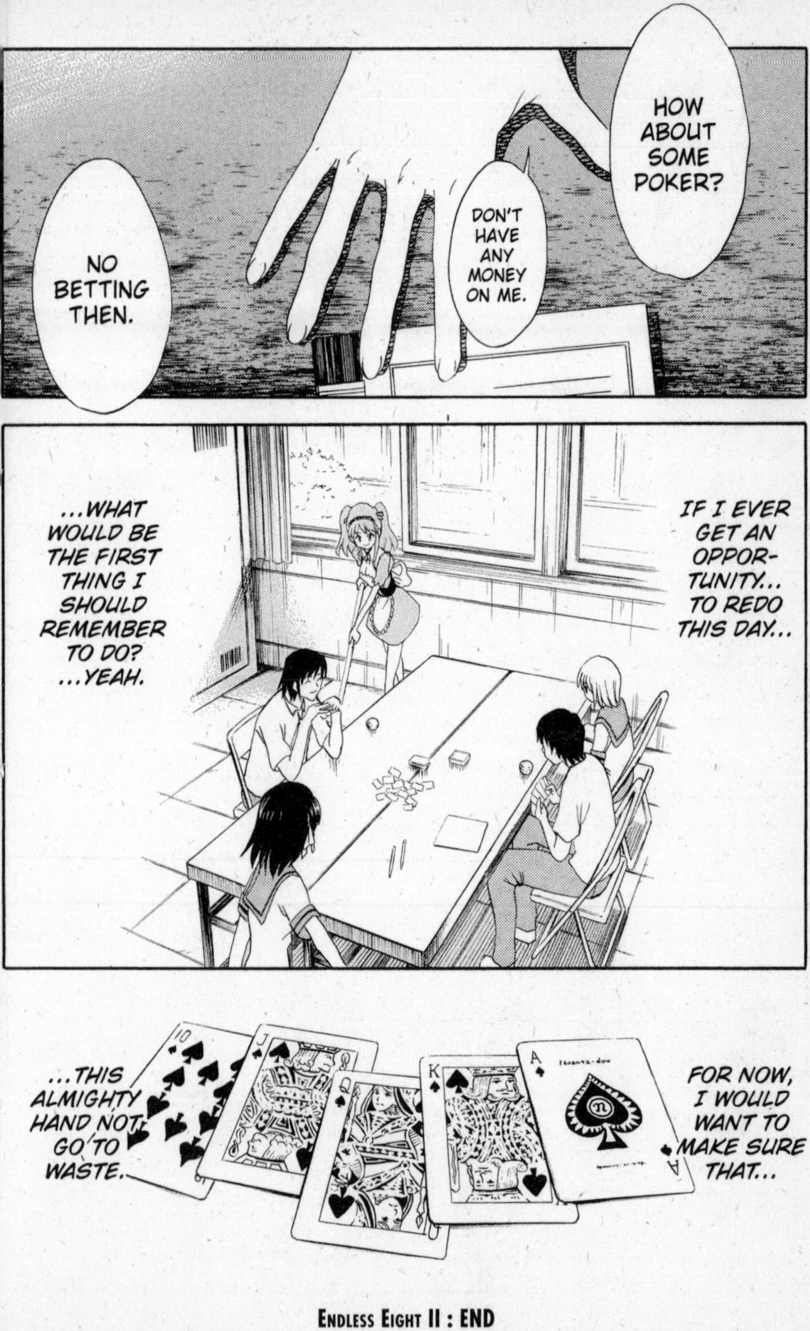
HOW ABOUT SOME POKER?
DON'T HAVE ANY MONEY ON ME.
NO BETTING THEN.
IF I EVER GET AN OPPORTUNITY... TO REDO THIS DAY...
...WHAT WOULD BE THE FIRST THING I SHOULD REMEMBER TO DO? ...YEAH.
FOR NOW, I WOULD WANT TO MAKE SURE THAT...
...THIS ALMIGHTY HAND NOT GO TO WASTE.

Endless Eight II : END

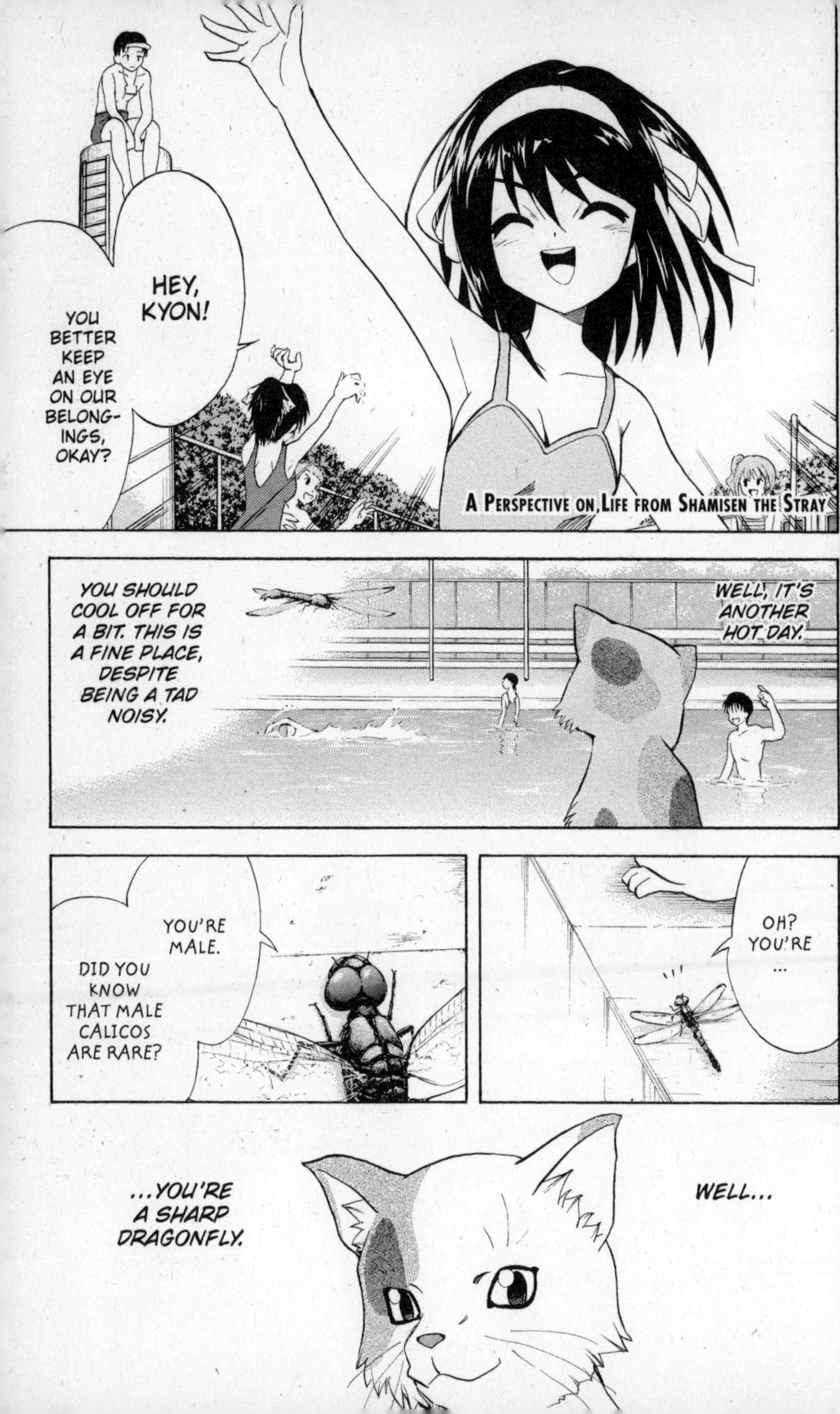
HEY, KYON! YOU BETTER KEEP AN EYE ON OUR BELONGINGS, OKAY?
A PERSPECTIVE ON LIFE FROM SHAMISEN THE STRAY
WELL, IT'S ANOTHER HOT DAY.
YOU SHOULD COOL OFF FOR A BIT. THIS IS A FINE PLACE, DESPITE BEING A TAD NOISY.
OH? YOU'RE ...
YOU'RE MALE.
DID YOU KNOW THAT MALE CALICOS ARE RARE?
WELL...
...YOU'RE A SHARP DRAGONFLY.

A Perspective on Life from Shamisen the Stray

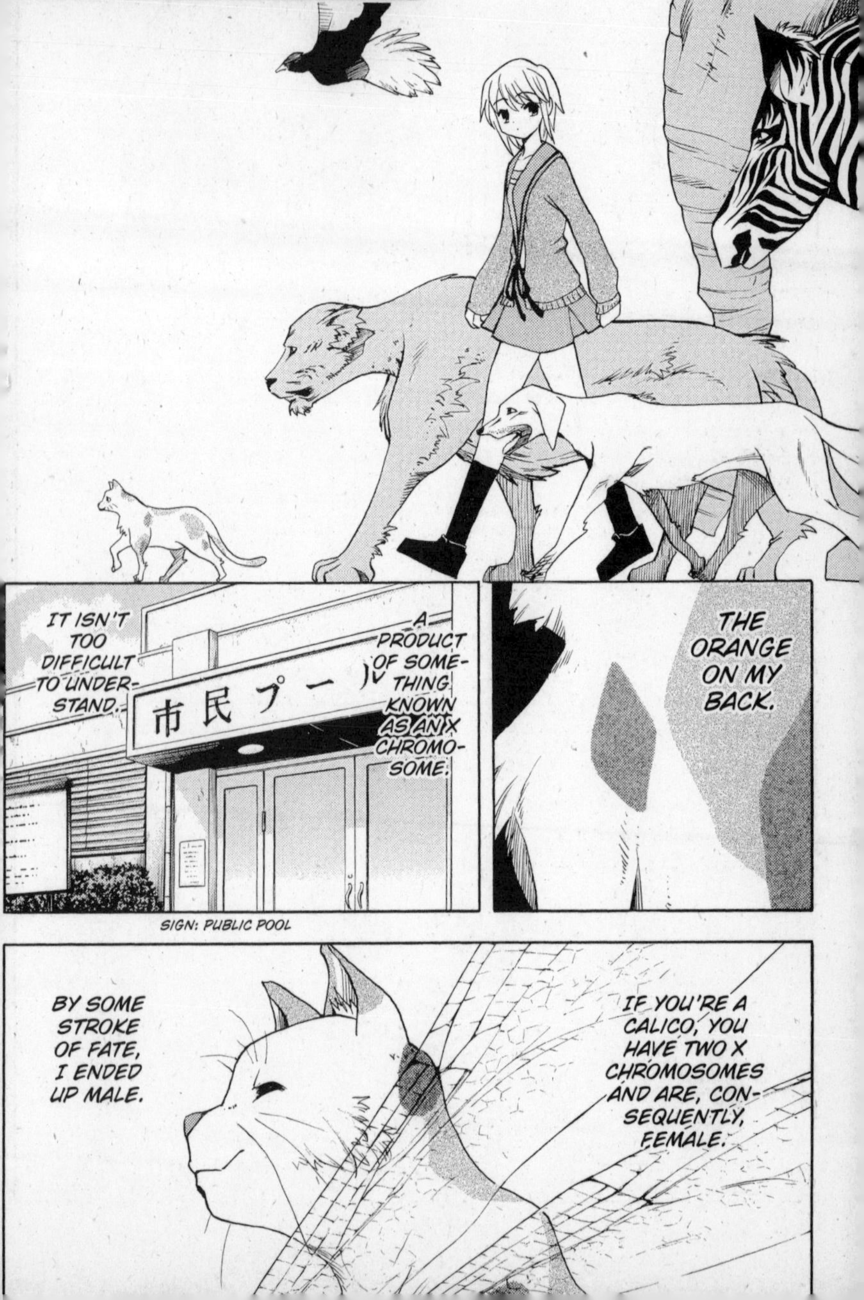
THE ORANGE ON MY BACK.
A PRODUCT OF SOMETHING KNOWN AS AN X CHROMOSOME.
IT ISN'T TOO DIFFICULT TO UNDERSTAND.
市民プール
SIGN: PUBLIC POOL
IF YOU'RE A CALICO, YOU HAVE TWO X CHROMOSOMES AND ARE, CONSEQUENTLY, FEMALE.
BY SOME STROKE OF FATE, I ENDED UP MALE.

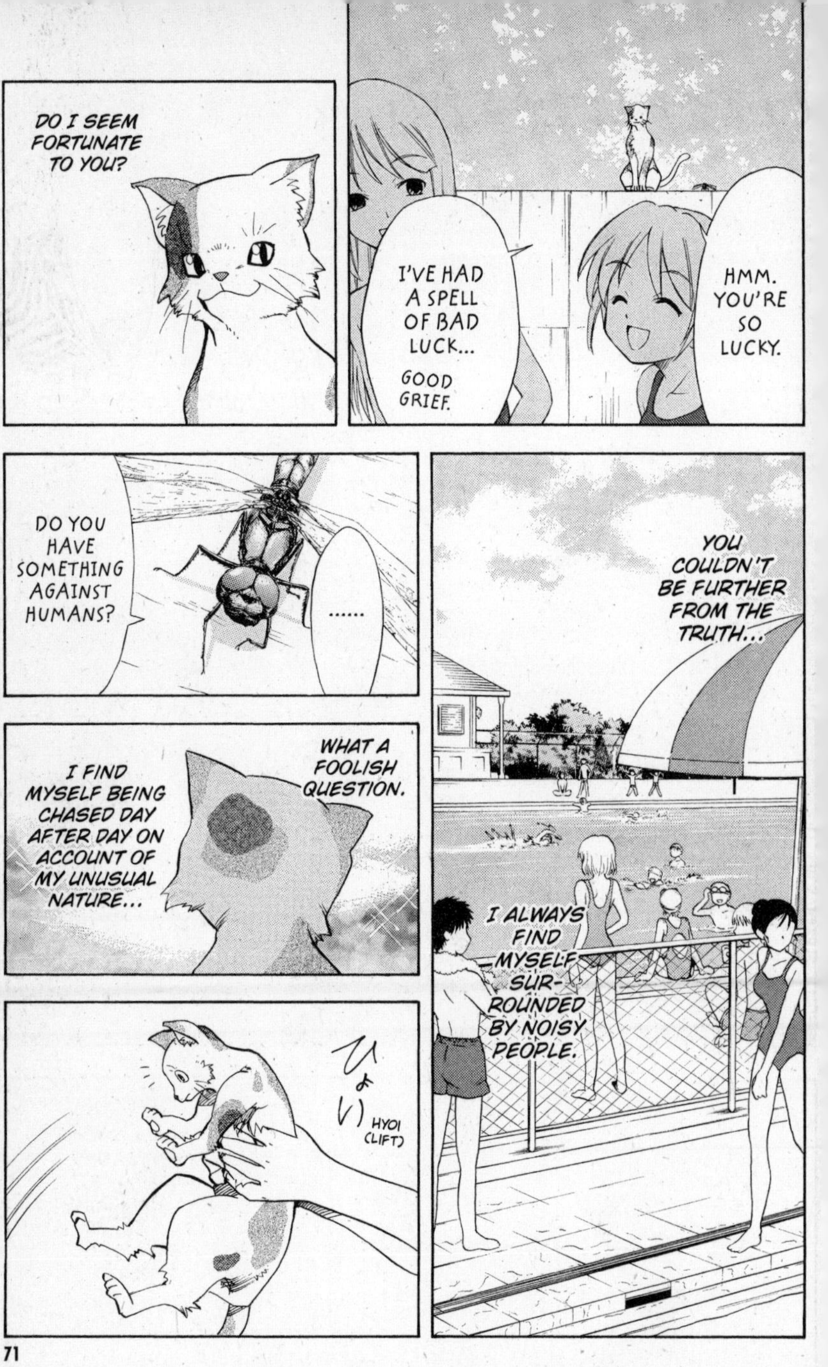
HMM. YOU'RE SO LUCKY.
I'VE HAD A SPELL OF BAD LUCK...
GOOD GRIEF.
DO I SEEM FORTUNATE TO YOU?
YOU COULDN'T BE FURTHER FROM THE TRUTH...
I ALWAYS FIND MYSELF SUR-ROUNDED BY NOISY PEOPLE.
DO YOU HAVE SOMETHING AGAINST HUMANS?
......
WHAT A FOOLISH QUESTION.
I FIND MYSELF BEING CHASED DAY AFTER DAY ON ACCOUNT OF MY UNUSUAL NATURE...
ひょい
HYOI (LIFT)

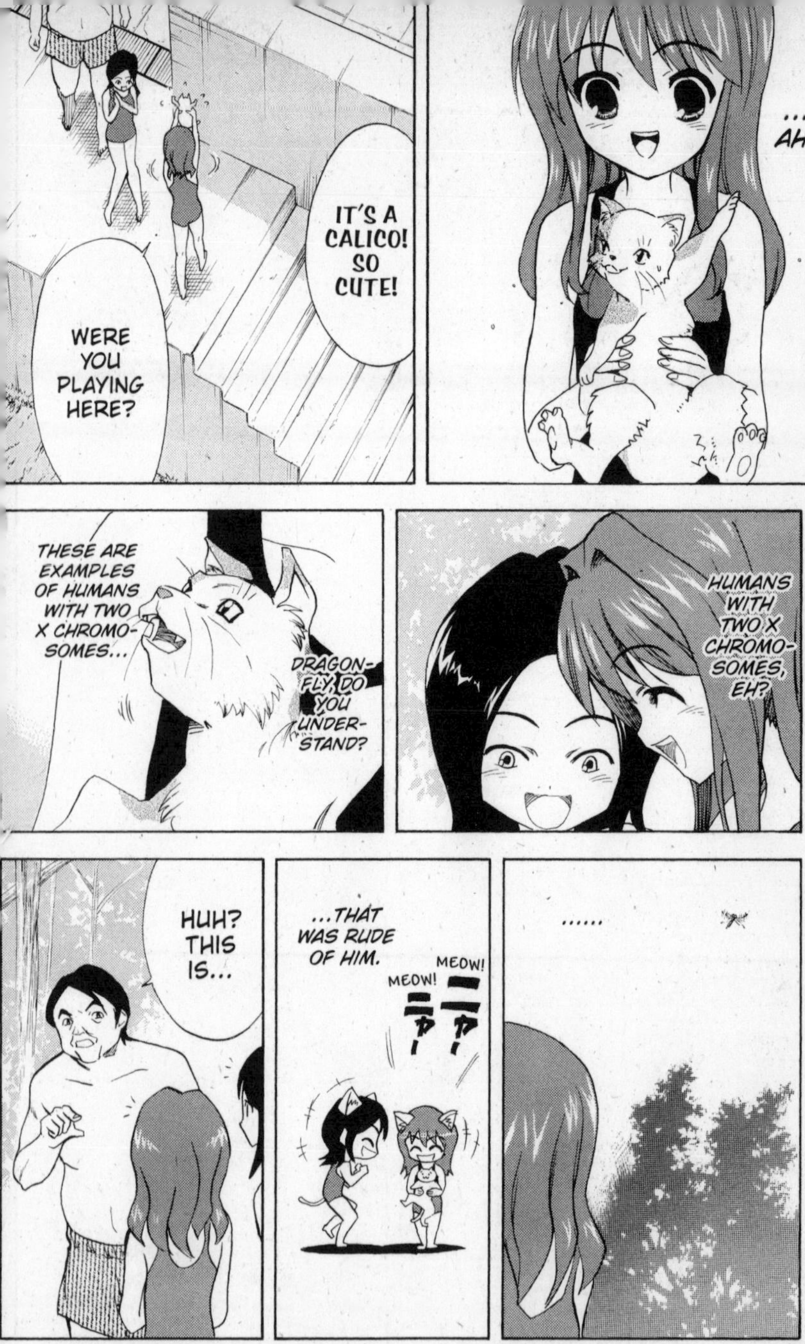
... AH.
IT'S A CALICO! SO CUTE!
WERE YOU PLAYING HERE?
HUMANS WITH TWO X CHROMOSOMES, EH?
THESE ARE EXAMPLES OF HUMANS WITH TWO X CHROMOSOMES...
DRAGONFLY, DO YOU UNDERSTAND?
......
...THAT WAS RUDE OF HIM.
MEOW!
ニャー
MEOW!
ニャー
HUH? THIS IS...

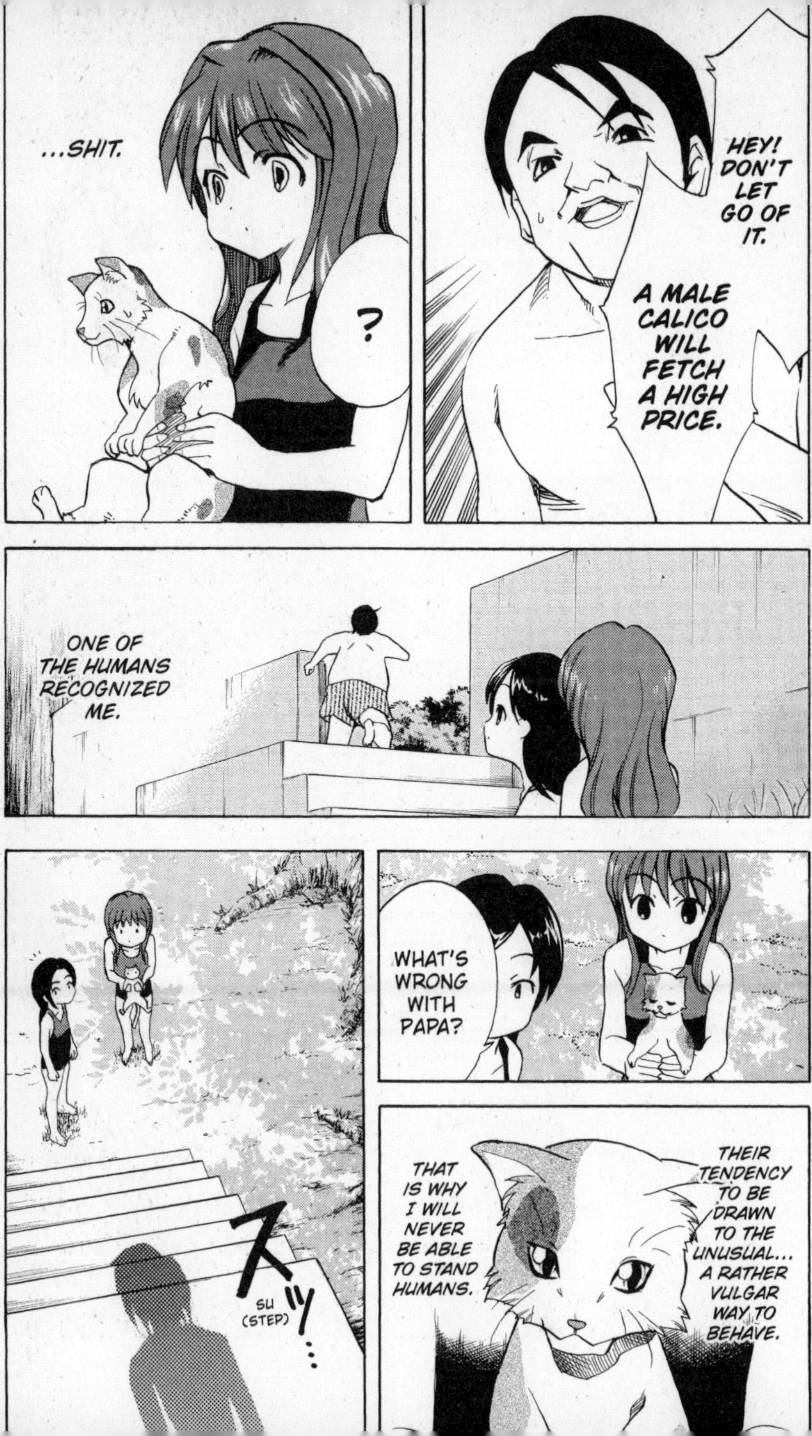
HEY! DON'T LET GO OF IT.
A MALE CALICO WILL FETCH A HIGH PRICE.
...SHIT.
?
ONE OF THE HUMANS RECOGNIZED ME.
WHAT'S WRONG WITH PAPA?
THEIR TENDENCY TO BE DRAWN TO THE UNUSUAL... A RATHER VULGAR WAY TO BEHAVE.
THAT IS WHY I WILL NEVER BE ABLE TO STAND HUMANS.
スッ…
SU (STEP)

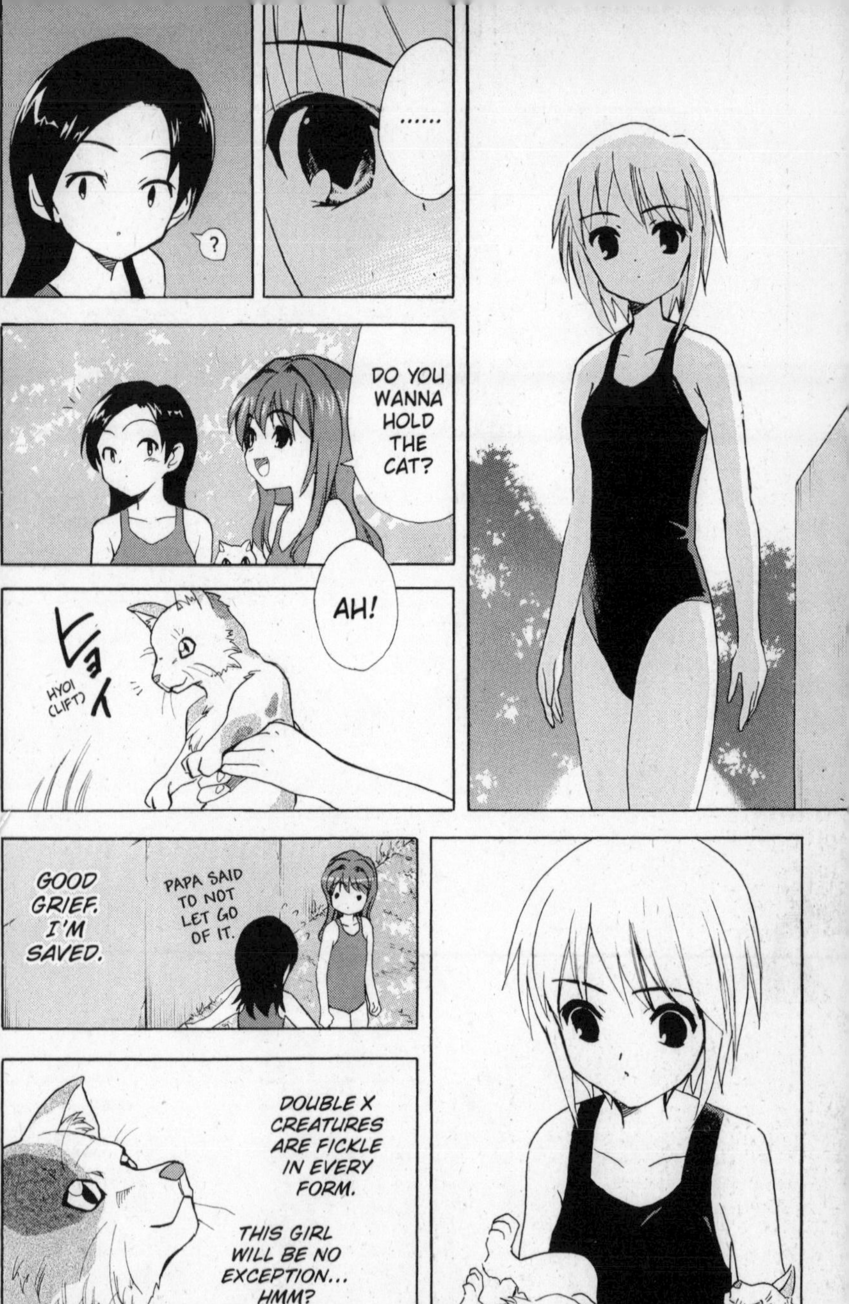
......
?
DO YOU WANNA HOLD THE CAT?
AH!
ヒョイ
HYOI (LIFT)
PAPA SAID TO NOT LET GO OF IT.
GOOD GRIEF. I'M SAVED.
DOUBLE X CREATURES ARE FICKLE IN EVERY FORM.
THIS GIRL WILL BE NO EXCEPTION... HMM?

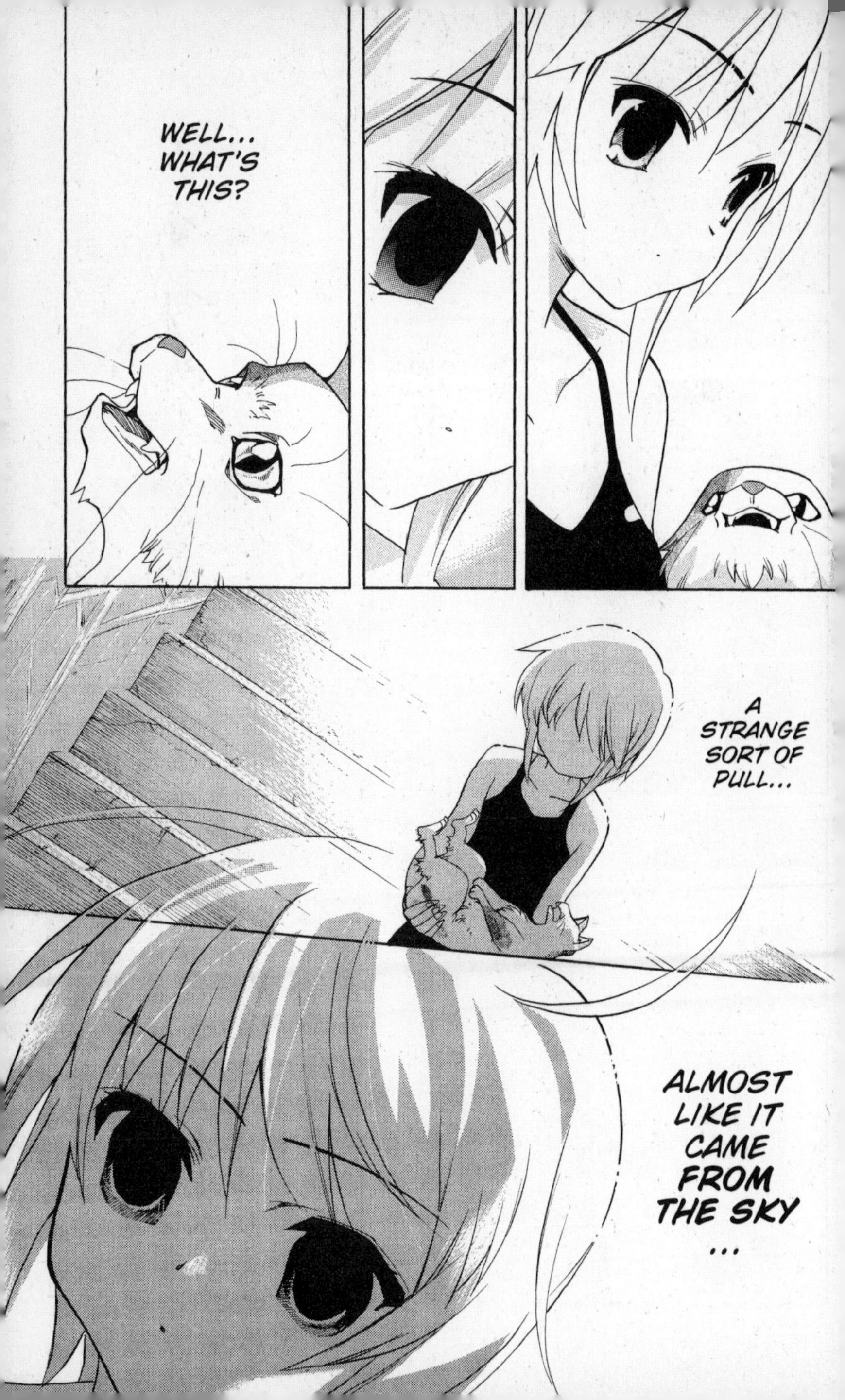
WELL... WHAT'S THIS?
A STRANGE SORT OF PULL...
ALMOST LIKE IT CAME FROM THE SKY...

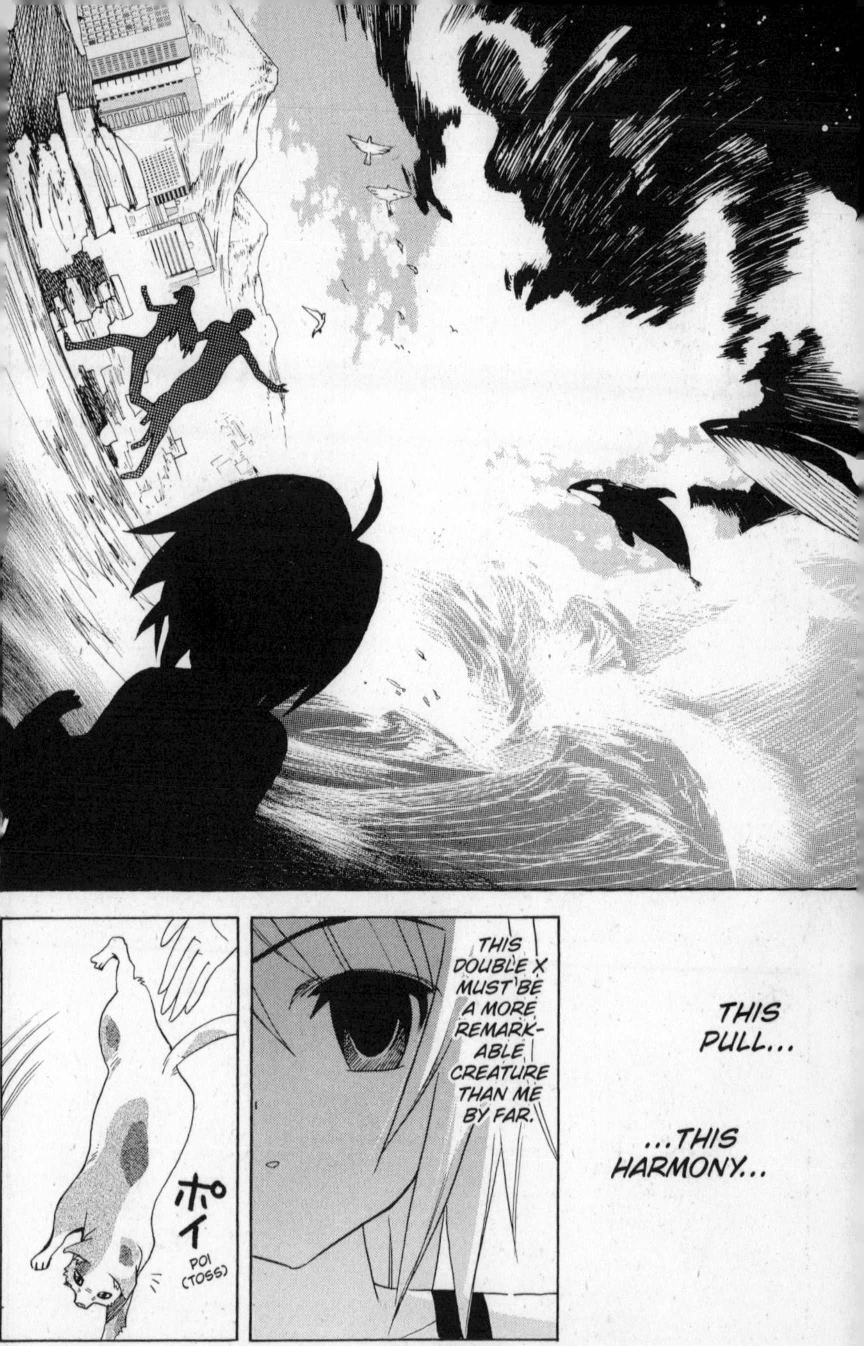
THIS PULL...
...THIS HARMONY...
THIS DOUBLE X MUST BE A MORE REMARKABLE CREATURE THAN ME BY FAR.
ポイ
POI (TOSS)

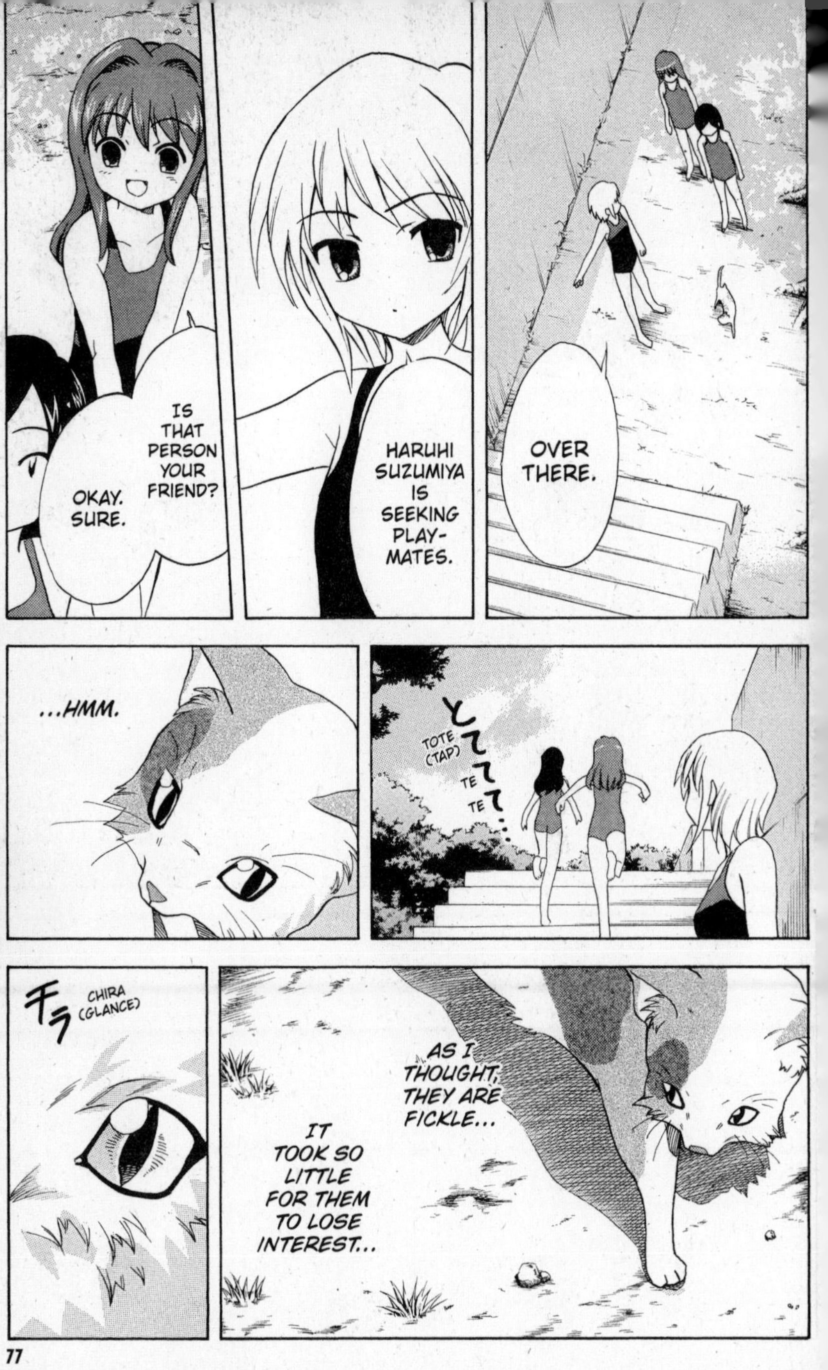
OVER THERE.
HARUHI SUZUMIYA IS SEEKING PLAY-MATES.
IS THAT PERSON YOUR FRIEND?
OKAY. SURE.
とててて
TOTE (TAP) TE TE
...HMM.
AS I THOUGHT, THEY ARE FICKLE...
IT TOOK SO LITTLE FOR THEM TO LOSE INTEREST...
チラ
CHIRA (GLANCE)

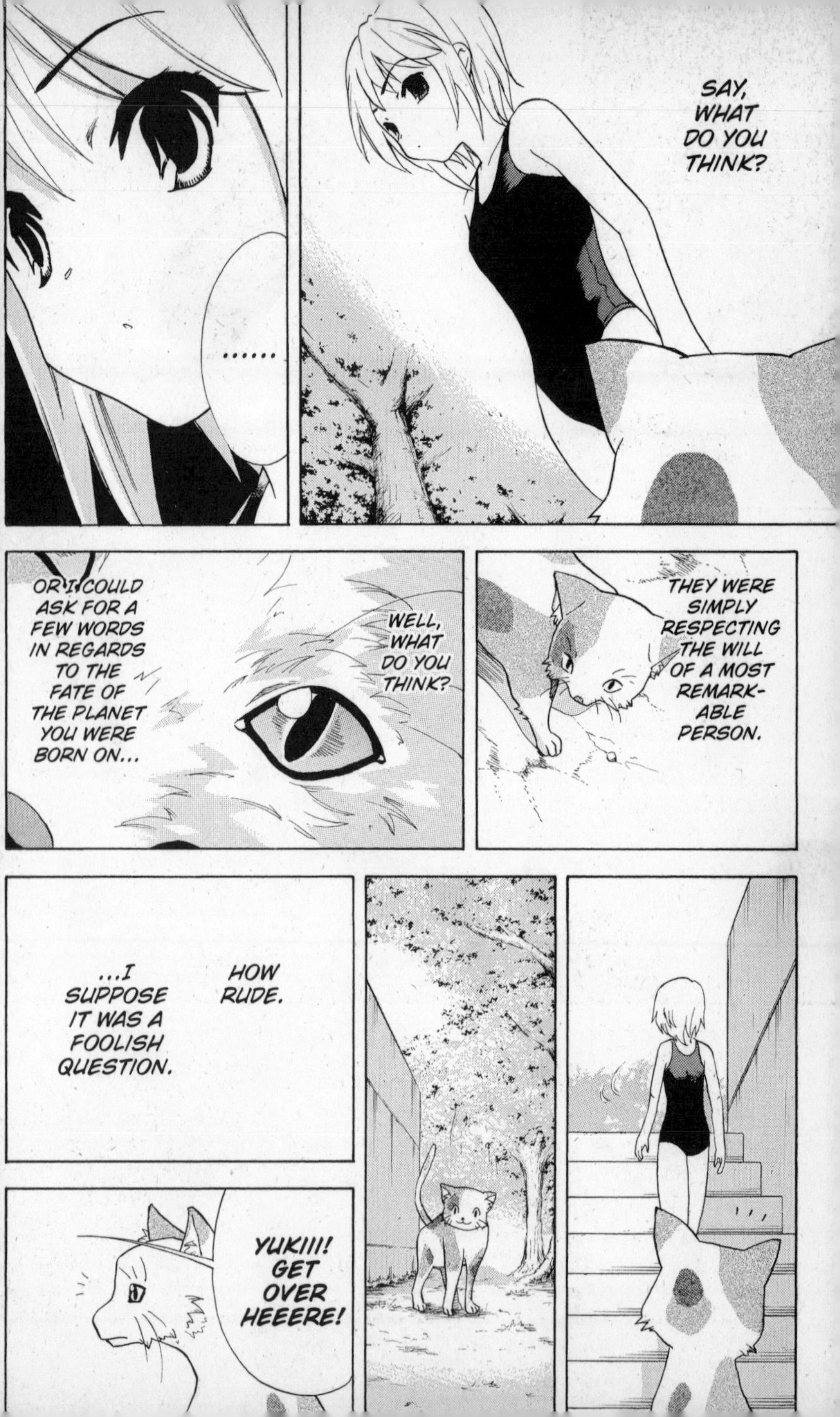
SAY, WHAT DO YOU THINK?
......
THEY WERE SIMPLY RESPECTING THE WILL OF A MOST REMARKABLE PERSON.
WELL, WHAT DO YOU THINK?
OR I COULD ASK FOR A FEW WORDS IN REGARDS TO THE FATE OF THE PLANET YOU WERE BORN ON...
HOW RUDE.
...I SUPPOSE IT WAS A FOOLISH QUESTION.
YUKIII! GET OVER HEEERE!

....

HONESTLY, WHAT AN INCREDIBLE DAY.

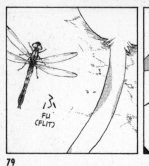

FU
(FLIT)

FROM THAT RETICENT GIRL TO THIS ONE...

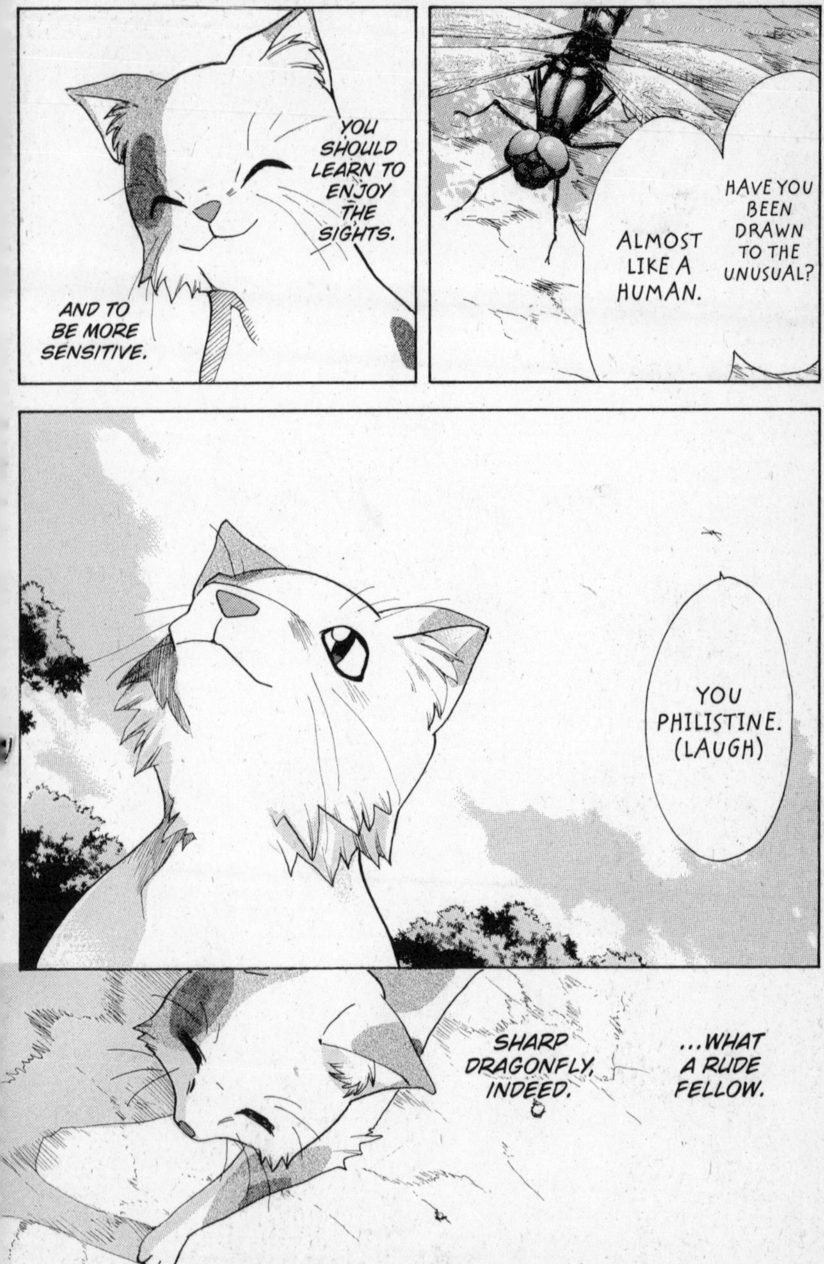
HAVE YOU BEEN DRAWN TO THE UNUSUAL?
ALMOST LIKE A HUMAN.
YOU SHOULD LEARN TO ENJOY THE SIGHTS.
AND TO BE MORE SENSITIVE.
YOU PHILISTINE. (LAUGH)
...WHAT A RUDE FELLOW.
SHARP DRAGONFLY, INDEED.

A Perspective on Life from Shamisen the Stray : END

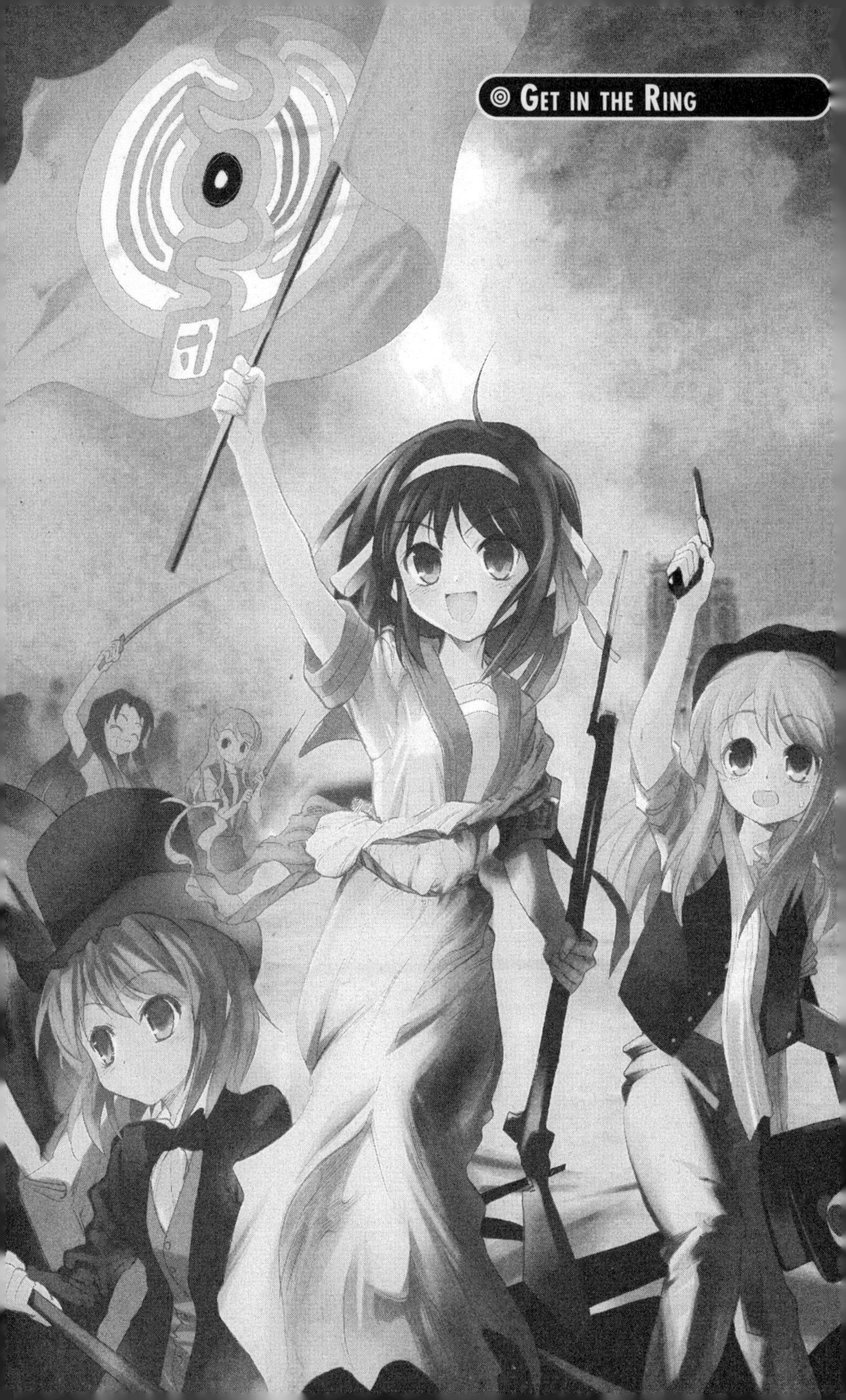
GET IN THE RING

THE MELANCHOLY OF HARUHI SUZUMIYA

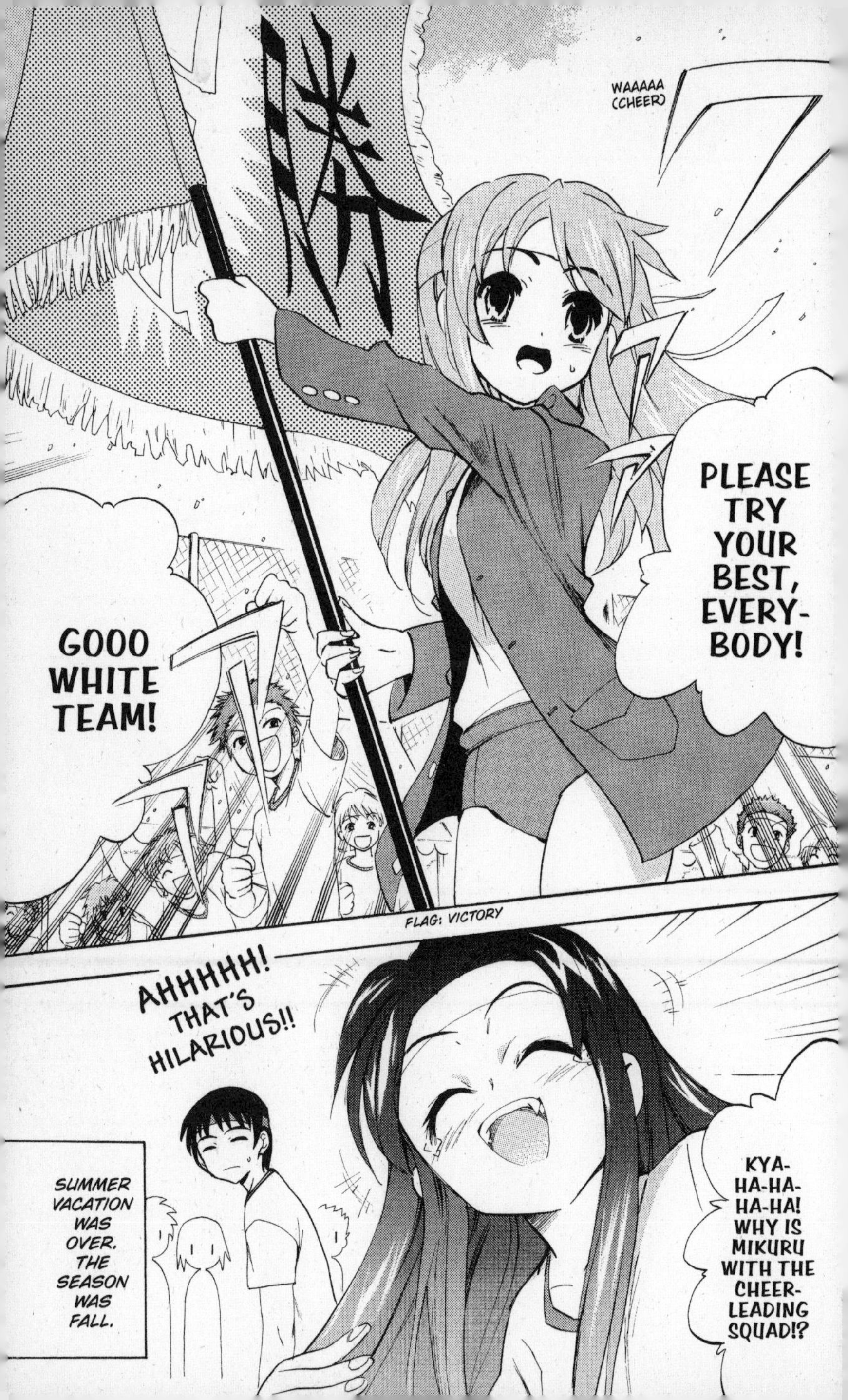
WAAAAA (CHEER)
PLEASE TRY YOUR BEST, EVERY-BODY!
GOOO WHITE TEAM!
FLAG: VICTORY
AHHHHH! THAT'S HILARIOUS!!
KYA-HA-HA-HA-HA! WHY IS MIKURU WITH THE CHEER-LEADING SQUAD!?
SUMMER VACATION WAS OVER. THE SEASON WAS FALL.

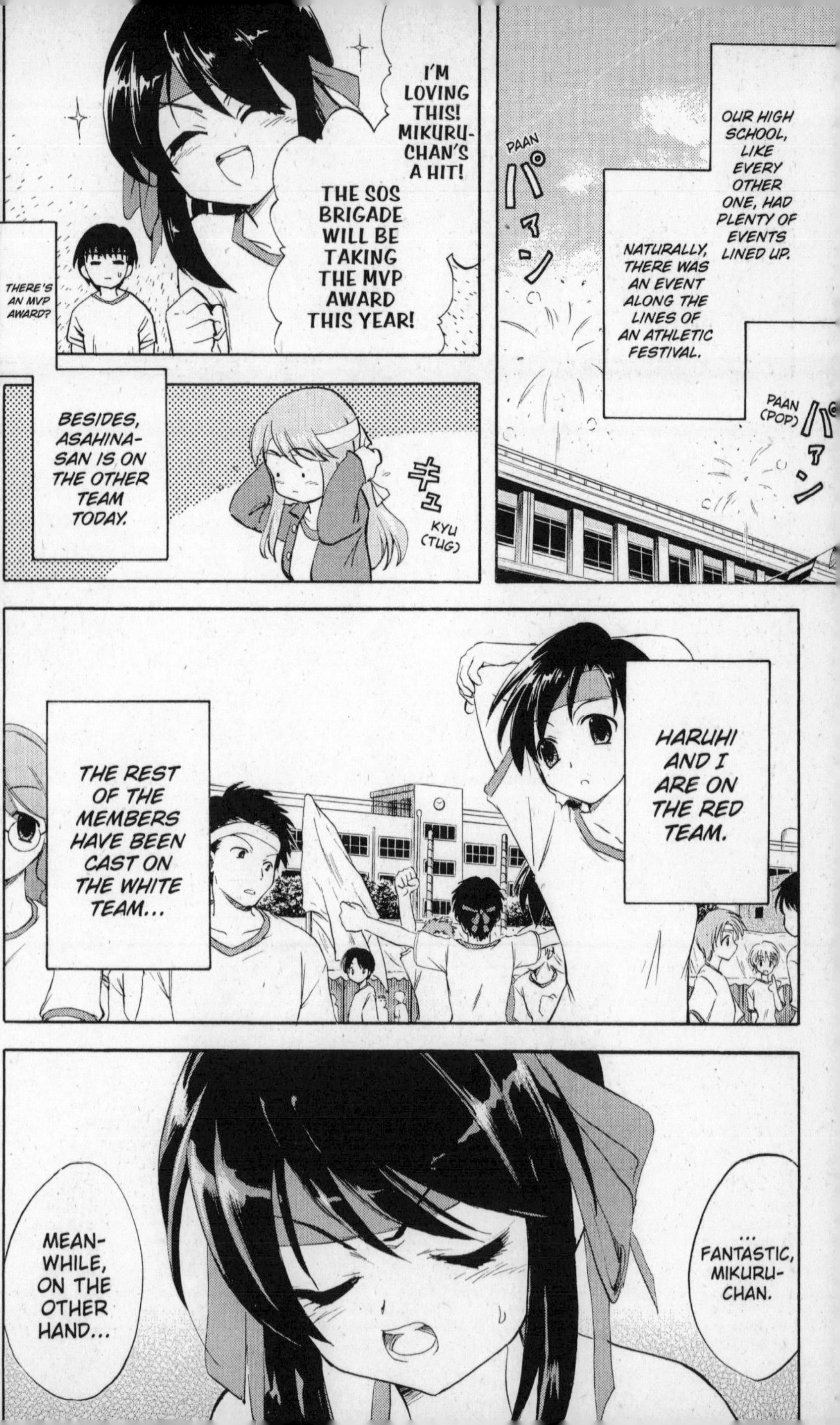
OUR HIGH SCHOOL, LIKE EVERY OTHER ONE, HAD PLENTY OF EVENTS LINED UP.
NATURALLY, THERE WAS AN EVENT ALONG THE LINES OF AN ATHLETIC FESTIVAL.
パァン PAAN
パァン PAAN (POP)
I'M LOVING THIS! MIKURU-CHAN'S A HIT!
THE SOS BRIGADE WILL BE TAKING THE MVP AWARD THIS YEAR!
THERE'S AN MVP AWARD?
BESIDES, ASAHINA-SAN IS ON THE OTHER TEAM TODAY.
キュ KYU (TUG)
HARUHI AND I ARE ON THE RED TEAM.
THE REST OF THE MEMBERS HAVE BEEN CAST ON THE WHITE TEAM...
...FANTASTIC, MIKURU-CHAN.
MEAN-WHILE, ON THE OTHER HAND...

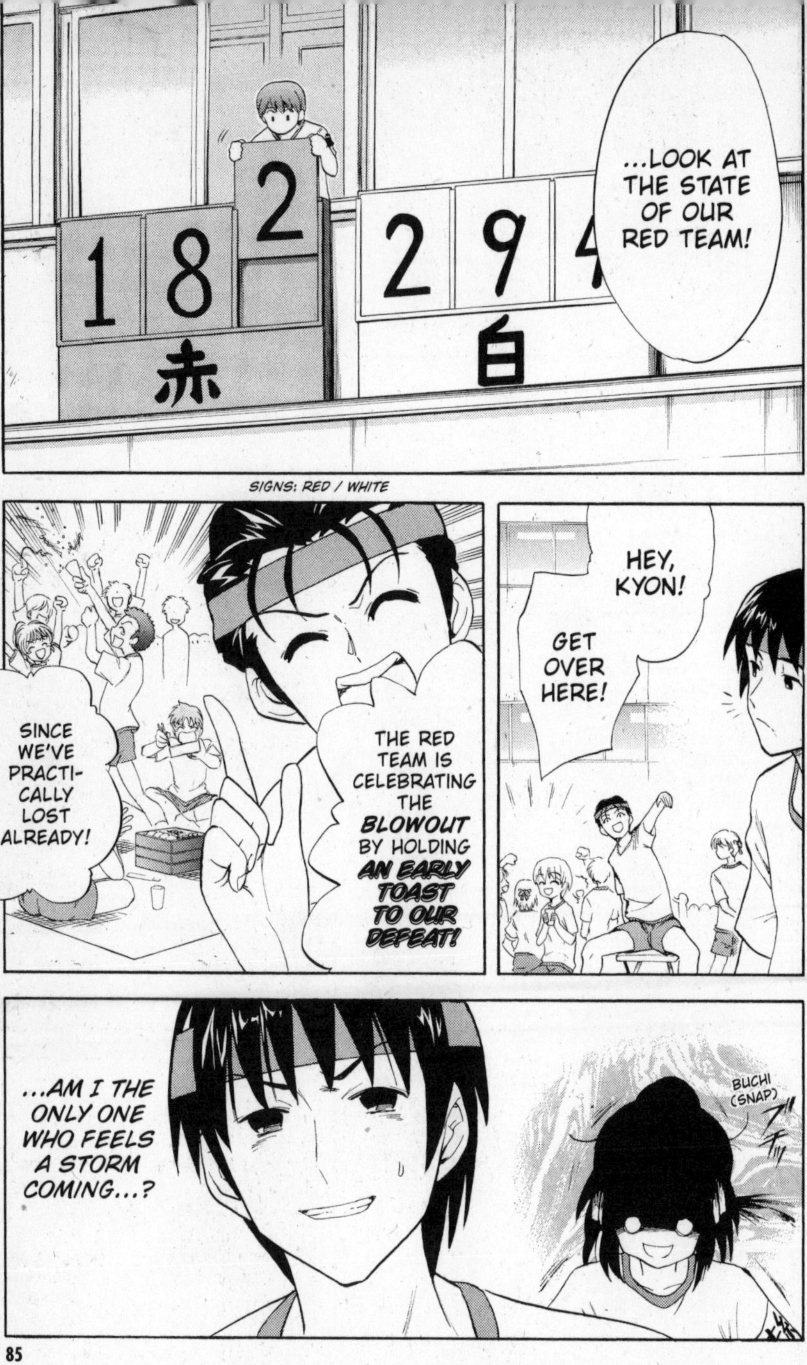
...LOOK AT THE STATE OF OUR RED TEAM!
赤
白
SIGNS: RED / WHITE
HEY, KYON!
GET OVER HERE!
THE RED TEAM IS CELEBRATING THE BLOWOUT BY HOLDING AN EARLY TOAST TO OUR DEFEAT!
SINCE WE'VE PRACTI-CALLY LOST ALREADY!
BUCHI (SNAP)
...AM I THE ONLY ONE WHO FEELS A STORM COMING...?

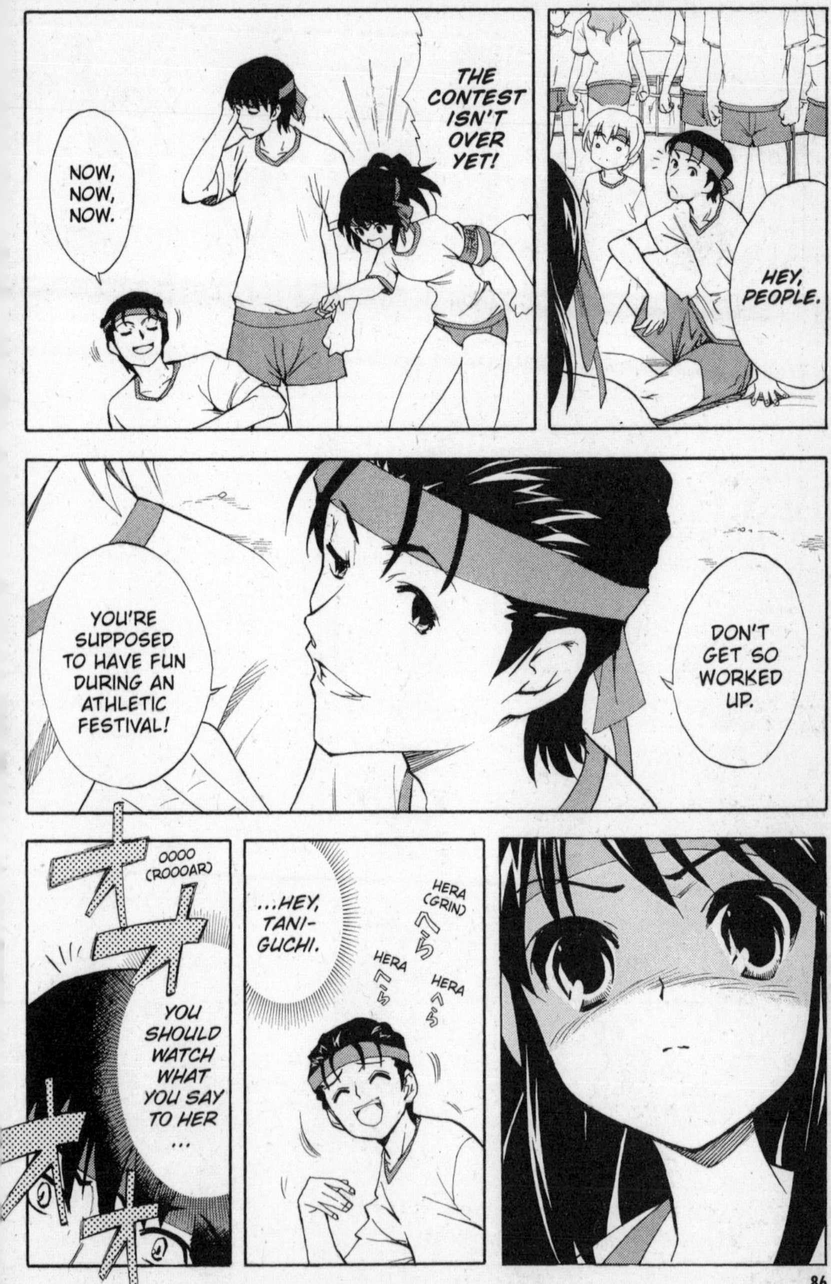
HEY, PEOPLE.
THE CONTEST ISN'T OVER YET!
NOW, NOW, NOW.
DON'T GET SO WORKED UP.
YOU'RE SUPPOSED TO HAVE FUN DURING AN ATHLETIC FESTIVAL!
HERA (GRIN)
...HEY, TANI-GUCHI.
HERA
HERA
OOOO (ROOOAR)
YOU SHOULD WATCH WHAT YOU SAY TO HER ...

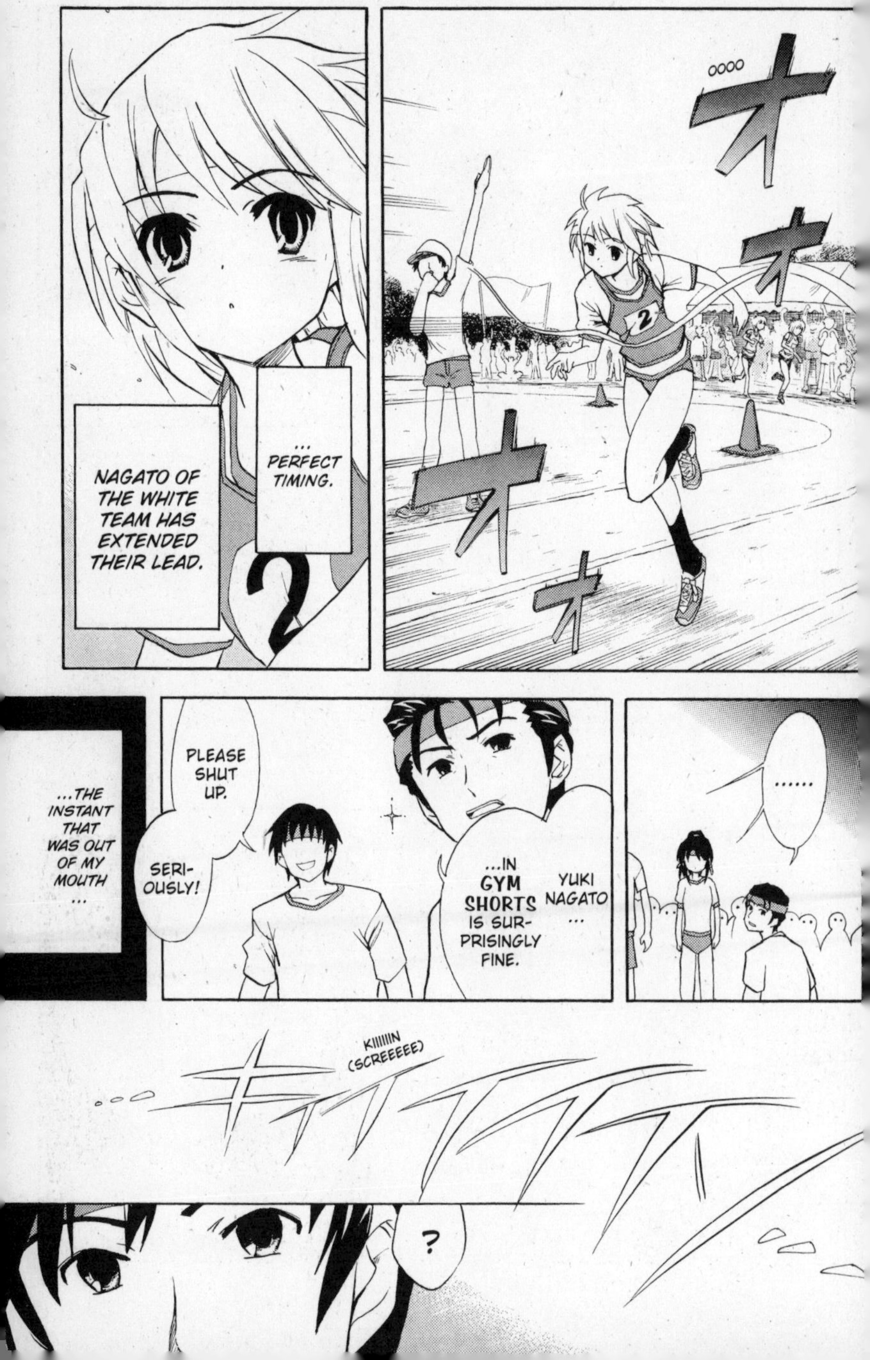
OOOO
... PERFECT TIMING.
NAGATO OF THE WHITE TEAM HAS EXTENDED THEIR LEAD.
......
YUKI NAGATO ...
...IN GYM SHORTS IS SURPRISINGLY FINE.
PLEASE SHUT UP.
SERIOUSLY!
...THE INSTANT THAT WAS OUT OF MY MOUTH ...
KIIIIIIN (SCREEEEE)
?

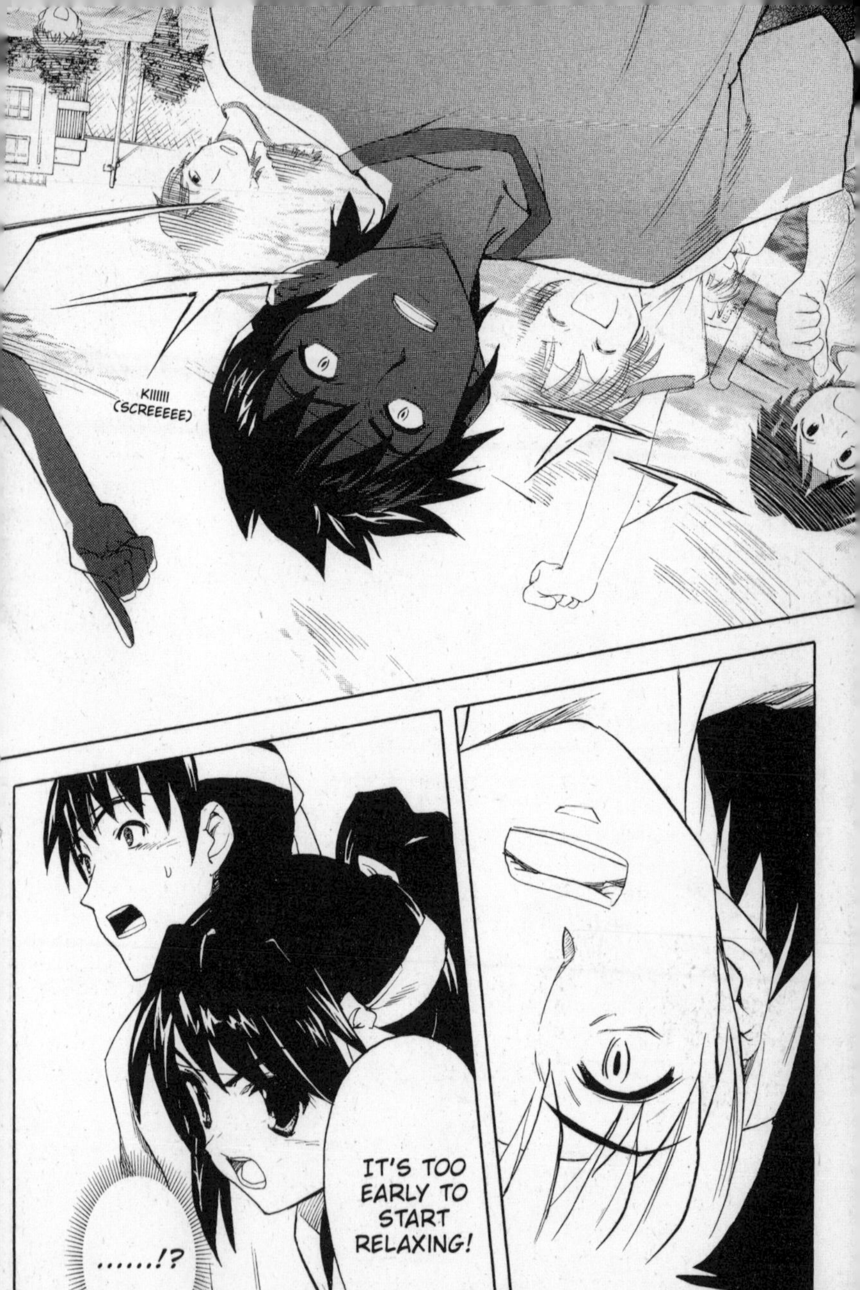
KIIIII
(SCREEEEE)
IT'S TOO EARLY TO START RELAXING!
......!?

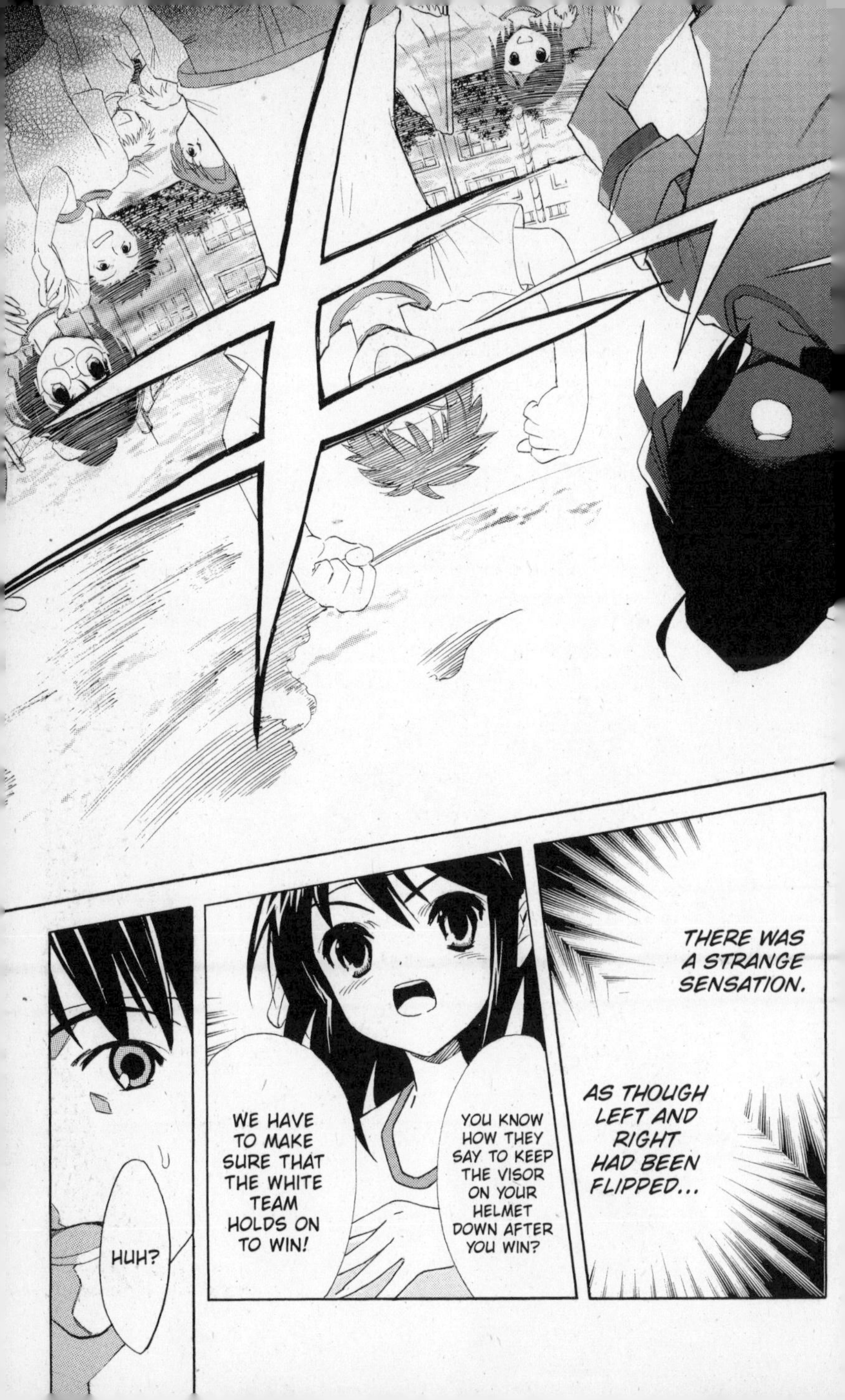
THERE WAS A STRANGE SENSATION.
AS THOUGH LEFT AND RIGHT HAD BEEN FLIPPED...
YOU KNOW HOW THEY SAY TO KEEP THE VISOR ON YOUR HELMET DOWN AFTER YOU WIN?
WE HAVE TO MAKE SURE THAT THE WHITE TEAM HOLDS ON TO WIN!
HUH?

ARMBAND: WHITE TEAM

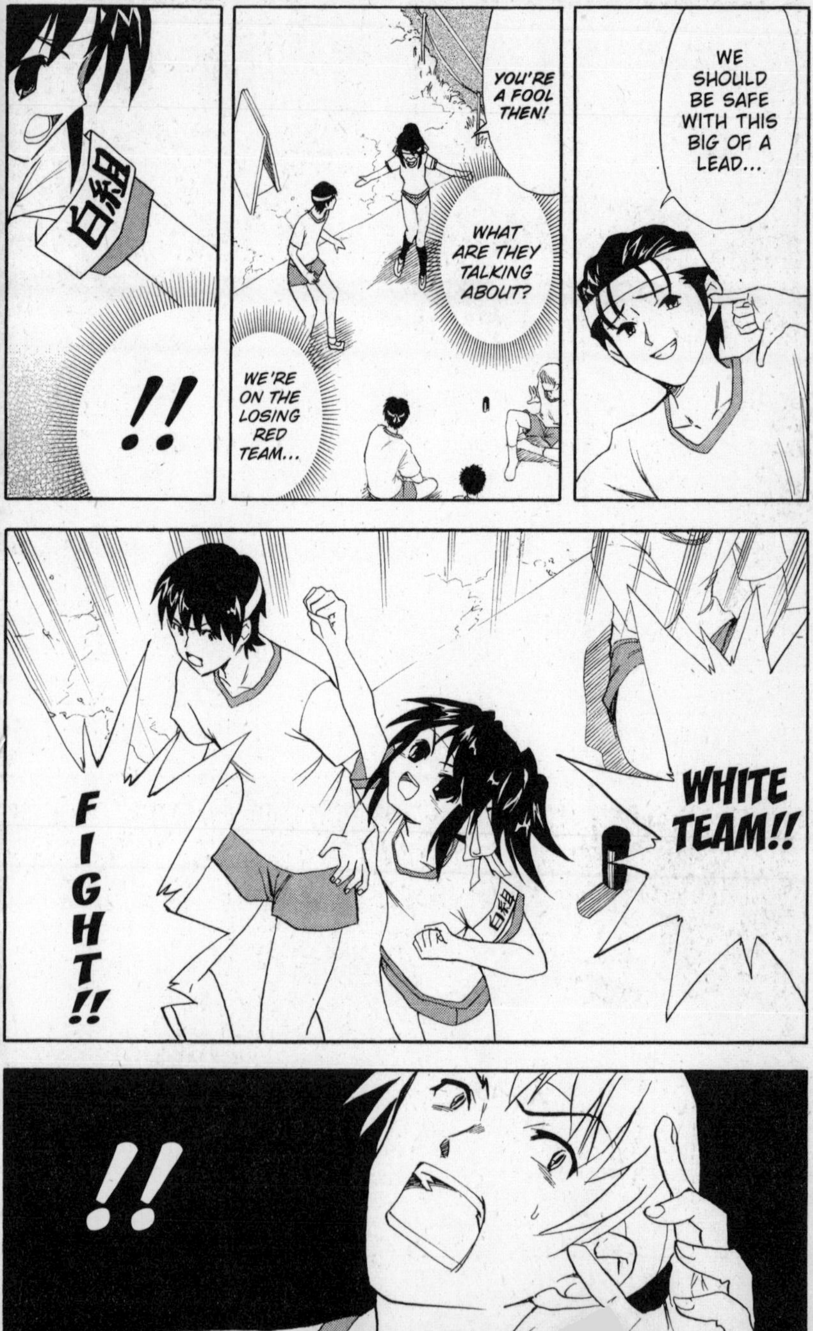
WE SHOULD BE SAFE WITH THIS BIG OF A LEAD...
YOU'RE A FOOL THEN!
WHAT ARE THEY TALKING ABOUT?
WE'RE ON THE LOSING RED TEAM...
!!
WHITE TEAM!!
FIGHT!!
!!

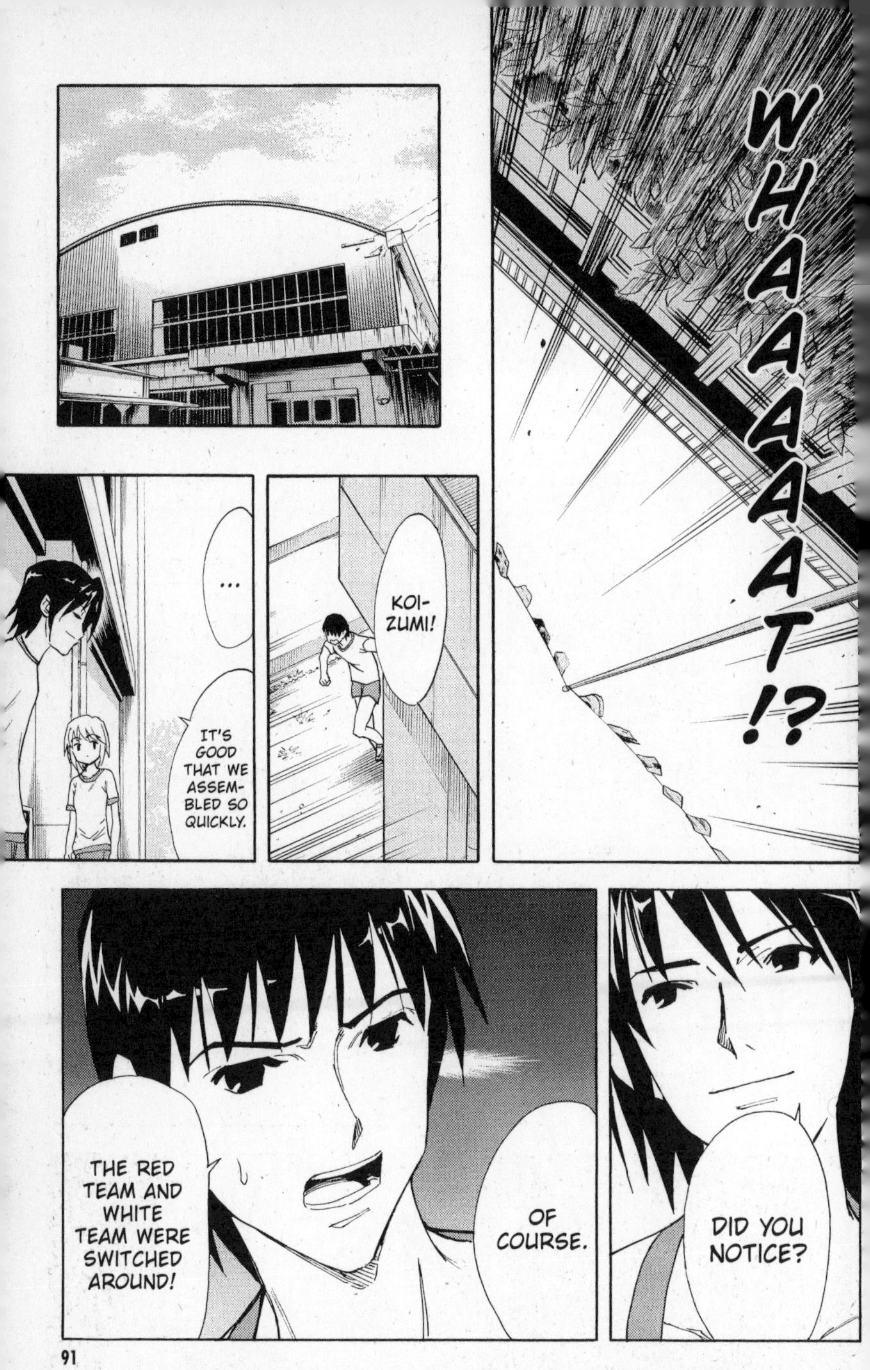
WHAAAAAAT!?
KOI-ZUMI!
...
IT'S GOOD THAT WE ASSEMBLED SO QUICKLY.
DID YOU NOTICE?
OF COURSE.
THE RED TEAM AND WHITE TEAM WERE SWITCHED AROUND!

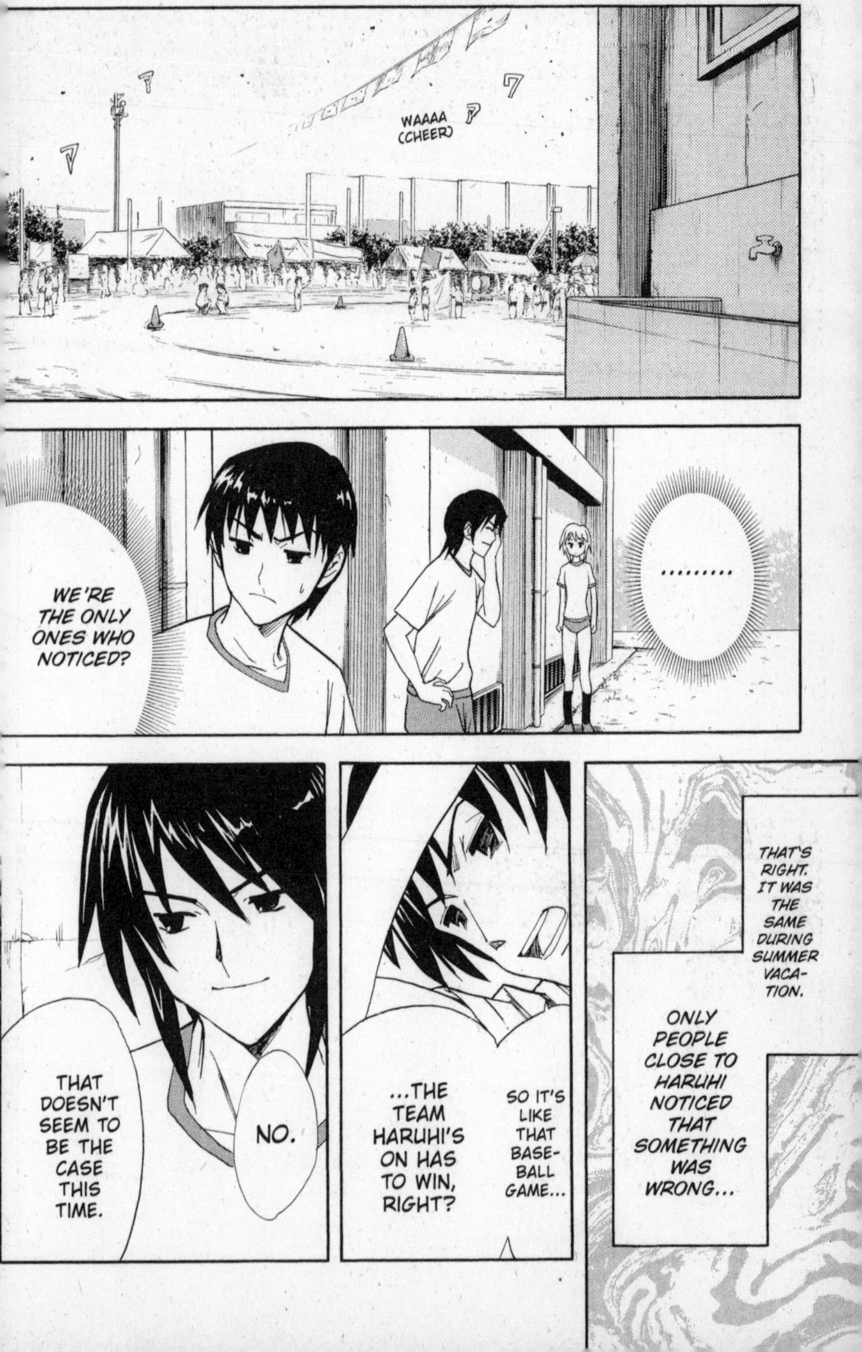
WAAAA (CHEER)
....
WE'RE THE ONLY ONES WHO NOTICED?
THAT'S RIGHT. IT WAS THE SAME DURING SUMMER VACATION.
ONLY PEOPLE CLOSE TO HARUHI NOTICED THAT SOMETHING WAS WRONG...
SO IT'S LIKE THAT BASEBALL GAME...
...THE TEAM HARUHI'S ON HAS TO WIN, RIGHT?
NO.
THAT DOESN'T SEEM TO BE THE CASE THIS TIME.

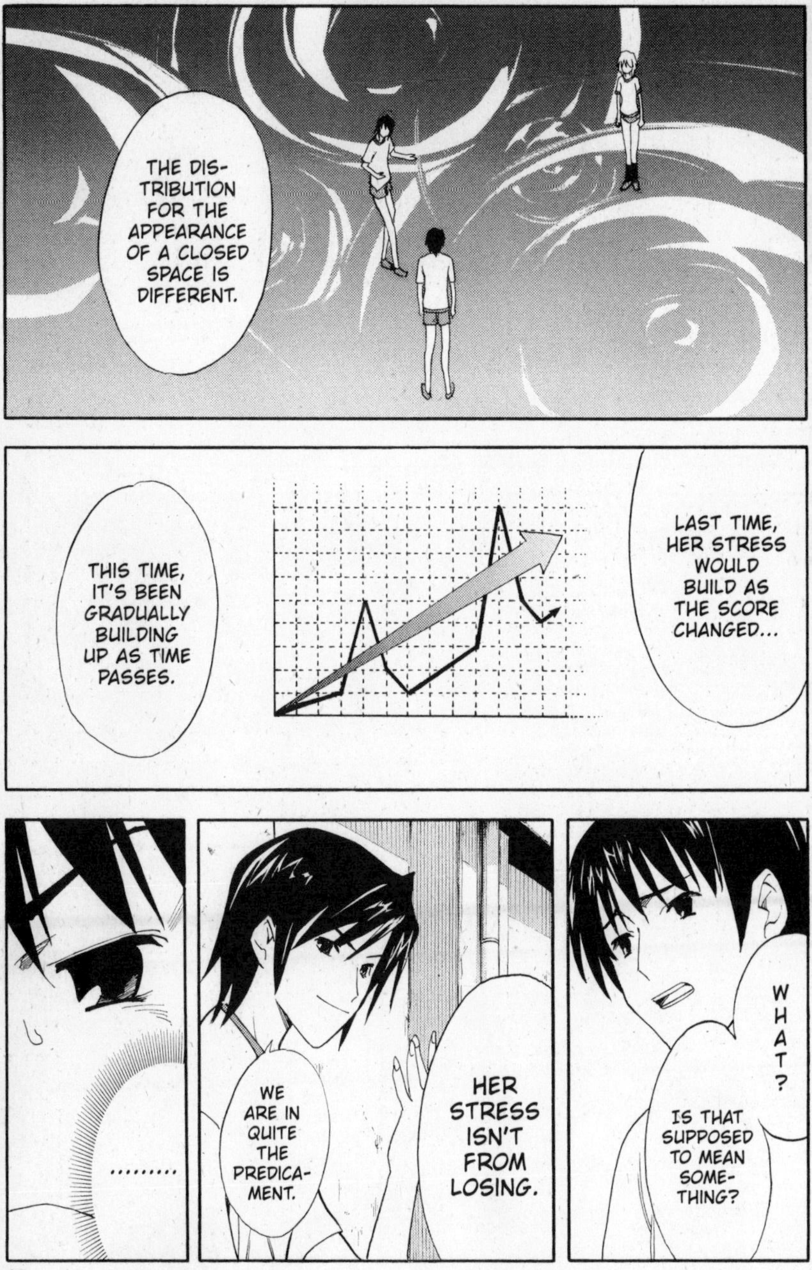
THE DIS-TRIBUTION FOR THE APPEARANCE OF A CLOSED SPACE IS DIFFERENT.
LAST TIME, HER STRESS WOULD BUILD AS THE SCORE CHANGED...
THIS TIME, IT'S BEEN GRADUALLY BUILDING UP AS TIME PASSES.
WHAT?
IS THAT SUPPOSED TO MEAN SOME-THING?
HER STRESS ISN'T FROM LOSING.
WE ARE IN QUITE THE PREDICA-MENT.
....

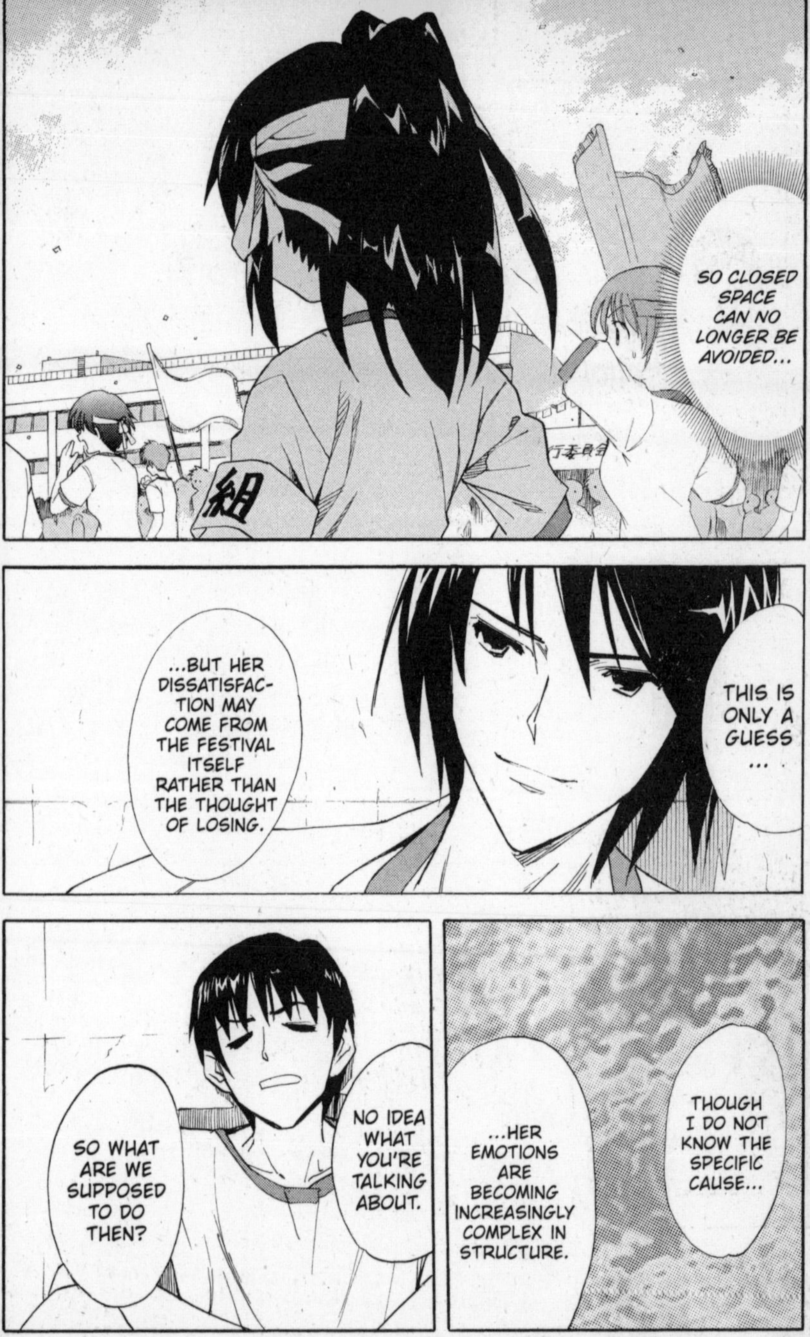
SO CLOSED SPACE CAN NO LONGER BE AVOIDED...
THIS IS ONLY A GUESS ...
...BUT HER DISSATISFACTION MAY COME FROM THE FESTIVAL ITSELF RATHER THAN THE THOUGHT OF LOSING.
THOUGH I DO NOT KNOW THE SPECIFIC CAUSE...
...HER EMOTIONS ARE BECOMING INCREASINGLY COMPLEX IN STRUCTURE.
NO IDEA WHAT YOU'RE TALKING ABOUT.
SO WHAT ARE WE SUPPOSED TO DO THEN?

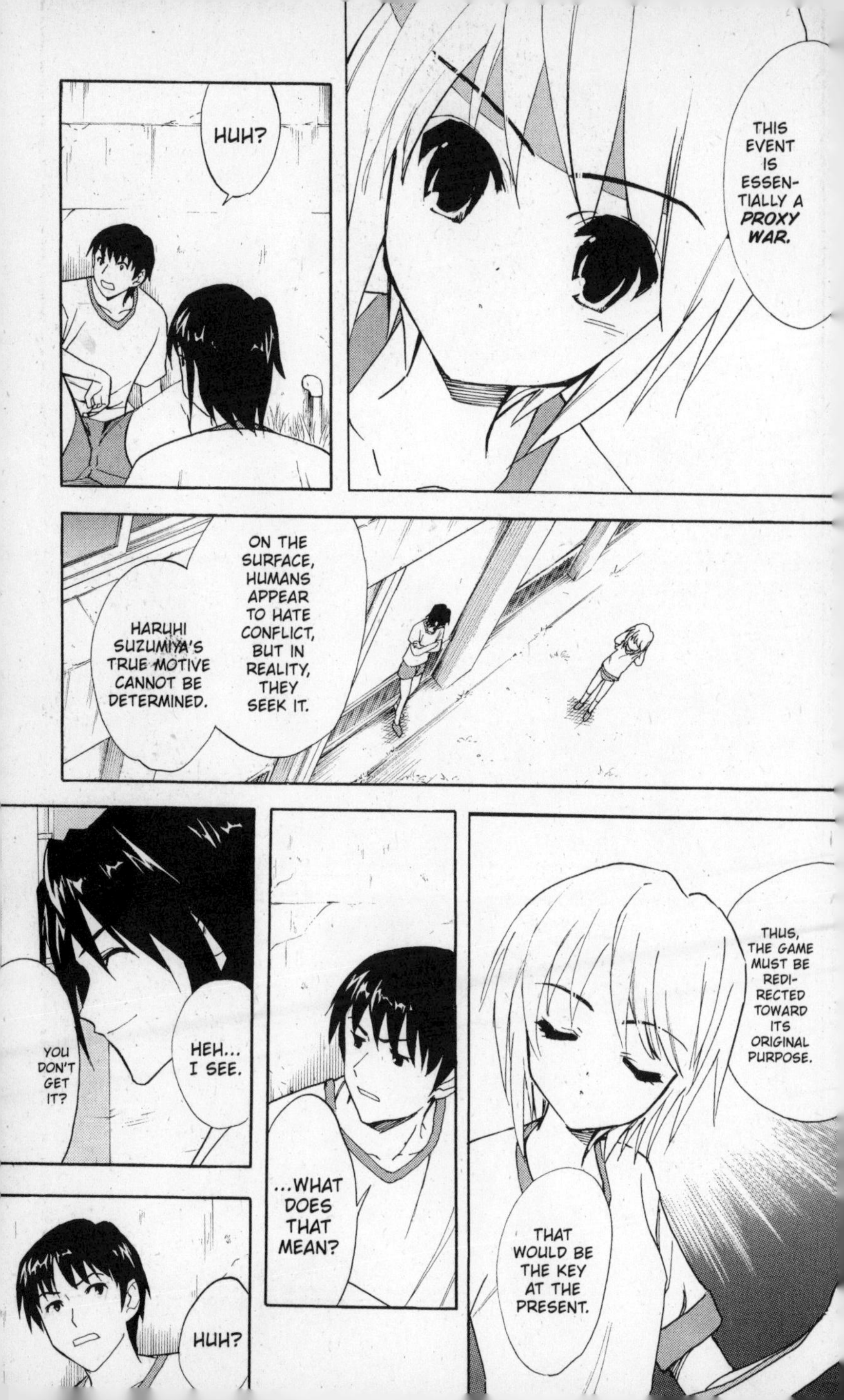
THIS EVENT IS ESSENTIALLY A ***PROXY WAR.***
HUH?
ON THE SURFACE, HUMANS APPEAR TO HATE CONFLICT, BUT IN REALITY, THEY SEEK IT.
HARUHI SUZUMIYA'S TRUE MOTIVE CANNOT BE DETERMINED.
THUS, THE GAME MUST BE REDIRECTED TOWARD ITS ORIGINAL PURPOSE.
THAT WOULD BE THE KEY AT THE PRESENT.
...WHAT DOES THAT MEAN?
HEH... I SEE.
YOU DON'T GET IT?
HUH?

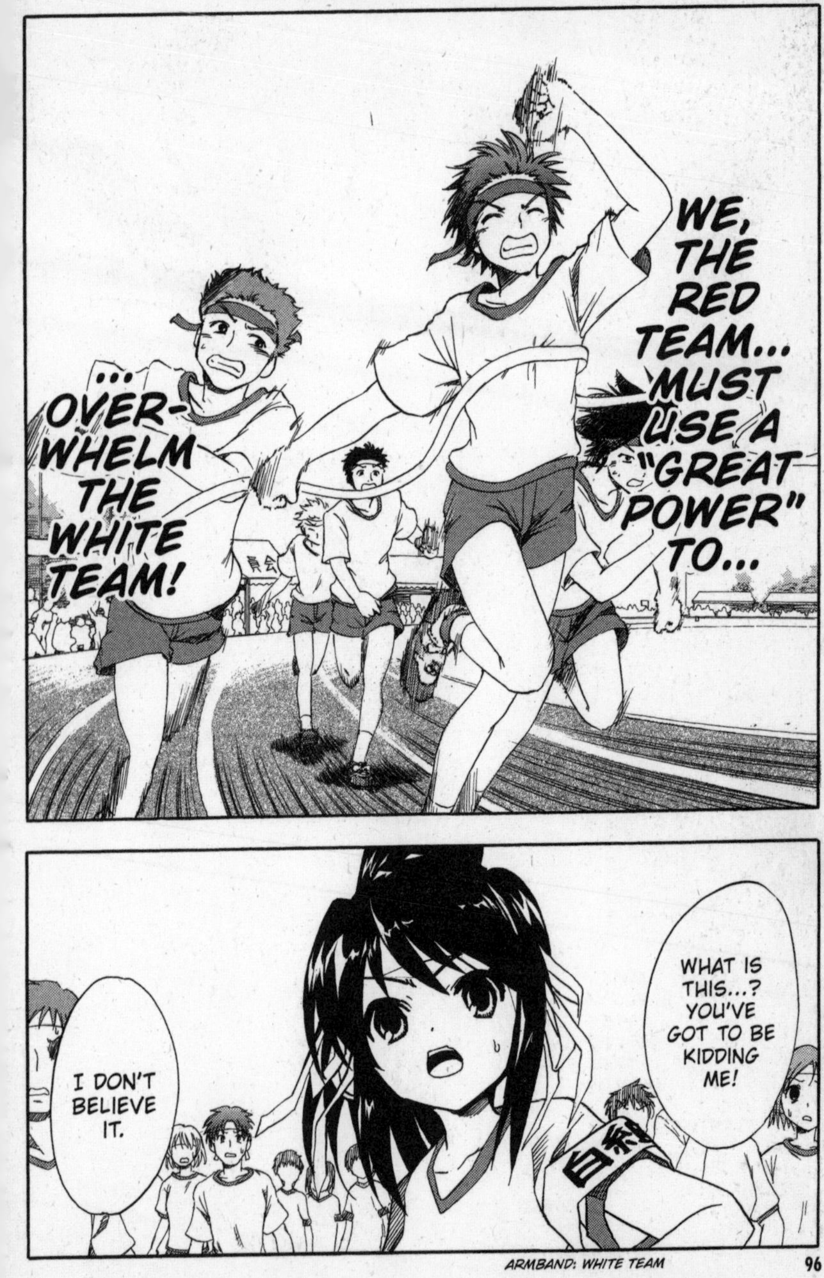
WE, THE RED TEAM... MUST USE A "GREAT POWER" TO...
...OVER-WHELM THE WHITE TEAM!
WHAT IS THIS...? YOU'VE GOT TO BE KIDDING ME!
I DON'T BELIEVE IT.

ARMBAND: WHITE TEAM

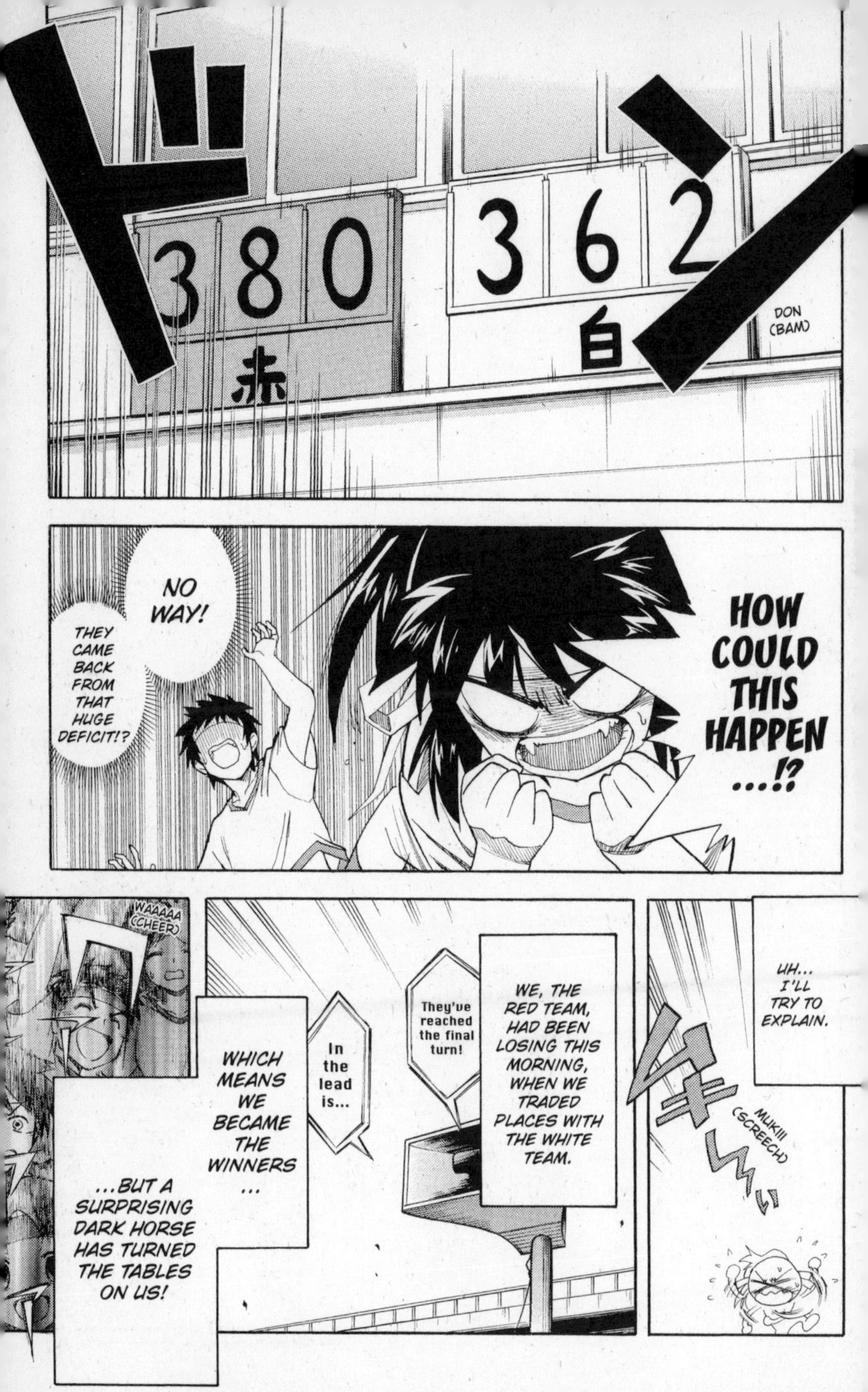
380
赤
362
白
DON (BAM)
HOW COULD THIS HAPPEN...!?
NO WAY!
THEY CAME BACK FROM THAT HUGE DEFICIT!?
UH... I'LL TRY TO EXPLAIN.
MUKIII (SCREECH)
WE, THE RED TEAM, HAD BEEN LOSING THIS MORNING, WHEN WE TRADED PLACES WITH THE WHITE TEAM.
They've reached the final turn!
In the lead is...
WHICH MEANS WE BECAME THE WINNERS...
WAAAAA (CHEER)
...BUT A SURPRISING DARK HORSE HAS TURNED THE TABLES ON US!

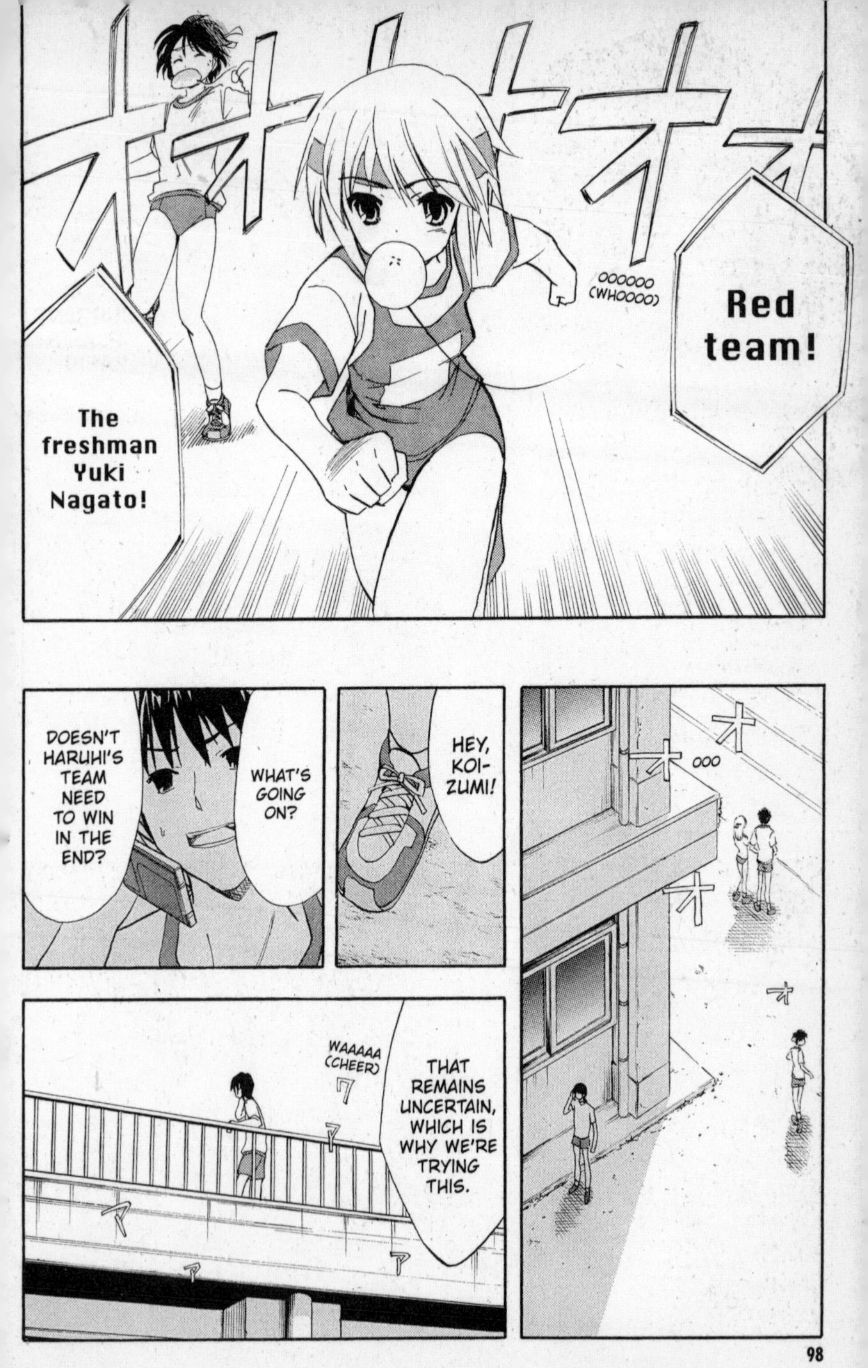
Red team!
OOOOOO (WHOOOO)
The freshman Yuki Nagato!
OOO
HEY, KOI-ZUMI!
WHAT'S GOING ON?
DOESN'T HARUHI'S TEAM NEED TO WIN IN THE END?
THAT REMAINS UNCERTAIN, WHICH IS WHY WE'RE TRYING THIS.
WAAAAA (CHEER)

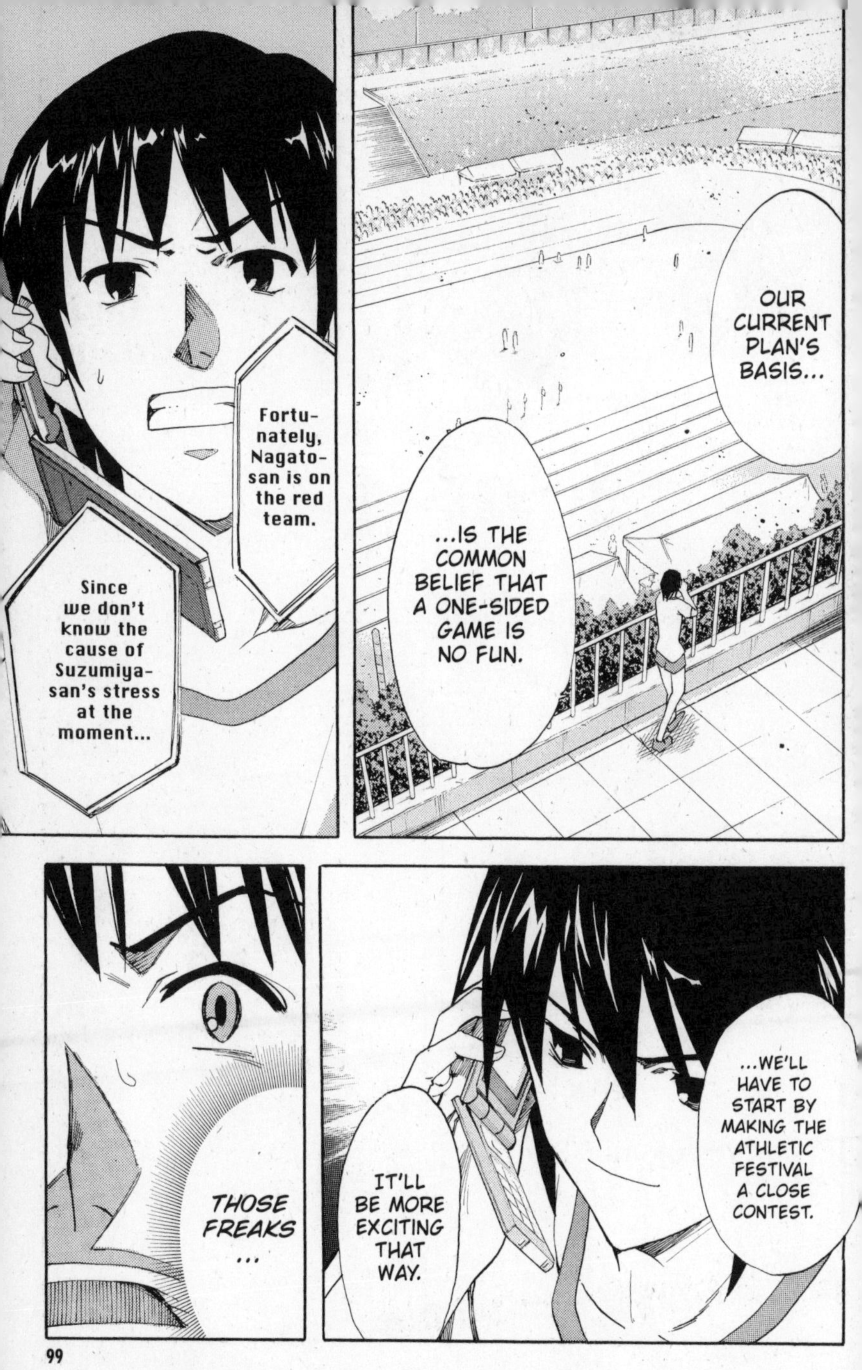
OUR CURRENT PLAN'S BASIS...
...IS THE COMMON BELIEF THAT A ONE-SIDED GAME IS NO FUN.
Fortunately, Nagato-san is on the red team.
Since we don't know the cause of Suzumiya-san's stress at the moment...
...WE'LL HAVE TO START BY MAKING THE ATHLETIC FESTIVAL A CLOSE CONTEST.
IT'LL BE MORE EXCITING THAT WAY.
THOSE FREAKS ...

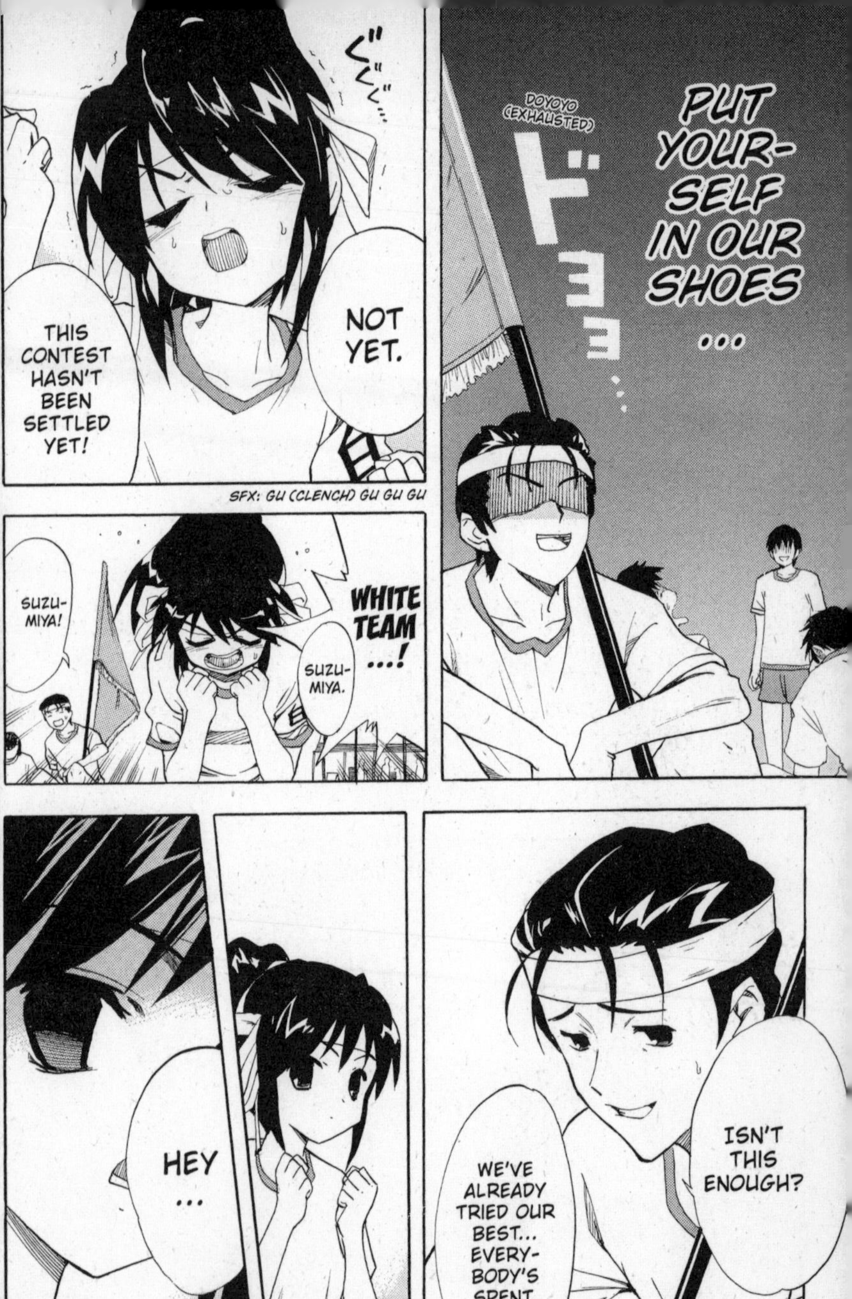
PUT YOUR-SELF IN OUR SHOES ...
DOYOYO (EXHAUSTED)
NOT YET.
THIS CONTEST HASN'T BEEN SETTLED YET!
SFX: GU (CLENCH) GU GU GU
WHITE TEAM ...!
SUZU-MIYA.
SUZU-MIYA!
ISN'T THIS ENOUGH?
WE'VE ALREADY TRIED OUR BEST... EVERY-BODY'S SPENT.
HEY ...

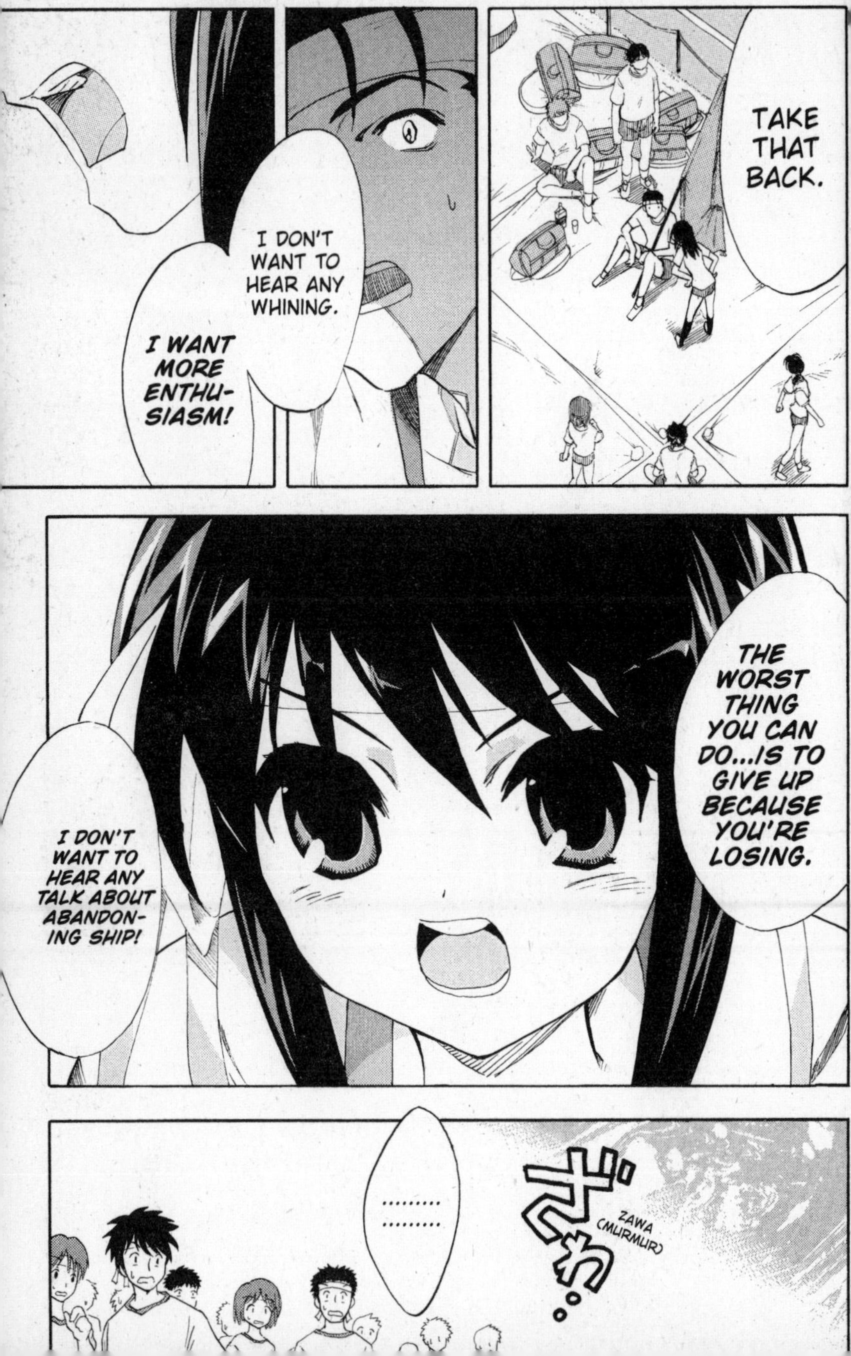
TAKE THAT BACK.
I DON'T WANT TO HEAR ANY WHINING.
I WANT MORE ENTHU-SIASM!
THE WORST THING YOU CAN DO...IS TO GIVE UP BECAUSE YOU'RE LOSING.
I DON'T WANT TO HEAR ANY TALK ABOUT ABANDON-ING SHIP!
ざわ。。。
ZAWA (MURMUR)
....
....

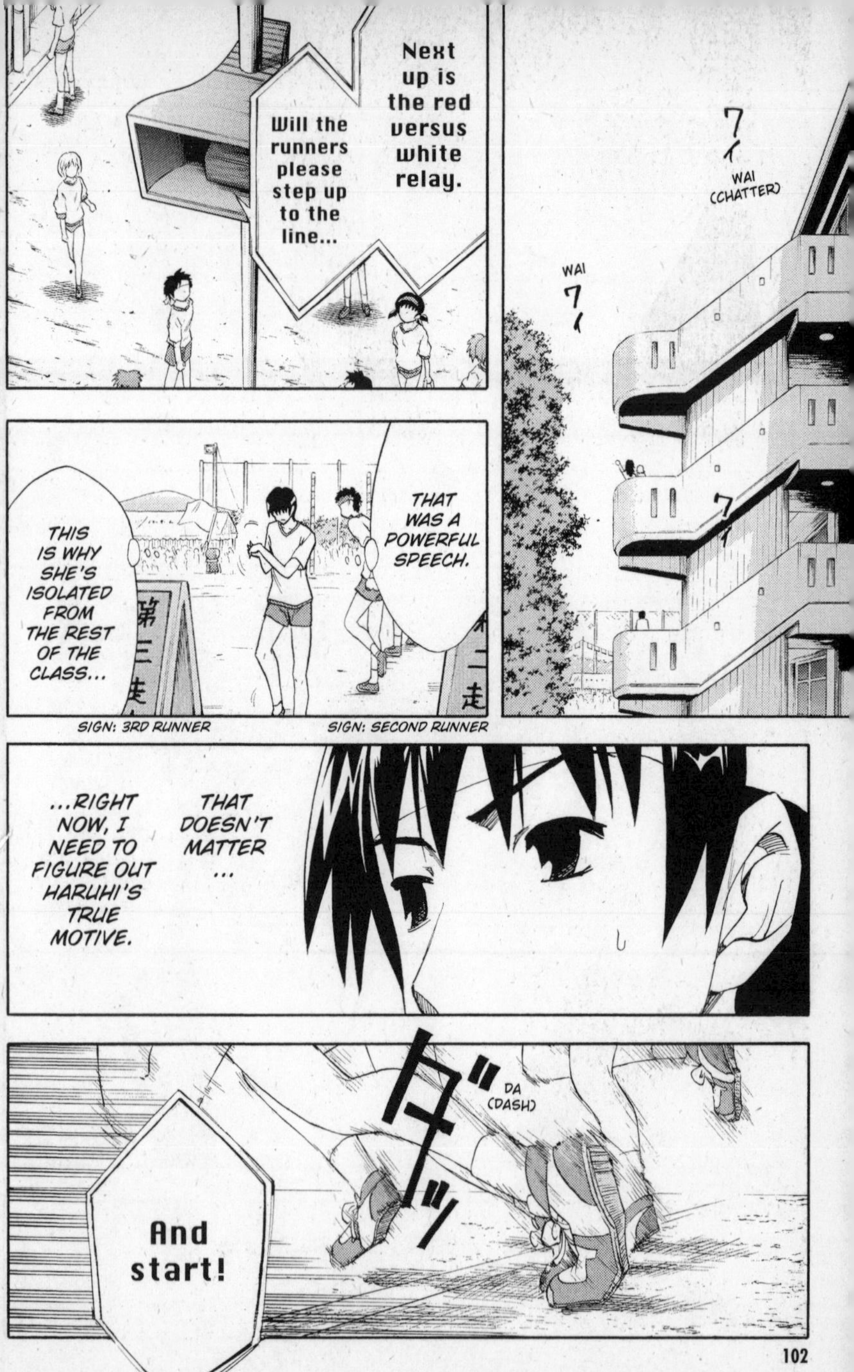
ワイ
WAI (CHATTER)
ワイ
WAI
Next up is the red versus white relay.
Will the runners please step up to the line...
THAT WAS A POWERFUL SPEECH.
THIS IS WHY SHE'S ISOLATED FROM THE REST OF THE CLASS...
SIGN: SECOND RUNNER
SIGN: 3RD RUNNER
THAT DOESN'T MATTER...
...RIGHT NOW, I NEED TO FIGURE OUT HARUHI'S TRUE MOTIVE.
ダッ
DA (DASH)
And start!

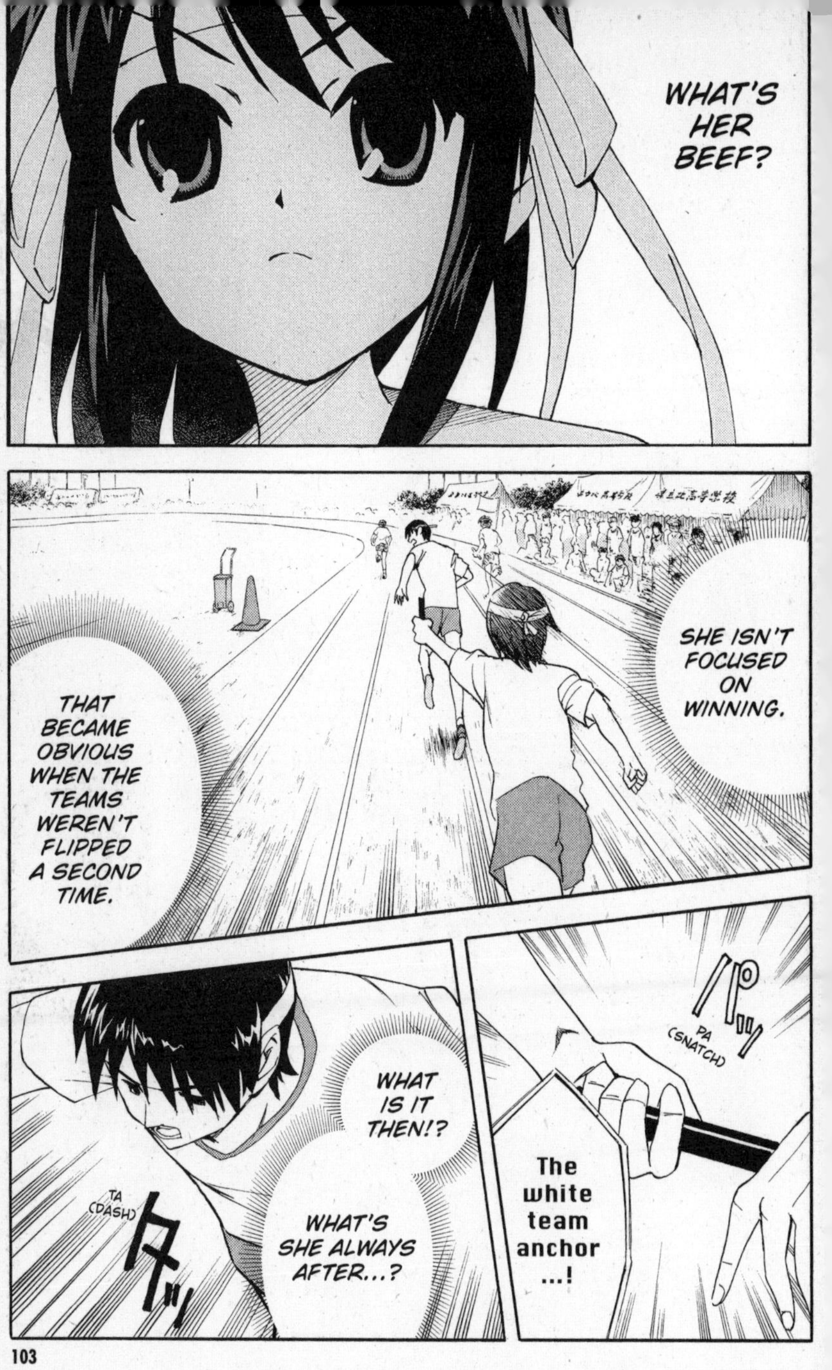
WHAT'S HER BEEF?
SHE ISN'T FOCUSED ON WINNING.
THAT BECAME OBVIOUS WHEN THE TEAMS WEREN'T FLIPPED A SECOND TIME.
PA (SNATCH)
The white team anchor ...!
WHAT IS IT THEN!?
WHAT'S SHE ALWAYS AFTER...?
TA (DASH)

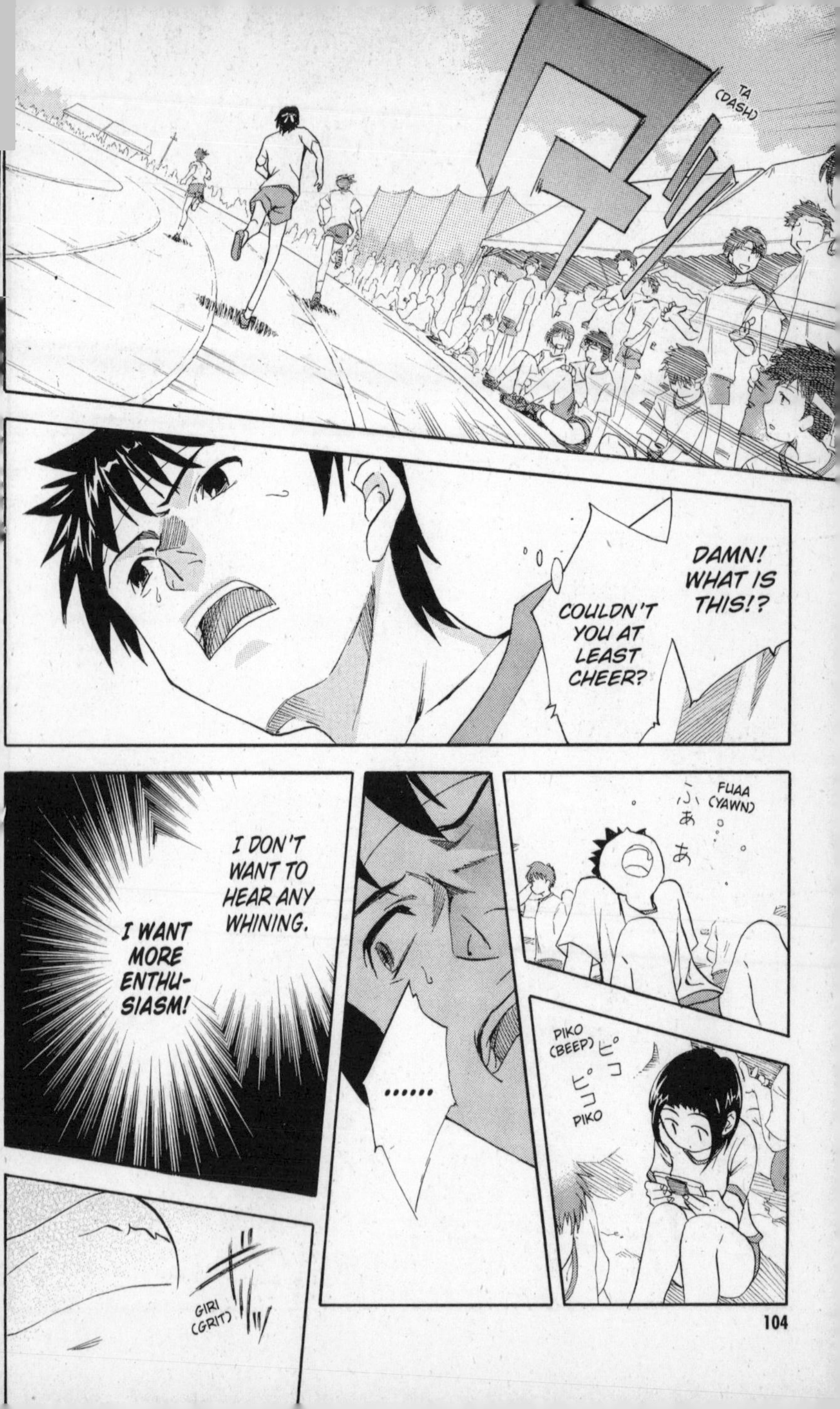
TA (DASH)
DAMN! WHAT IS THIS!?
COULDN'T YOU AT LEAST CHEER?
ふあぁ
FUAA (YAWN)
ピコ ピコ
PIKO (BEEP) PIKO
……
I DON'T WANT TO HEAR ANY WHINING.
I WANT MORE ENTHU-SIASM!
GIRI (GRIT)

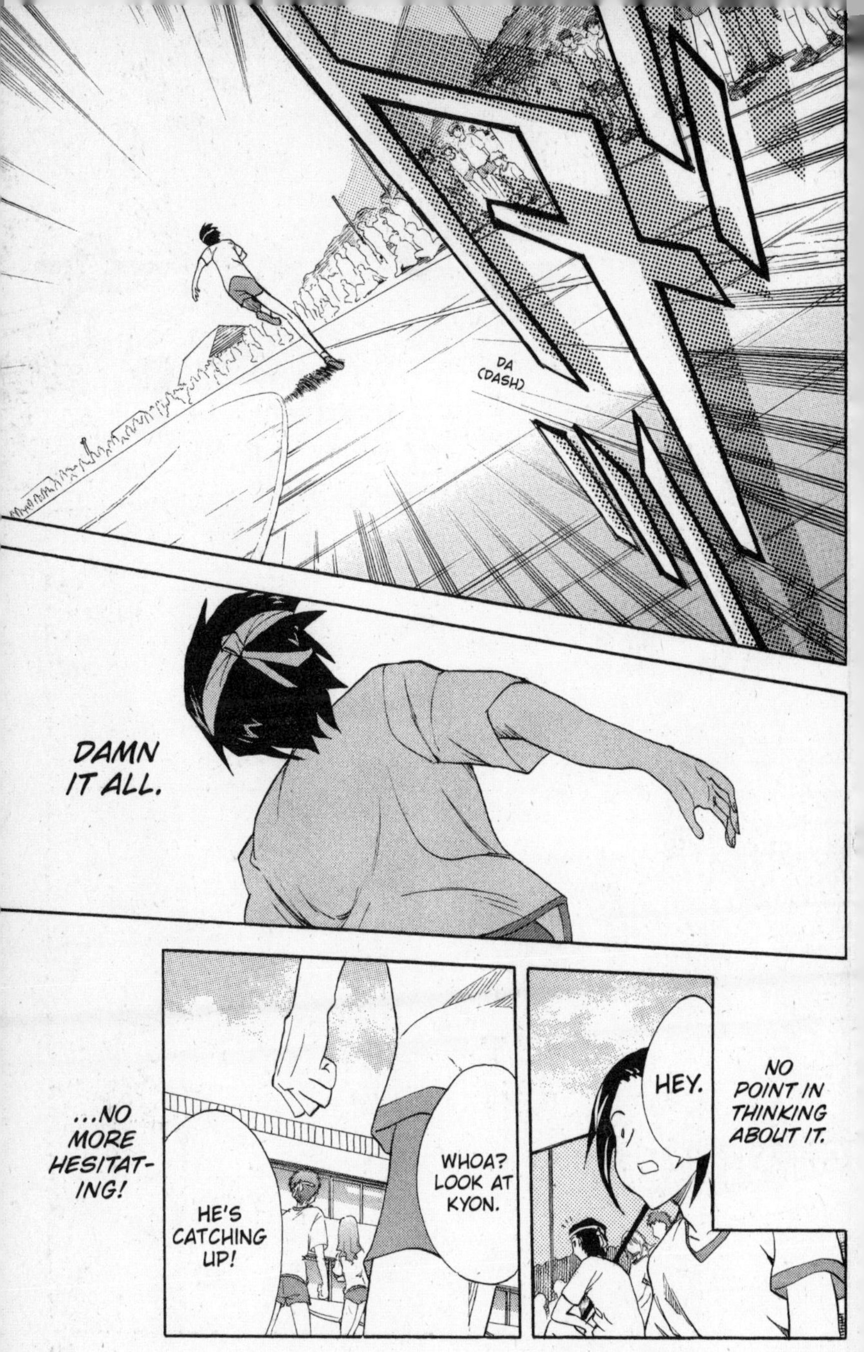
DA (DASH)
DAMN IT ALL.
NO POINT IN THINKING ABOUT IT.
HEY.
WHOA? LOOK AT KYON.
HE'S CATCHING UP!
...NO MORE HESITATING!

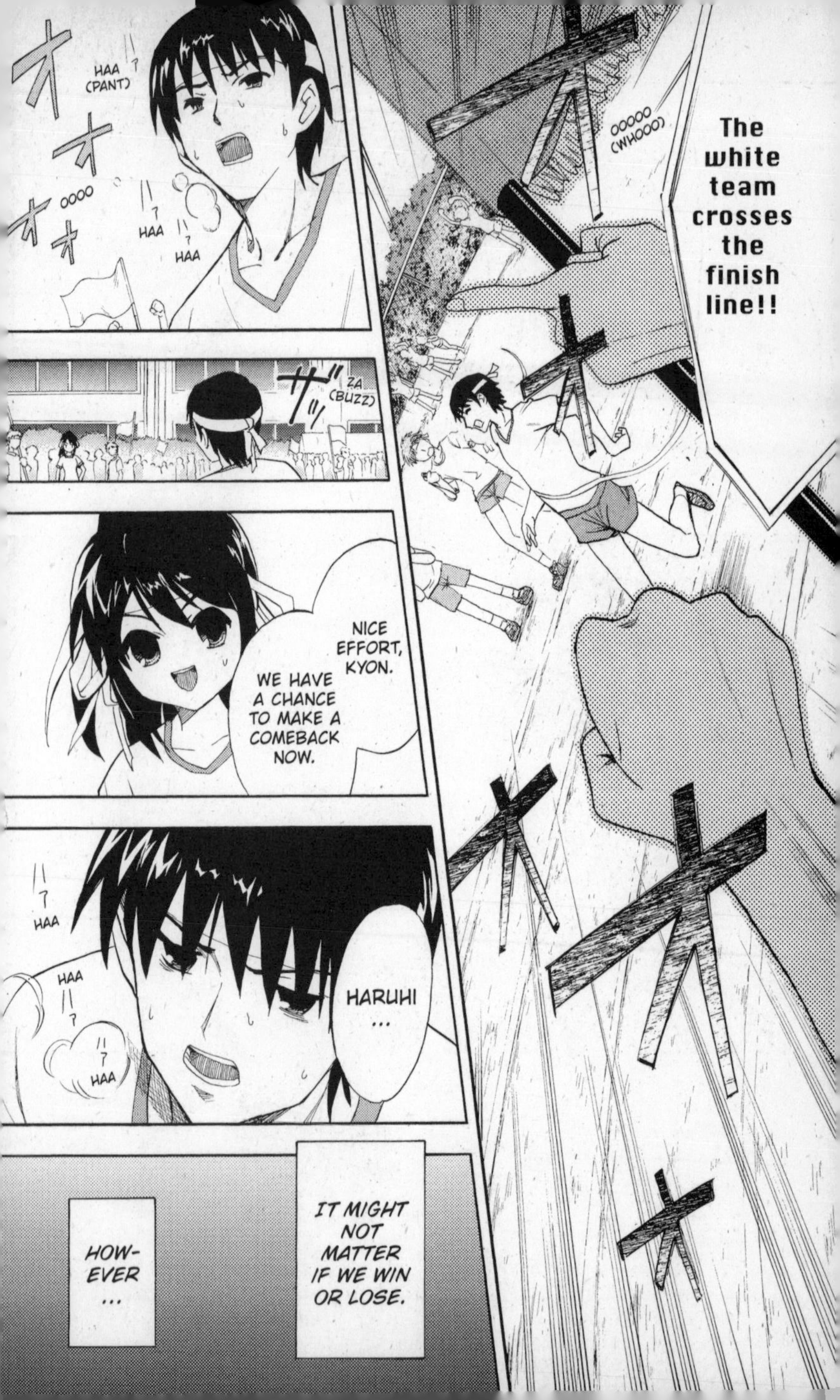
OOOOO (WHOOO)
The white team crosses the finish line!!
HAA (PANT)
OOOO
HAA
HAA
ZA (BUZZ)
NICE EFFORT, KYON.
WE HAVE A CHANCE TO MAKE A COMEBACK NOW.
HARUHI ...
HAA
HAA
HAA
IT MIGHT NOT MATTER IF WE WIN OR LOSE.
HOW-EVER ...

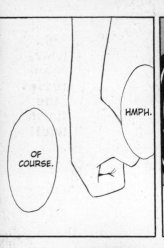

OF COURSE.

HMPH.

LET'S WIN.

WE'RE AIMING TO WALK AWAY VICTORIOUS!!

NOBODY LIKES TO LOSE.

ISN'T IT ONLY NATURAL TO FEEL THAT WAY?

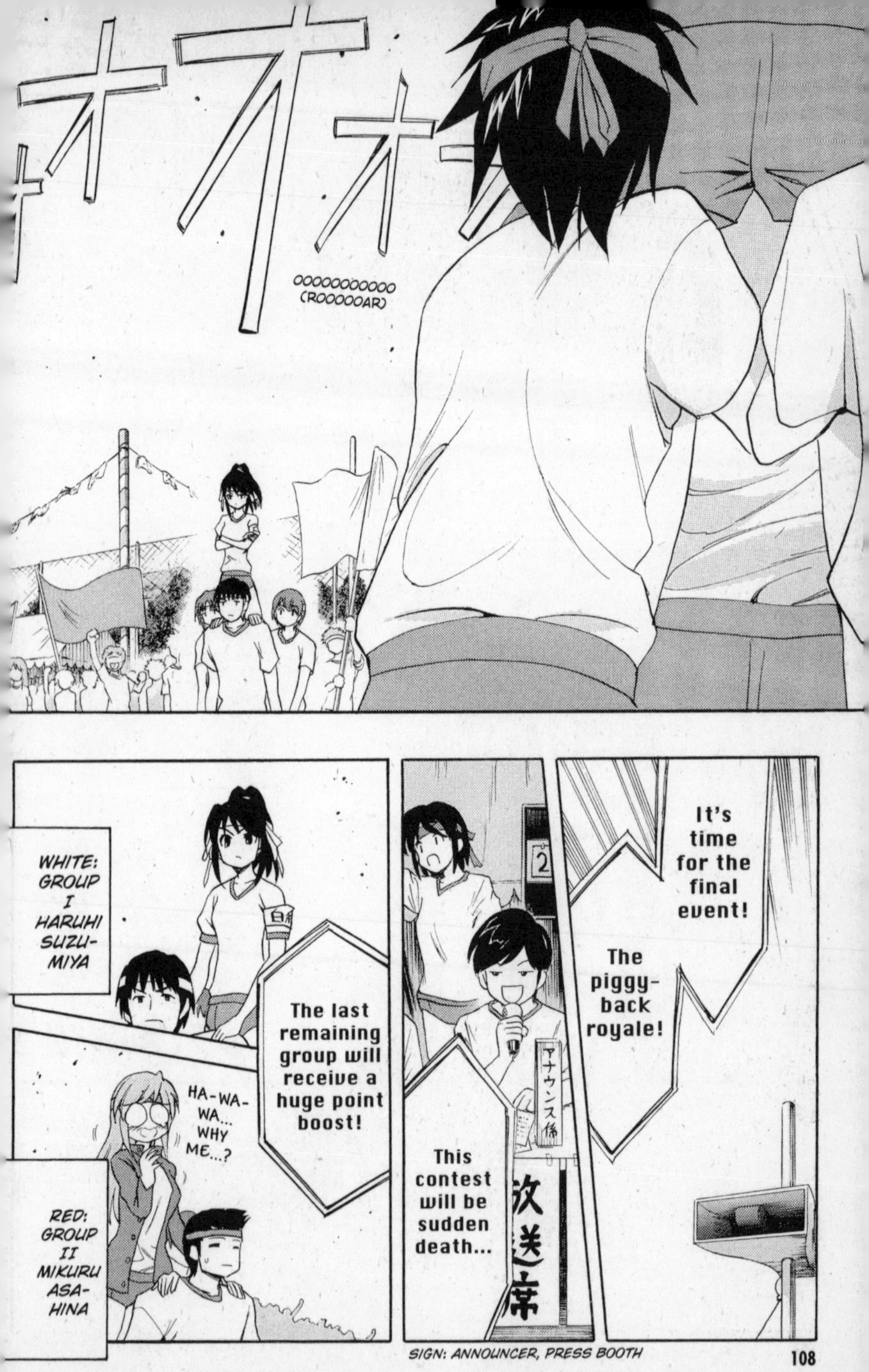
OOOOOOOOOOO
(ROOOOOAR)
It's time for the final event!
The piggy-back royale!
アナウンス係
放送席
This contest will be sudden death...
The last remaining group will receive a huge point boost!
WHITE: GROUP I HARUHI SUZU-MIYA
HA-WA-WA... WHY ME...?
RED: GROUP II MIKURU ASA-HINA

SIGN: ANNOUNCER, PRESS BOOTH

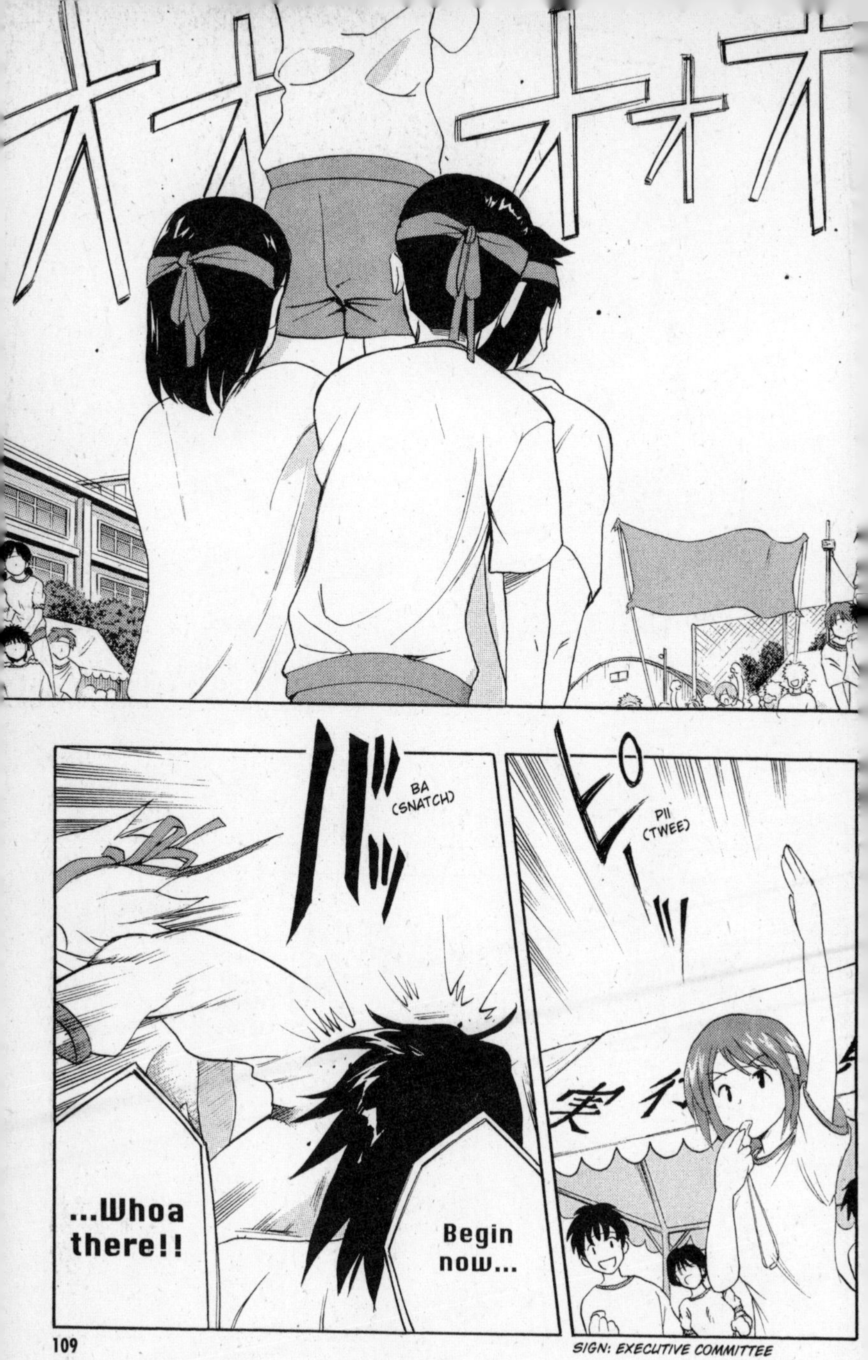
オオオォォオ
ピー
PII (TWEE)
実行
バッ
BA (SNATCH)
Begin now...
...Whoa there!!

SIGN: EXECUTIVE COMMITTEE

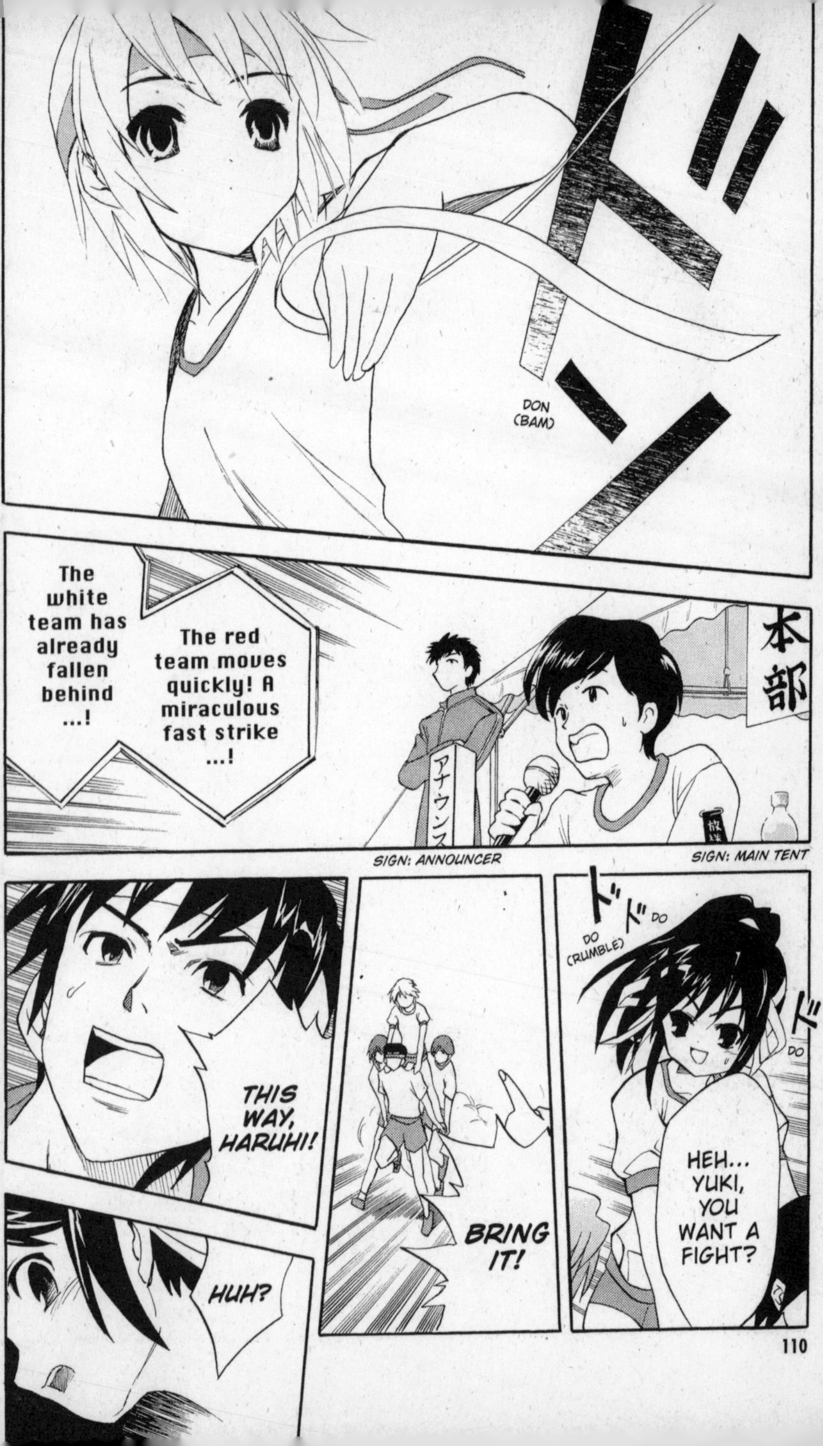
DON
(BAM)
The red team moves quickly! A miraculous fast strike ...!
The white team has already fallen behind ...!
本部
SIGN: MAIN TENT
SIGN: ANNOUNCER
DO
DO
(RUMBLE)
DO
HEH... YUKI, YOU WANT A FIGHT?
BRING IT!
THIS WAY, HARUHI!
HUH?

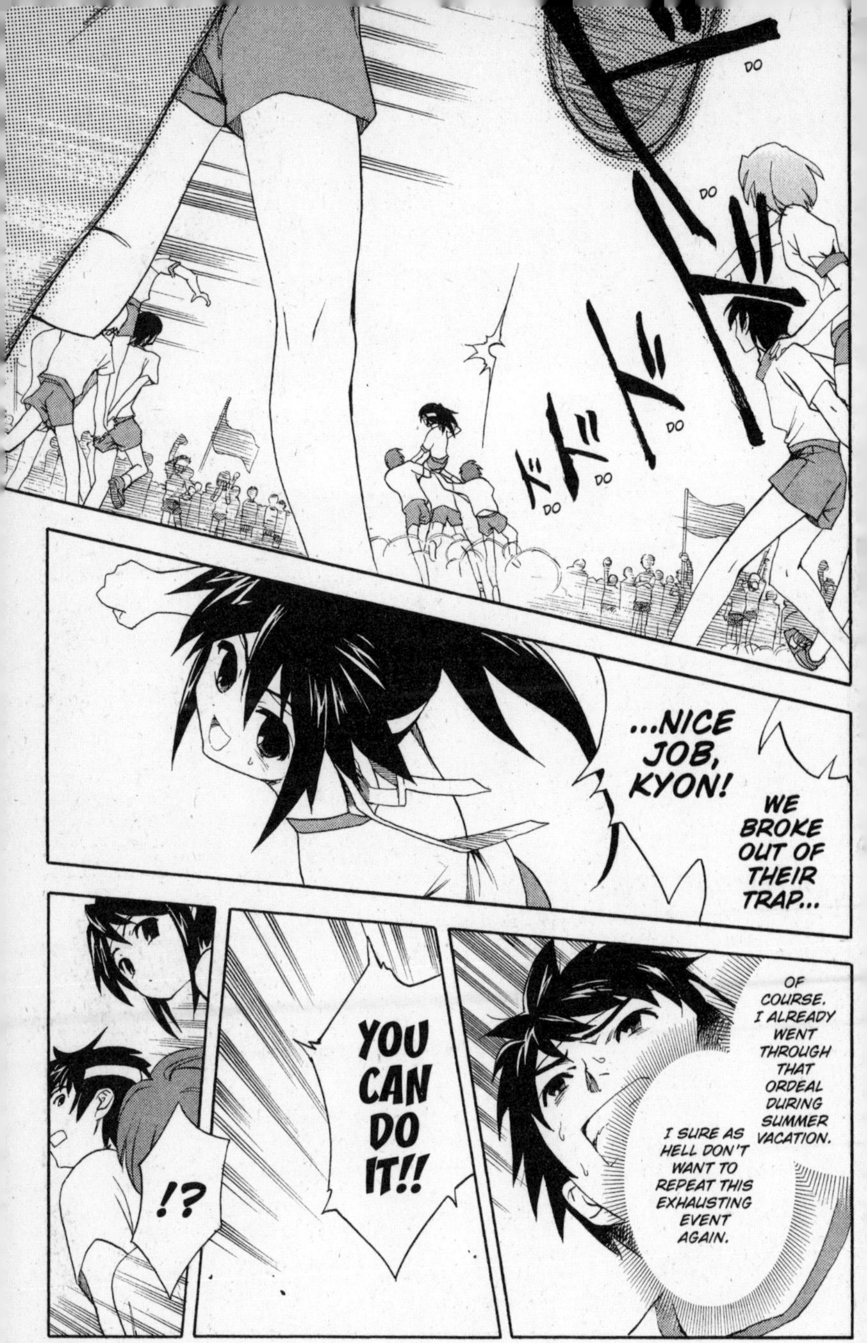
DO
DO
DO
DO
DO
...NICE JOB, KYON!
WE BROKE OUT OF THEIR TRAP...
OF COURSE. I ALREADY WENT THROUGH THAT ORDEAL DURING SUMMER VACATION.
I SURE AS HELL DON'T WANT TO REPEAT THIS EXHAUSTING EVENT AGAIN.
YOU CAN DO IT!!
!?

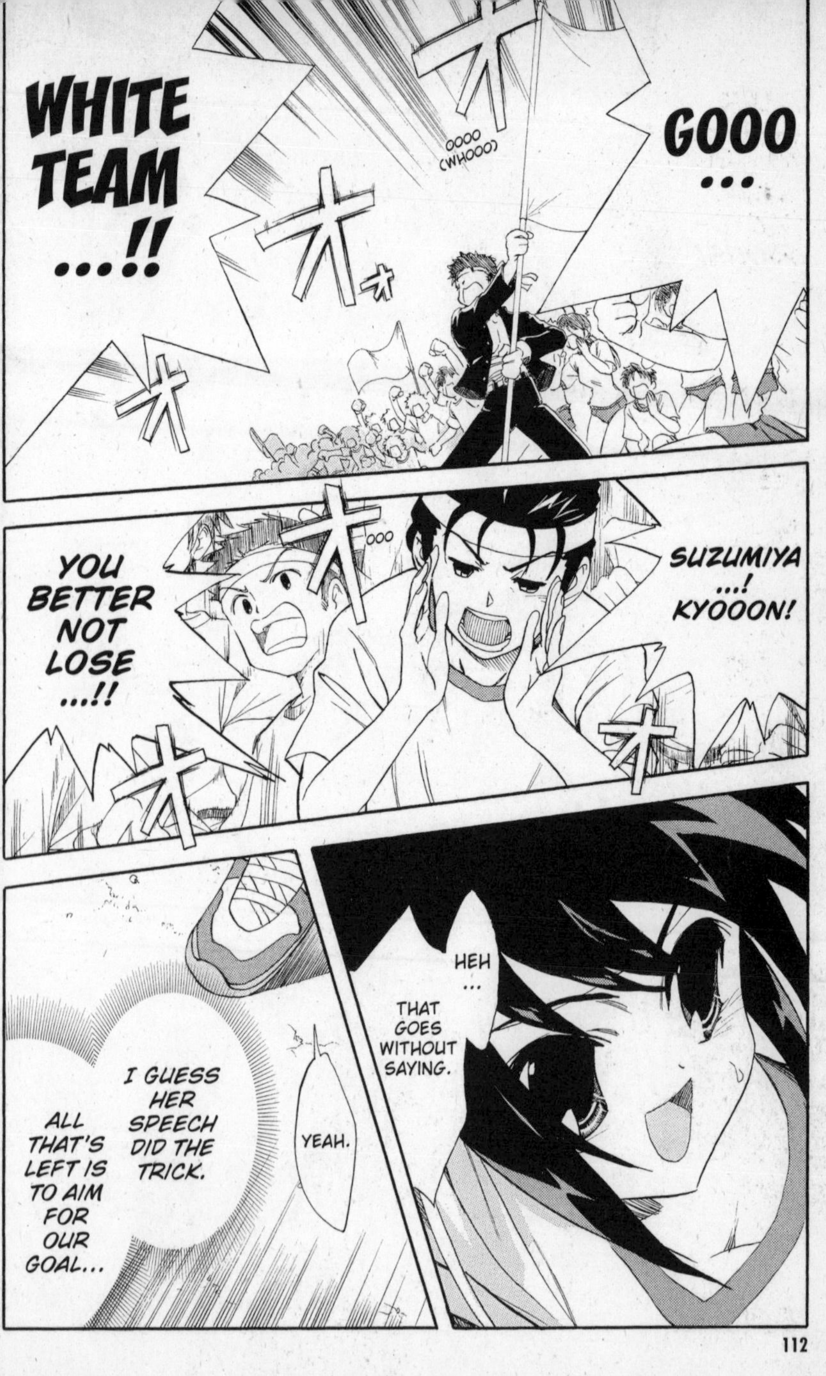
GOOO ...
OOOO (WHOOO)
WHITE TEAM ...!!
SUZUMIYA ...! KYOOON!
YOU BETTER NOT LOSE ...!!
HEH ...
THAT GOES WITHOUT SAYING.
YEAH.
I GUESS HER SPEECH DID THE TRICK.
ALL THAT'S LEFT IS TO AIM FOR OUR GOAL...

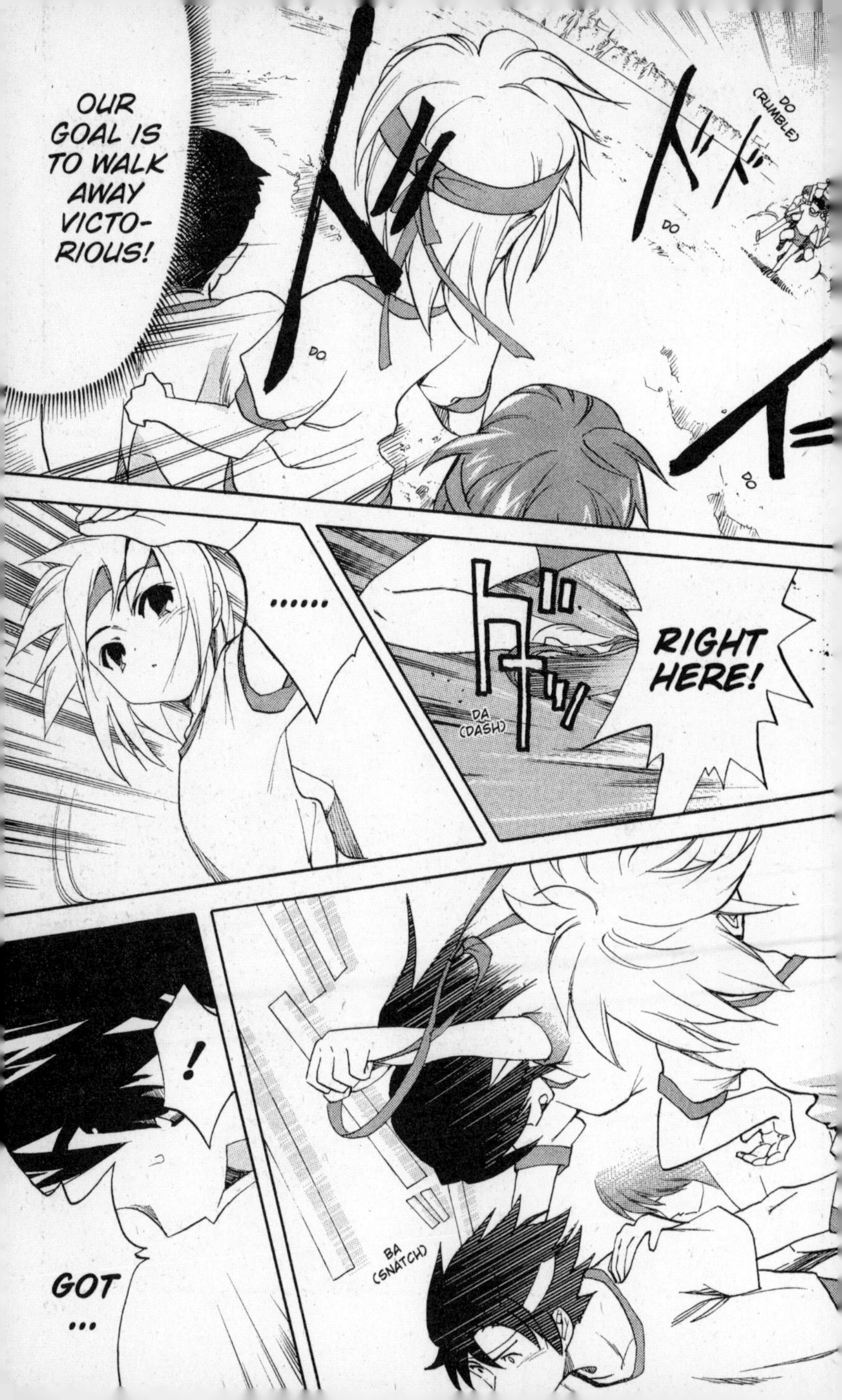

DO (RUMBLE)
DO
OUR GOAL IS TO WALK AWAY VICTORIOUS!
DO
DO
RIGHT HERE!
DA (DASH)
......
BA (SNATCH)
!
GOT ...

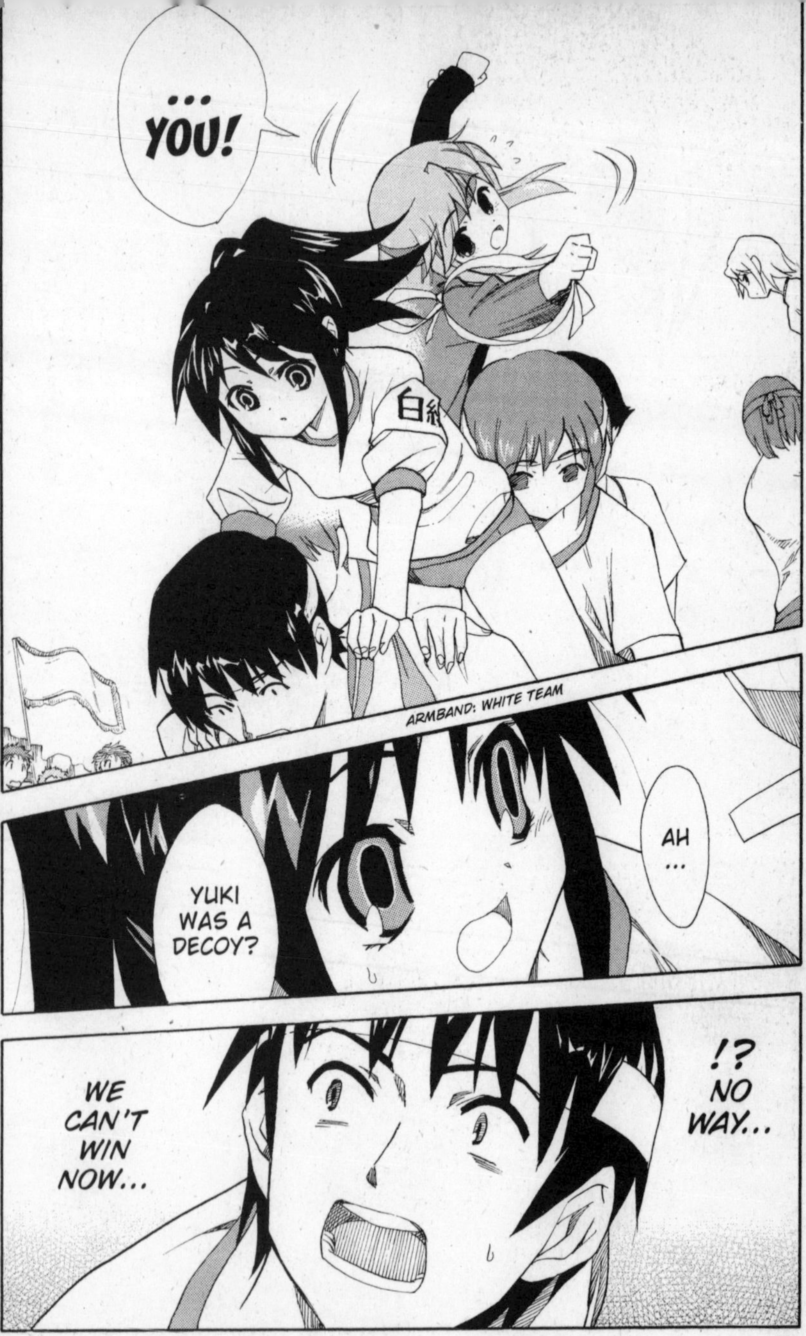
...YOU!
白組
ARMBAND: WHITE TEAM
AH...
YUKI WAS A DECOY?
!? NO WAY...
WE CAN'T WIN NOW...

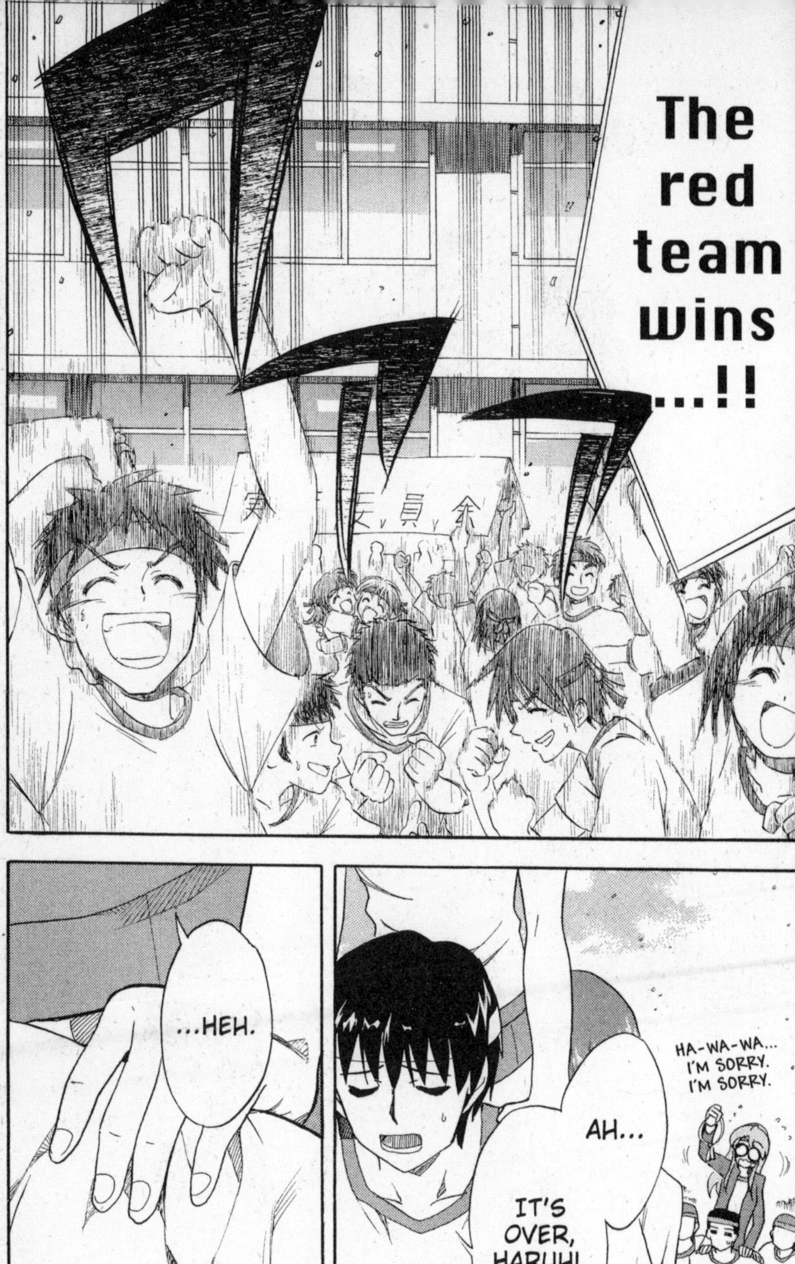
The red team wins...!!
HA-WA-WA... I'M SORRY. I'M SORRY.
AH...
IT'S OVER, HARUHI.
...HEH.

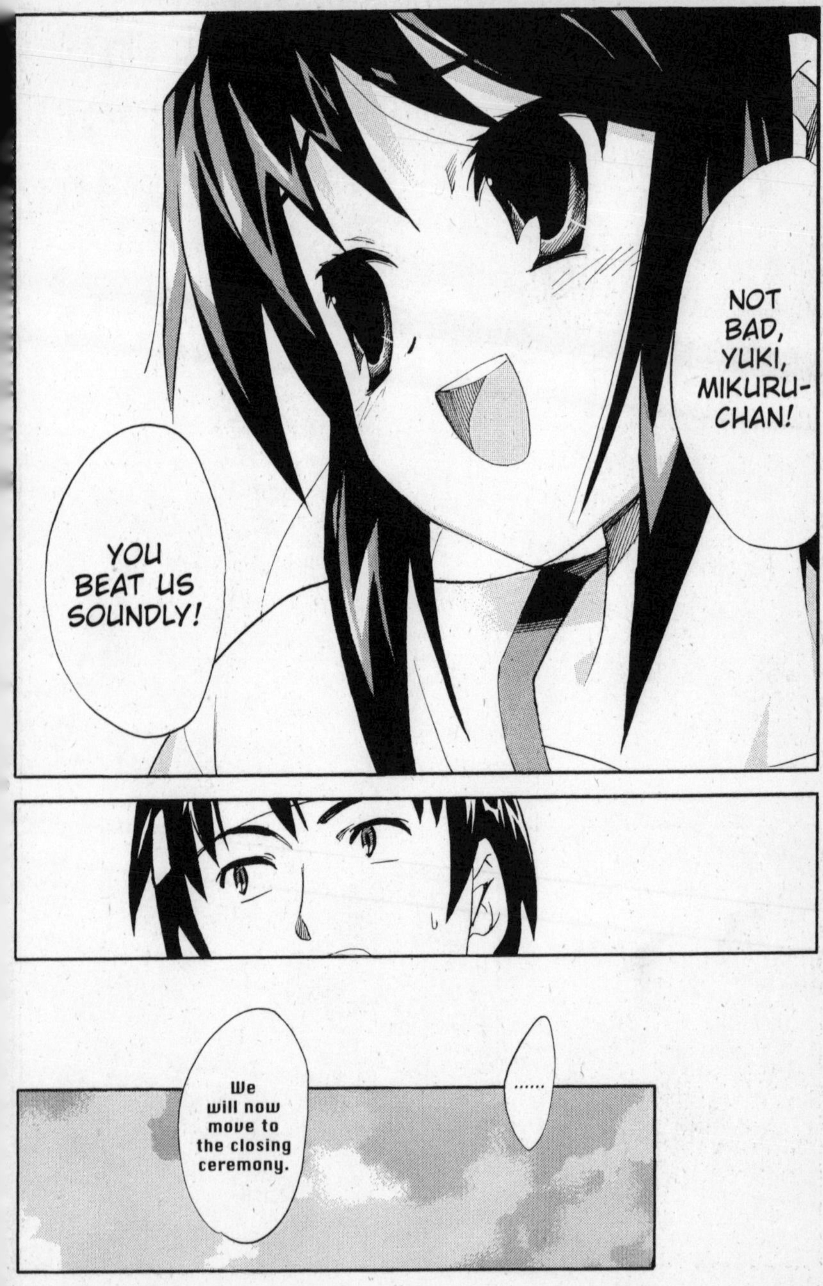
NOT BAD, YUKI, MIKURU-CHAN!
YOU BEAT US SOUNDLY!
......
We will now move to the closing ceremony.

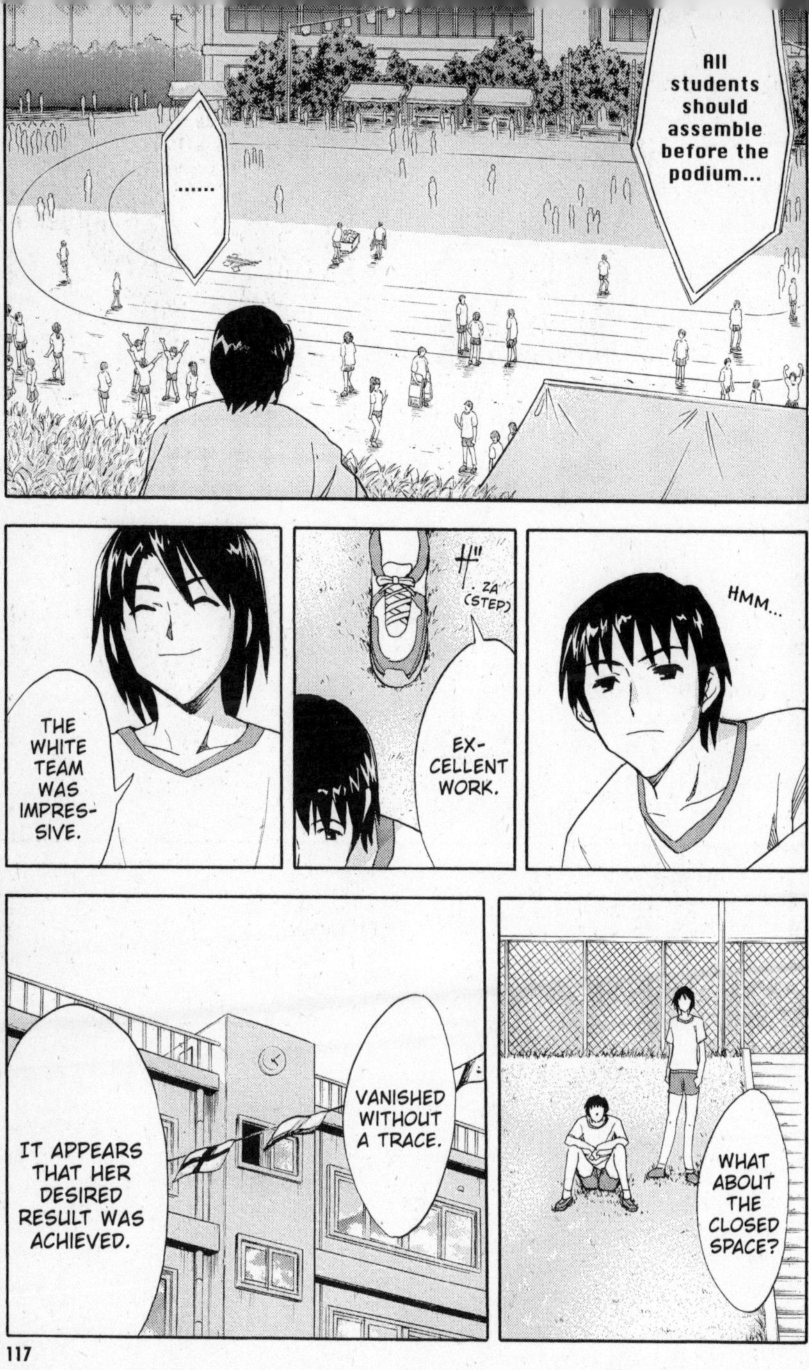
All students should assemble before the podium...
......
HMM...
ザ"
ZA (STEP)
EX-CELLENT WORK.
THE WHITE TEAM WAS IMPRES-SIVE.
WHAT ABOUT THE CLOSED SPACE?
VANISHED WITHOUT A TRACE.
IT APPEARS THAT HER DESIRED RESULT WAS ACHIEVED.

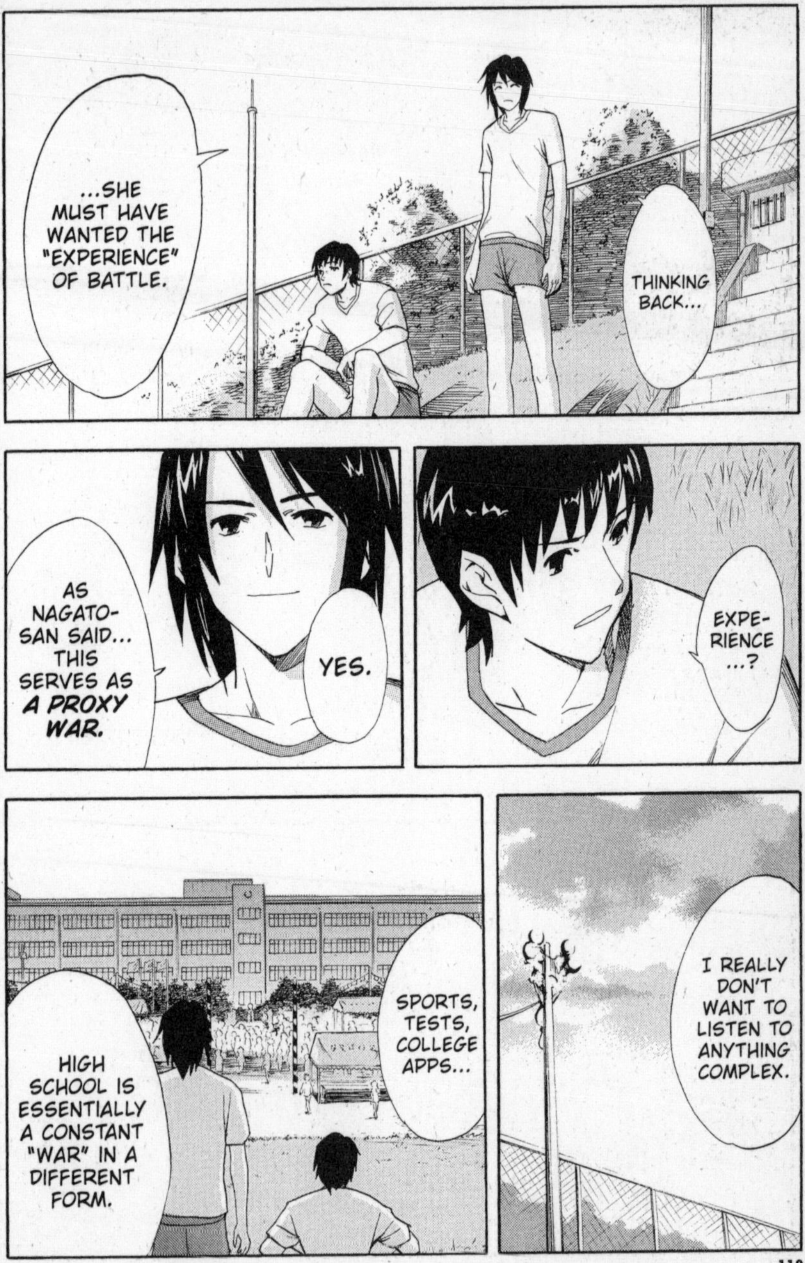
THINKING BACK...
...SHE MUST HAVE WANTED THE "EXPERIENCE" OF BATTLE.
EXPE-RIENCE ...?
YES.
AS NAGATO-SAN SAID... THIS SERVES AS **A PROXY WAR.**
I REALLY DON'T WANT TO LISTEN TO ANYTHING COMPLEX.
SPORTS, TESTS, COLLEGE APPS...
HIGH SCHOOL IS ESSENTIALLY A CONSTANT "WAR" IN A DIFFERENT FORM.

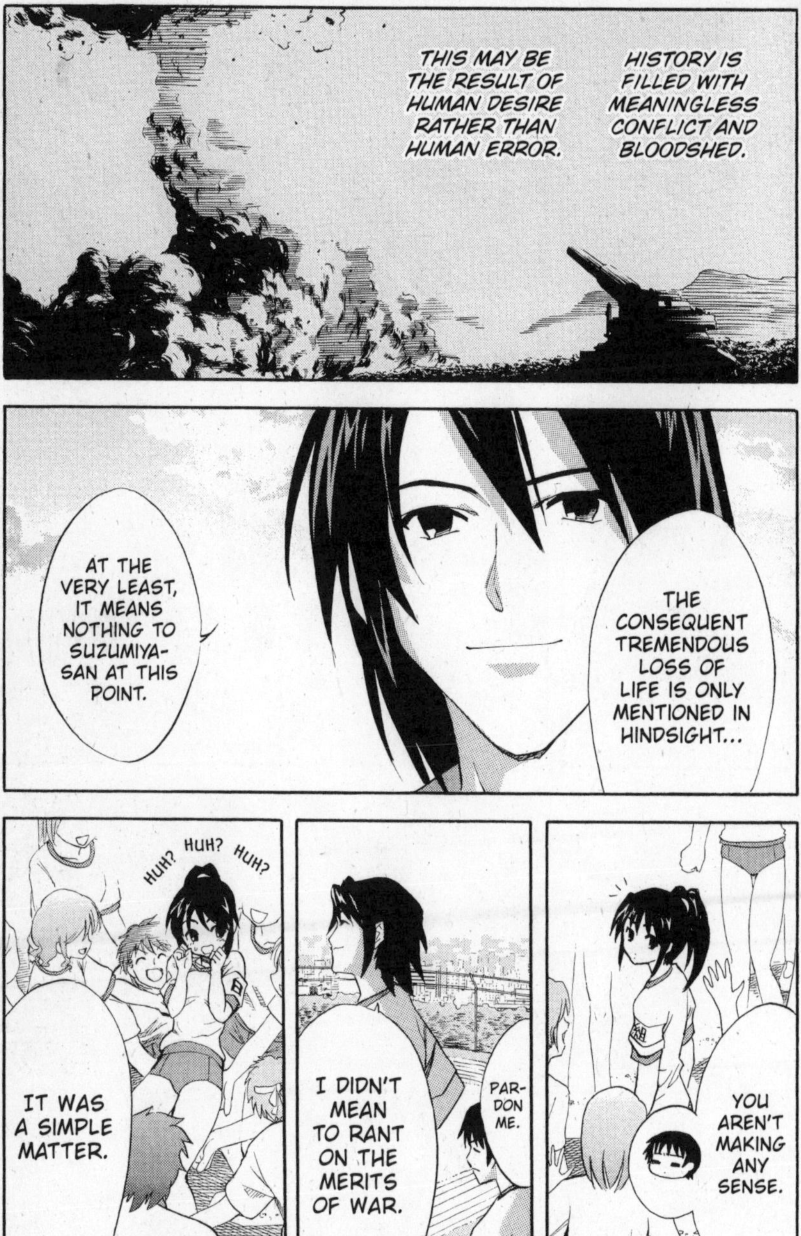
HISTORY IS FILLED WITH MEANINGLESS CONFLICT AND BLOODSHED.
THIS MAY BE THE RESULT OF HUMAN DESIRE RATHER THAN HUMAN ERROR.
THE CONSEQUENT TREMENDOUS LOSS OF LIFE IS ONLY MENTIONED IN HINDSIGHT...
AT THE VERY LEAST, IT MEANS NOTHING TO SUZUMIYA-SAN AT THIS POINT.
YOU AREN'T MAKING ANY SENSE.
PAR-DON ME.
I DIDN'T MEAN TO RANT ON THE MERITS OF WAR.
HUH? HUH? HUH?
IT WAS A SIMPLE MATTER.

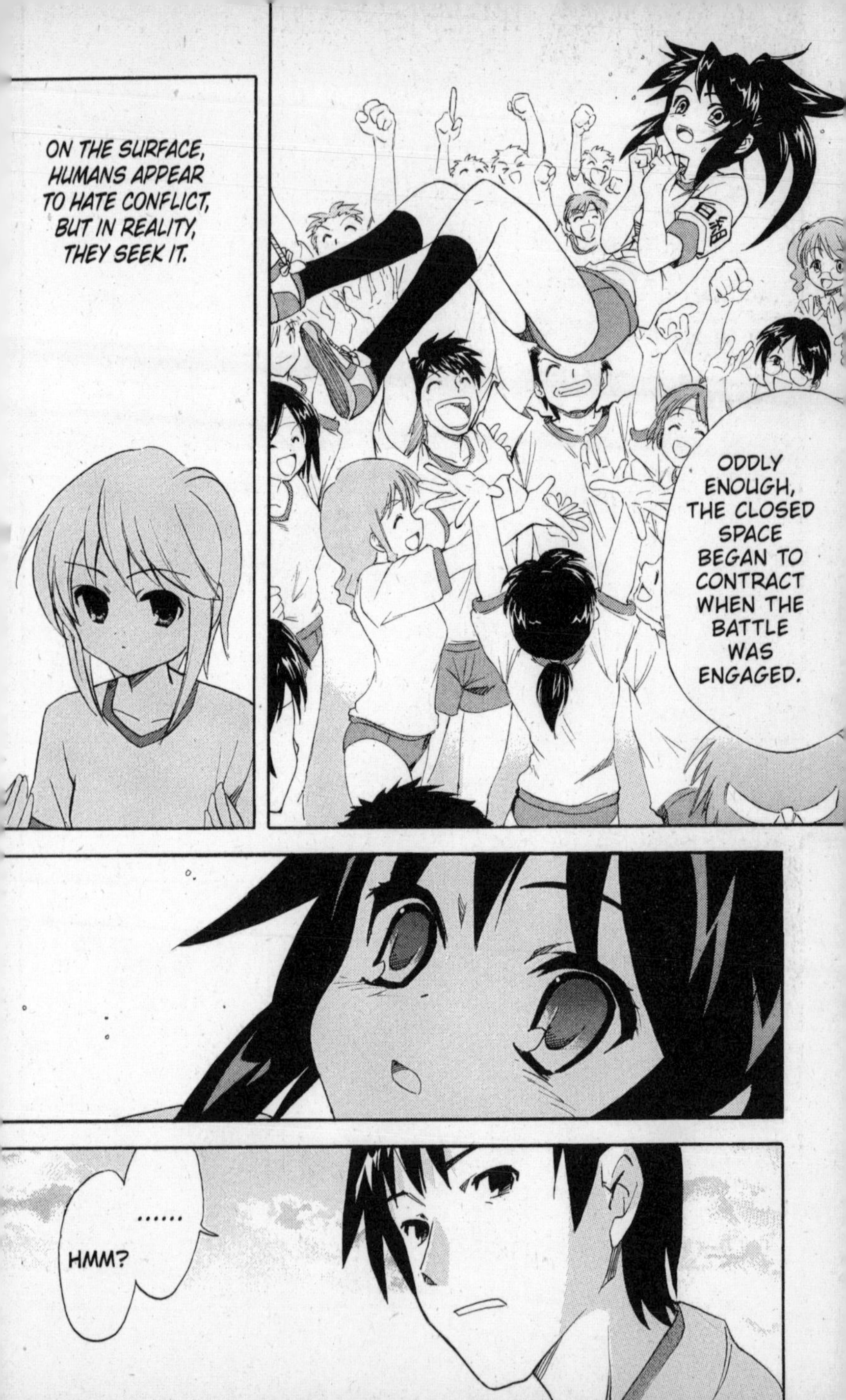
ODDLY ENOUGH, THE CLOSED SPACE BEGAN TO CONTRACT WHEN THE BATTLE WAS ENGAGED.
ON THE SURFACE, HUMANS APPEAR TO HATE CONFLICT, BUT IN REALITY, THEY SEEK IT.
......
HMM?

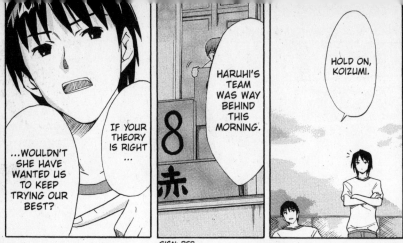

HOLD ON, KOIZUMI.
HARUHI'S TEAM WAS WAY BEHIND THIS MORNING.
8
赤
SIGN: RED
IF YOUR THEORY IS RIGHT ...
...WOULDN'T SHE HAVE WANTED US TO KEEP TRYING OUR BEST?
......
IN THEORY, YES.
HOWEVER, WOULD THE RED TEAM HAVE BEEN ABLE TO STAGE A COMEBACK WITHOUT NAGATO-SAN?
ふぅ…
FUU (SIGH)
THERE IS NOTHING AS BORING AS A ONE-SIDED GAME.
....

...THAT'S SOME PRETTY ARBITRARY REASONING.

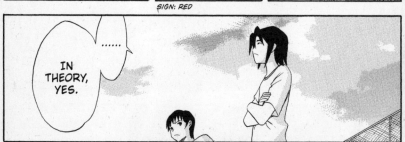

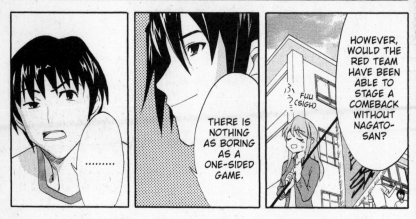

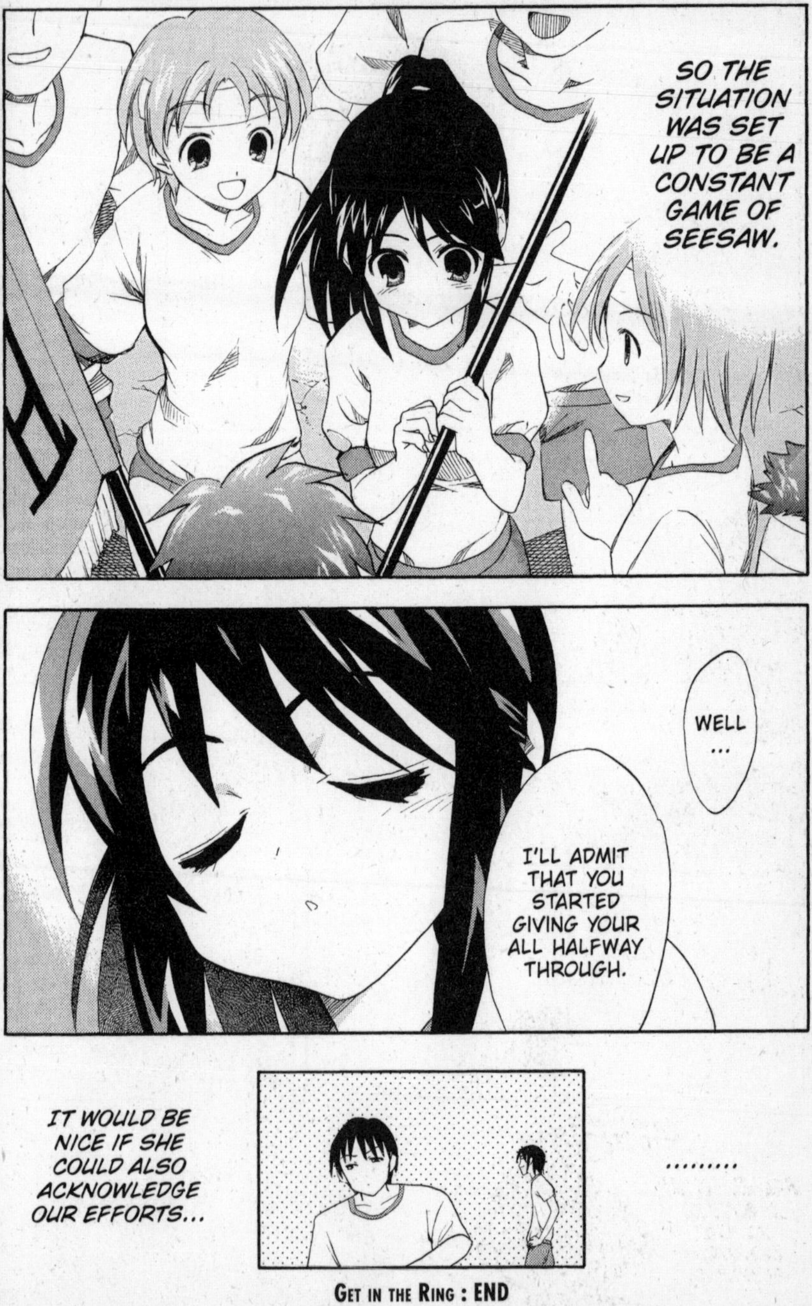
SO THE SITUATION WAS SET UP TO BE A CONSTANT GAME OF SEESAW.
WELL...
I'LL ADMIT THAT YOU STARTED GIVING YOUR ALL HALFWAY THROUGH.
....
IT WOULD BE NICE IF SHE COULD ALSO ACKNOWLEDGE OUR EFFORTS...

Get in the Ring : END

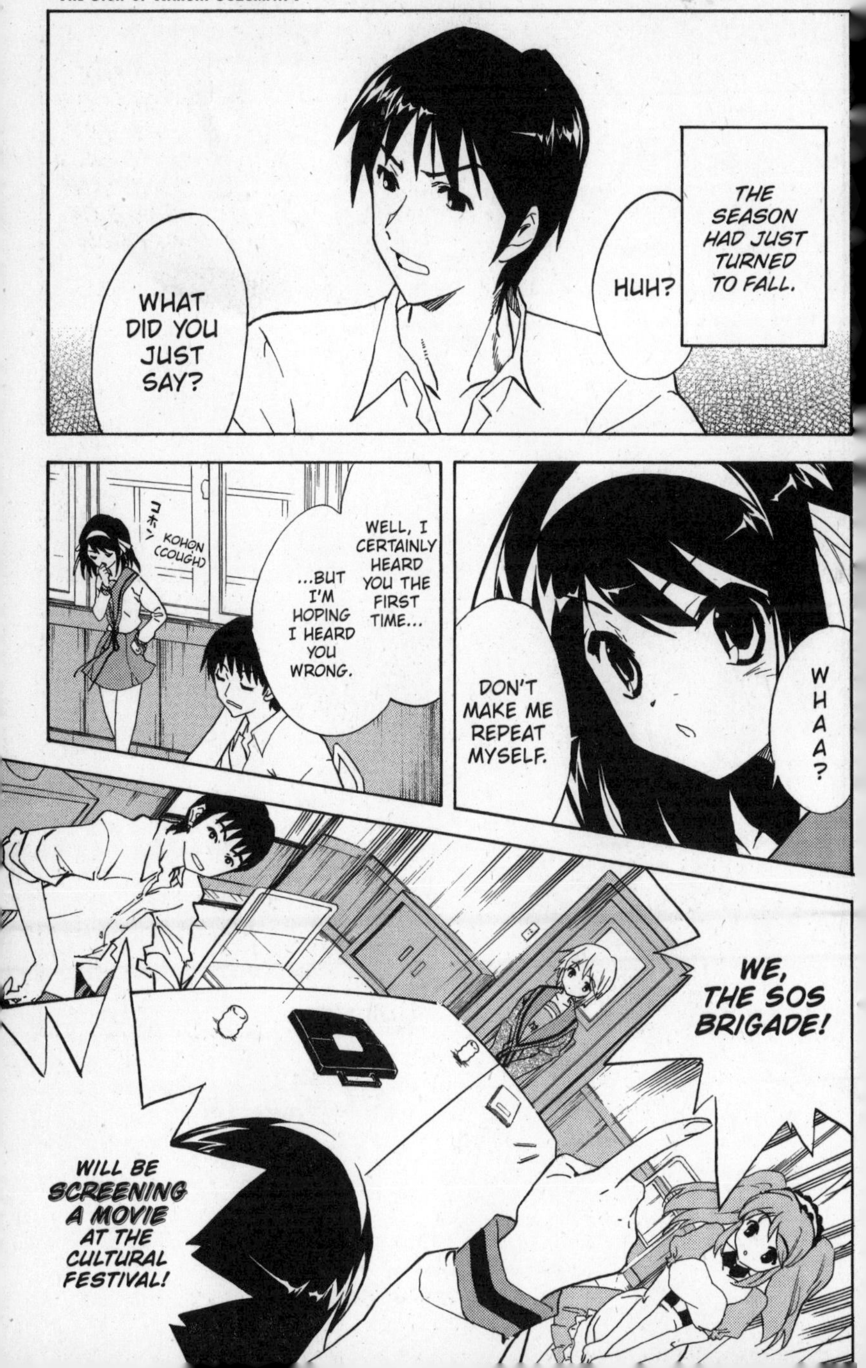
THE SEASON HAD JUST TURNED TO FALL.
HUH?
WHAT DID YOU JUST SAY?
WHAA?
DON'T MAKE ME REPEAT MYSELF.
WELL, I CERTAINLY HEARD YOU THE FIRST TIME...
...BUT I'M HOPING I HEARD YOU WRONG.
コホン KOHON (COUGH)
WE, THE SOS BRIGADE!
WILL BE SCREENING A MOVIE AT THE CULTURAL FESTIVAL!

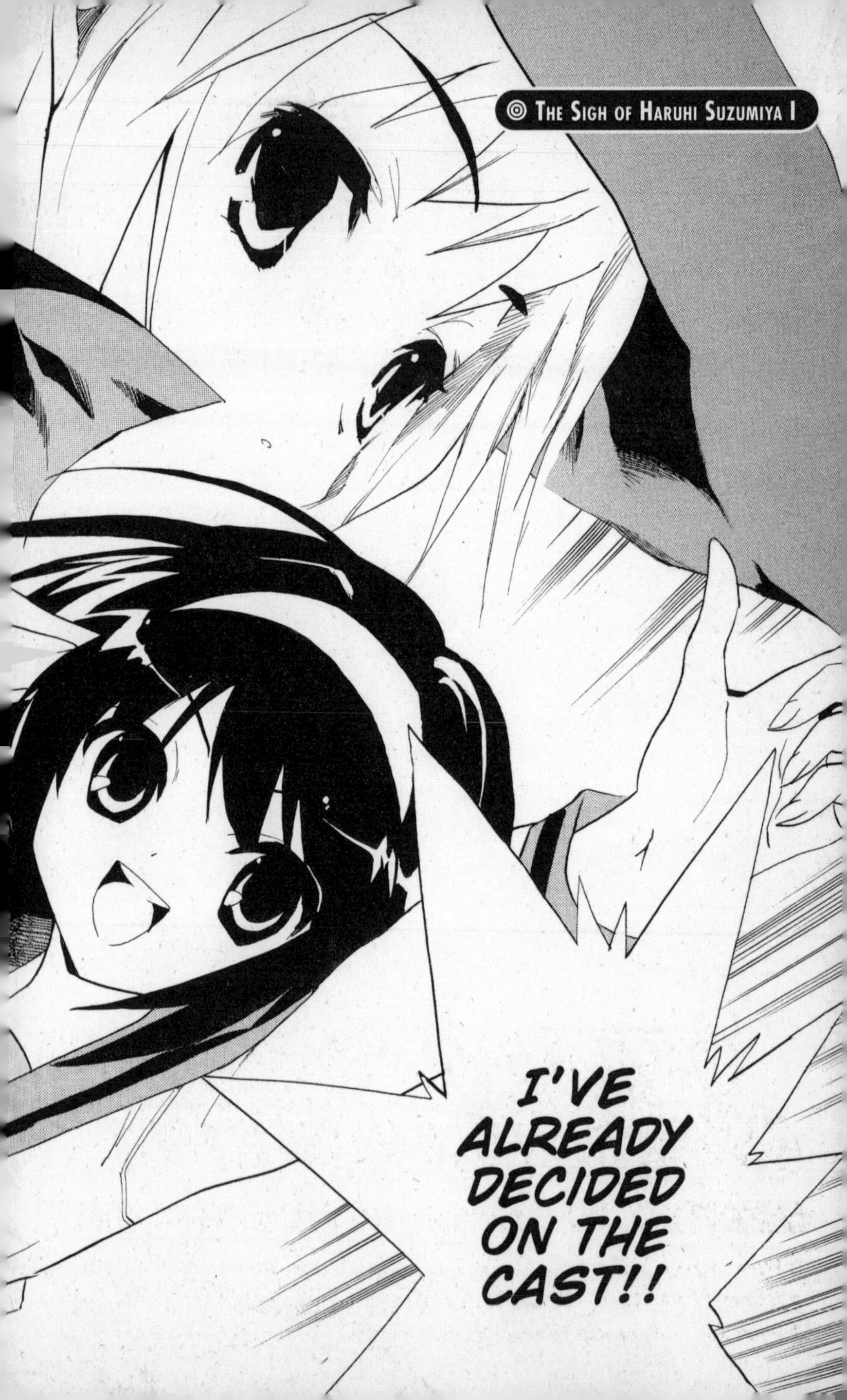
I'VE ALREADY DECIDED ON THE CAST!!

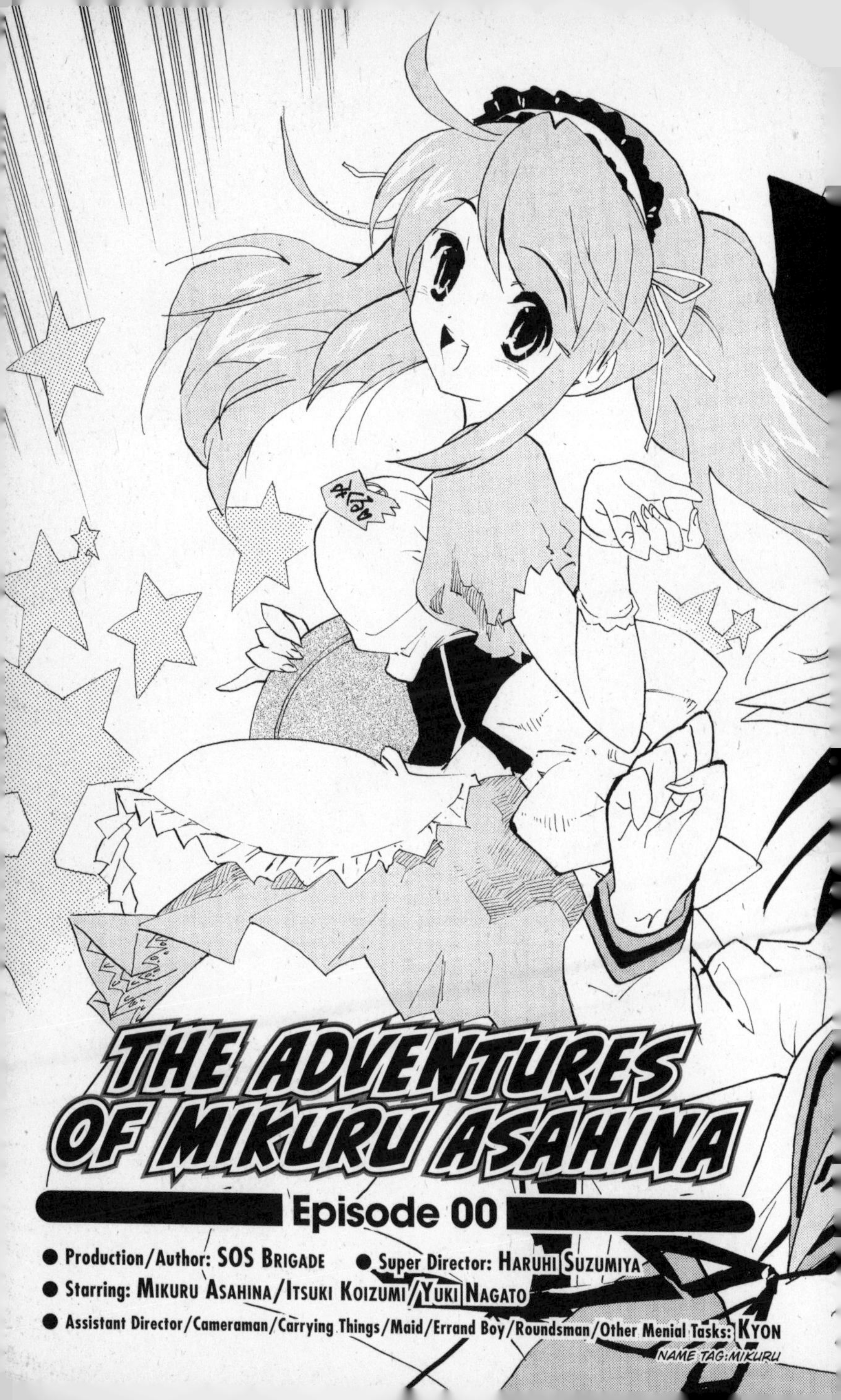

THE ADVENTURES OF MIKURU ASAHINA
Episode 00
● Production/Author: SOS Brigade ● Super Director: Haruhi Suzumiya
● Starring: Mikuru Asahina/Itsuki Koizumi/Yuki Nagato
● Assistant Director/Cameraman/Carrying Things/Maid/Errand Boy/Roundsman/Other Menial Tasks: Kyon
NAME TAG:MIKURU

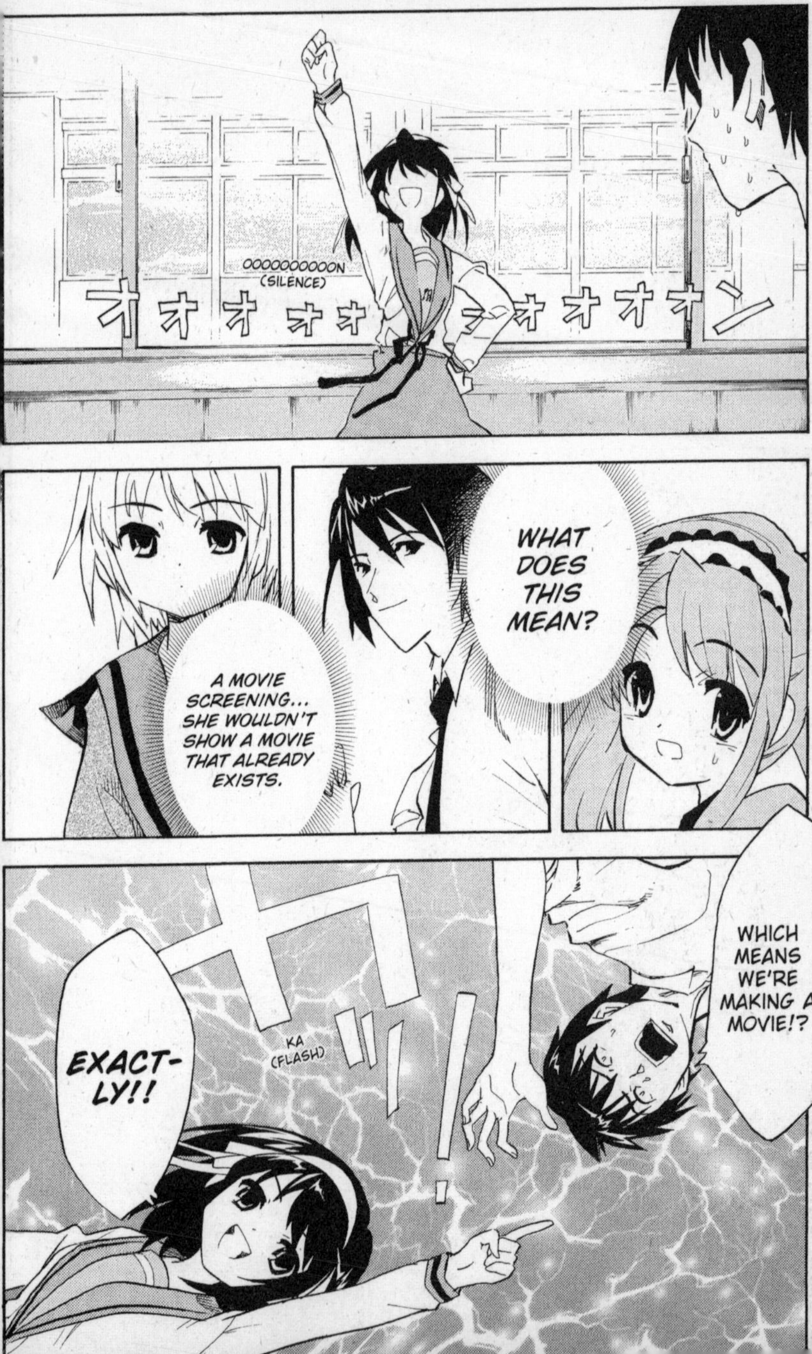

OOOOOOOOOOON (SILENCE)
オオオオオ オオオオン
WHAT DOES THIS MEAN?
A MOVIE SCREENING... SHE WOULDN'T SHOW A MOVIE THAT ALREADY EXISTS.
WHICH MEANS WE'RE MAKING A MOVIE!?
KA (FLASH)
EXACT-LY!!

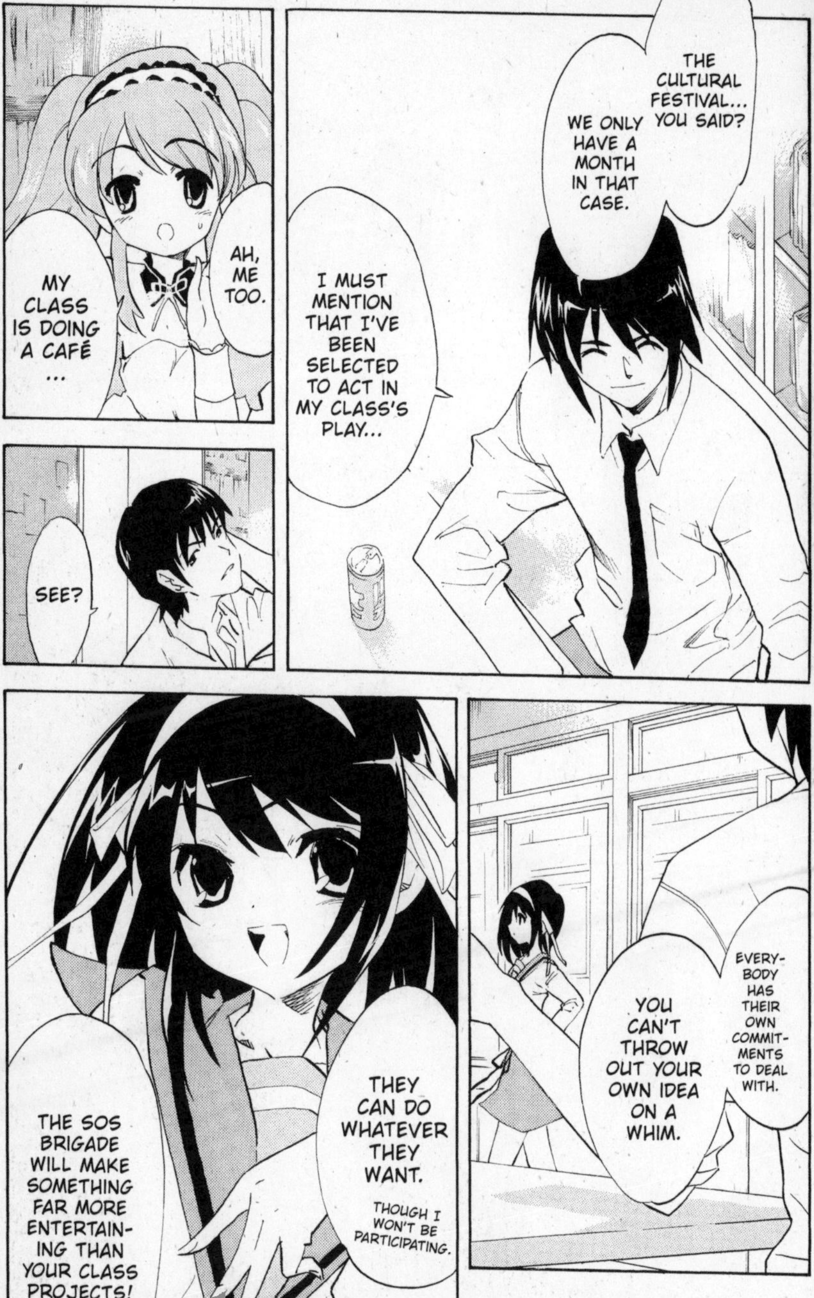
THE CULTURAL FESTIVAL... YOU SAID?
WE ONLY HAVE A MONTH IN THAT CASE.
I MUST MENTION THAT I'VE BEEN SELECTED TO ACT IN MY CLASS'S PLAY...
AH, ME TOO.
MY CLASS IS DOING A CAFÉ ...
SEE?
EVERY-BODY HAS THEIR OWN COMMIT-MENTS TO DEAL WITH.
YOU CAN'T THROW OUT YOUR OWN IDEA ON A WHIM.
THEY CAN DO WHATEVER THEY WANT.
THOUGH I WON'T BE PARTICIPATING.
THE SOS BRIGADE WILL MAKE SOMETHING FAR MORE ENTERTAIN-ING THAN YOUR CLASS PROJECTS!

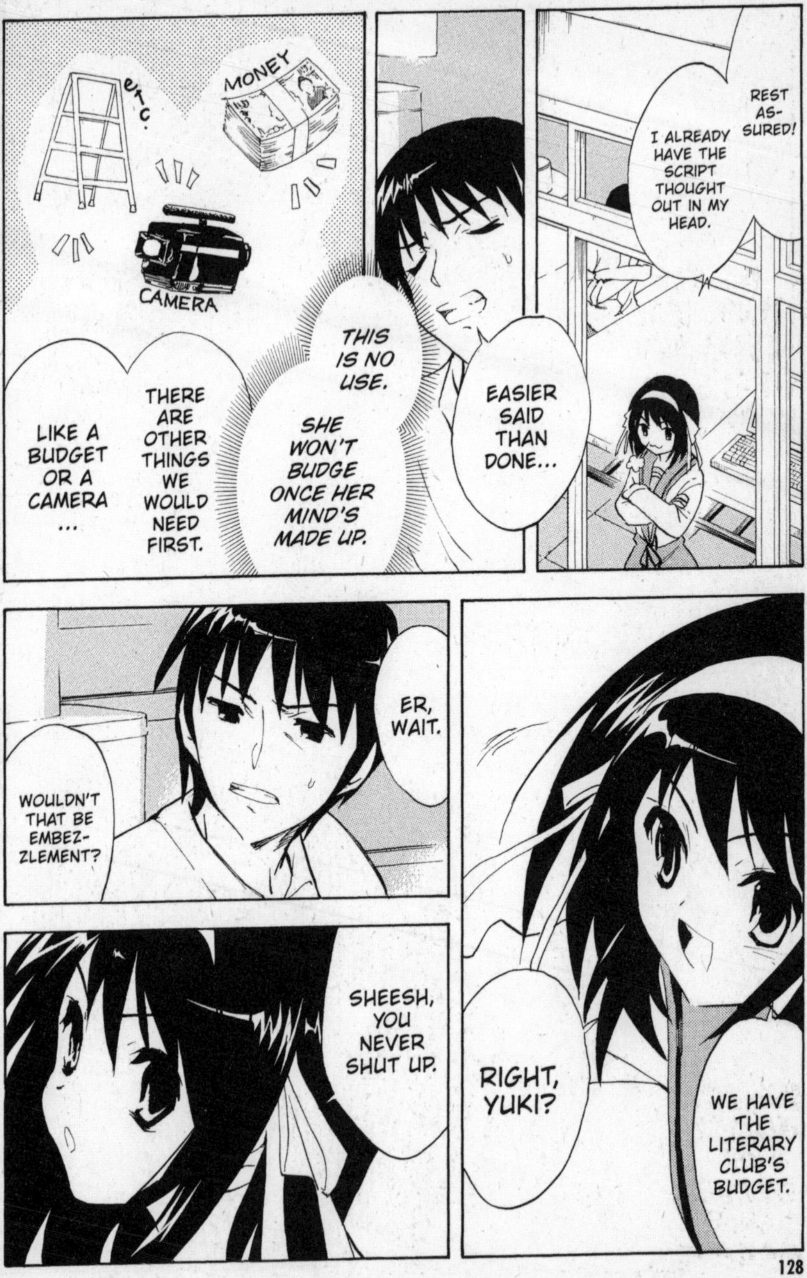
REST AS-SURED!
I ALREADY HAVE THE SCRIPT THOUGHT OUT IN MY HEAD.
EASIER SAID THAN DONE...
THIS IS NO USE.
SHE WON'T BUDGE ONCE HER MIND'S MADE UP.
MONEY
etc.
CAMERA
THERE ARE OTHER THINGS WE WOULD NEED FIRST.
LIKE A BUDGET OR A CAMERA ...
WE HAVE THE LITERARY CLUB'S BUDGET.
RIGHT, YUKI?
ER, WAIT.
WOULDN'T THAT BE EMBEZ-ZLEMENT?
SHEESH, YOU NEVER SHUT UP.

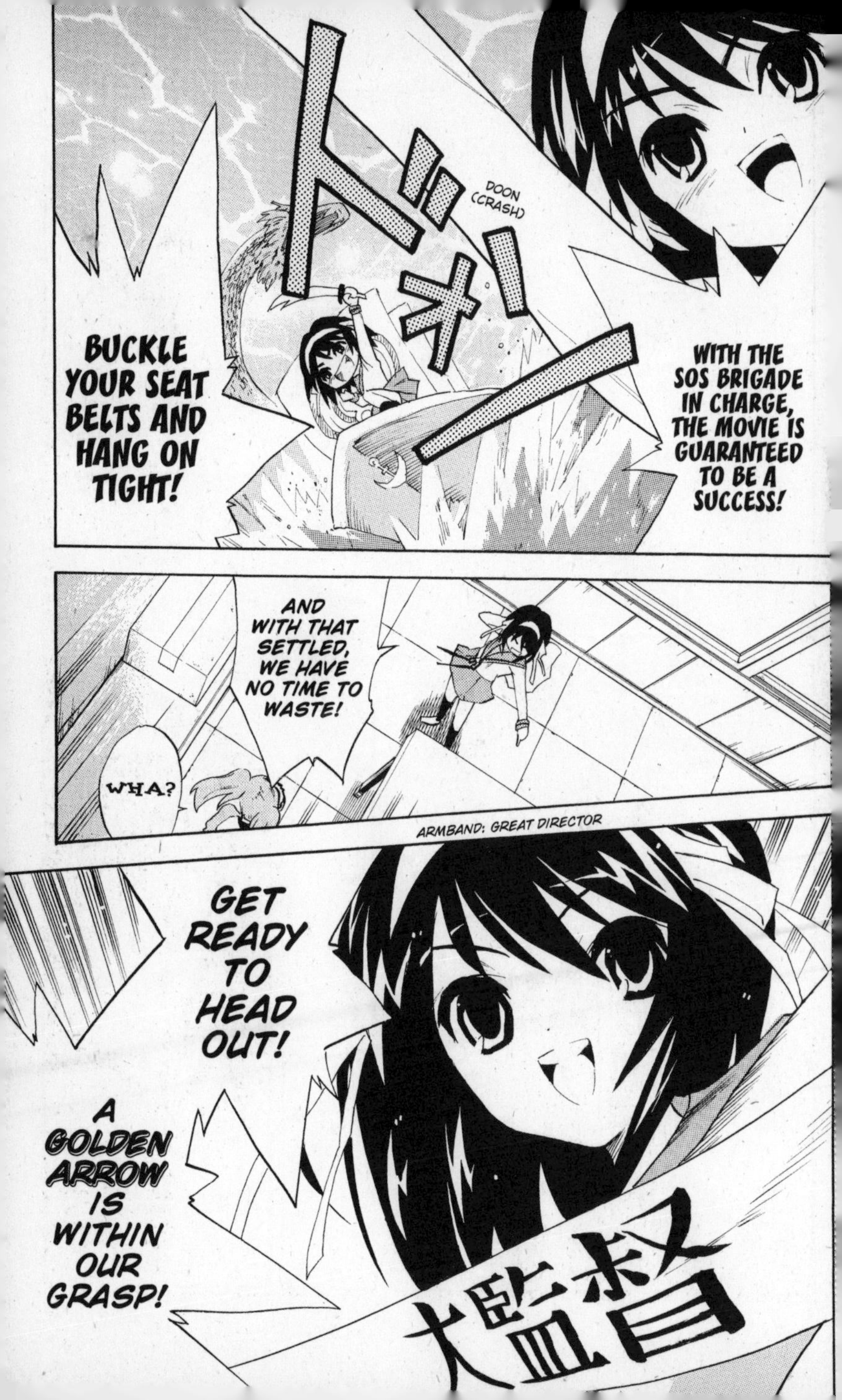
WITH THE SOS BRIGADE IN CHARGE, THE MOVIE IS GUARANTEED TO BE A SUCCESS!
DOON (CRASH)
BUCKLE YOUR SEAT BELTS AND HANG ON TIGHT!
AND WITH THAT SETTLED, WE HAVE NO TIME TO WASTE!
WHA?
ARMBAND: GREAT DIRECTOR
GET READY TO HEAD OUT!
A GOLDEN ARROW IS WITHIN OUR GRASP!
大監督

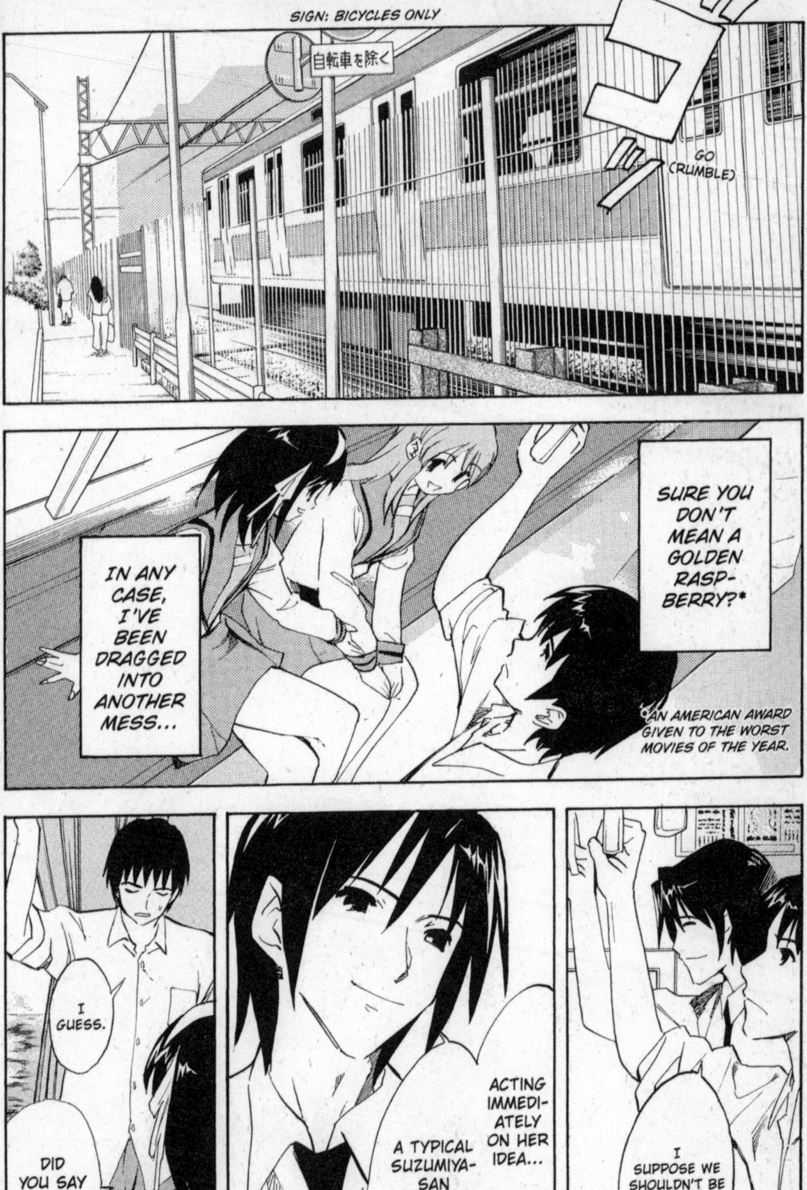
SIGN: BICYCLES ONLY
自転車を除く
GO (RUMBLE)
SURE YOU DON'T MEAN A GOLDEN RASPBERRY?*
*AN AMERICAN AWARD GIVEN TO THE WORST MOVIES OF THE YEAR.
IN ANY CASE, I'VE BEEN DRAGGED INTO ANOTHER MESS...
I SUPPOSE WE SHOULDN'T BE SURPRISED.
ACTING IMMEDIATELY ON HER IDEA...
A TYPICAL SUZUMIYA-SAN RESPONSE.
I GUESS.
DID YOU SAY SOMETHING?

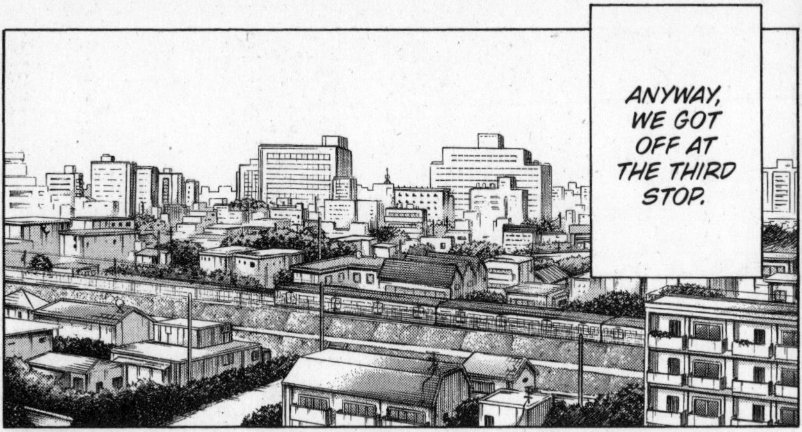
ANYWAY, WE GOT OFF AT THE THIRD STOP.

BUILDING: CENTRAL SHOPPING DISTRICT, FIRST DISTRICT, UMEYA

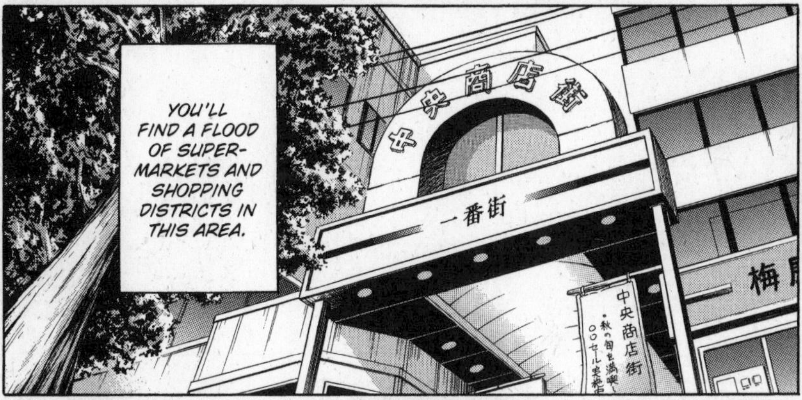
YOU'LL FIND A FLOOD OF SUPER-MARKETS AND SHOPPING DISTRICTS IN THIS AREA.
中央商店街
一番街
中央商店街

BANNER: CENTRAL SHOPPING DISTRICT, HAVING A SPECIAL SALE TO CELEBRATE THE COMING OF THE FALL SEASON

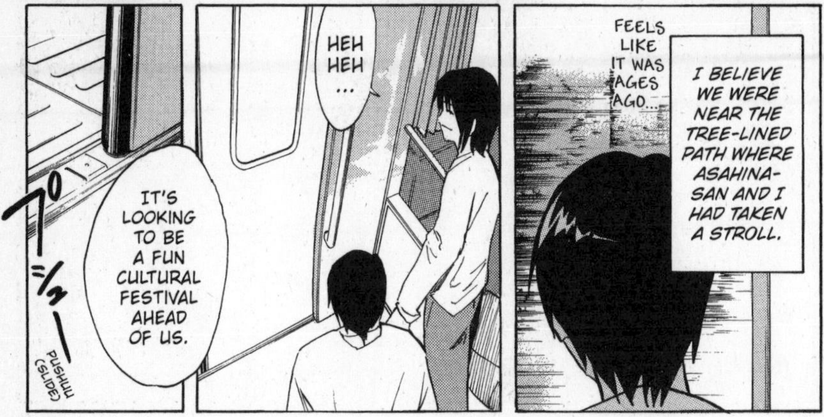
I BELIEVE WE WERE NEAR THE TREE-LINED PATH WHERE ASAHINA-SAN AND I HAD TAKEN A STROLL.
FEELS LIKE IT WAS AGES AGO...
HEH HEH ...
IT'S LOOKING TO BE A FUN CULTURAL FESTIVAL AHEAD OF US.
PUSHUU (SLIDE)

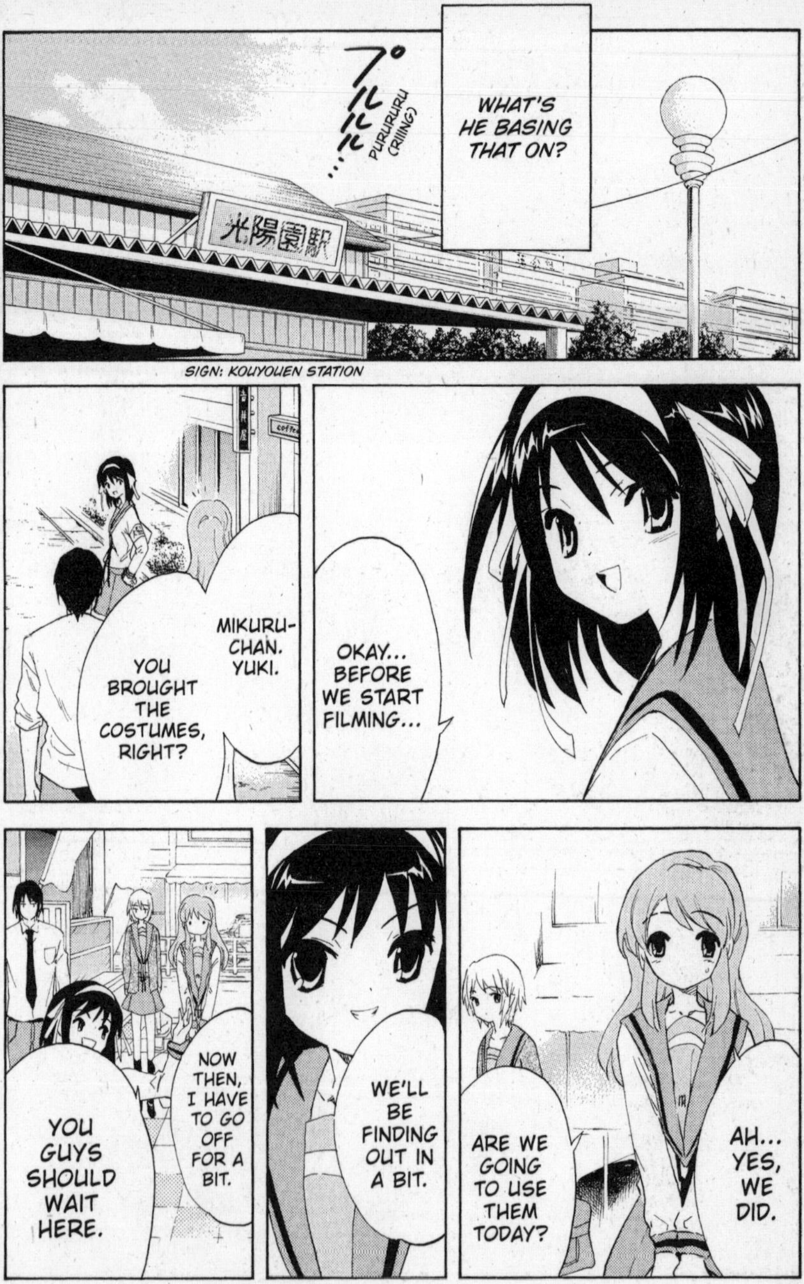
WHAT'S HE BASING THAT ON?
プルルル…
PURURURU (RIIING)
光陽園駅
SIGN: KOUYOUEN STATION
OKAY... BEFORE WE START FILMING...
MIKURU-CHAN. YUKI.
YOU BROUGHT THE COSTUMES, RIGHT?
AH... YES, WE DID.
ARE WE GOING TO USE THEM TODAY?
WE'LL BE FINDING OUT IN A BIT.
NOW THEN, I HAVE TO GO OFF FOR A BIT.
YOU GUYS SHOULD WAIT HERE.

SIGN: OHMORI ELECTRONICS

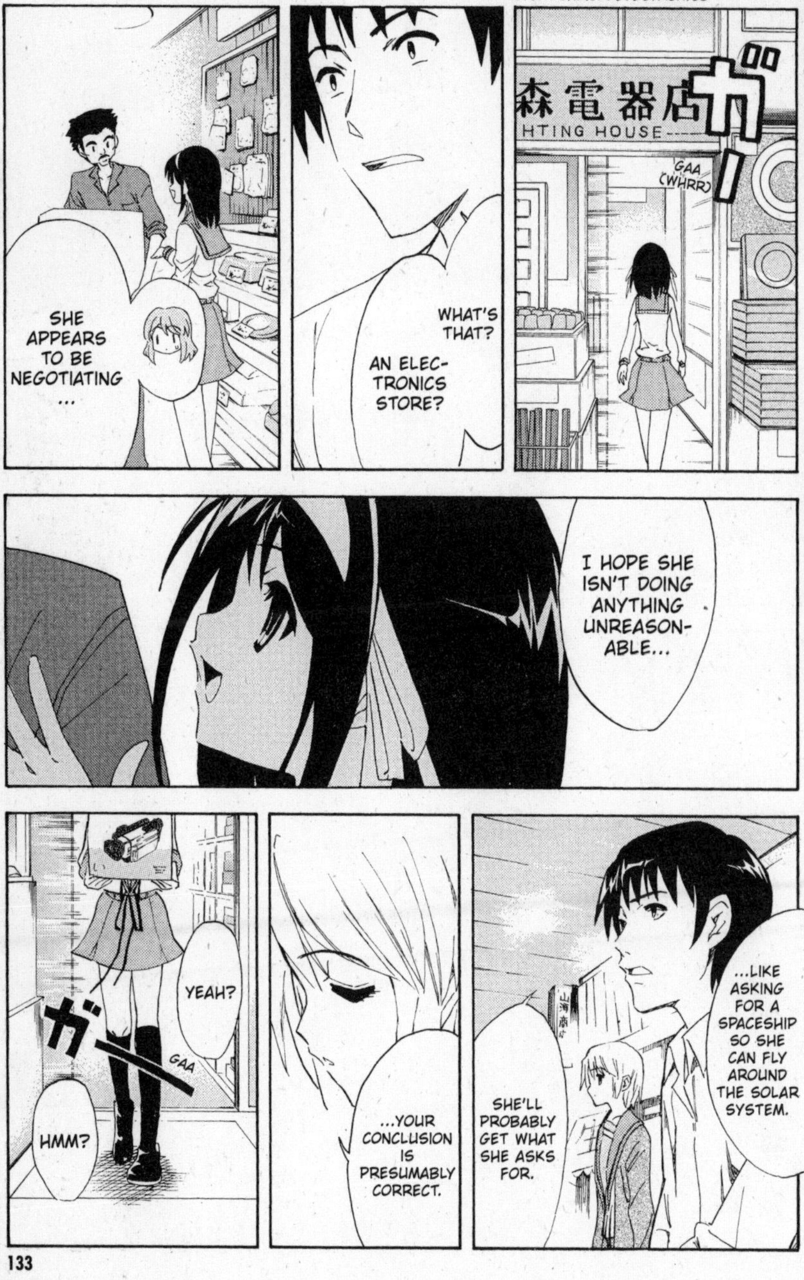

森電器店
HTING HOUSE
ガ
GAA (WHRR)
WHAT'S THAT?
AN ELEC-TRONICS STORE?
SHE APPEARS TO BE NEGOTIATING ...
I HOPE SHE ISN'T DOING ANYTHING UNREASON-ABLE...
...LIKE ASKING FOR A SPACESHIP SO SHE CAN FLY AROUND THE SOLAR SYSTEM.
SHE'LL PROBABLY GET WHAT SHE ASKS FOR.
...YOUR CONCLUSION IS PRESUMABLY CORRECT.
YEAH?
ガー
GAA
HMM?

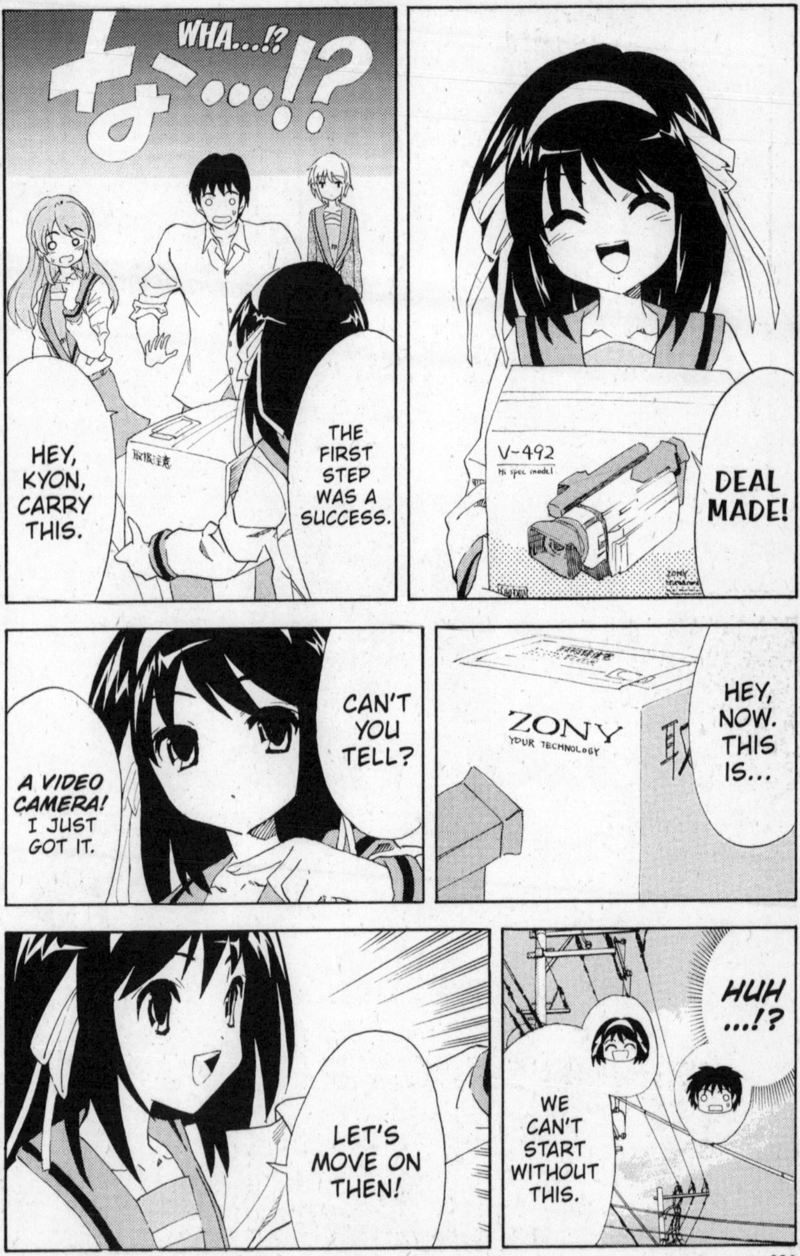
V-492
Hi spec model
DEAL MADE!
な…!?
WHA...!?
THE FIRST STEP WAS A SUCCESS.
取扱注意
HEY, KYON, CARRY THIS.
HEY, NOW. THIS IS...
ZONY
YOUR TECHNOLOGY
CAN'T YOU TELL?
A VIDEO CAMERA! I JUST GOT IT.
HUH ...!?
WE CAN'T START WITHOUT THIS.
LET'S MOVE ON THEN!

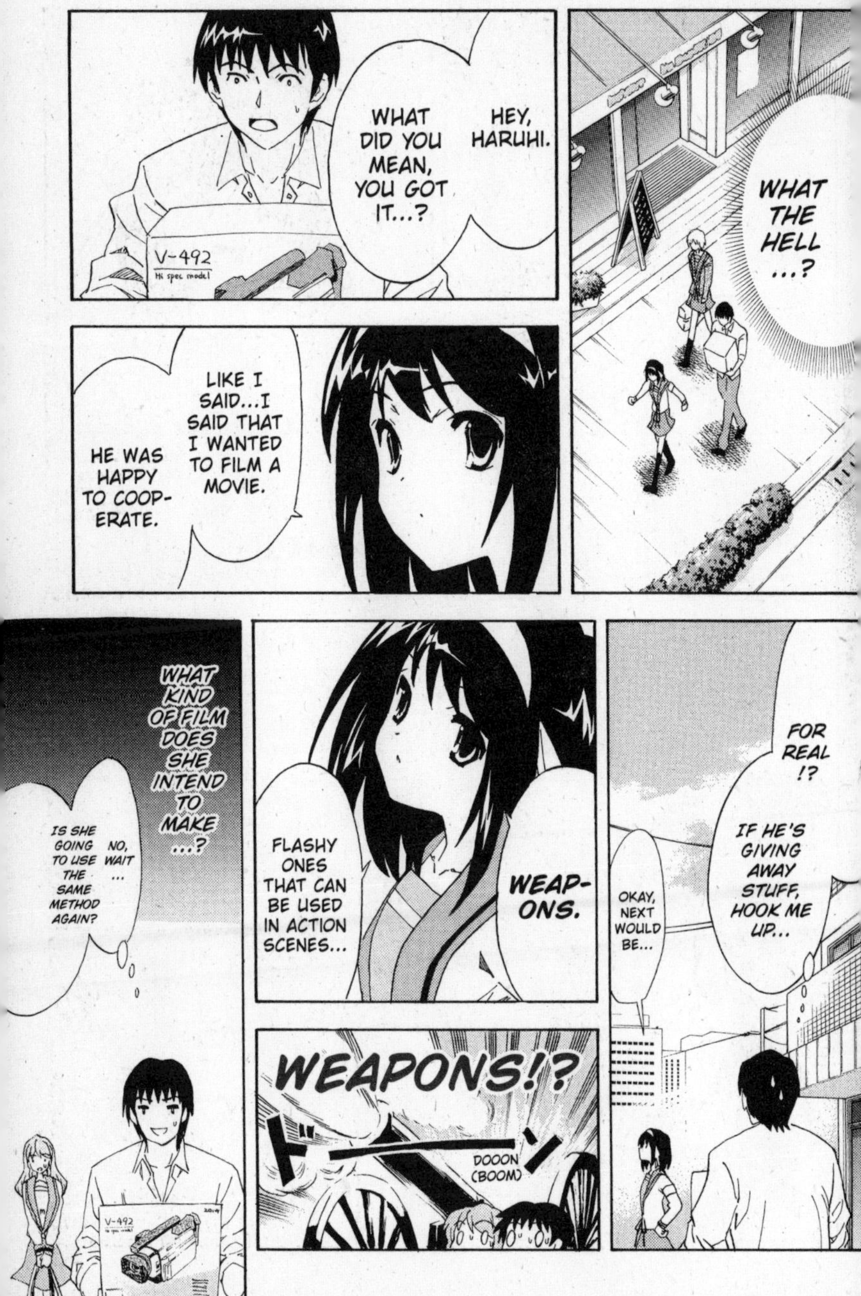
WHAT THE HELL ...?
HEY, HARUHI.
WHAT DID YOU MEAN, YOU GOT IT...?
V-492
Hi spec model
LIKE I SAID...I SAID THAT I WANTED TO FILM A MOVIE.
HE WAS HAPPY TO COOP-ERATE.
FOR REAL !?
IF HE'S GIVING AWAY STUFF, HOOK ME UP...
OKAY, NEXT WOULD BE...
WEAP-ONS.
FLASHY ONES THAT CAN BE USED IN ACTION SCENES...
WEAPONS!?
DOOON (BOOM)
WHAT KIND OF FILM DOES SHE INTEND TO MAKE ...?
NO, WAIT ...
IS SHE GOING TO USE THE SAME METHOD AGAIN?
V-492

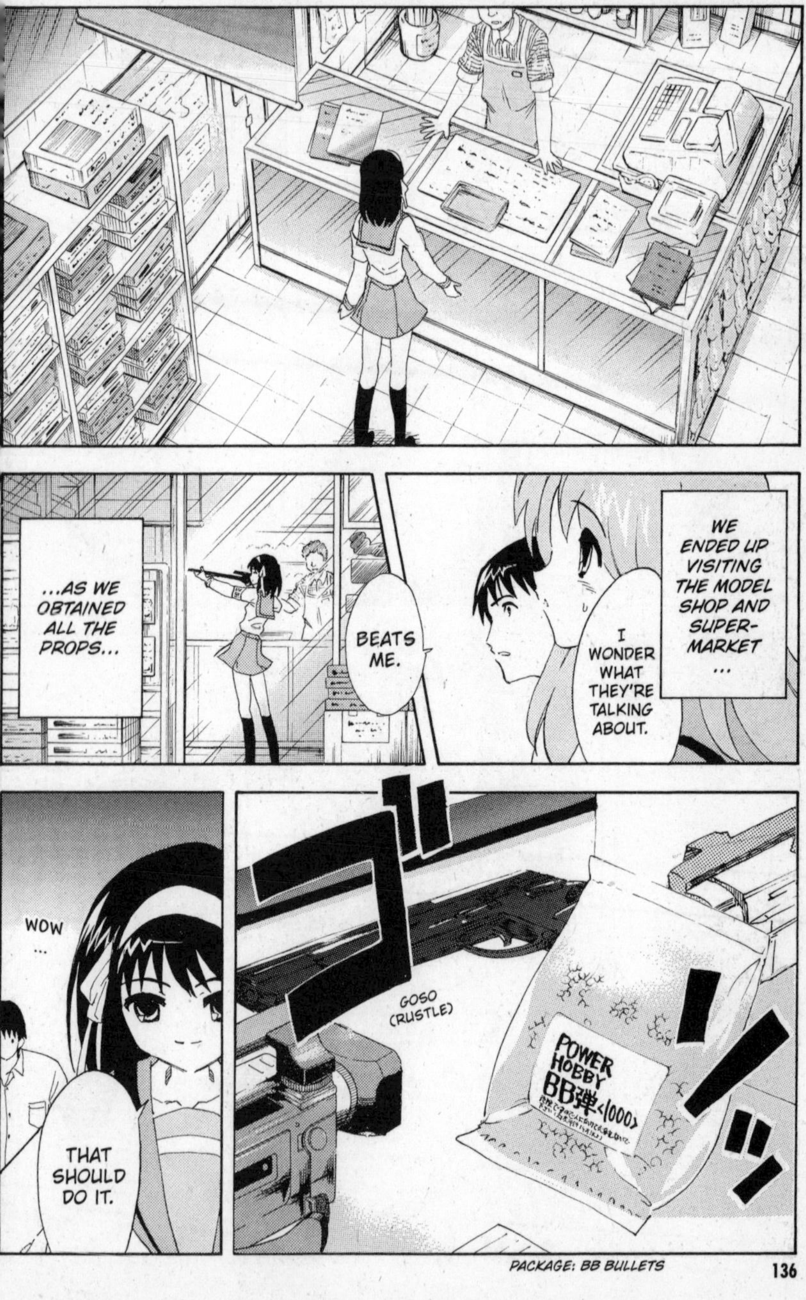

WE ENDED UP VISITING THE MODEL SHOP AND SUPER-MARKET ...
I WONDER WHAT THEY'RE TALKING ABOUT.
BEATS ME.
...AS WE OBTAINED ALL THE PROPS...
GOSO (RUSTLE)
POWER HOBBY BB弾<1000>
WOW ...
THAT SHOULD DO IT.

PACKAGE: BB BULLETS

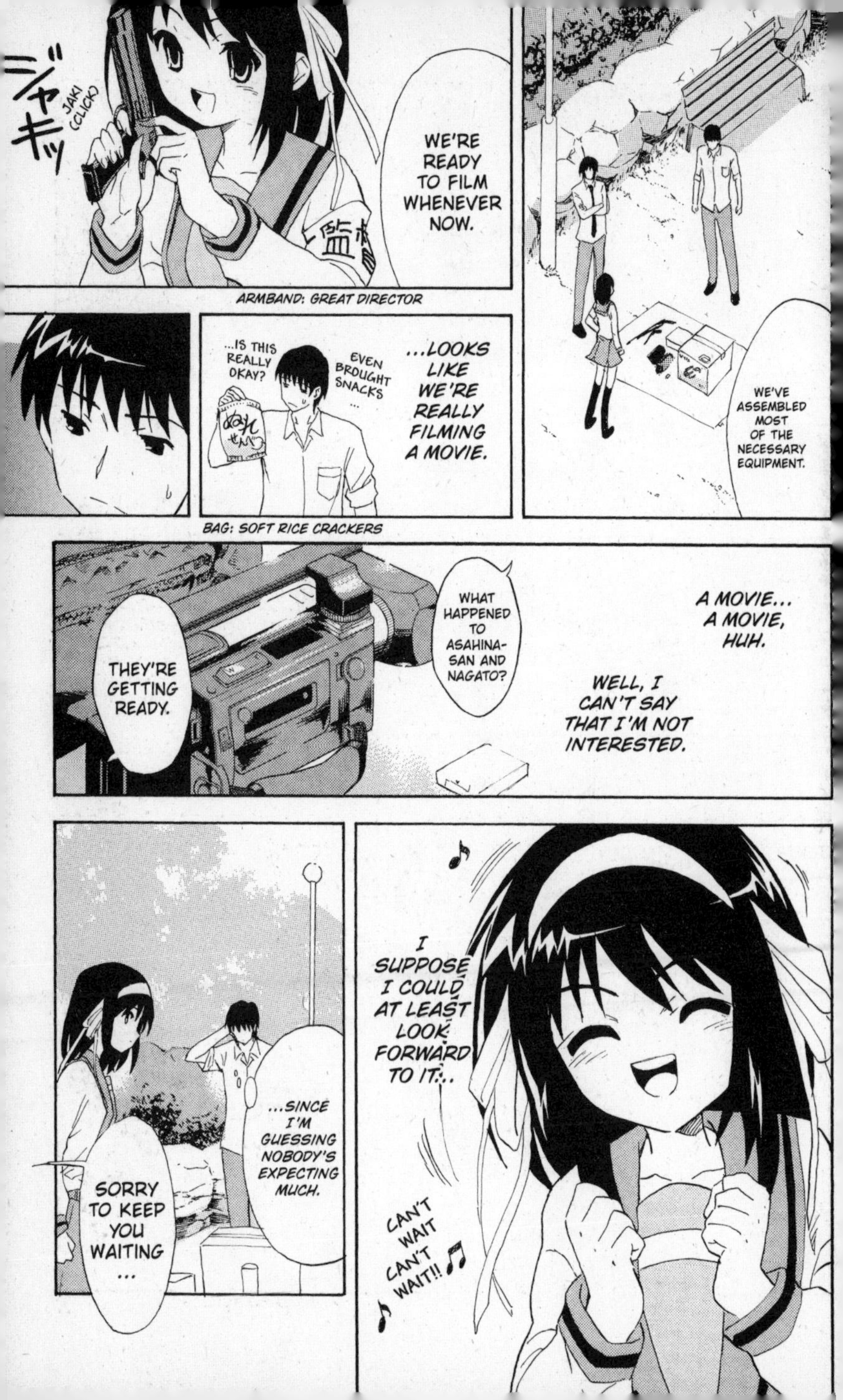
WE'VE ASSEMBLED MOST OF THE NECESSARY EQUIPMENT.
WE'RE READY TO FILM WHENEVER NOW.
ジャキッ
JAKI (CLICK)
ARMBAND: GREAT DIRECTOR
...LOOKS LIKE WE'RE REALLY FILMING A MOVIE.
EVEN BROUGHT SNACKS ...
...IS THIS REALLY OKAY?
BAG: SOFT RICE CRACKERS
A MOVIE... A MOVIE, HUH.
WELL, I CAN'T SAY THAT I'M NOT INTERESTED.
WHAT HAPPENED TO ASAHINA-SAN AND NAGATO?
THEY'RE GETTING READY.
I SUPPOSE I COULD AT LEAST LOOK FORWARD TO IT...
CAN'T WAIT CAN'T WAIT!!
...SINCE I'M GUESSING NOBODY'S EXPECTING MUCH.
SORRY TO KEEP YOU WAITING ...

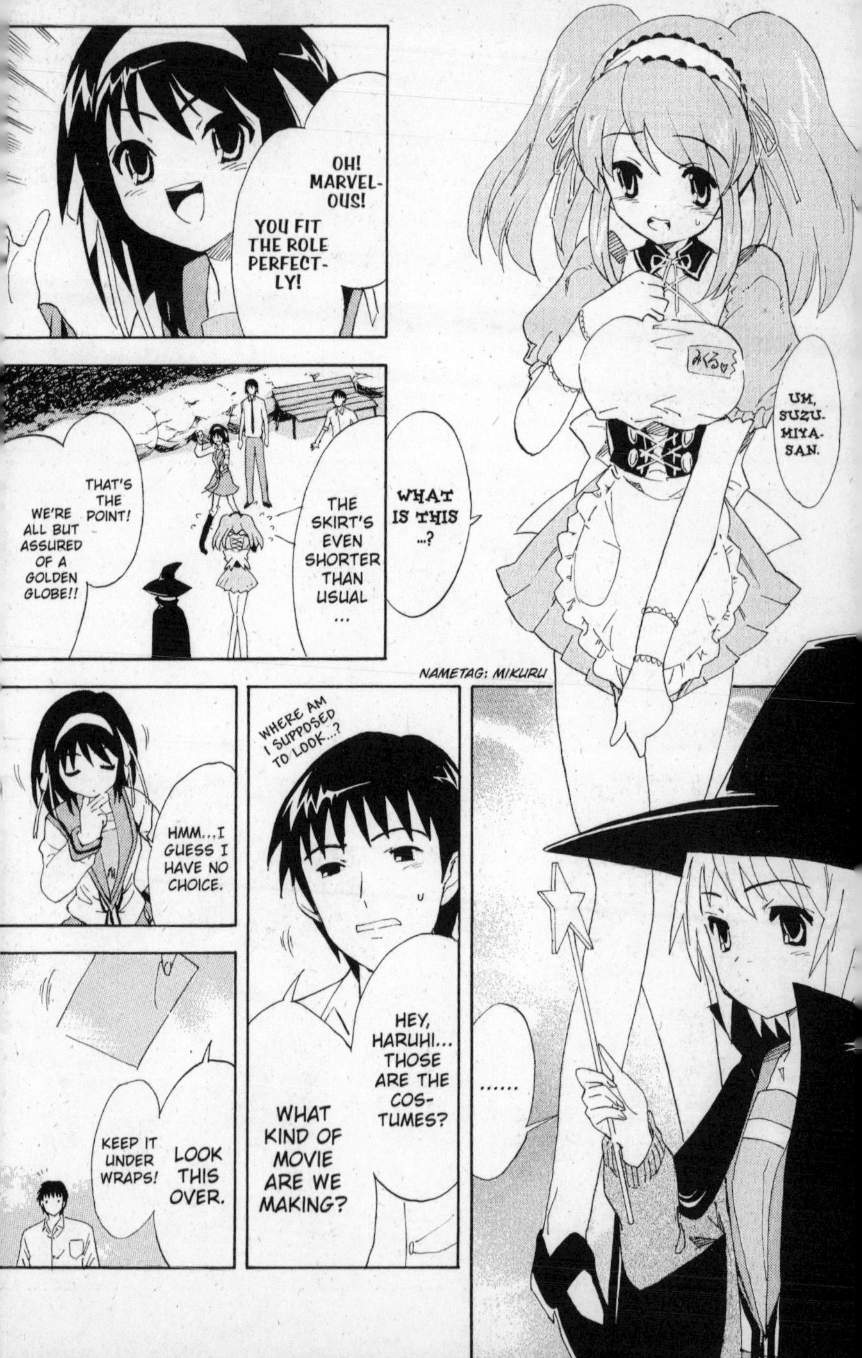
UM, SUZU-MIYA-SAN.
NAMETAG: MIKURU
OH! MARVEL-OUS!
YOU FIT THE ROLE PERFECT-LY!
WHAT IS THIS ...?
THE SKIRT'S EVEN SHORTER THAN USUAL ...
THAT'S THE POINT!
WE'RE ALL BUT ASSURED OF A GOLDEN GLOBE!!
......
WHERE AM I SUPPOSED TO LOOK...?
HEY, HARUHI... THOSE ARE THE COS-TUMES?
WHAT KIND OF MOVIE ARE WE MAKING?
HMM...I GUESS I HAVE NO CHOICE.
LOOK THIS OVER.
KEEP IT UNDER WRAPS!

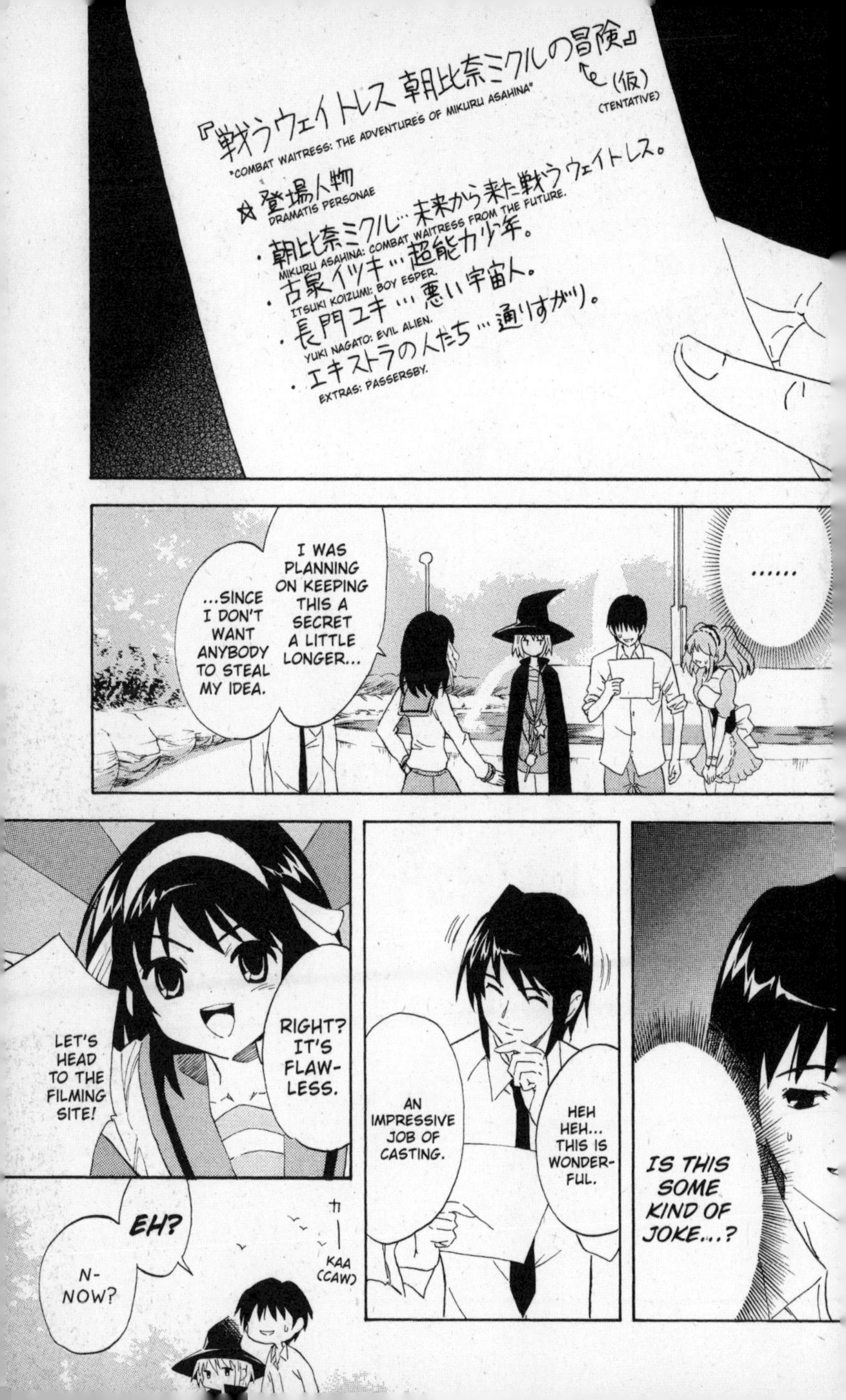
『戦うウェイトレス 朝比奈ミクルの冒険』
(仮)
(TENTATIVE)
"COMBAT WAITRESS: THE ADVENTURES OF MIKURU ASAHINA"
☆登場人物
DRAMATIS PERSONAE
・朝比奈ミクル…未来から来た戦うウェイトレス。
MIKURU ASAHINA: COMBAT WAITRESS FROM THE FUTURE.
・古泉イツキ…超能力少年。
ITSUKI KOIZUMI: BOY ESPER.
・長門ユキ…悪い宇宙人。
YUKI NAGATO: EVIL ALIEN.
・エキストラの人たち…通りすがり。
EXTRAS: PASSERSBY.
......
I WAS PLANNING ON KEEPING THIS A SECRET A LITTLE LONGER...
...SINCE I DON'T WANT ANYBODY TO STEAL MY IDEA.
IS THIS SOME KIND OF JOKE...?
HEH HEH... THIS IS WONDERFUL.
AN IMPRESSIVE JOB OF CASTING.
RIGHT? IT'S FLAWLESS.
LET'S HEAD TO THE FILMING SITE!
カー
KAA (CAW)
EH?
N-NOW?

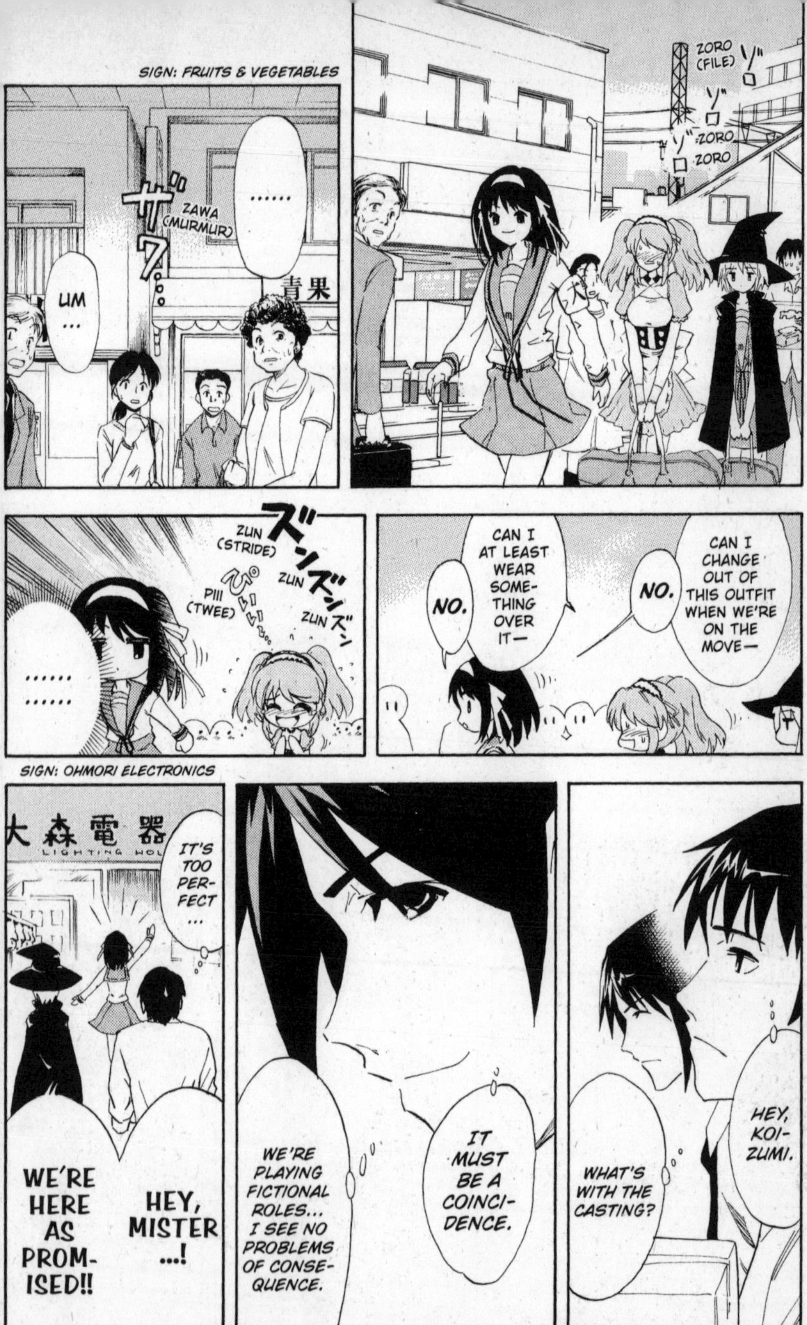

ZORO (FILE)
ゾロ
ゾロ
ZORO
ゾロ
ZORO
SIGN: FRUITS & VEGETABLES
青果
......
ザワ
ZAWA (MURMUR)
UM ...
CAN I CHANGE OUT OF THIS OUTFIT WHEN WE'RE ON THE MOVE—
NO.
CAN I AT LEAST WEAR SOMETHING OVER IT—
NO.
ズン
ZUN (STRIDE)
ズン
ZUN
ズン
ZUN
PIII (TWEE)
....
HEY, KOI-ZUMI.
WHAT'S WITH THE CASTING?
IT MUST BE A COINCI-DENCE.
WE'RE PLAYING FICTIONAL ROLES... I SEE NO PROBLEMS OF CONSE-QUENCE.
SIGN: OHMORI ELECTRONICS
大森電器
IT'S TOO PER-FECT ...
HEY, MISTER ...!
WE'RE HERE AS PROM-ISED!!

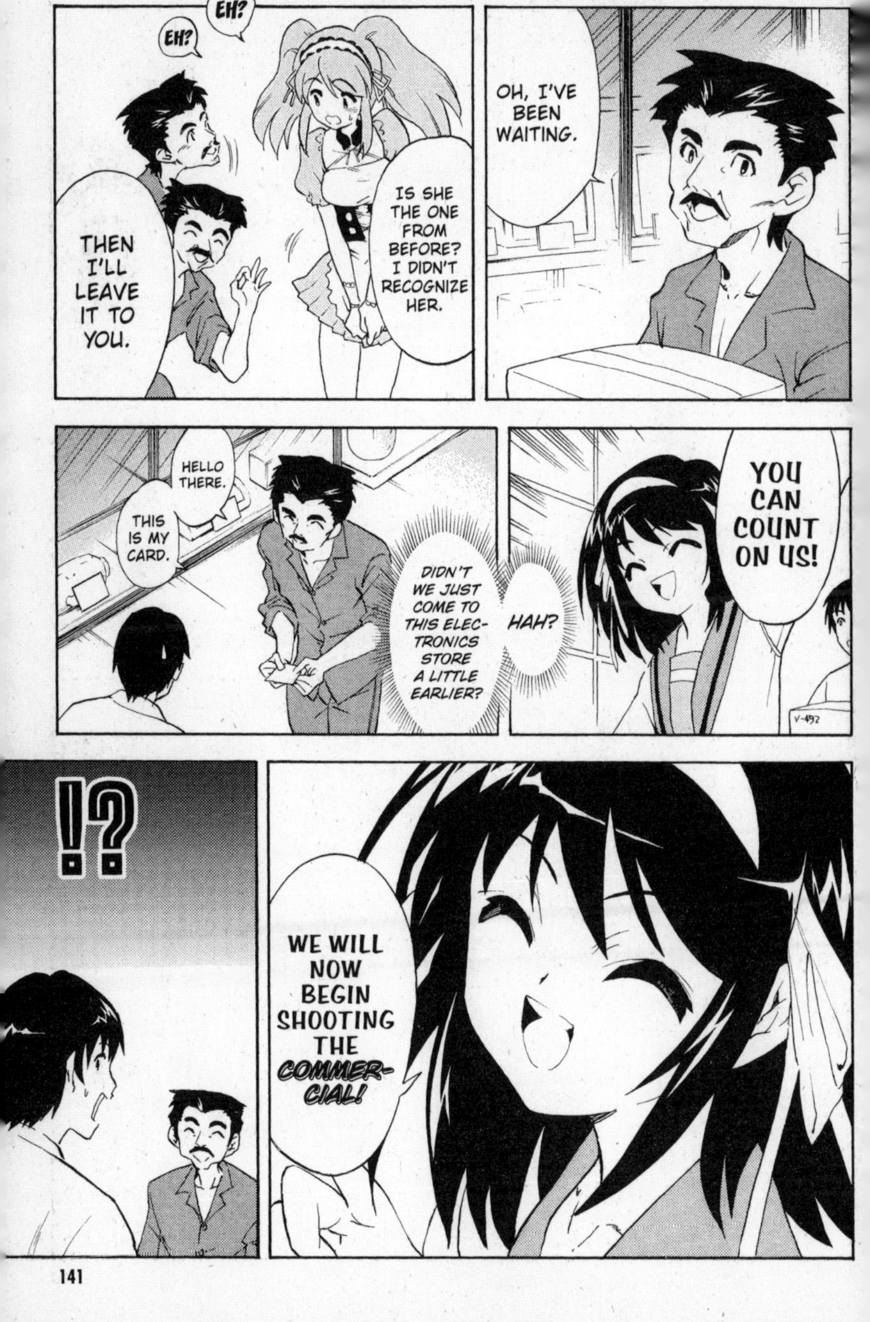
OH, I'VE BEEN WAITING.
EH?
EH?
IS SHE THE ONE FROM BEFORE? I DIDN'T RECOGNIZE HER.
THEN I'LL LEAVE IT TO YOU.
YOU CAN COUNT ON US!
V-492
HAH?
DIDN'T WE JUST COME TO THIS ELEC-TRONICS STORE A LITTLE EARLIER?
HELLO THERE.
THIS IS MY CARD.
WE WILL NOW BEGIN SHOOTING THE COMMER-CIAL!
!?

BANNER: SPECIAL SALE

SIGNS: OHMORI ELECTRONICS

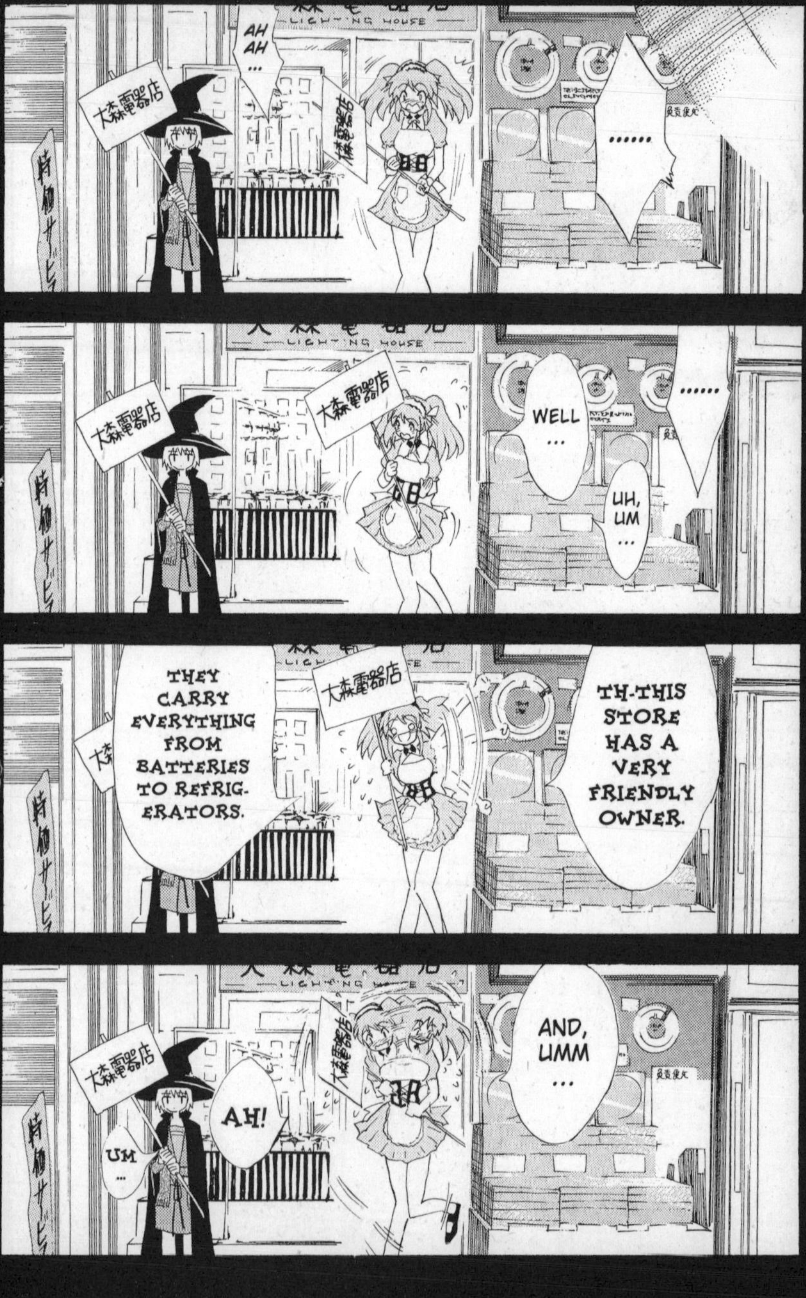
......
AH AH ...
......
WELL ...
UH, UM ...
TH-THIS STORE HAS A VERY FRIENDLY OWNER.
THEY CARRY EVERYTHING FROM BATTERIES TO REFRIG-ERATORS.
AND, UMM ...
AH!
UM ...

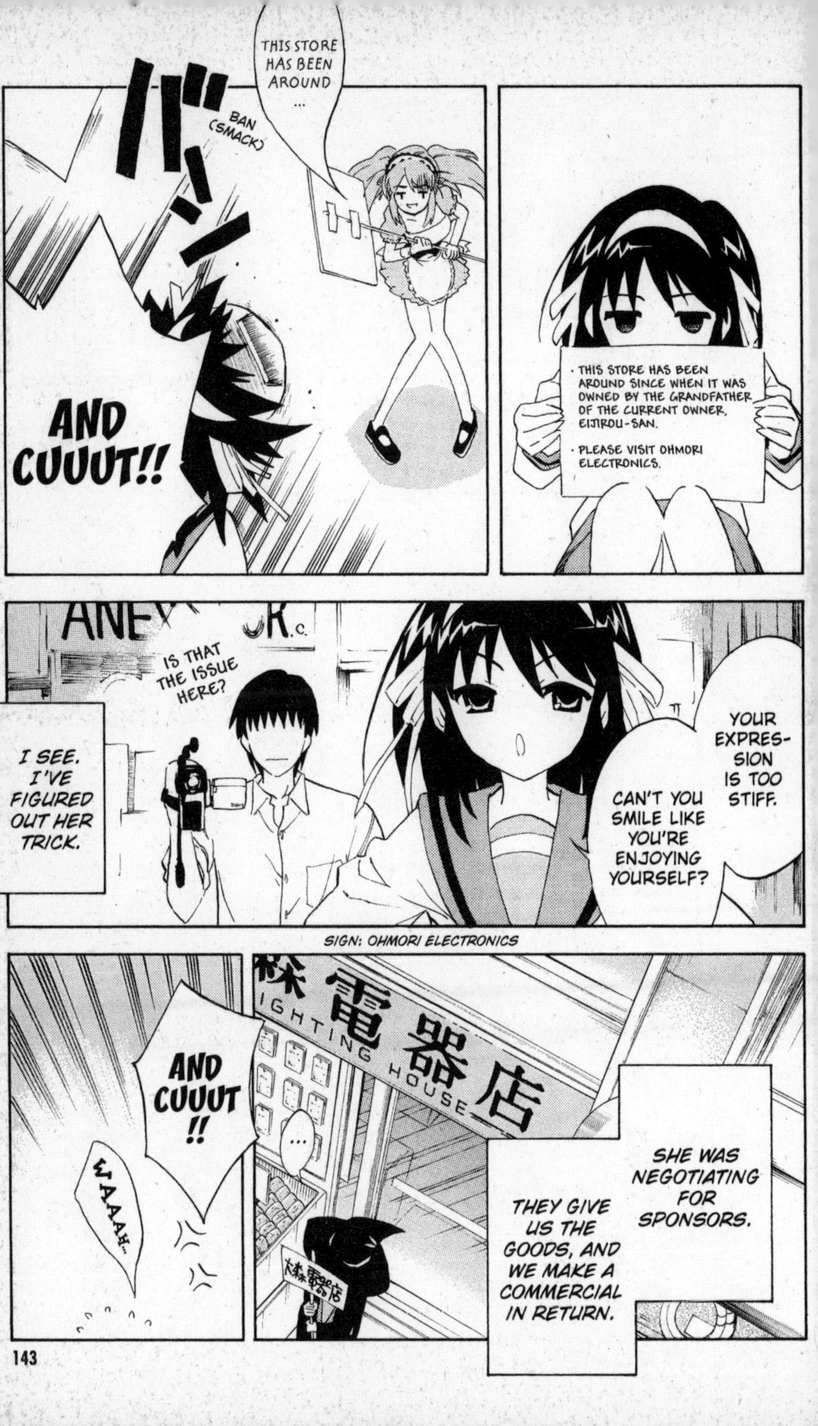

· THIS STORE HAS BEEN AROUND SINCE WHEN IT WAS OWNED BY THE GRANDFATHER OF THE CURRENT OWNER, EIJIROU-SAN.
· PLEASE VISIT OHMORI ELECTRONICS.
THIS STORE HAS BEEN AROUND ...
BAN (SMACK)
AND CUUUT!!
YOUR EXPRESSION IS TOO STIFF.
CAN'T YOU SMILE LIKE YOU'RE ENJOYING YOURSELF?
IS THAT THE ISSUE HERE?
I SEE. I'VE FIGURED OUT HER TRICK.
SIGN: OHMORI ELECTRONICS
SHE WAS NEGOTIATING FOR SPONSORS.
THEY GIVE US THE GOODS, AND WE MAKE A COMMERCIAL IN RETURN.
...
AND CUUUT!!
WAAAH...

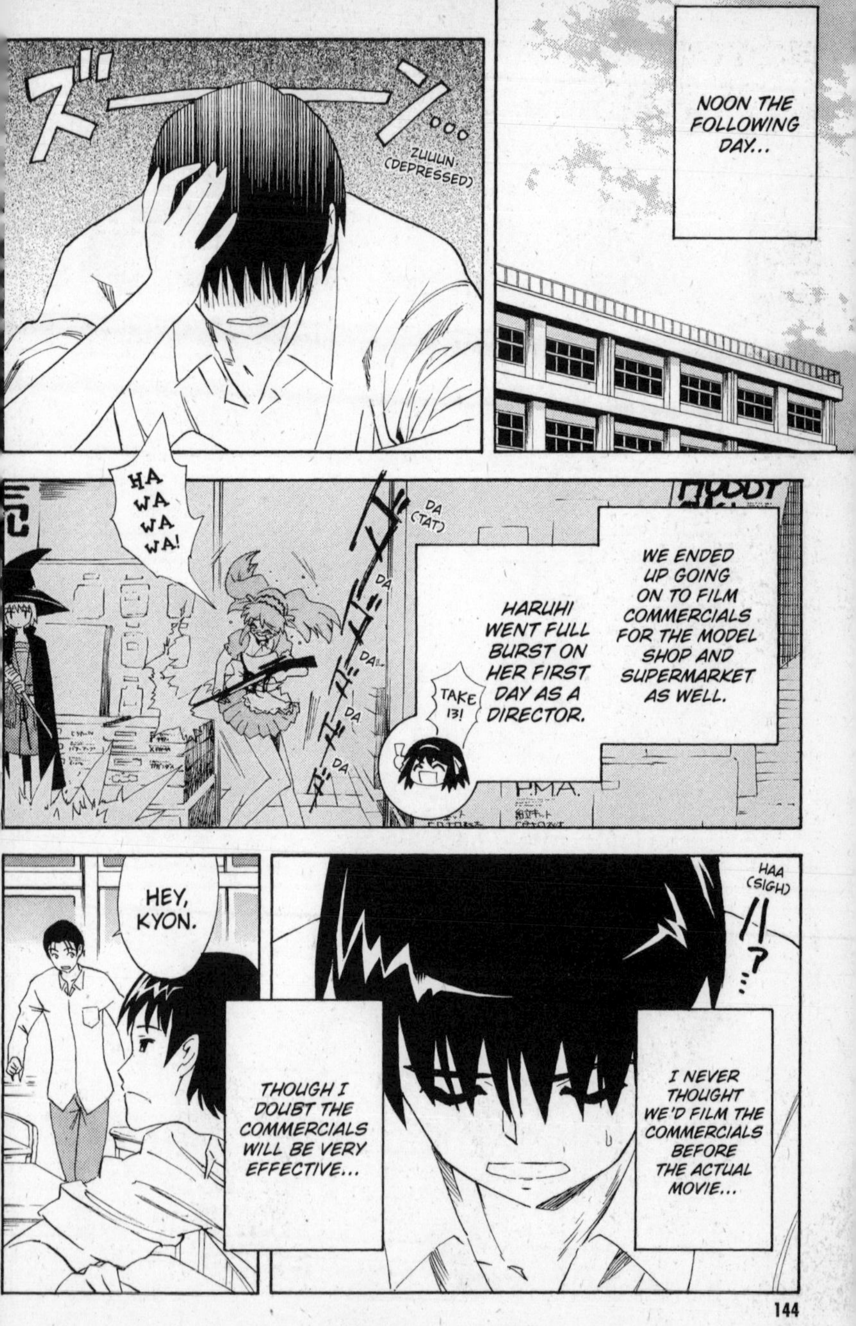
NOON THE FOLLOWING DAY...
ZUUUN (DEPRESSED)
DA (TAT)
WE ENDED UP GOING ON TO FILM COMMERCIALS FOR THE MODEL SHOP AND SUPERMARKET AS WELL.
HARUHI WENT FULL BURST ON HER FIRST DAY AS A DIRECTOR.
DA DA DA DA
TAKE 13!
HA WA WA WA!
HAA (SIGH)
I NEVER THOUGHT WE'D FILM THE COMMERCIALS BEFORE THE ACTUAL MOVIE...
THOUGH I DOUBT THE COMMERCIALS WILL BE VERY EFFECTIVE...
HEY, KYON.

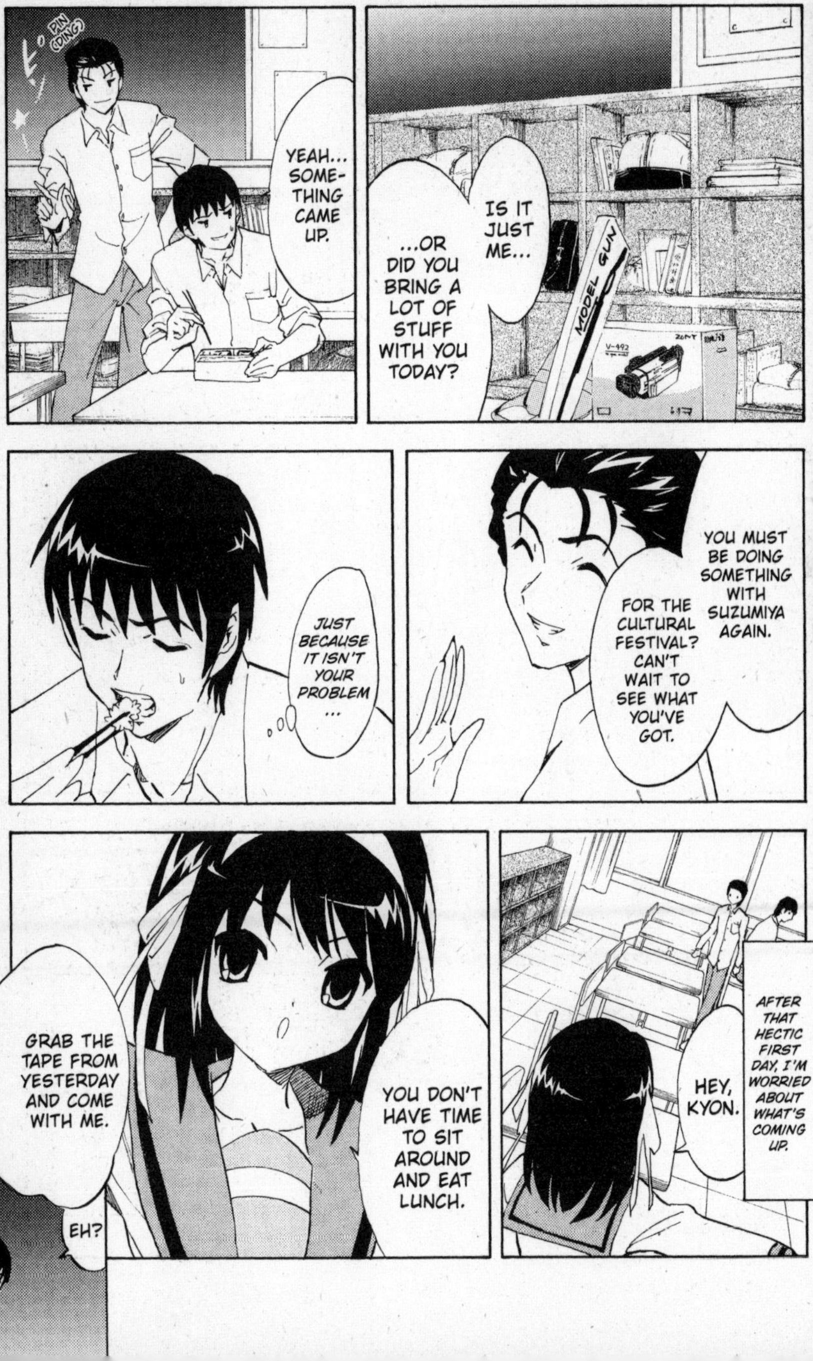
IS IT JUST ME...
...OR DID YOU BRING A LOT OF STUFF WITH YOU TODAY?
MODEL GUN
PIN (DING)
YEAH... SOME-THING CAME UP.
YOU MUST BE DOING SOMETHING WITH SUZUMIYA AGAIN.
FOR THE CULTURAL FESTIVAL? CAN'T WAIT TO SEE WHAT YOU'VE GOT.
JUST BECAUSE IT ISN'T YOUR PROBLEM...
AFTER THAT HECTIC FIRST DAY, I'M WORRIED ABOUT WHAT'S COMING UP.
HEY, KYON.
YOU DON'T HAVE TIME TO SIT AROUND AND EAT LUNCH.
GRAB THE TAPE FROM YESTERDAY AND COME WITH ME.
EH?

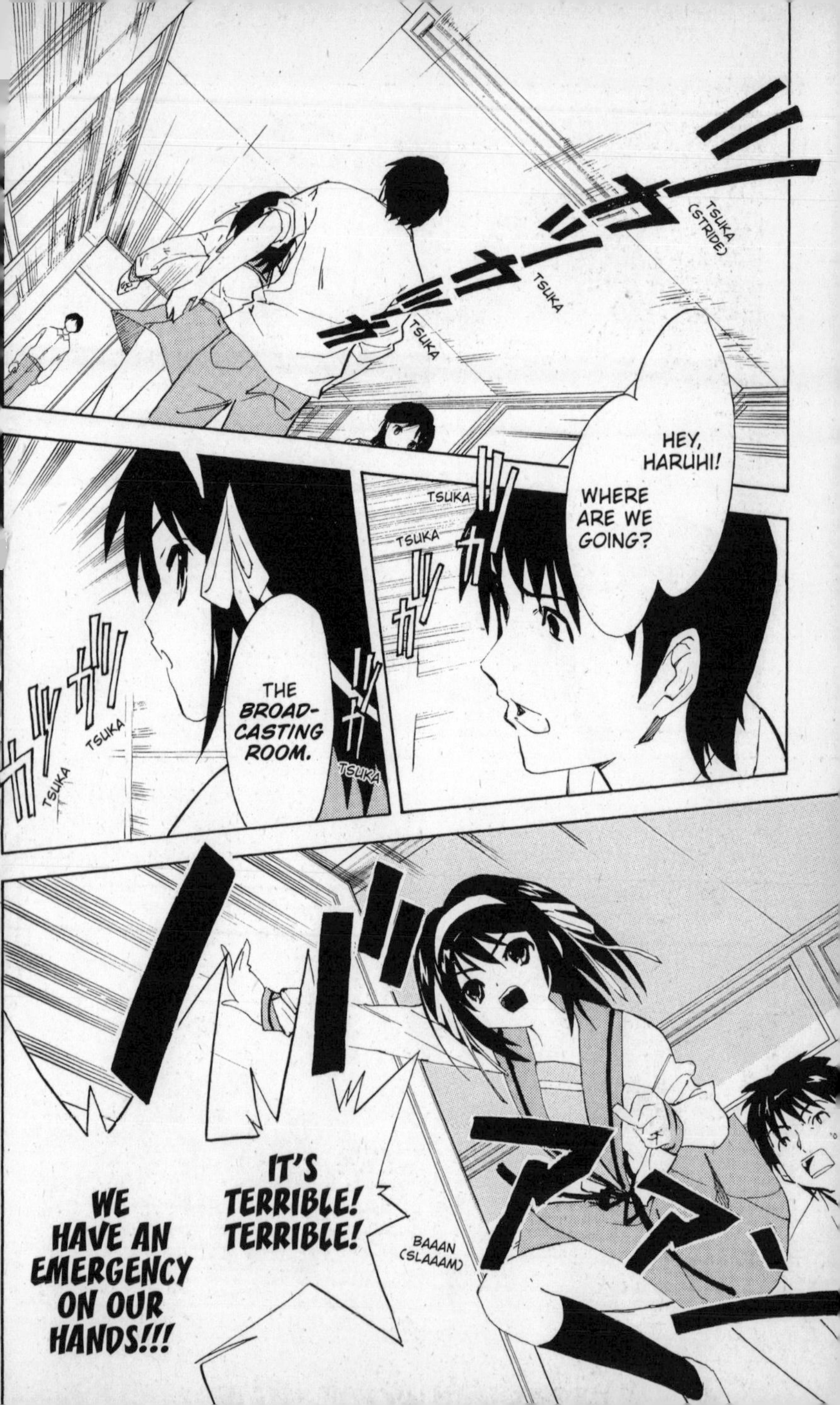
TSUKA (STRIDE)
TSUKA
TSUKA
HEY, HARUHI!
WHERE ARE WE GOING?
TSUKA
TSUKA
THE BROAD-CASTING ROOM.
TSUKA
TSUKA
TSUKA
BAAAN (SLAAAM)
IT'S TERRIBLE! TERRIBLE!
WE HAVE AN EMERGENCY ON OUR HANDS!!!

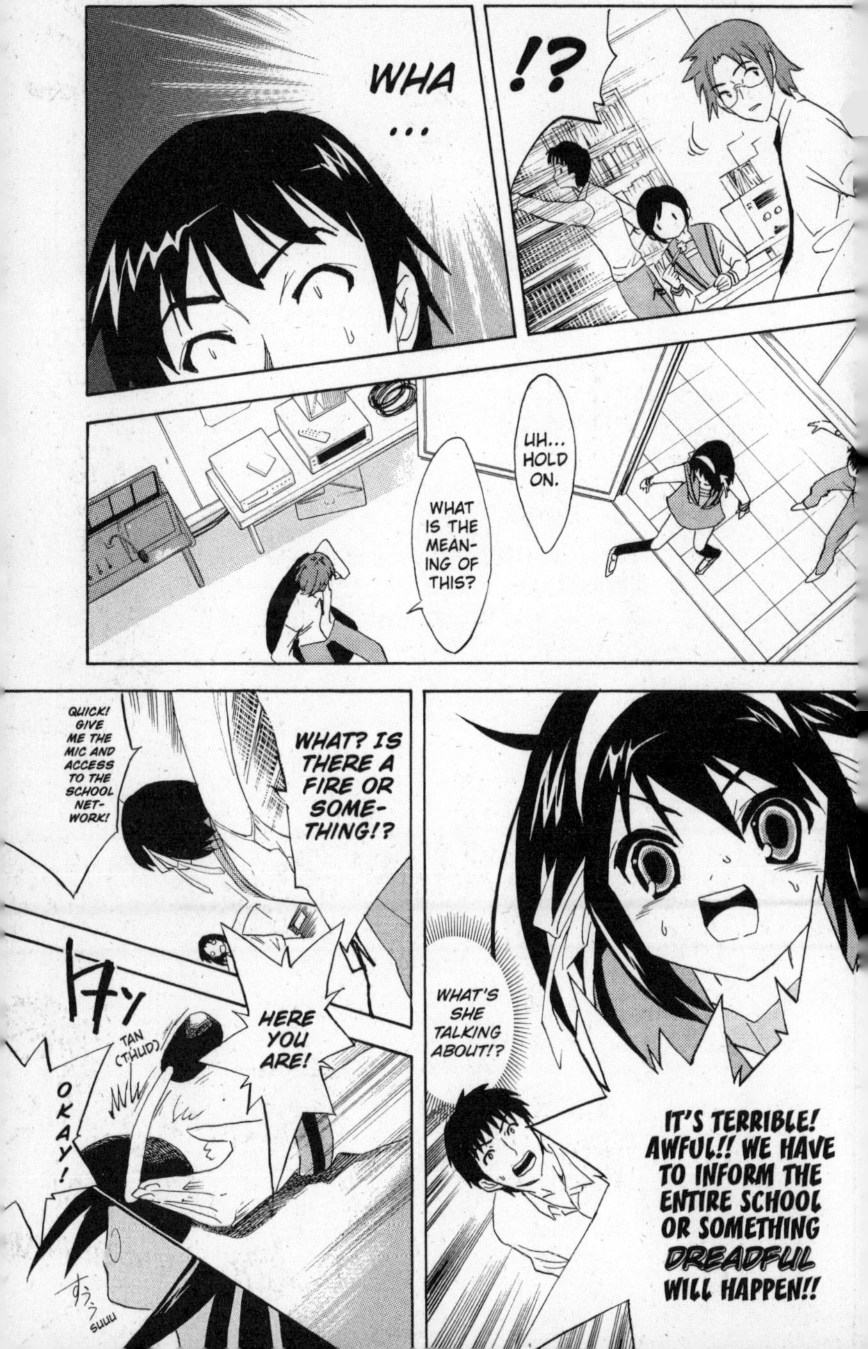
!?
WHA ...
UH... HOLD ON.
WHAT IS THE MEANING OF THIS?
IT'S TERRIBLE! AWFUL!! WE HAVE TO INFORM THE ENTIRE SCHOOL OR SOMETHING DREADFUL WILL HAPPEN!!
WHAT'S SHE TALKING ABOUT!?
WHAT? IS THERE A FIRE OR SOME-THING!?
QUICK! GIVE ME THE MIC AND ACCESS TO THE SCHOOL NET-WORK!
HERE YOU ARE!
TAN (THUD)
OKAY!
SUUU

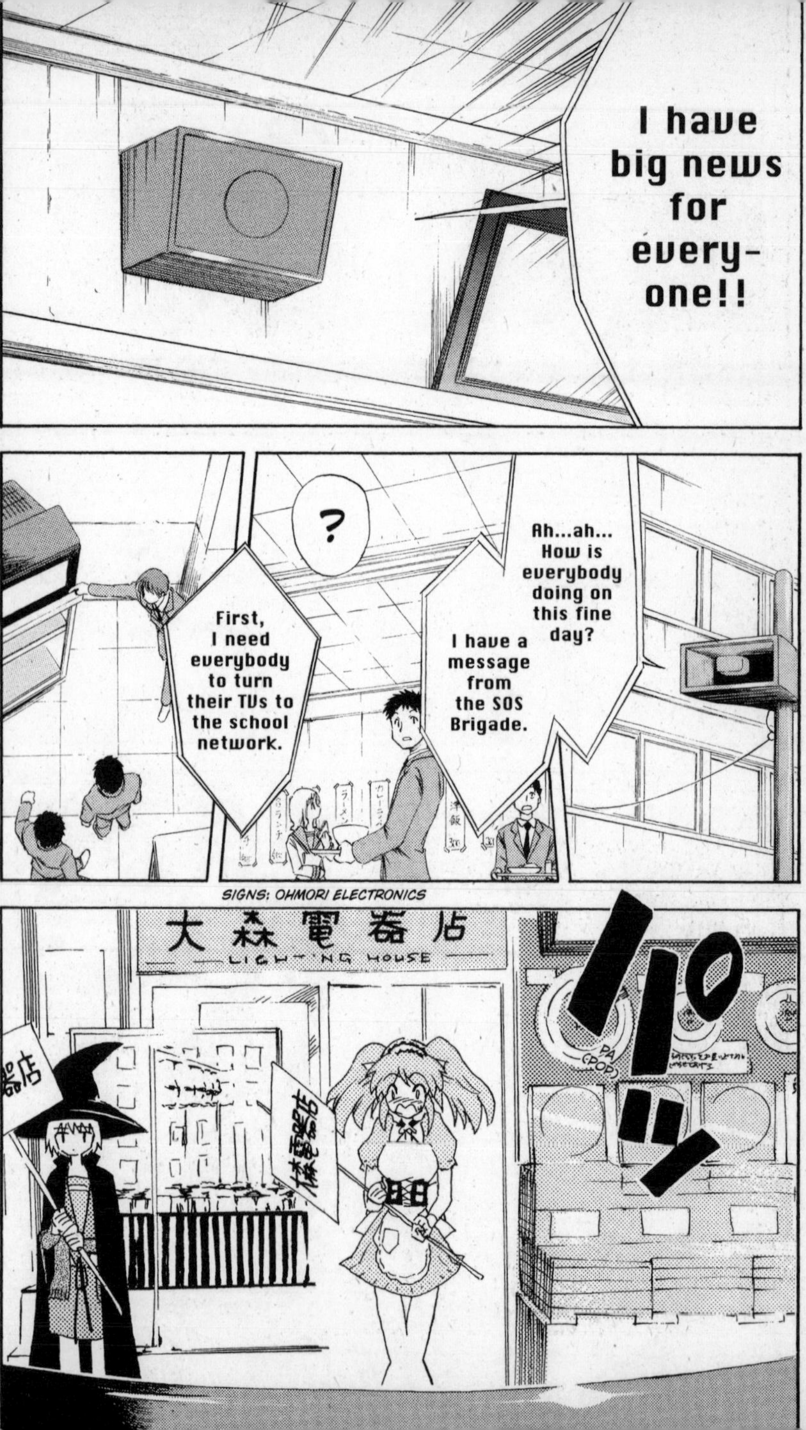
I have big news for everyone!!
Ah...ah... How is everybody doing on this fine day?
I have a message from the SOS Brigade.
?
First, I need everybody to turn their TVs to the school network.
SIGNS: OHMORI ELECTRONICS
大森電器店
PA (POP)

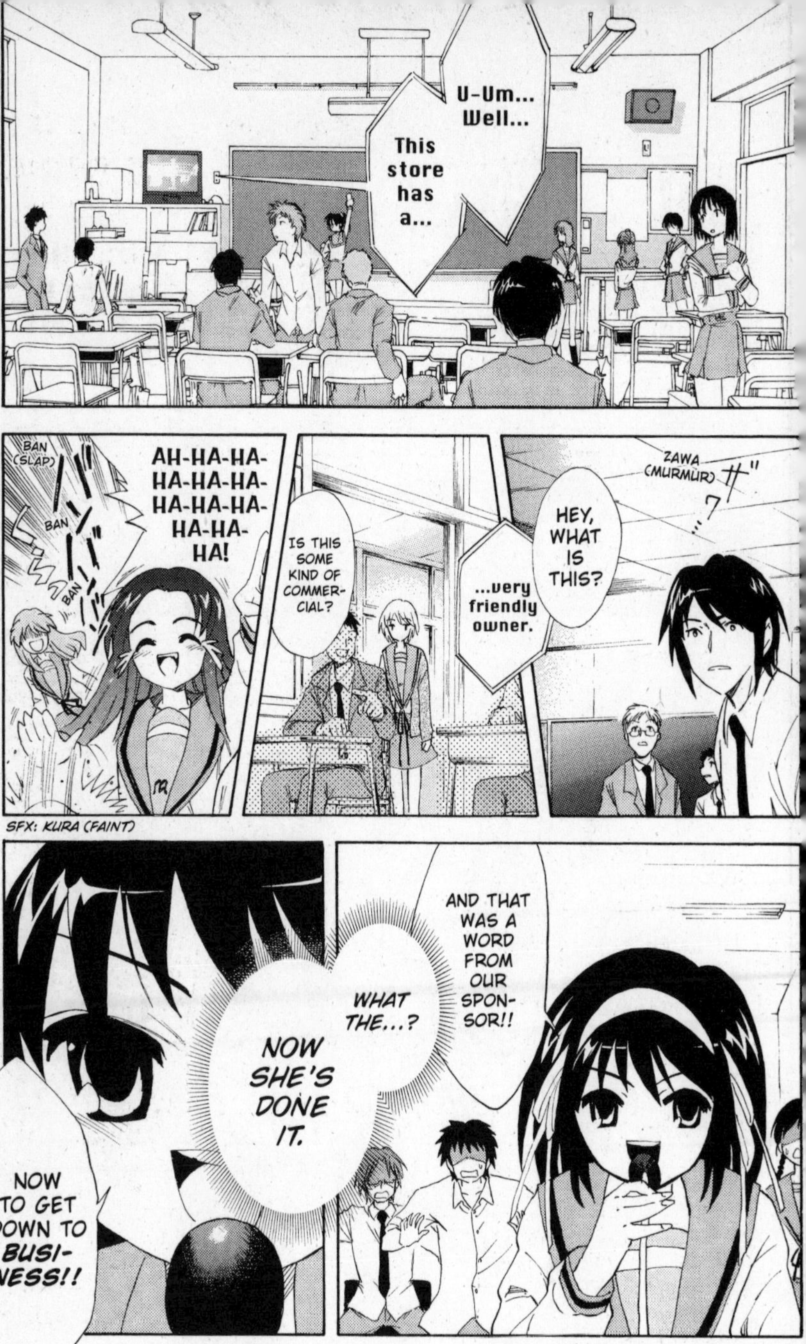
U-Um... Well...
This store has a...
ZAWA (MURMUR)
HEY, WHAT IS THIS?
...very friendly owner.
IS THIS SOME KIND OF COMMERCIAL?
BAN (SLAP)
BAN
BAN
AH-HA-HA-HA-HA-HA-HA-HA-HA-HA-HA-HA!
SFX: KURA (FAINT)
AND THAT WAS A WORD FROM OUR SPONSOR!!
WHAT THE...?
NOW SHE'S DONE IT.
NOW TO GET DOWN TO BUSINESS!!

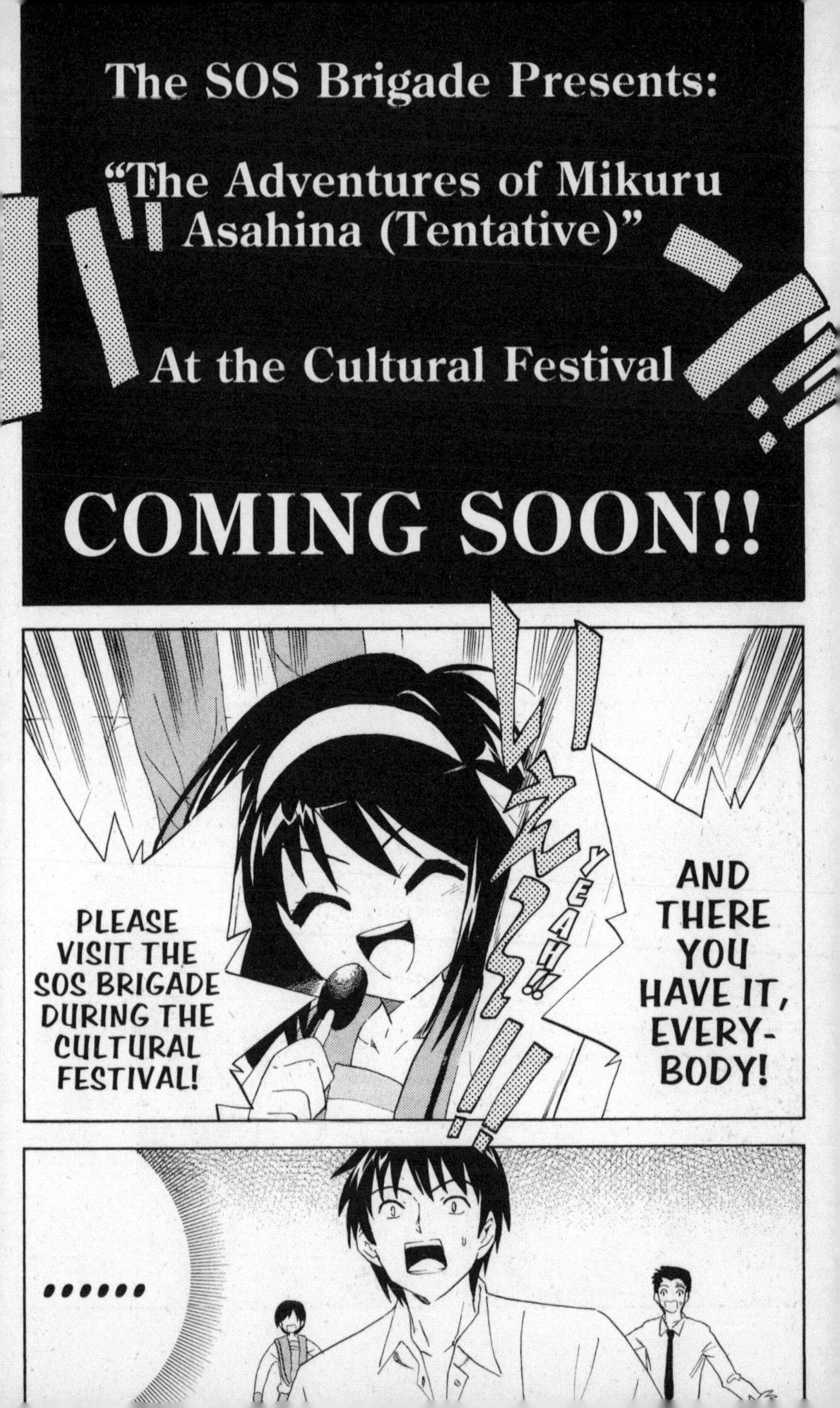
The SOS Brigade Presents:
"The Adventures of Mikuru Asahina (Tentative)"
At the Cultural Festival
COMING SOON!!
AND THERE YOU HAVE IT, EVERY-BODY!
YEAH!!
PLEASE VISIT THE SOS BRIGADE DURING THE CULTURAL FESTIVAL!
......

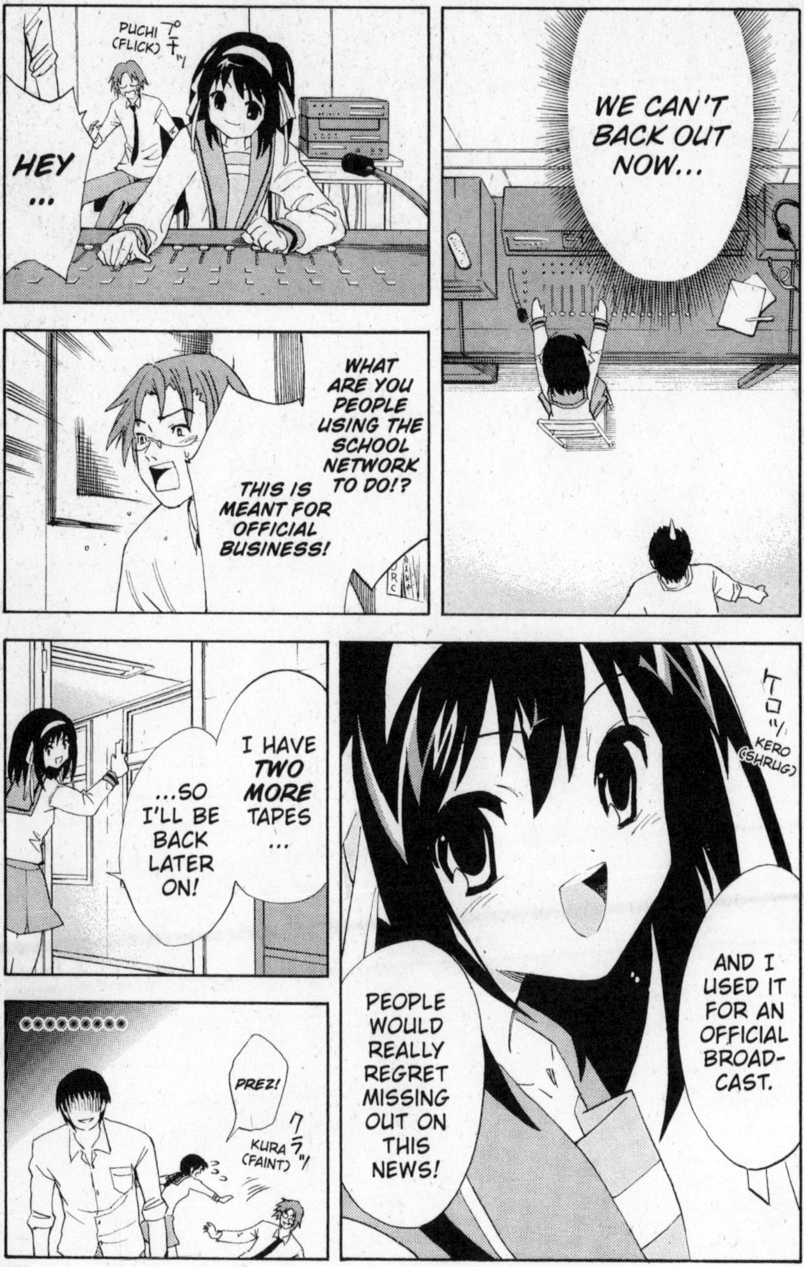
WE CAN'T BACK OUT NOW...
PUCHI (FLICK)
HEY ...
WHAT ARE YOU PEOPLE USING THE SCHOOL NETWORK TO DO!?
THIS IS MEANT FOR OFFICIAL BUSINESS!
KERO (SHRUG)
AND I USED IT FOR AN OFFICIAL BROADCAST.
PEOPLE WOULD REALLY REGRET MISSING OUT ON THIS NEWS!
I HAVE TWO MORE TAPES ...
...SO I'LL BE BACK LATER ON!
PREZ!
KURA (FAINT)

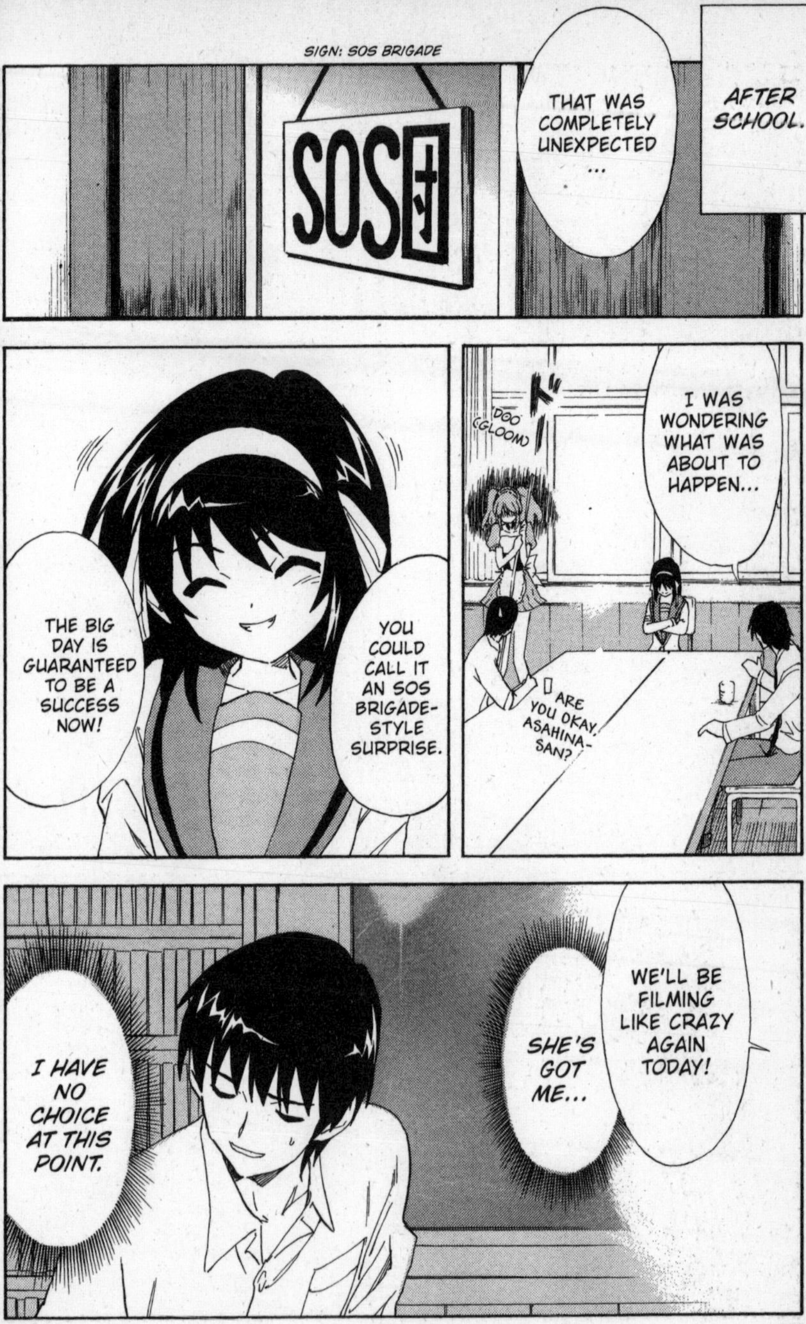
AFTER SCHOOL.
THAT WAS COMPLETELY UNEXPECTED ...
SIGN: SOS BRIGADE
SOS
I WAS WONDERING WHAT WAS ABOUT TO HAPPEN...
DOO (GLOOM)
ARE YOU OKAY, ASAHINA-SAN?
YOU COULD CALL IT AN SOS BRIGADE-STYLE SURPRISE.
THE BIG DAY IS GUARANTEED TO BE A SUCCESS NOW!
WE'LL BE FILMING LIKE CRAZY AGAIN TODAY!
SHE'S GOT ME...
I HAVE NO CHOICE AT THIS POINT.

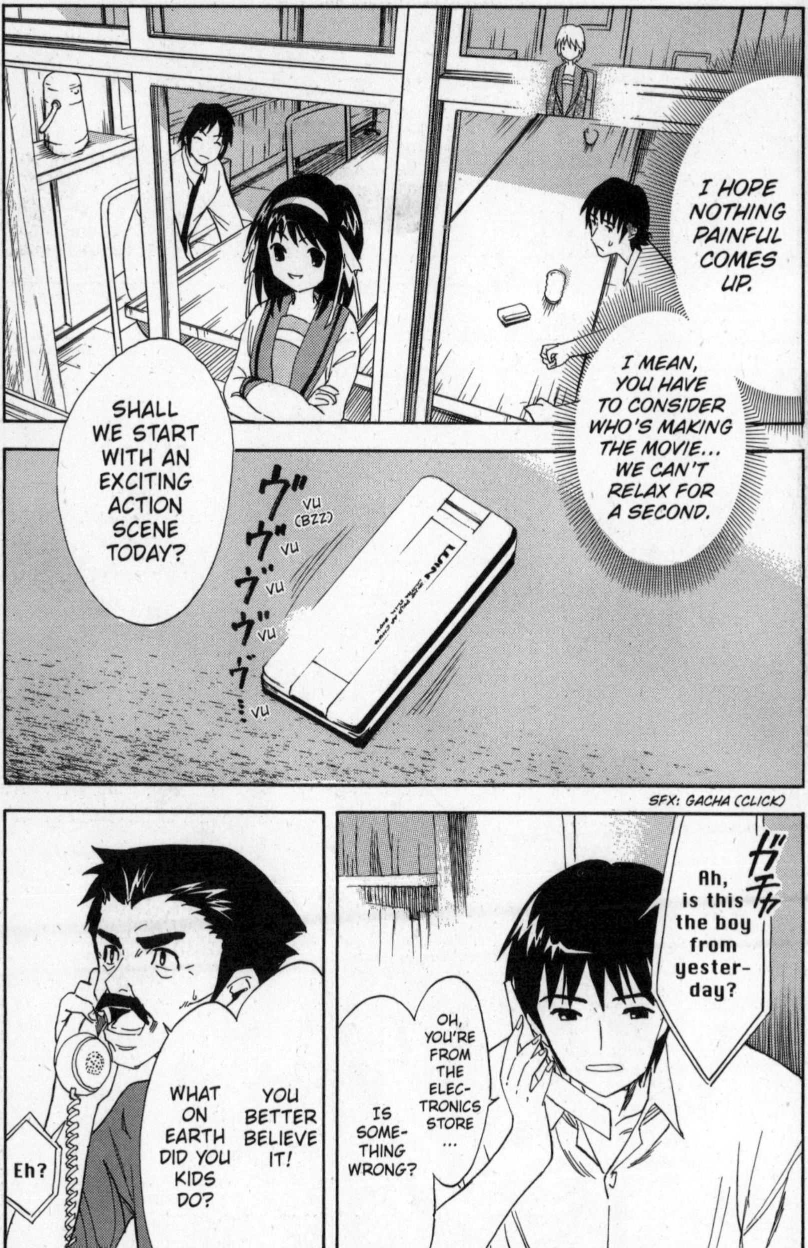
I HOPE NOTHING PAINFUL COMES UP.
I MEAN, YOU HAVE TO CONSIDER WHO'S MAKING THE MOVIE... WE CAN'T RELAX FOR A SECOND.
SHALL WE START WITH AN EXCITING ACTION SCENE TODAY?
ヴヴヴヴヴ…
VU (BZZ) VU VU VU VU
SFX: GACHA (CLICK)
ガチャ
Ah, is this the boy from yester-day?
OH, YOU'RE FROM THE ELEC-TRONICS STORE ...
IS SOME-THING WRONG?
YOU BETTER BELIEVE IT!
WHAT ON EARTH DID YOU KIDS DO?
Eh?

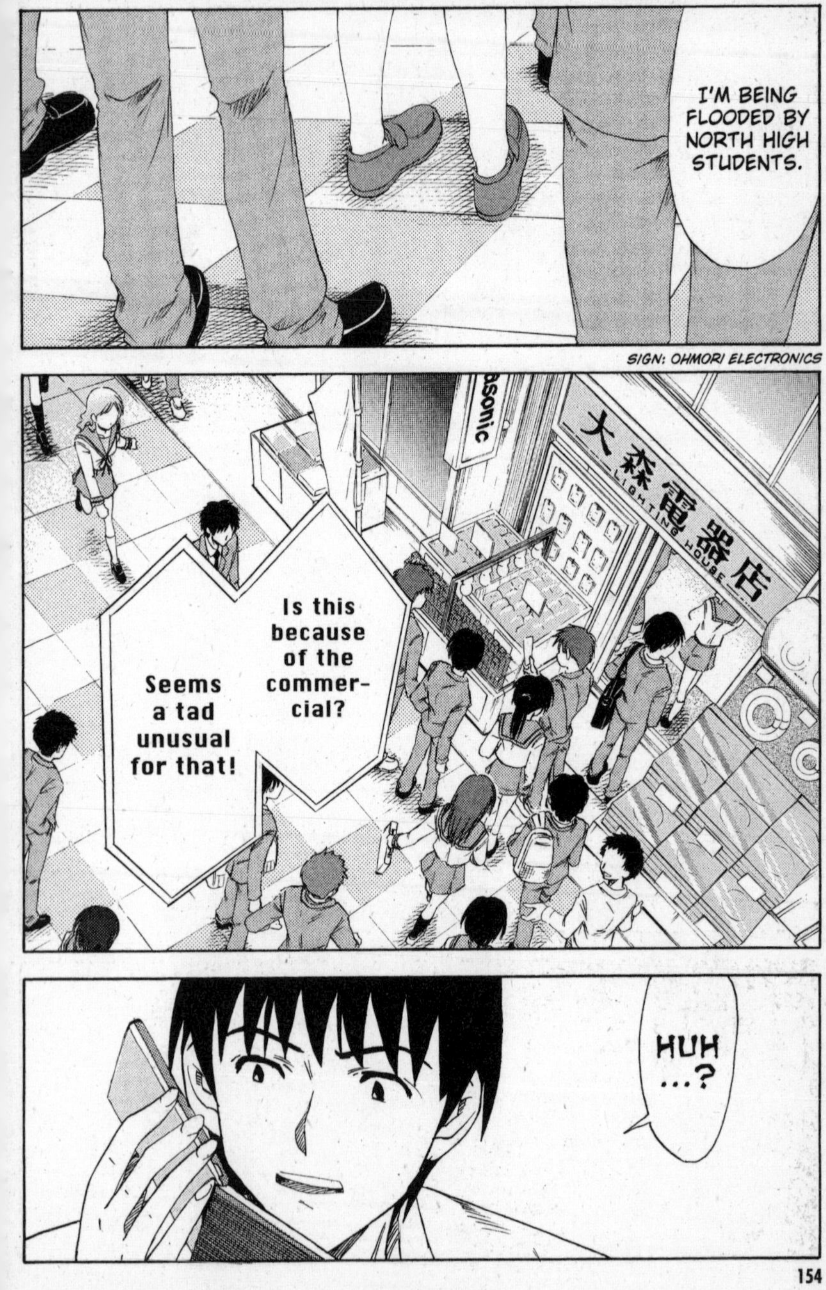
I'M BEING FLOODED BY NORTH HIGH STUDENTS.
SIGN: OHMORI ELECTRONICS
大森電器店
LIGHTING HOUSE
Is this because of the commercial?
Seems a tad unusual for that!
HUH ...?

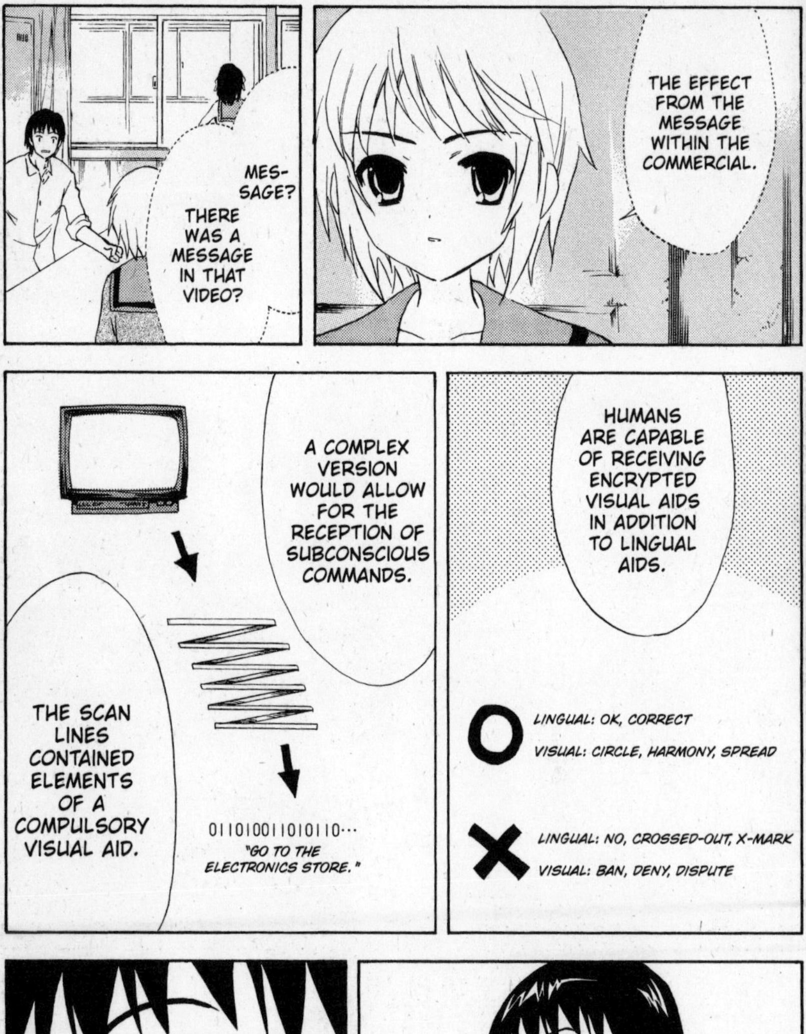
THE EFFECT FROM THE MESSAGE WITHIN THE COMMERCIAL.
MES-SAGE?
THERE WAS A MESSAGE IN THAT VIDEO?
HUMANS ARE CAPABLE OF RECEIVING ENCRYPTED VISUAL AIDS IN ADDITION TO LINGUAL AIDS.
LINGUAL: OK, CORRECT
VISUAL: CIRCLE, HARMONY, SPREAD
LINGUAL: NO, CROSSED-OUT, X-MARK
VISUAL: BAN, DENY, DISPUTE
A COMPLEX VERSION WOULD ALLOW FOR THE RECEPTION OF SUBCONSCIOUS COMMANDS.
01101001101010110···
"GO TO THE ELECTRONICS STORE."
THE SCAN LINES CONTAINED ELEMENTS OF A COMPULSORY VISUAL AID.
WHEN WAS IT ADDED IN...?
IT WASN'T ADDED IN.
THE MESSAGE WAS IN THE COMMERCIAL ONCE HARUHI SUZUMIYA FILMED IT.

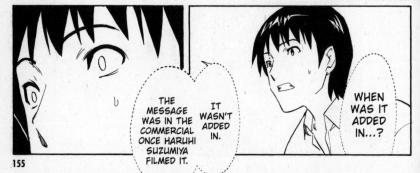

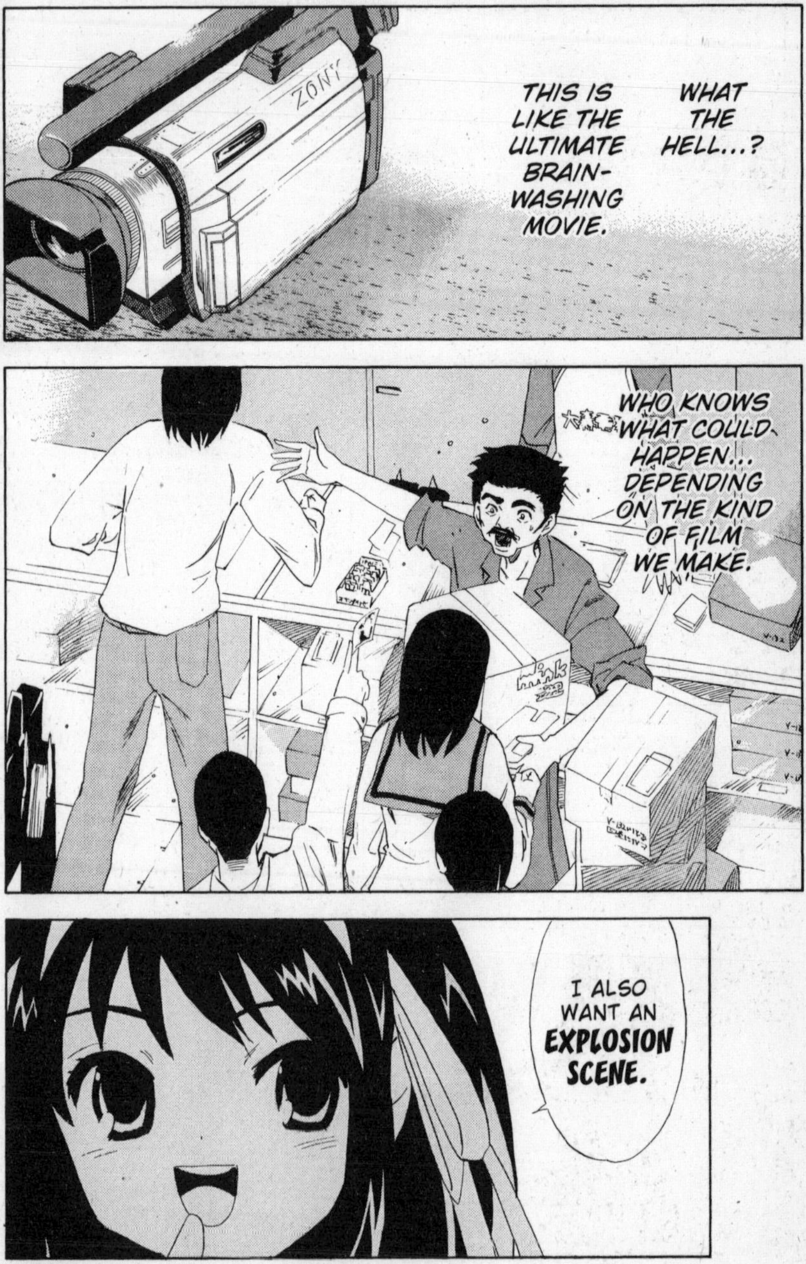
WHAT THE HELL...?
THIS IS LIKE THE ULTIMATE BRAIN-WASHING MOVIE.
ZONY
WHO KNOWS WHAT COULD HAPPEN... DEPENDING ON THE KIND OF FILM WE MAKE.
I ALSO WANT AN **EXPLOSION SCENE.**

The Sigh of Haruhi Suzumiya I : END

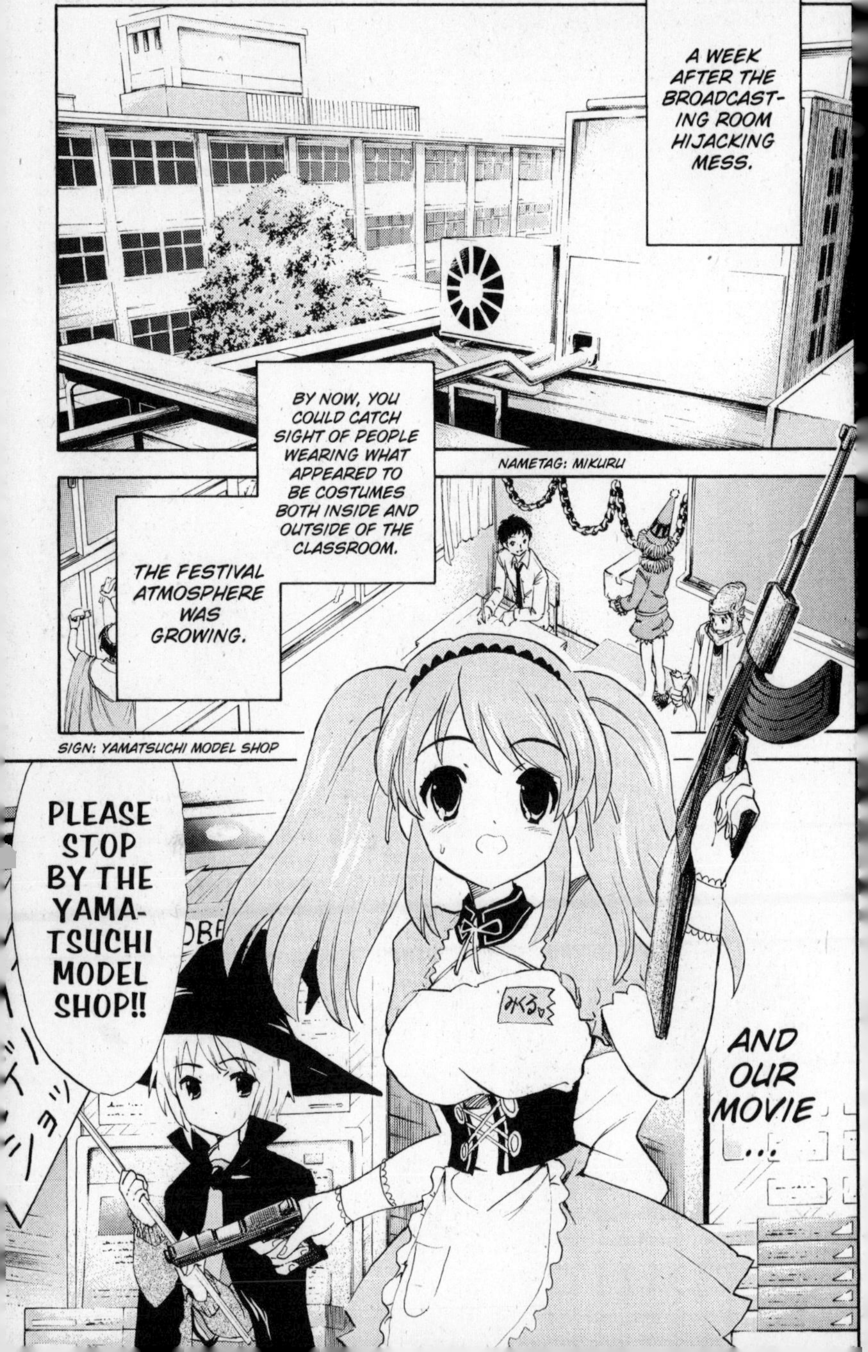
A WEEK AFTER THE BROADCASTING ROOM HIJACKING MESS.
BY NOW, YOU COULD CATCH SIGHT OF PEOPLE WEARING WHAT APPEARED TO BE COSTUMES BOTH INSIDE AND OUTSIDE OF THE CLASSROOM.
THE FESTIVAL ATMOSPHERE WAS GROWING.
NAMETAG: MIKURU
SIGN: YAMATSUCHI MODEL SHOP
AND OUR MOVIE...
PLEASE STOP BY THE YAMATSUCHI MODEL SHOP!!

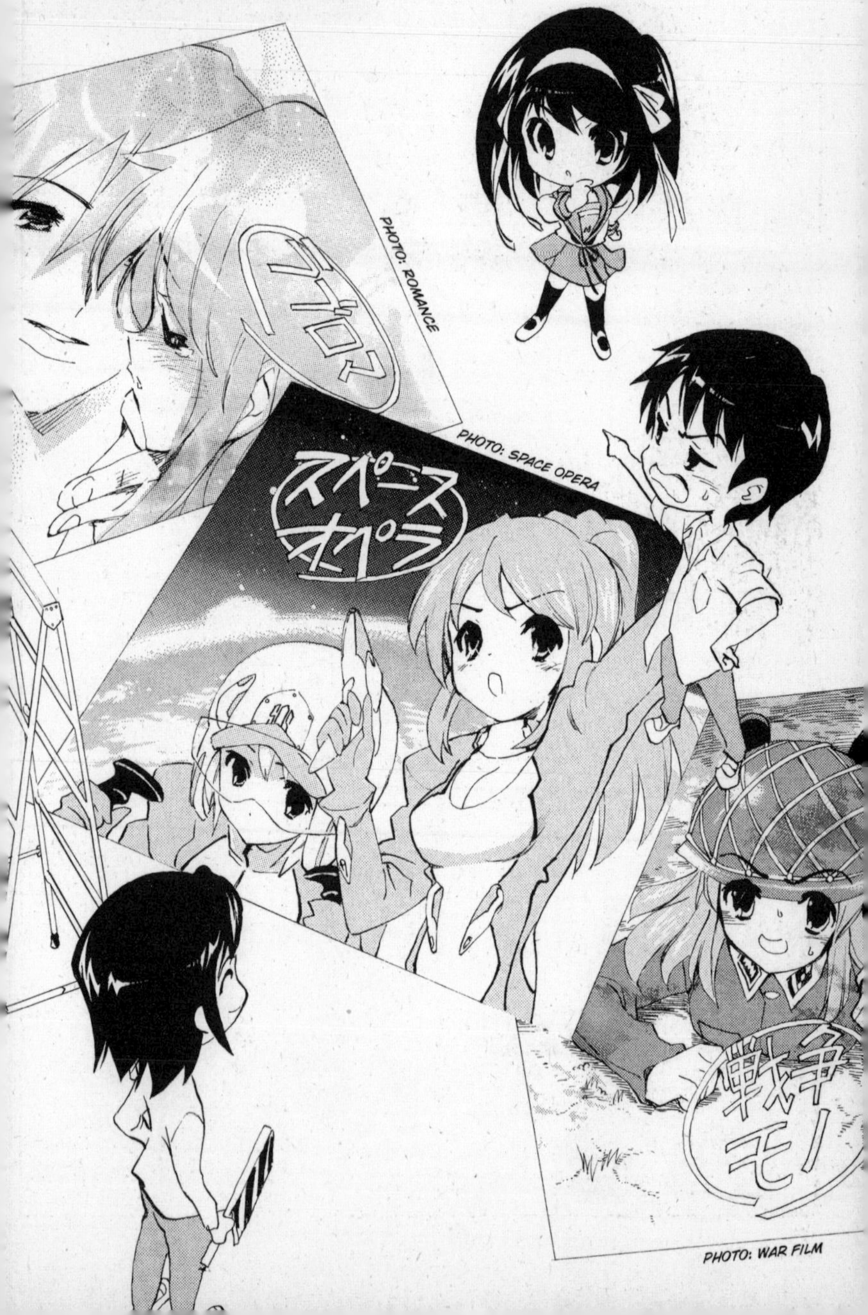
ラブロマ
PHOTO: ROMANCE
スペース オペラ
PHOTO: SPACE OPERA
戦争モノ
PHOTO: WAR FILM

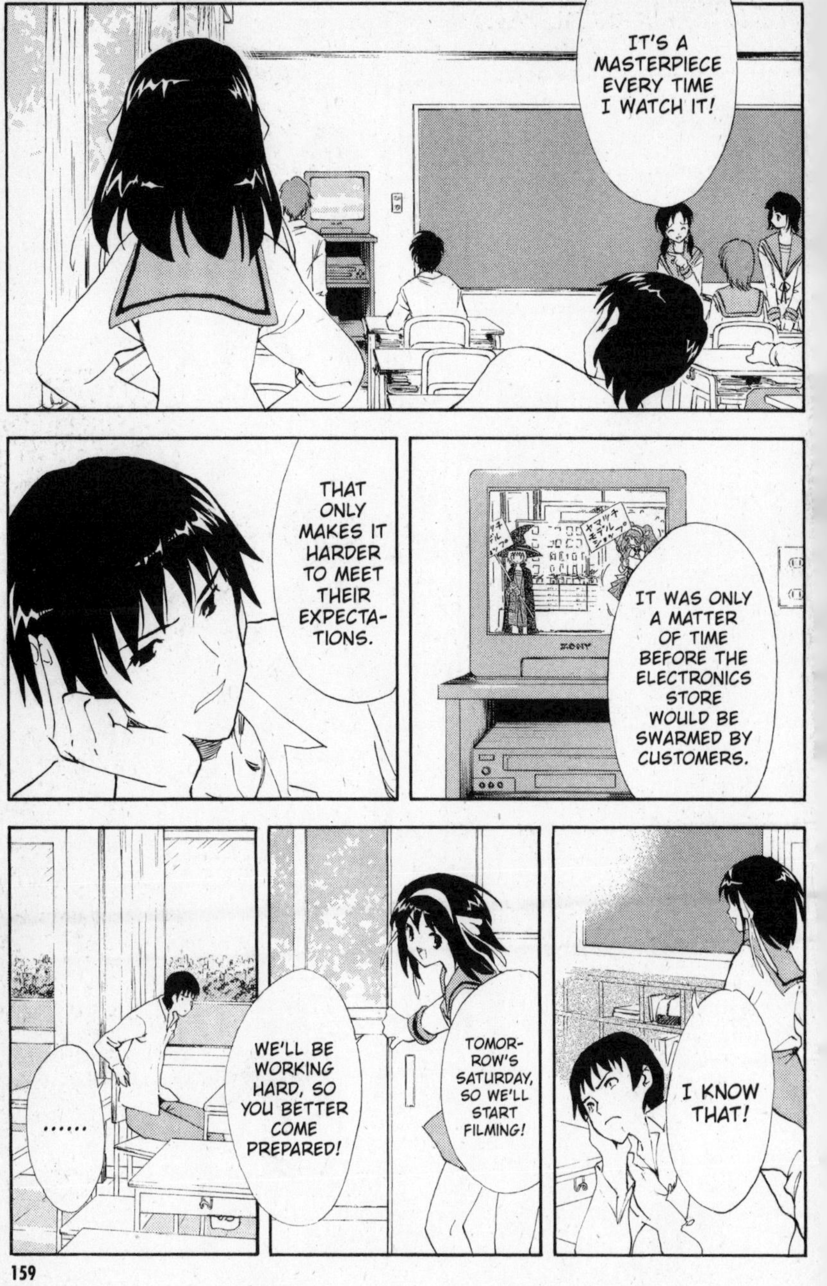
IT'S A MASTERPIECE EVERY TIME I WATCH IT!
IT WAS ONLY A MATTER OF TIME BEFORE THE ELECTRONICS STORE WOULD BE SWARMED BY CUSTOMERS.
THAT ONLY MAKES IT HARDER TO MEET THEIR EXPECTATIONS.
I KNOW THAT!
TOMORROW'S SATURDAY, SO WE'LL START FILMING!
WE'LL BE WORKING HARD, SO YOU BETTER COME PREPARED!
......

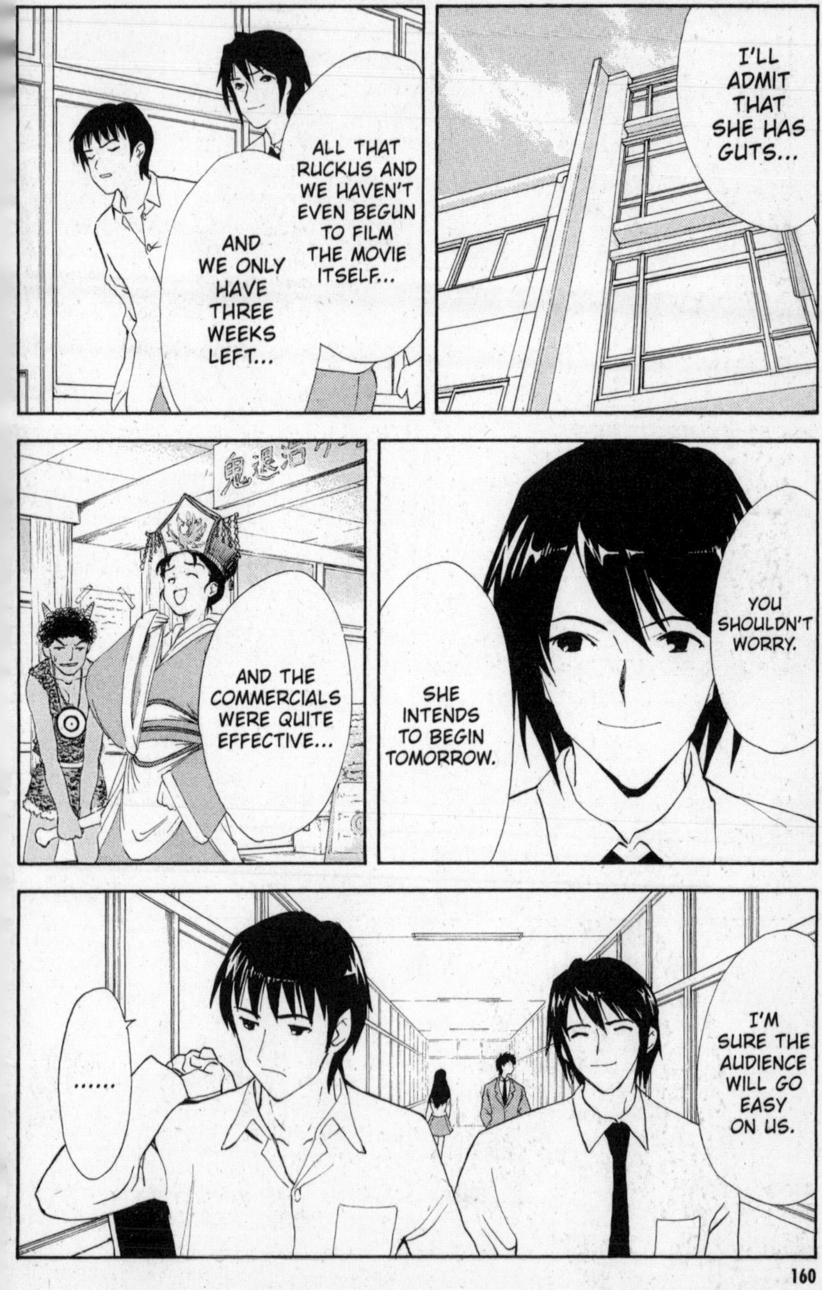
I'LL ADMIT THAT SHE HAS GUTS...
ALL THAT RUCKUS AND WE HAVEN'T EVEN BEGUN TO FILM THE MOVIE ITSELF...
AND WE ONLY HAVE THREE WEEKS LEFT...
YOU SHOULDN'T WORRY.
SHE INTENDS TO BEGIN TOMORROW.
鬼退治
AND THE COMMERCIALS WERE QUITE EFFECTIVE...
I'M SURE THE AUDIENCE WILL GO EASY ON US.
......

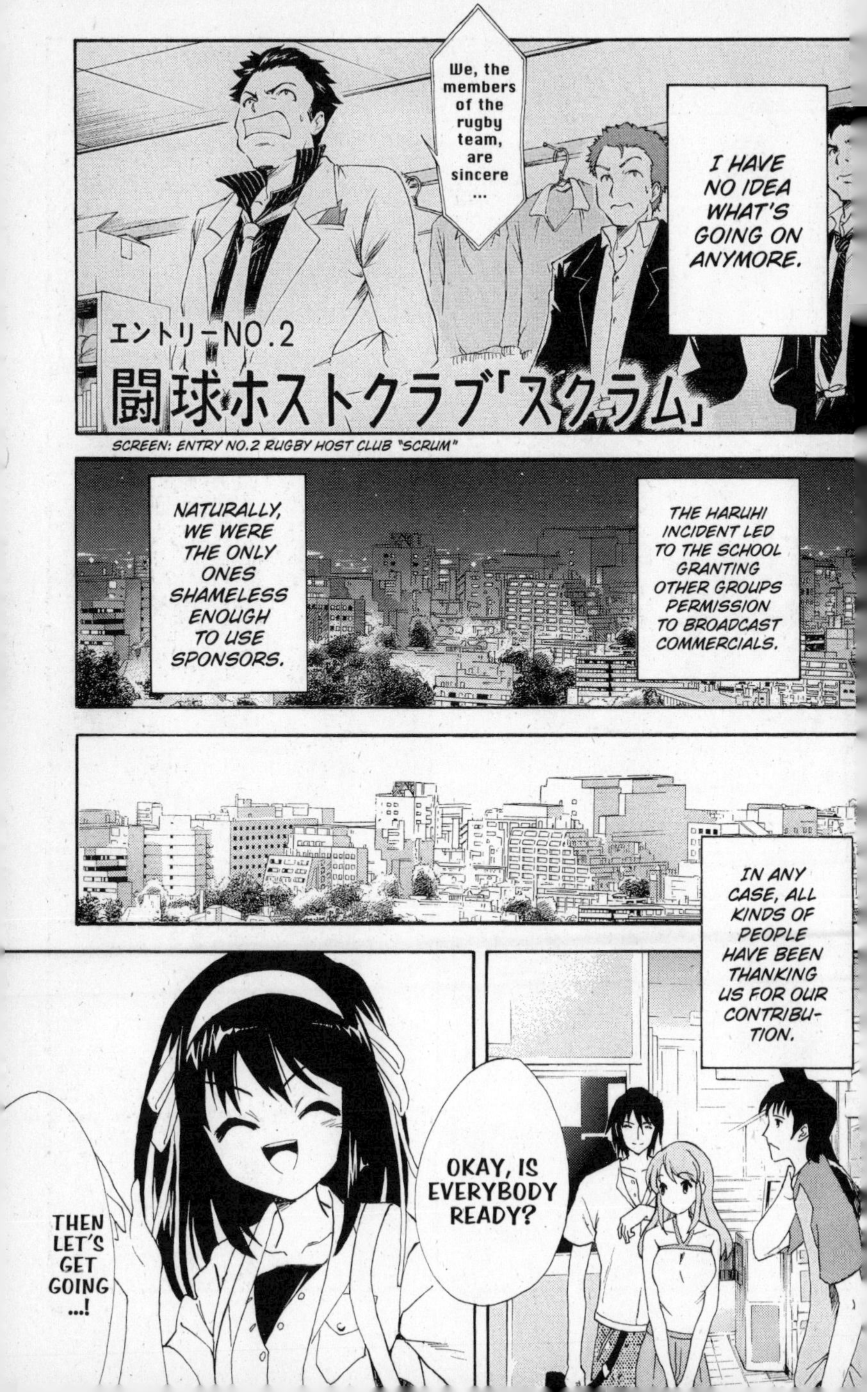
We, the members of the rugby team, are sincere ...
I HAVE NO IDEA WHAT'S GOING ON ANYMORE.
エントリーNO.2
闘球ホストクラブ「スクラム」
SCREEN: ENTRY NO.2 RUGBY HOST CLUB "SCRUM"
THE HARUHI INCIDENT LED TO THE SCHOOL GRANTING OTHER GROUPS PERMISSION TO BROADCAST COMMERCIALS.
NATURALLY, WE WERE THE ONLY ONES SHAMELESS ENOUGH TO USE SPONSORS.
IN ANY CASE, ALL KINDS OF PEOPLE HAVE BEEN THANKING US FOR OUR CONTRIBU-TION.
OKAY, IS EVERYBODY READY?
THEN LET'S GET GOING ...!

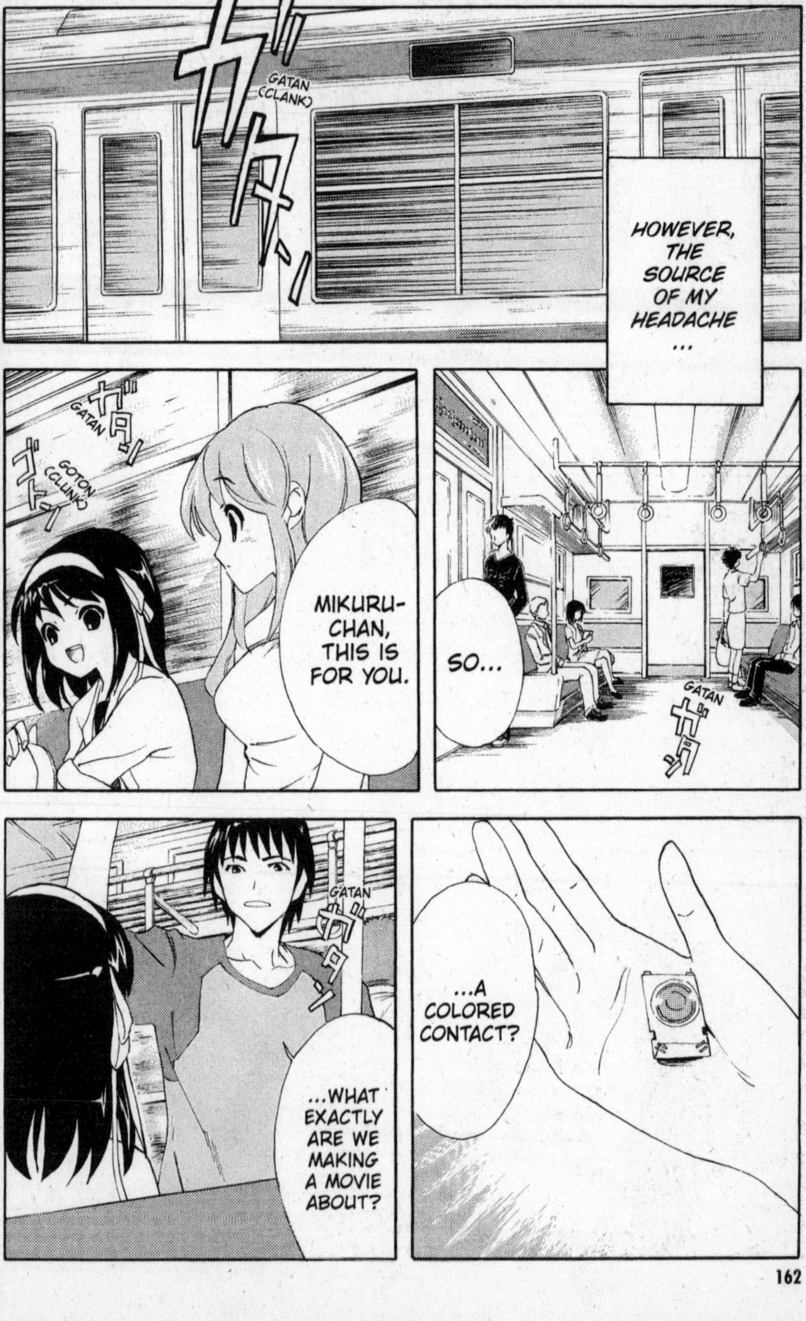
GATAN (CLANK)
HOWEVER, THE SOURCE OF MY HEADACHE ...
SO...
GATAN
GATAN
GOTON (CLUNK)
MIKURU-CHAN, THIS IS FOR YOU.
...A COLORED CONTACT?
GATAN
...WHAT EXACTLY ARE WE MAKING A MOVIE ABOUT?

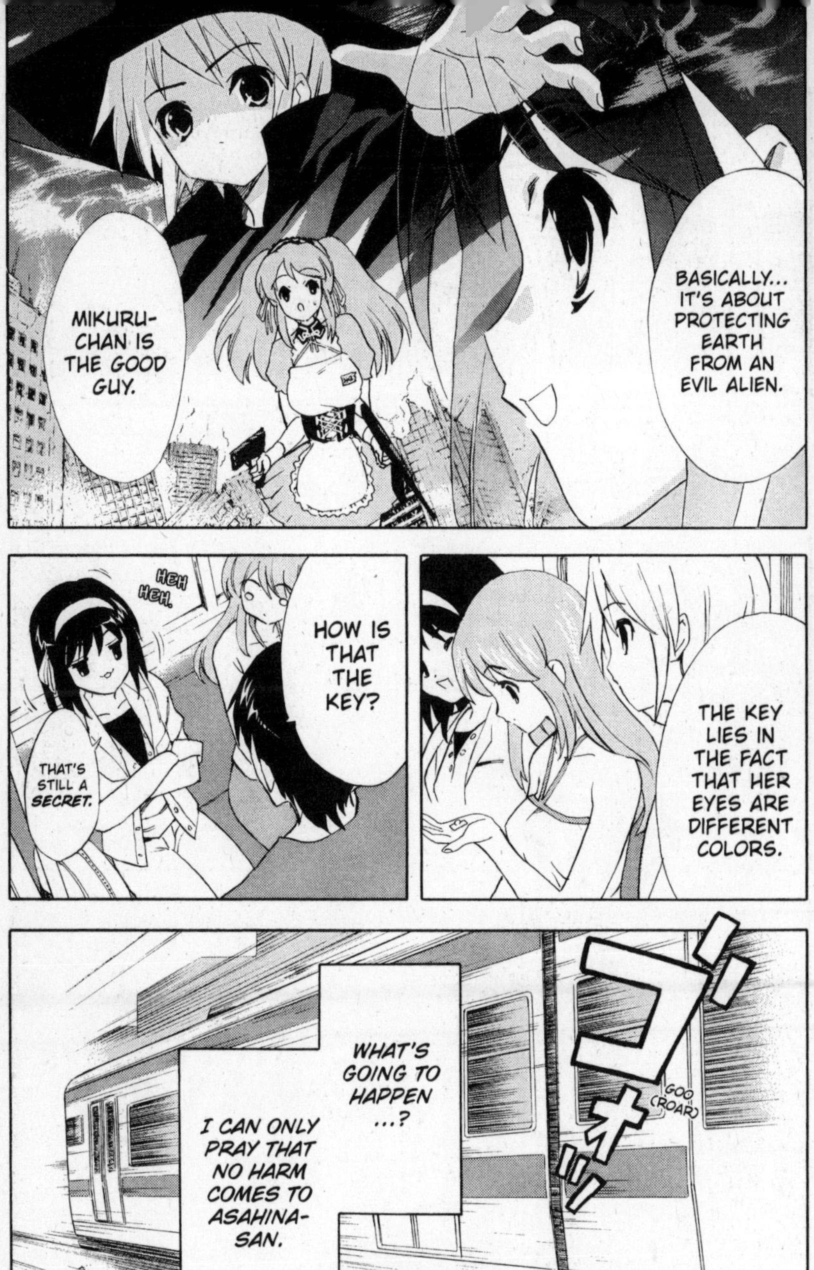
BASICALLY... IT'S ABOUT PROTECTING EARTH FROM AN EVIL ALIEN.
MIKURU-CHAN IS THE GOOD GUY.
THE KEY LIES IN THE FACT THAT HER EYES ARE DIFFERENT COLORS.
HOW IS THAT THE KEY?
HEH HEH.
THAT'S STILL A SECRET.
GOO (ROAR)
WHAT'S GOING TO HAPPEN ...?
I CAN ONLY PRAY THAT NO HARM COMES TO ASAHINA-SAN.

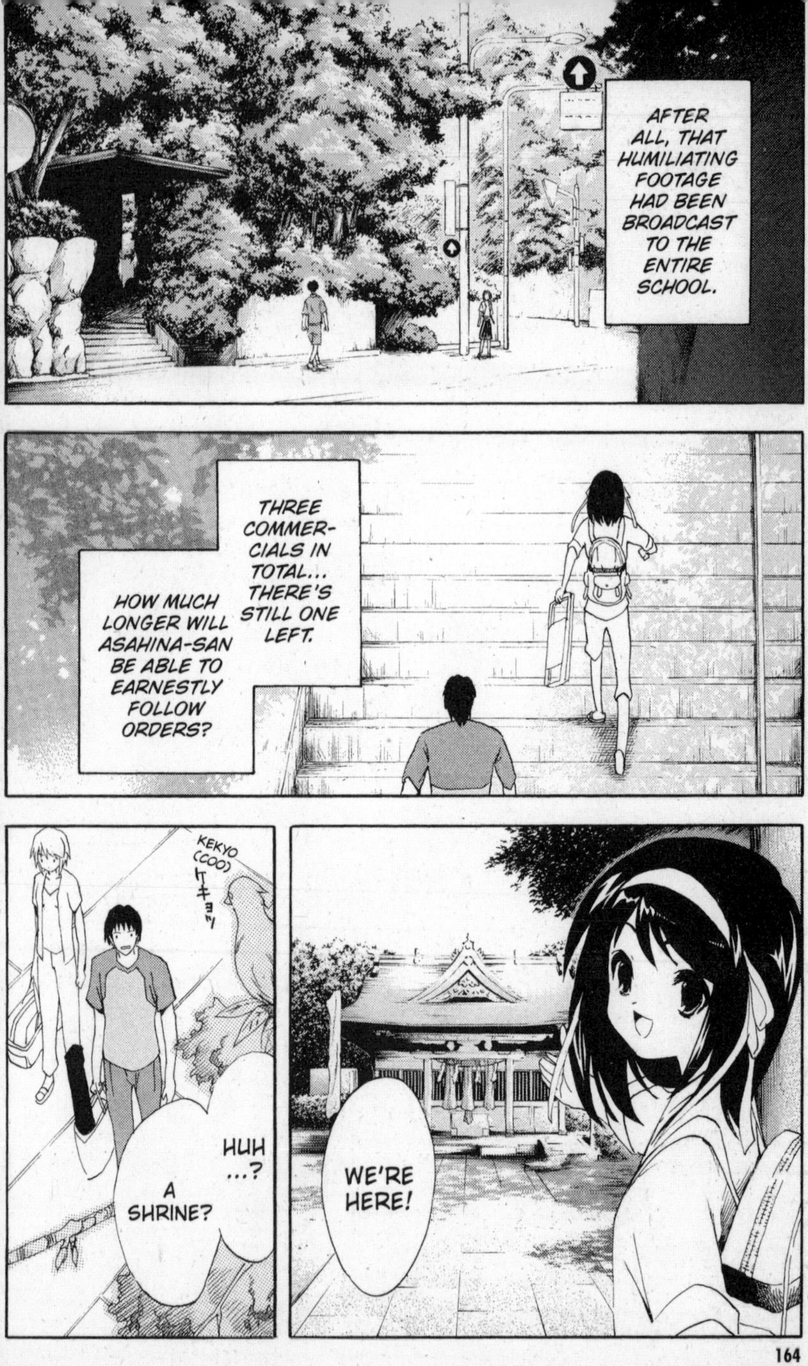
AFTER ALL, THAT HUMILIATING FOOTAGE HAD BEEN BROADCAST TO THE ENTIRE SCHOOL.
THREE COMMERCIALS IN TOTAL... THERE'S STILL ONE LEFT.
HOW MUCH LONGER WILL ASAHINA-SAN BE ABLE TO EARNESTLY FOLLOW ORDERS?
WE'RE HERE!
KEKYO (COO)
ケキョッ
HUH...?
A SHRINE?

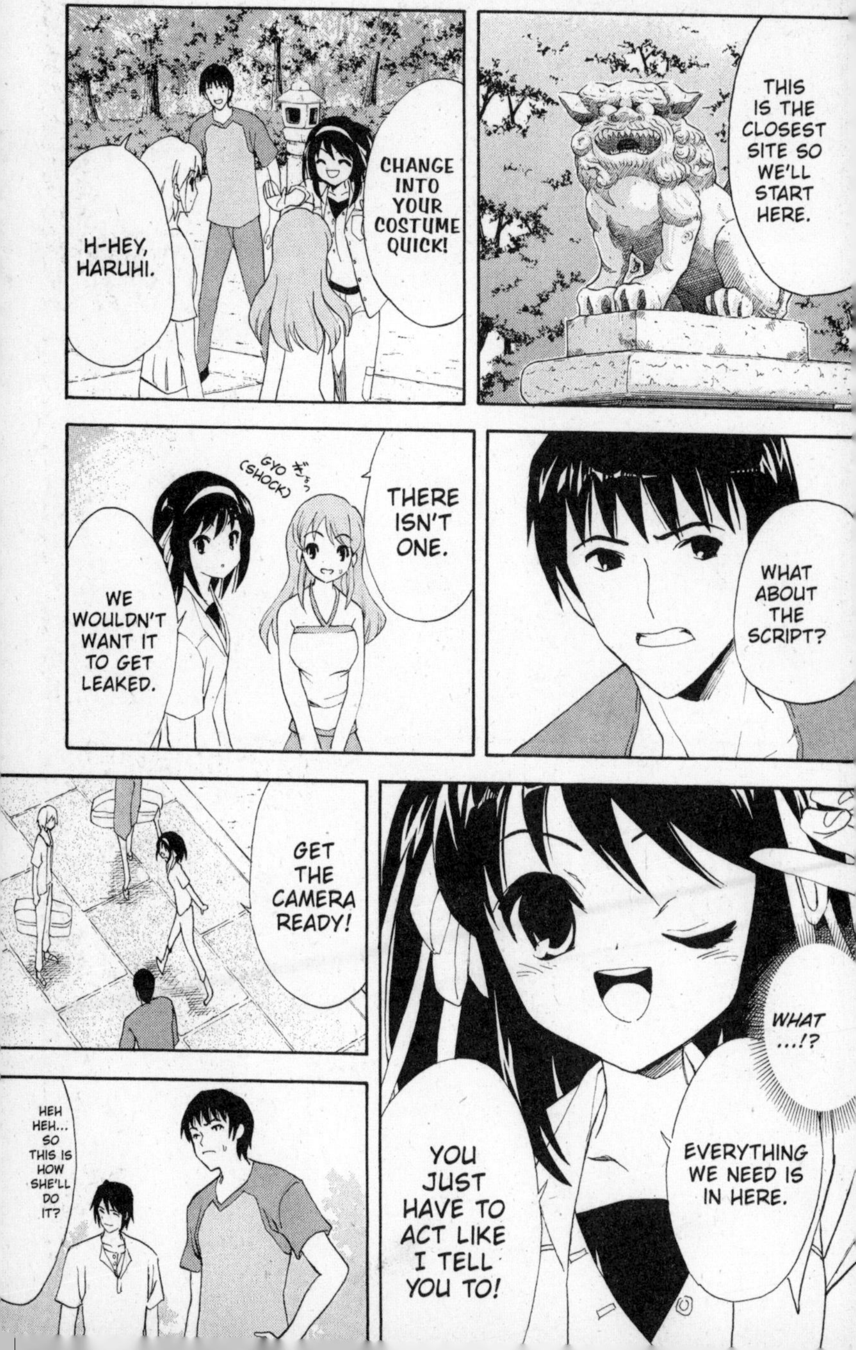
THIS IS THE CLOSEST SITE SO WE'LL START HERE.
CHANGE INTO YOUR COSTUME QUICK!
H-HEY, HARUHI.
WHAT ABOUT THE SCRIPT?
THERE ISN'T ONE.
GYO ぎょっ (SHOCK)
WE WOULDN'T WANT IT TO GET LEAKED.
WHAT ...!?
EVERYTHING WE NEED IS IN HERE.
YOU JUST HAVE TO ACT LIKE I TELL YOU TO!
GET THE CAMERA READY!
HEH HEH... SO THIS IS HOW SHE'LL DO IT?

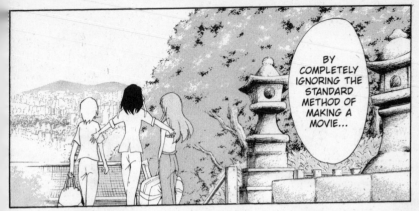

BY COMPLETELY IGNORING THE STANDARD METHOD OF MAKING A MOVIE...
THOUGH IT MAY WORK OUT BETTER THIS WAY.
BOLD IDEAS LEAD TO GREAT MASTER-PIECES.
DO WE HAVE TIME TO BE STANDING AROUND CHATTING?
THE COM-MERCIAL'S BRAIN-WASHING EFFECT HAS GUARANTEED US AN AUDIENCE.
WE'RE GOING TO BE LAUGHING-STOCKS.
?
ARE YOU SURE ABOUT THAT?

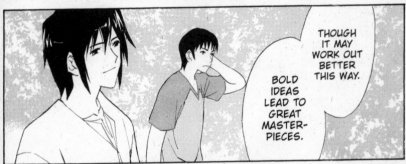

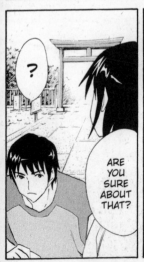

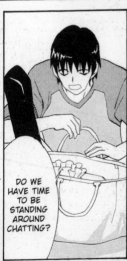

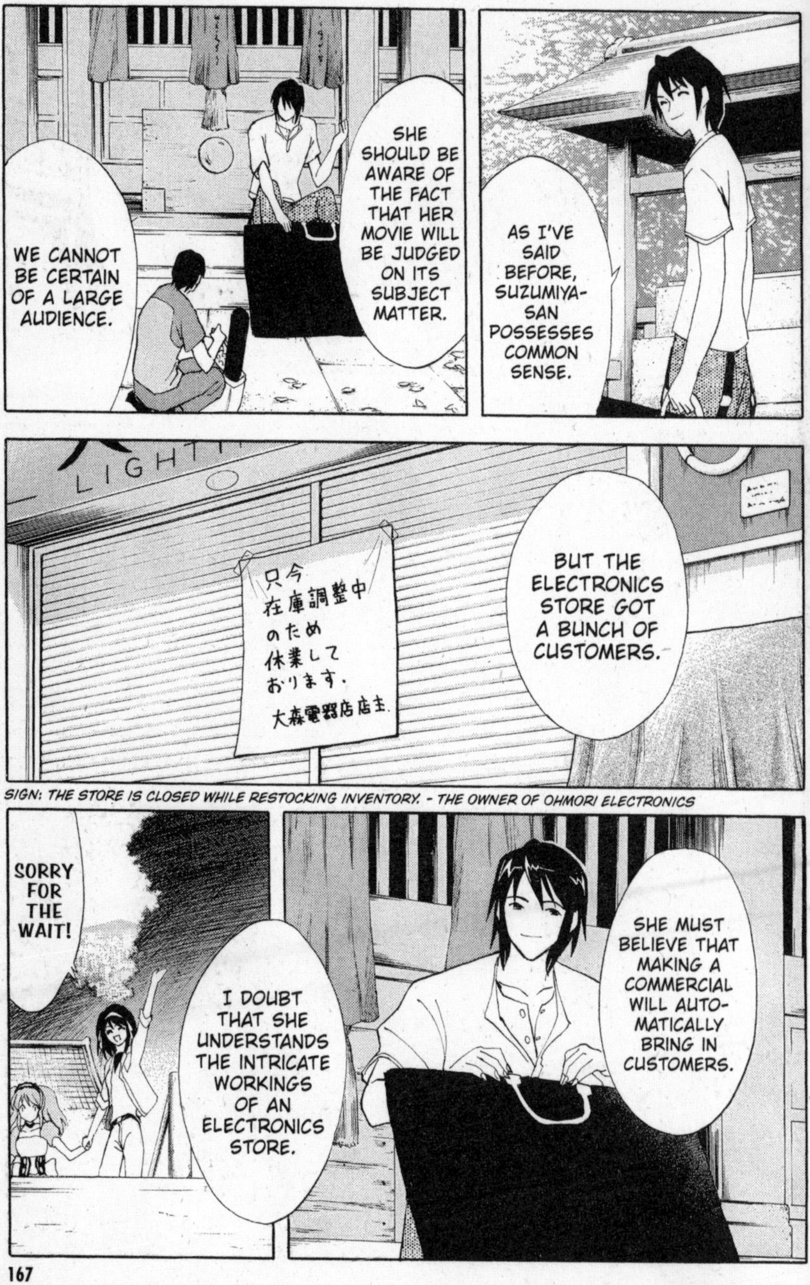
AS I'VE SAID BEFORE, SUZUMIYA-SAN POSSESSES COMMON SENSE.
SHE SHOULD BE AWARE OF THE FACT THAT HER MOVIE WILL BE JUDGED ON ITS SUBJECT MATTER.
WE CANNOT BE CERTAIN OF A LARGE AUDIENCE.
BUT THE ELECTRONICS STORE GOT A BUNCH OF CUSTOMERS.
只今
在庫調整中
のため
休業して
おります。
大森電器店店主
SIGN: THE STORE IS CLOSED WHILE RESTOCKING INVENTORY. - THE OWNER OF OHMORI ELECTRONICS
SHE MUST BELIEVE THAT MAKING A COMMERCIAL WILL AUTO-MATICALLY BRING IN CUSTOMERS.
I DOUBT THAT SHE UNDERSTANDS THE INTRICATE WORKINGS OF AN ELECTRONICS STORE.
SORRY FOR THE WAIT!

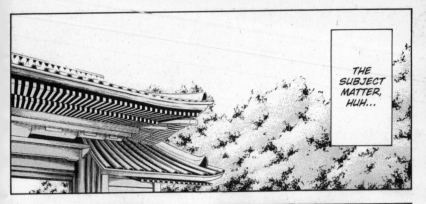

THE SUBJECT MATTER, HUH...
LET'S GO CATCH A CAT.
I'D PREFER A **BLACK** ONE.
CAT?
ONE THAT FITS THE IMAGE OF AN EVIL WITCH'S FAMILIAR.
WE'LL USE IT WHEN YUKI SHOWS UP!

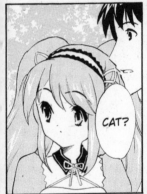

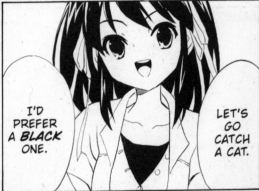

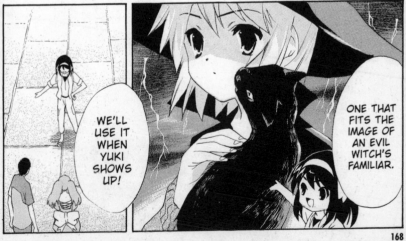

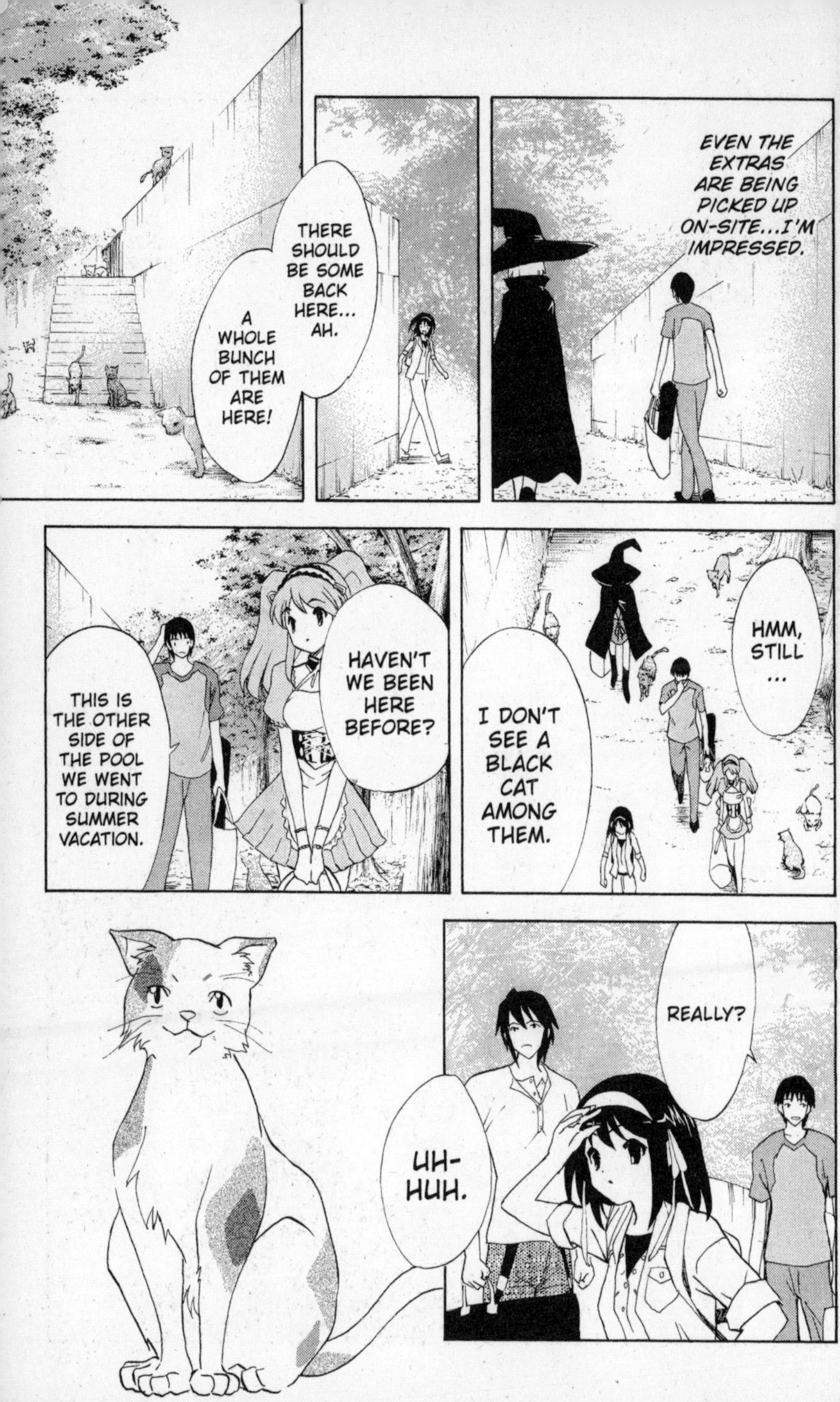
EVEN THE EXTRAS ARE BEING PICKED UP ON-SITE...I'M IMPRESSED.
THERE SHOULD BE SOME BACK HERE... AH.
A WHOLE BUNCH OF THEM ARE HERE!
HMM, STILL ...
I DON'T SEE A BLACK CAT AMONG THEM.
HAVEN'T WE BEEN HERE BEFORE?
THIS IS THE OTHER SIDE OF THE POOL WE WENT TO DURING SUMMER VACATION.
REALLY?
UH-HUH.

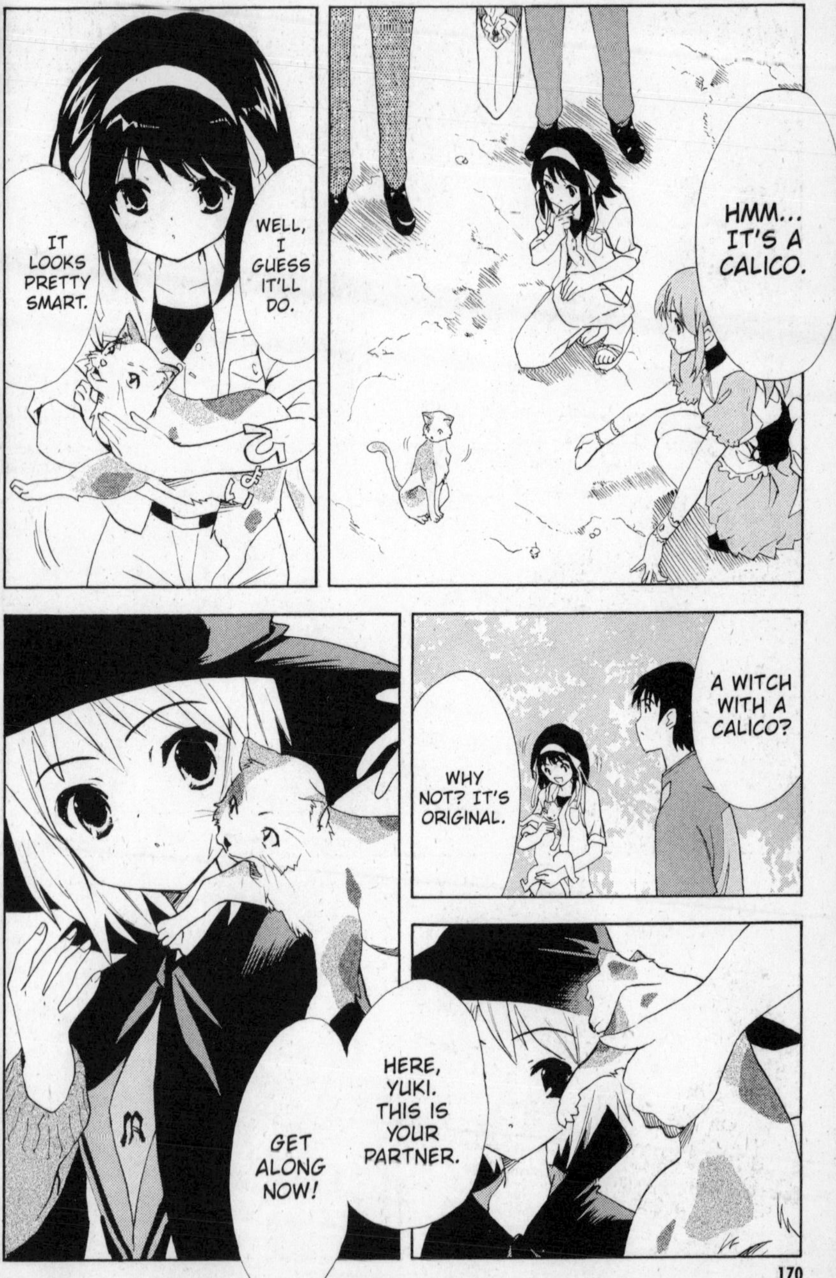
HMM... IT'S A CALICO.
WELL, I GUESS IT'LL DO.
IT LOOKS PRETTY SMART.
A WITCH WITH A CALICO?
WHY NOT? IT'S ORIGINAL.
HERE, YUKI. THIS IS YOUR PARTNER.
GET ALONG NOW!

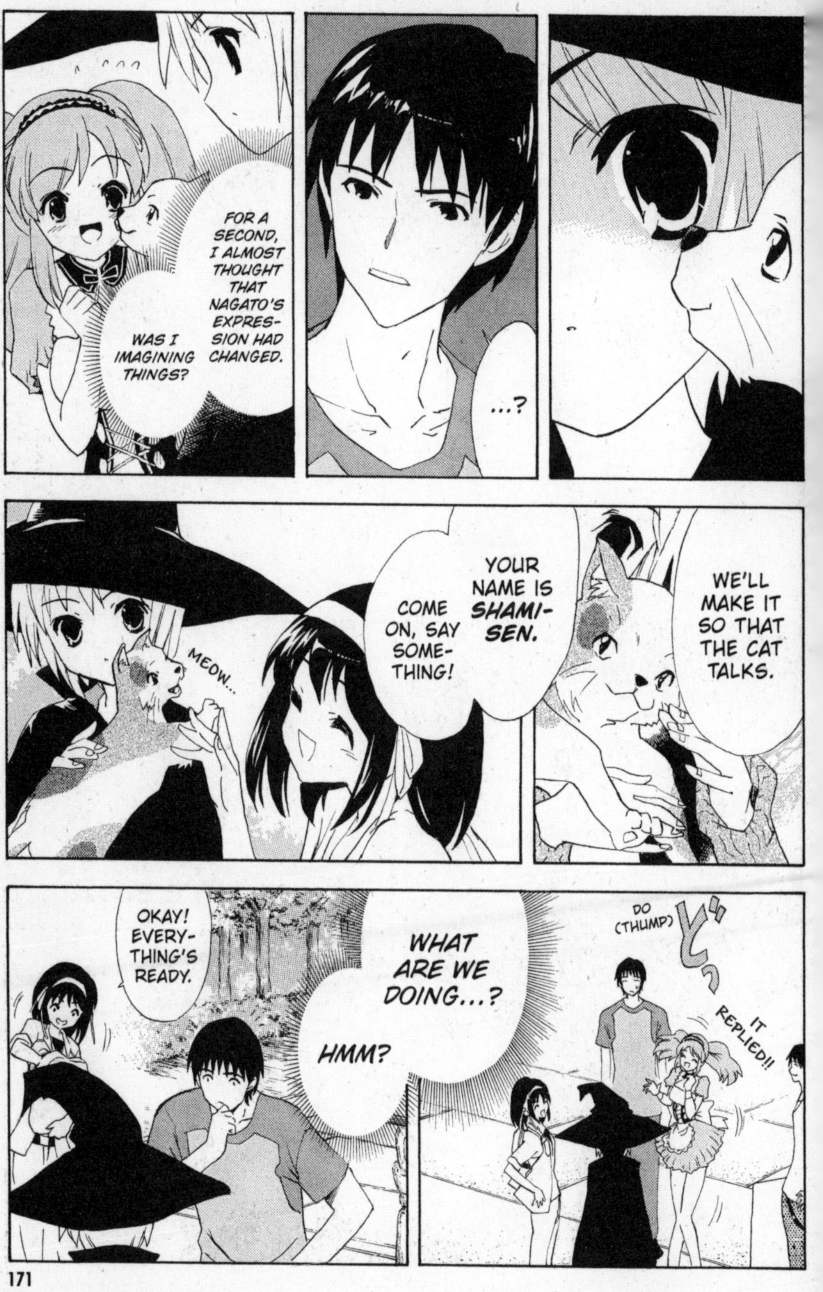
...?
FOR A SECOND, I ALMOST THOUGHT THAT NAGATO'S EXPRES-SION HAD CHANGED.
WAS I IMAGINING THINGS?
WE'LL MAKE IT SO THAT THE CAT TALKS.
YOUR NAME IS SHAMI-SEN.
COME ON, SAY SOME-THING!
MEOW...
DO (THUMP)
IT REPLIED!!
WHAT ARE WE DOING...?
HMM?
OKAY! EVERY-THING'S READY.

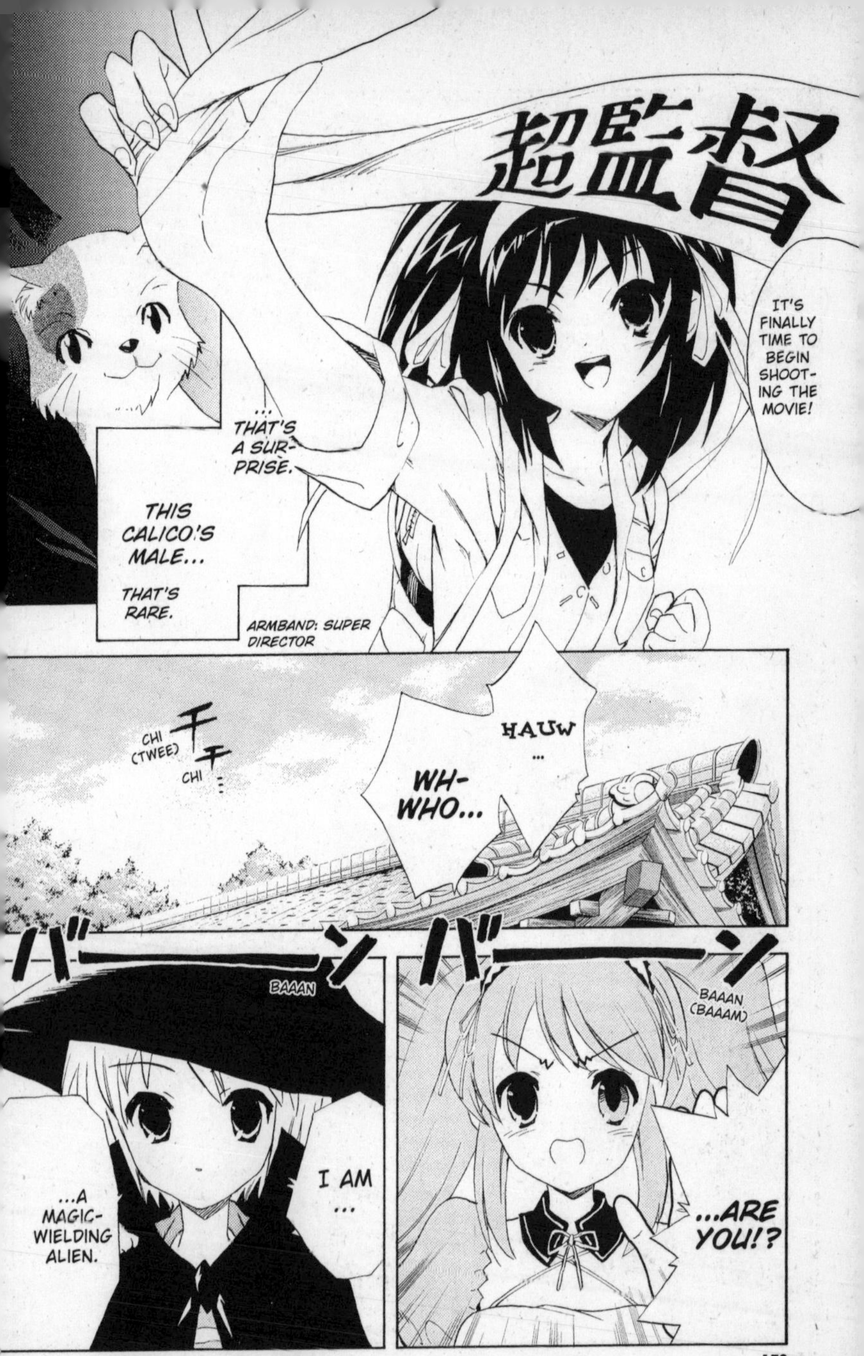
IT'S FINALLY TIME TO BEGIN SHOOTING THE MOVIE!
超監督
...THAT'S A SURPRISE.
THIS CALICO'S MALE...
THAT'S RARE.
ARMBAND: SUPER DIRECTOR
HAUW...
WH-WHO...
チ CHI (TWEE)
チ CHI
バーン
BAAAN (BAAAM)
...ARE YOU!?
バーン
BAAAN
I AM...
...A MAGIC-WIELDING ALIEN.

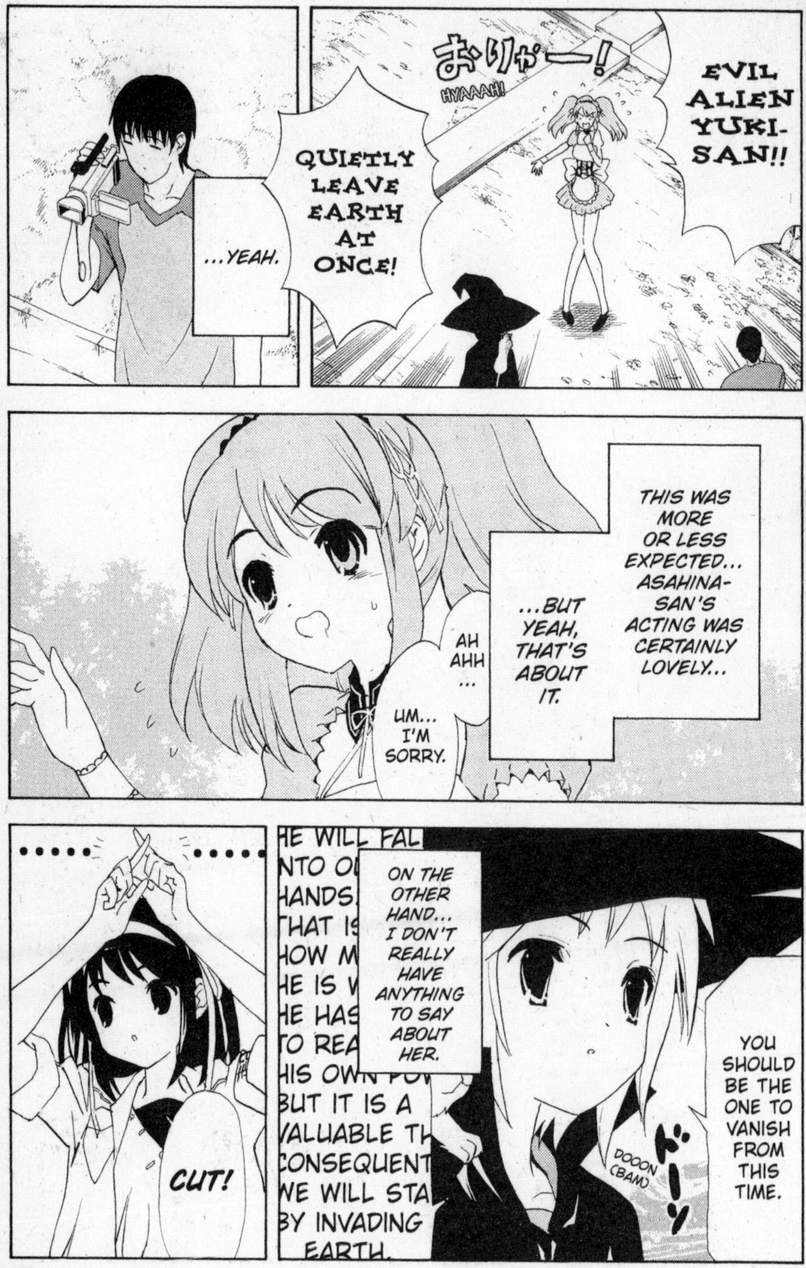

おりゃー!
HYAAAH!
EVIL ALIEN YUKI-SAN!!
QUIETLY LEAVE EARTH AT ONCE!
...YEAH.
THIS WAS MORE OR LESS EXPECTED... ASAHINA-SAN'S ACTING WAS CERTAINLY LOVELY...
...BUT YEAH, THAT'S ABOUT IT.
AH AHH ...
UM... I'M SORRY.
YOU SHOULD BE THE ONE TO VANISH FROM THIS TIME.
ドーッ
DOOON (BAM)
ON THE OTHER HAND... I DON'T REALLY HAVE ANYTHING TO SAY ABOUT HER.
.....
.....
CUT!

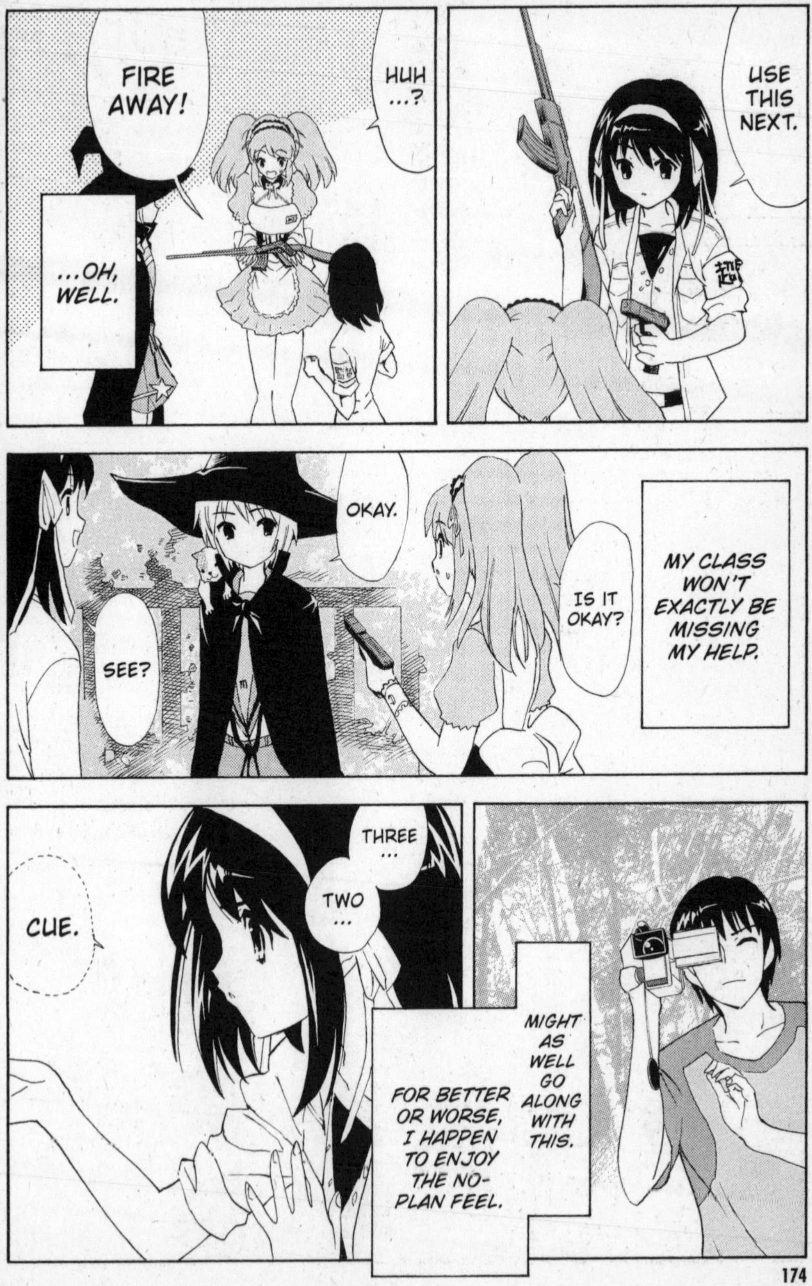
USE THIS NEXT.
HUH ...?
FIRE AWAY!
...OH, WELL.
MY CLASS WON'T EXACTLY BE MISSING MY HELP.
IS IT OKAY?
OKAY.
SEE?
MIGHT AS WELL GO ALONG WITH THIS.
FOR BETTER OR WORSE, I HAPPEN TO ENJOY THE NO-PLAN FEEL.
THREE ...
TWO ...
CUE.

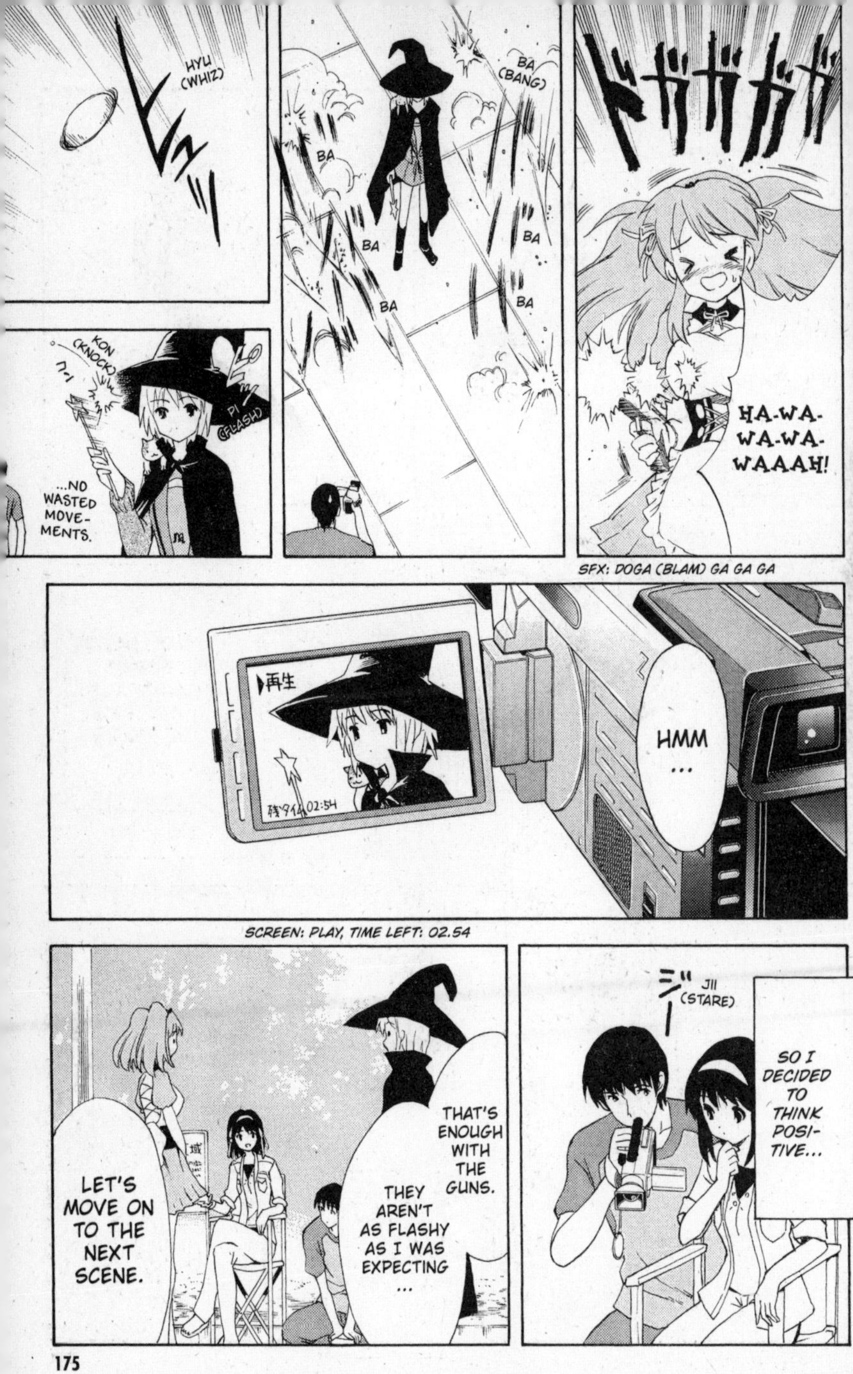
ドガガガガ
HA-WA-WA-WA-WAAAH!
SFX: DOGA (BLAM) GA GA GA
BA (BANG)
BA
BA
BA
BA
BA
HYU (WHIZ)
ヒュッ
KON (KNOCK)
コッ
PI (FLASH)
...NO WASTED MOVEMENTS.
HMM ...
▶再生
SCREEN: PLAY, TIME LEFT: 02.54
JII (STARE)
ジー
SO I DECIDED TO THINK POSITIVE...
THAT'S ENOUGH WITH THE GUNS.
THEY AREN'T AS FLASHY AS I WAS EXPECTING ...
LET'S MOVE ON TO THE NEXT SCENE.

YUKI'S COUNTER-ATTACK!
USE MAGIC TO WRECK MIKURU-CHAN!
NO NEED TO HOLD BACK.
チラ
CHIRA (GLANCE)
......
DON'T ACTUALLY DO IT.
ゾ
ZO (SHIVER)
COME ON, YUKI. GIVE IT TO HER GOOD.
THREE...
TWO...
CUE!

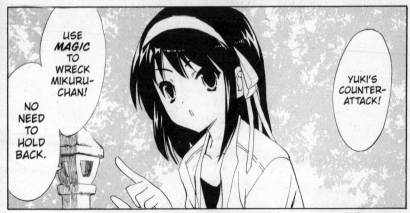

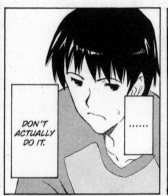

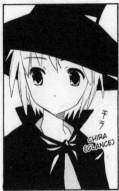

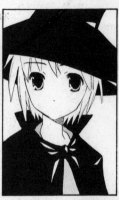

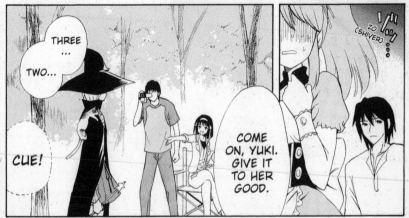

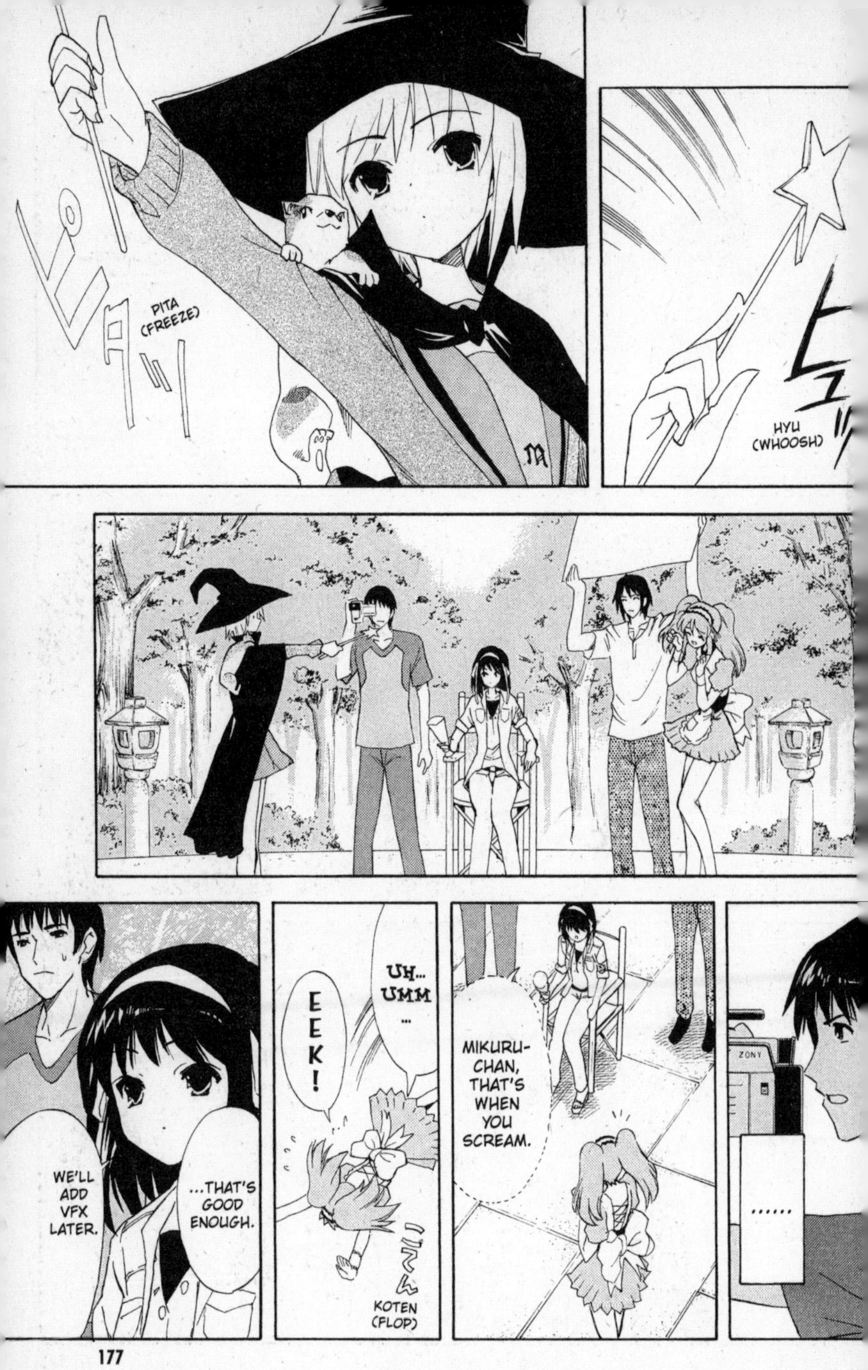
ヒュッ
HYU (WHOOSH)
ピタッ
PITA (FREEZE)
......
ZONY
MIKURU-CHAN, THAT'S WHEN YOU SCREAM.
UH... UMM ...
EEK!
こてん
KOTEN (FLOP)
...THAT'S GOOD ENOUGH.
WE'LL ADD VFX LATER.

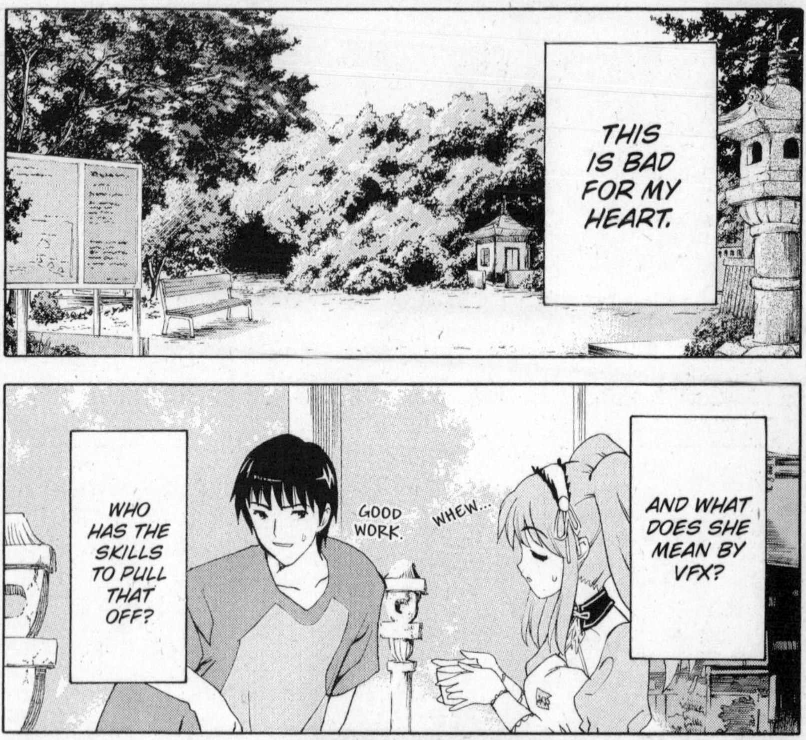
THIS IS BAD FOR MY HEART.
AND WHAT DOES SHE MEAN BY VFX?
WHEW...
GOOD WORK.
WHO HAS THE SKILLS TO PULL THAT OFF?

*VFX (VISUAL EFFECTS): SPECIAL EFFECTS THAT ARE ADDED INTO THE VIDEO AFTERWARD.

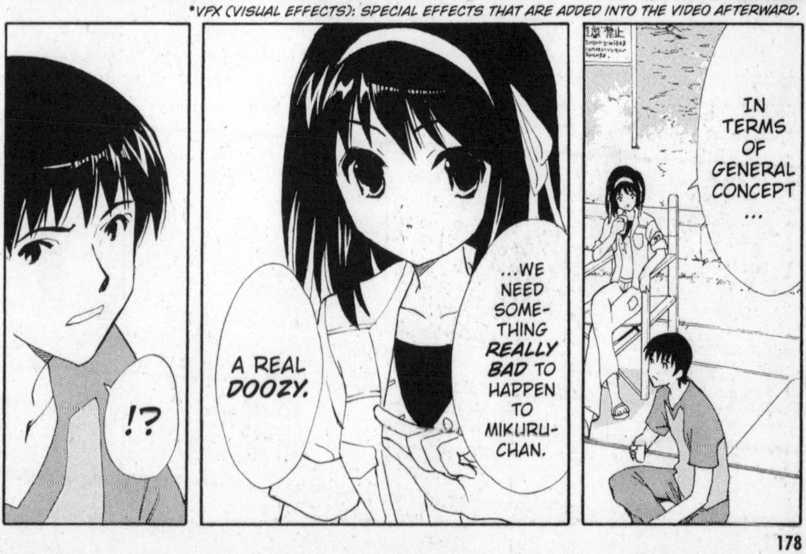
IN TERMS OF GENERAL CONCEPT...
...WE NEED SOMETHING REALLY BAD TO HAPPEN TO MIKURU-CHAN.
A REAL DOOZY.
!?

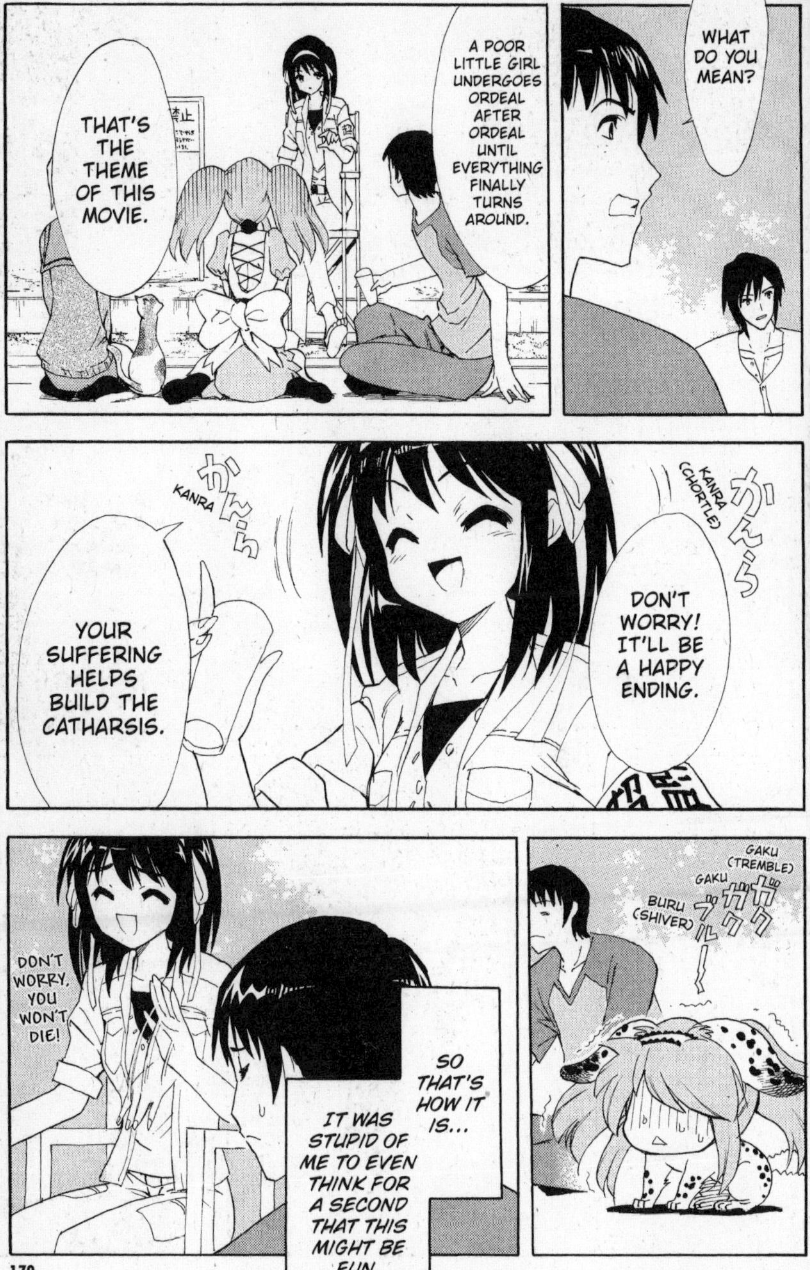
WHAT DO YOU MEAN?
A POOR LITTLE GIRL UNDERGOES ORDEAL AFTER ORDEAL UNTIL EVERYTHING FINALLY TURNS AROUND.
THAT'S THE THEME OF THIS MOVIE.
かんら
KANRA (CHORTLE)
DON'T WORRY! IT'LL BE A HAPPY ENDING.
かんら
KANRA
YOUR SUFFERING HELPS BUILD THE CATHARSIS.
ガクガク
GAKU (TREMBLE)
GAKU
ブルー
BURU (SHIVER)
DON'T WORRY, YOU WON'T DIE!
SO THAT'S HOW IT IS...
IT WAS STUPID OF ME TO EVEN THINK FOR A SECOND THAT THIS MIGHT BE FUN.

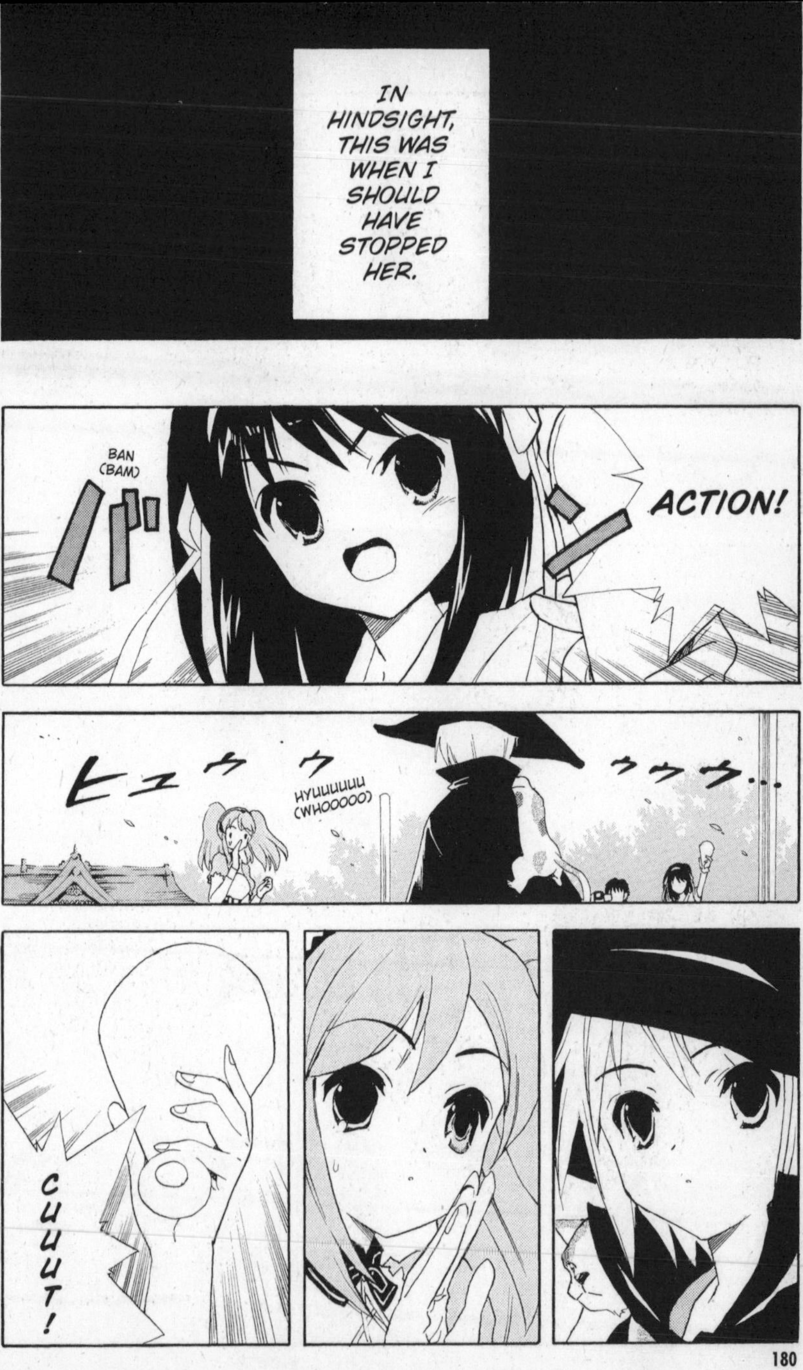

IN HINDSIGHT, THIS WAS WHEN I SHOULD HAVE STOPPED HER.
BAN (BAM)
ACTION!
ヒュウウ ウウウ...
HYUUUUUU (WHOOOOO)
CUUUUT!

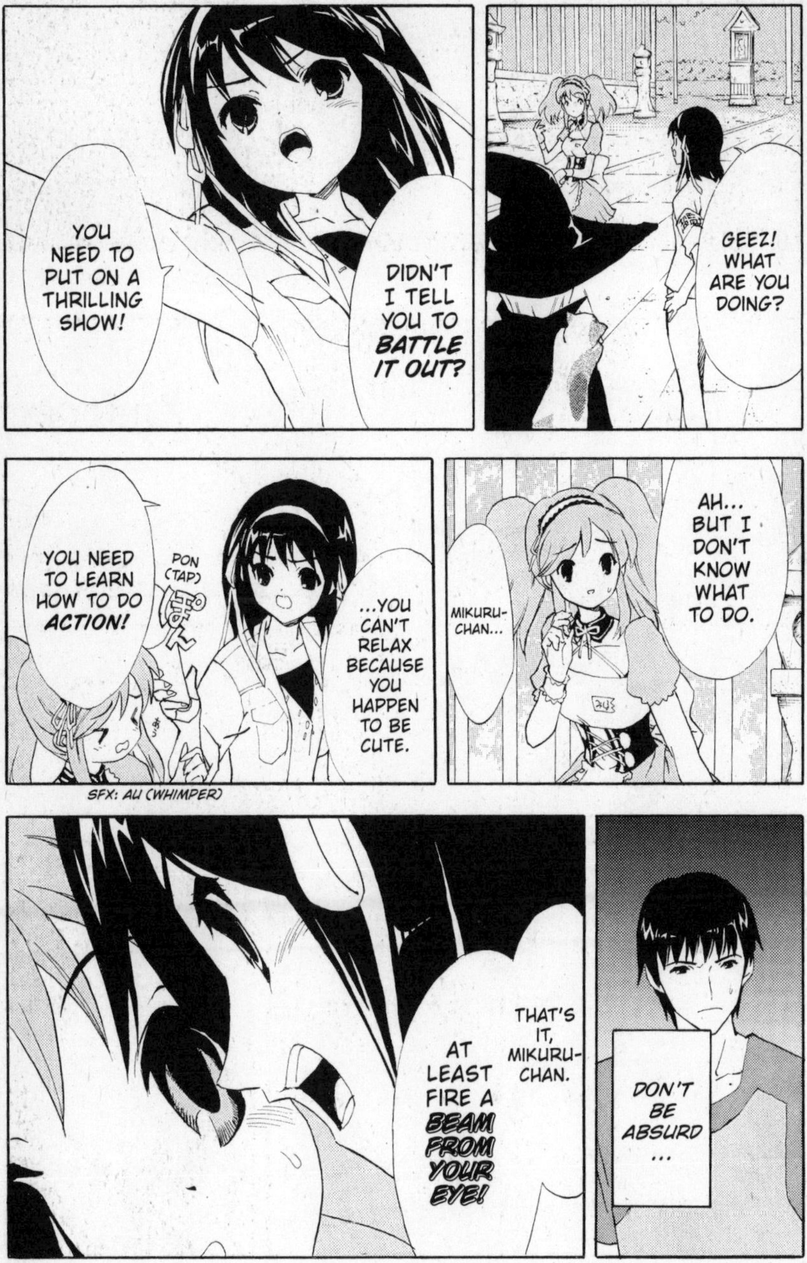
GEEZ! WHAT ARE YOU DOING?
DIDN'T I TELL YOU TO BATTLE IT OUT?
YOU NEED TO PUT ON A THRILLING SHOW!
AH... BUT I DON'T KNOW WHAT TO DO.
MIKURU-CHAN...
...YOU CAN'T RELAX BECAUSE YOU HAPPEN TO BE CUTE.
PON (TAP)
YOU NEED TO LEARN HOW TO DO ACTION!
SFX: AU (WHIMPER)
DON'T BE ABSURD...
THAT'S IT, MIKURU-CHAN.
AT LEAST FIRE A BEAM FROM YOUR EYE!

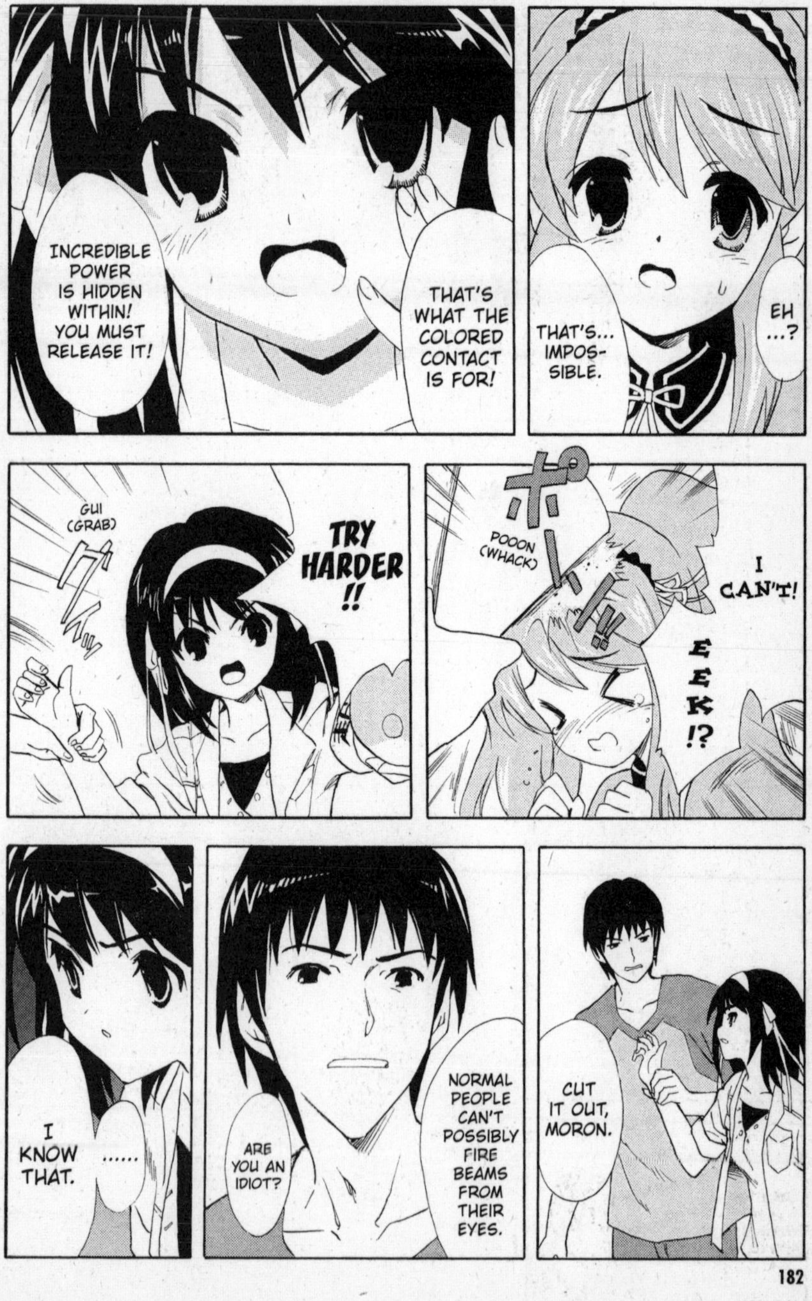

EH ...?
THAT'S... IMPOSSIBLE.
THAT'S WHAT THE COLORED CONTACT IS FOR!
INCREDIBLE POWER IS HIDDEN WITHIN! YOU MUST RELEASE IT!
I CAN'T!
POOON (WHACK)
EEK!?
TRY HARDER!!
GUI (GRAB)
CUT IT OUT, MORON.
NORMAL PEOPLE CAN'T POSSIBLY FIRE BEAMS FROM THEIR EYES.
ARE YOU AN IDIOT?
......
I KNOW THAT.

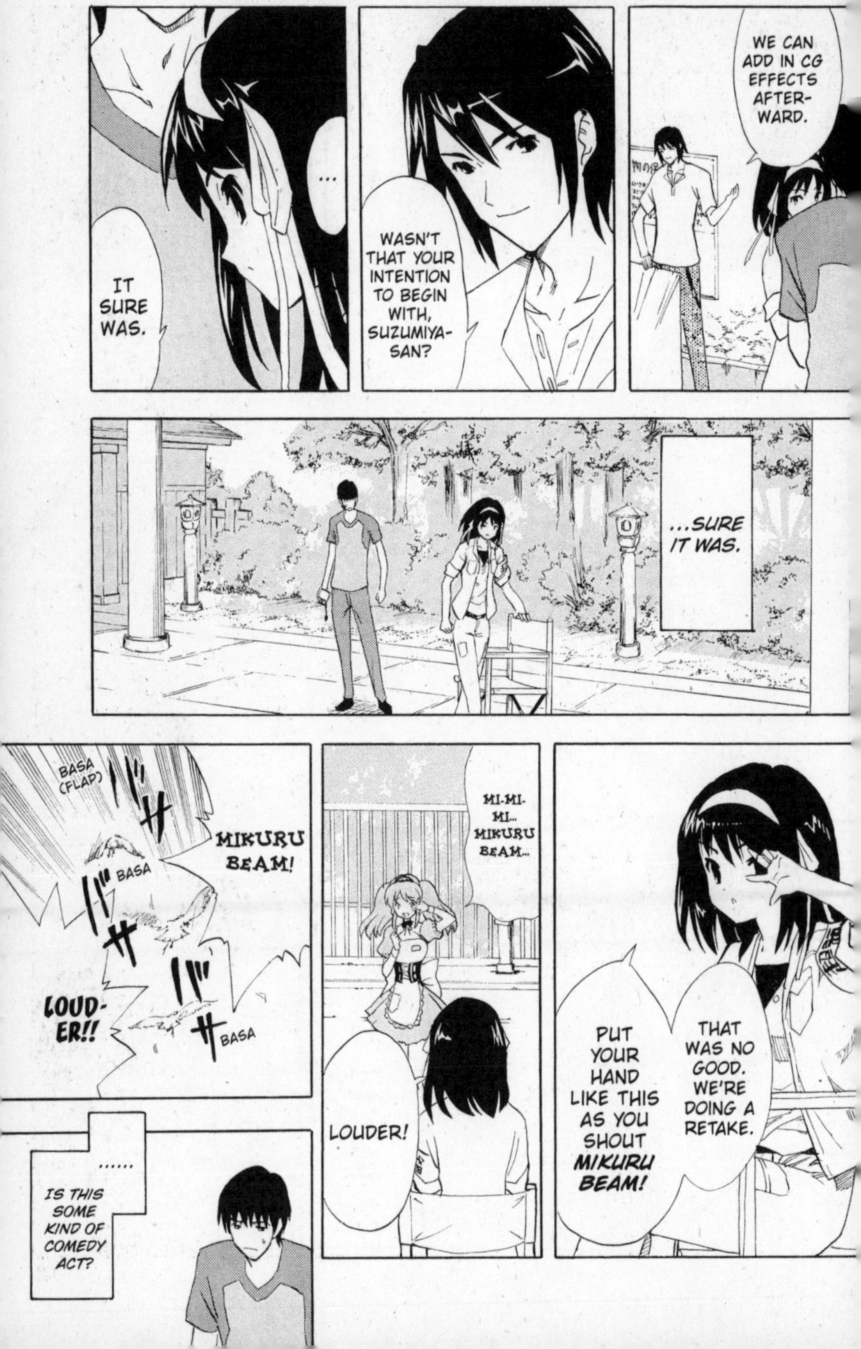
WE CAN ADD IN CG EFFECTS AFTER-WARD.
WASN'T THAT YOUR INTENTION TO BEGIN WITH, SUZUMIYA-SAN?
...
IT SURE WAS.
...SURE IT WAS.
THAT WAS NO GOOD. WE'RE DOING A RETAKE.
PUT YOUR HAND LIKE THIS AS YOU SHOUT *MIKURU BEAM!*
MI-MI-MI... MIKURU BEAM...
LOUDER!
BASA (FLAP)
MIKURU BEAM!
BASA
LOUDER!!
BASA
......
IS THIS SOME KIND OF COMEDY ACT?

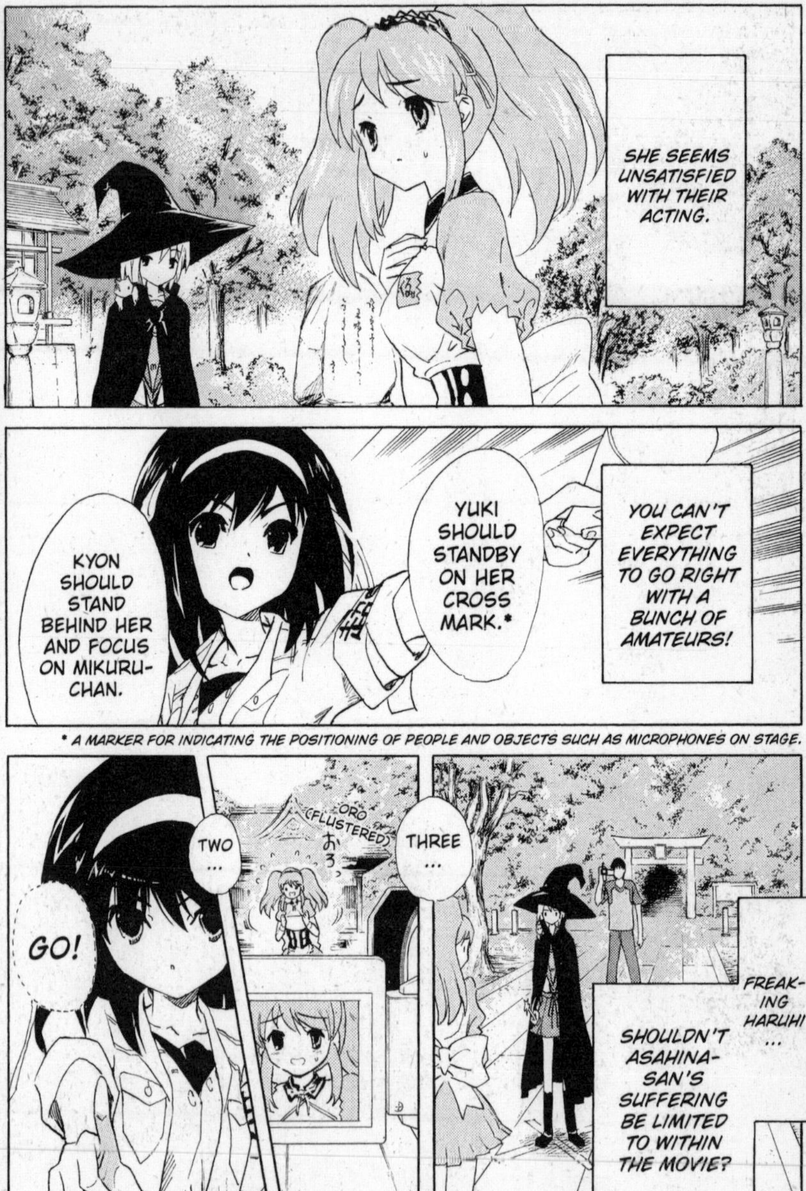
SHE SEEMS UNSATISFIED WITH THEIR ACTING.
YOU CAN'T EXPECT EVERYTHING TO GO RIGHT WITH A BUNCH OF AMATEURS!
YUKI SHOULD STANDBY ON HER CROSS MARK.*
KYON SHOULD STAND BEHIND HER AND FOCUS ON MIKURU-CHAN.
FREAK-ING HARUHI ...
SHOULDN'T ASAHINA-SAN'S SUFFERING BE LIMITED TO WITHIN THE MOVIE?
THREE ...
ORO (FLUSTERED)
TWO ...
GO!

* A MARKER FOR INDICATING THE POSITIONING OF PEOPLE AND OBJECTS SUCH AS MICROPHONES ON STAGE.

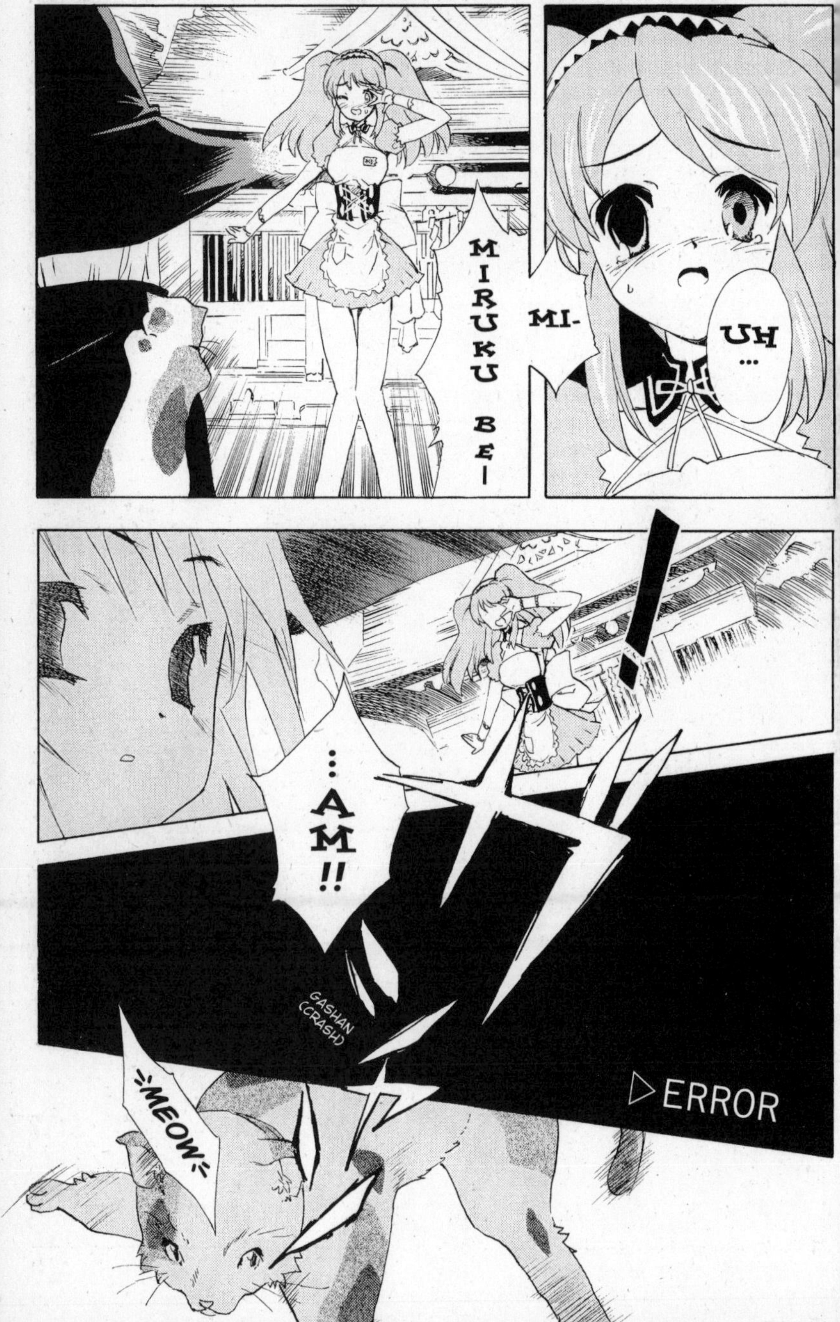
UH ...
MI-
MIRUKU BE-
...AM!!
!
GASHAN (CRASH)
▷ERROR
MEOW

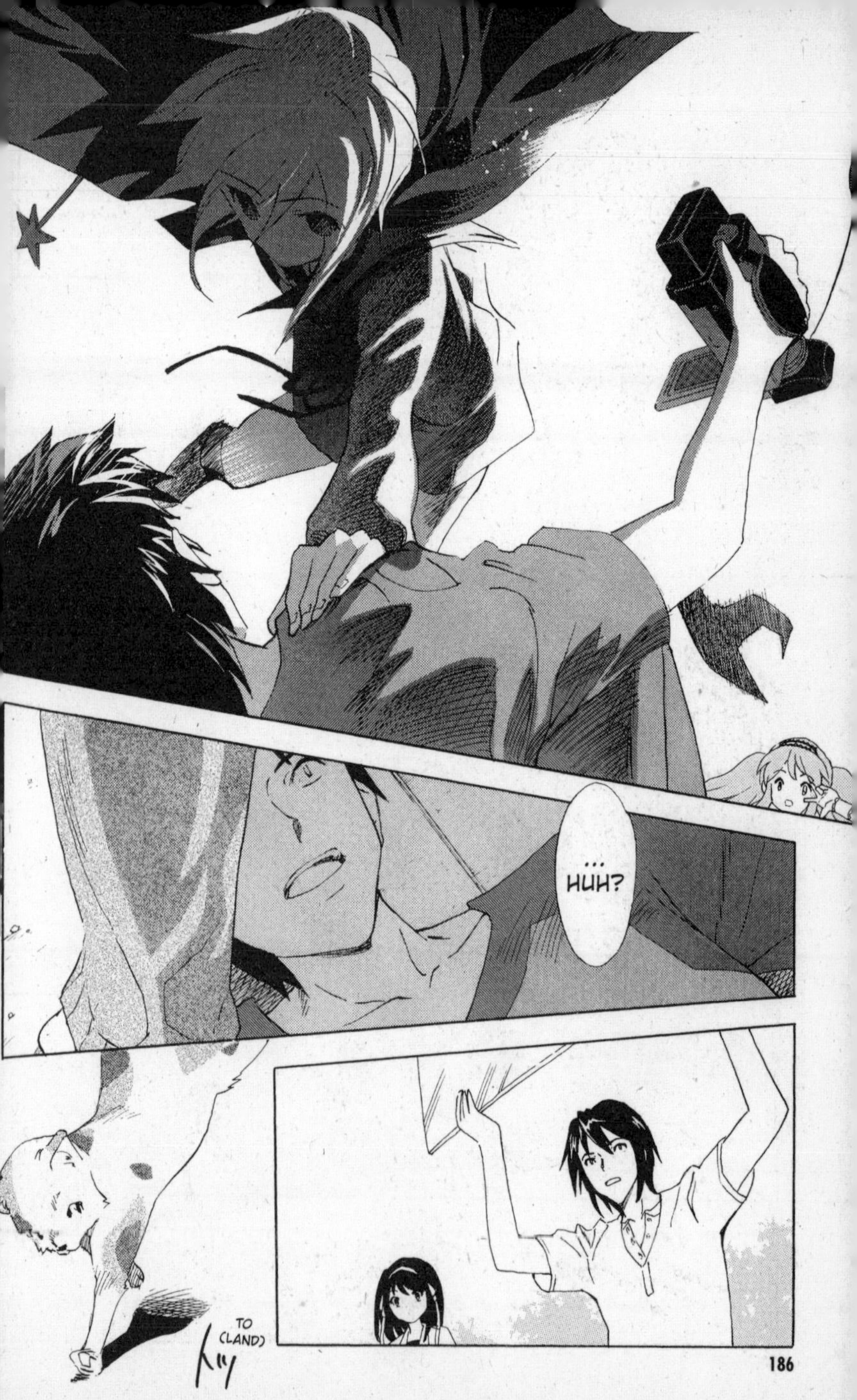

...
HUH?
TO (LAND)
トッ

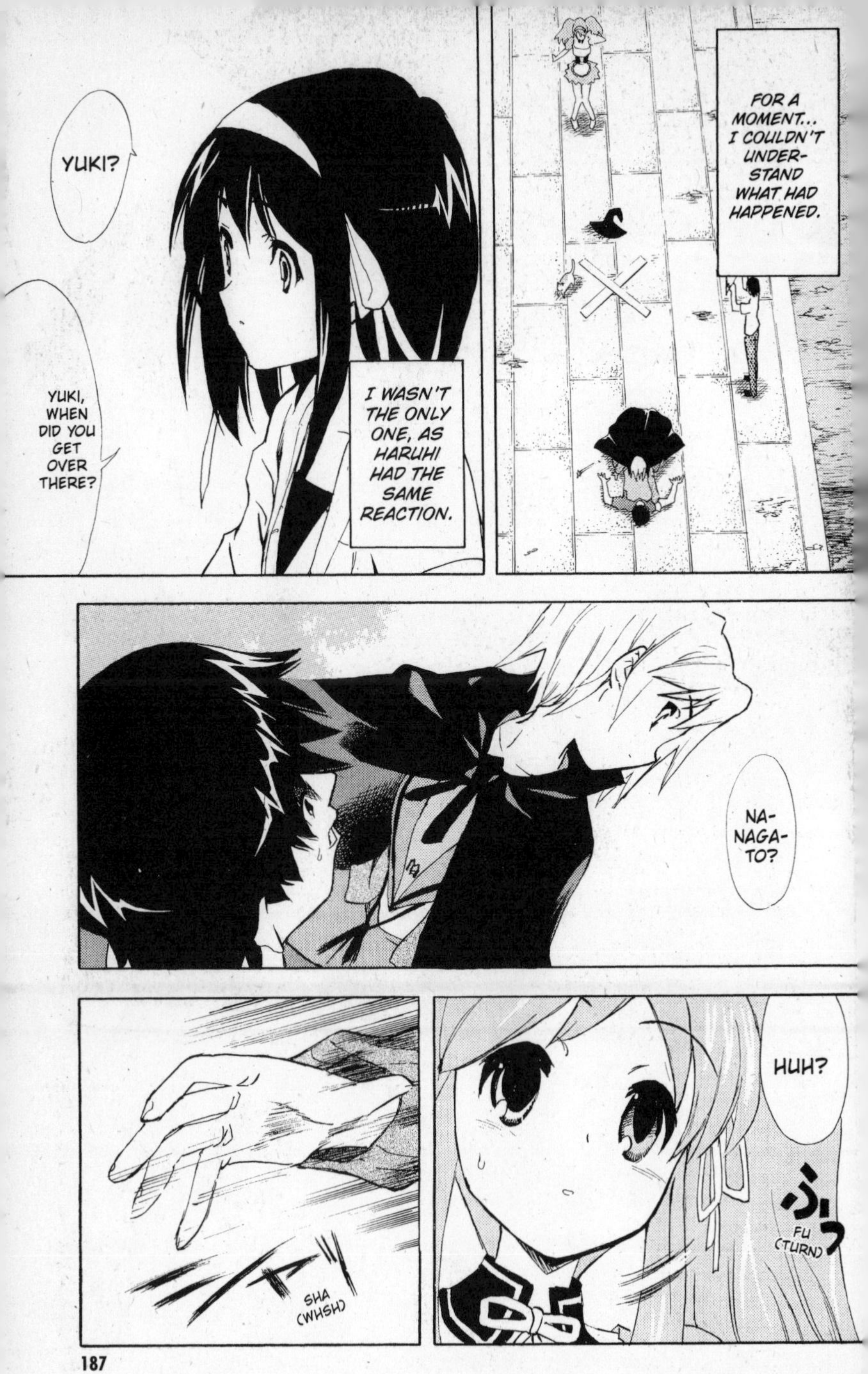
FOR A MOMENT... I COULDN'T UNDER-STAND WHAT HAD HAPPENED.
I WASN'T THE ONLY ONE, AS HARUHI HAD THE SAME REACTION.
YUKI?
YUKI, WHEN DID YOU GET OVER THERE?
NA-NAGATO?
HUH?
ふっ
FU (TURN)
SHA (WHSH)

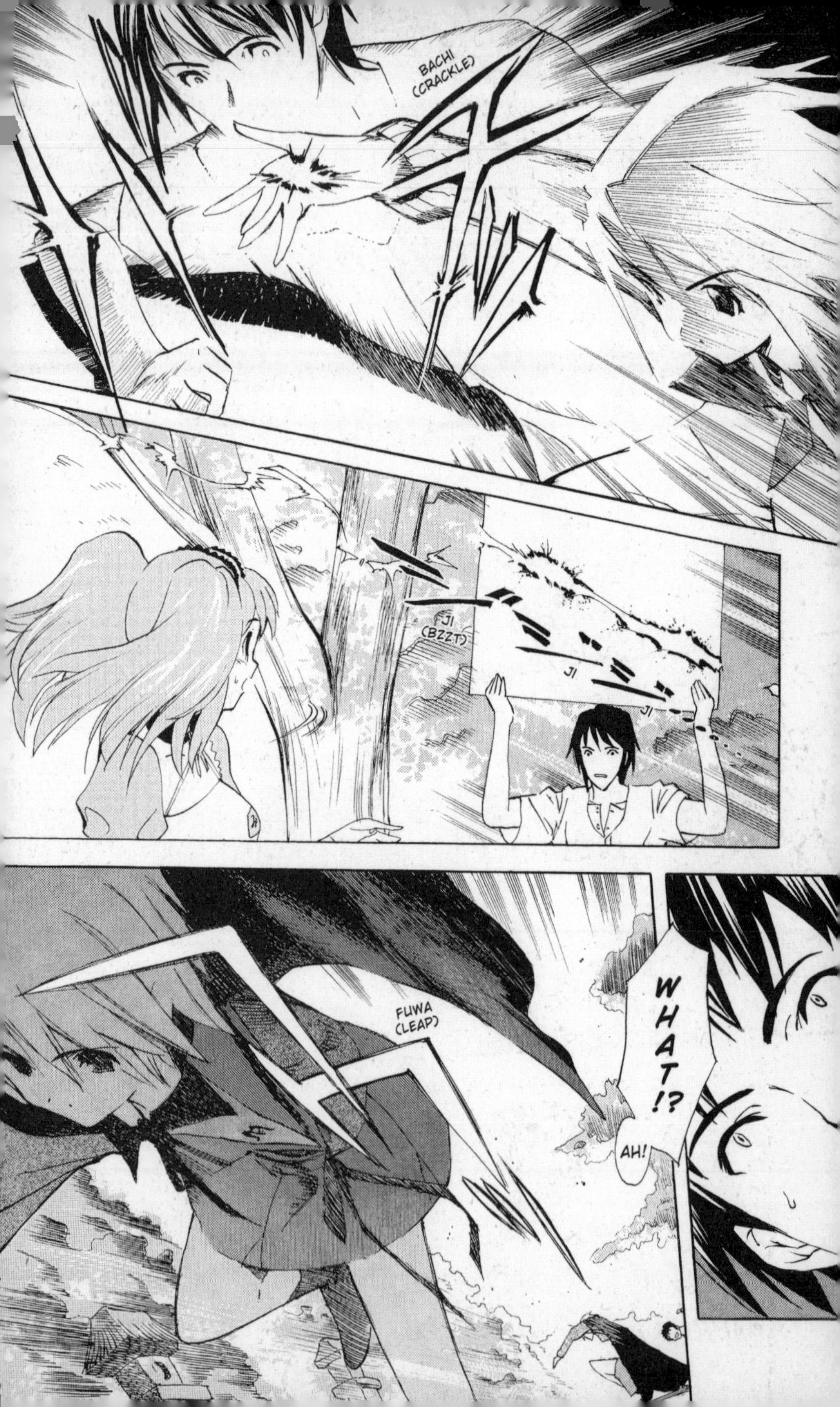
BACHI (CRACKLE)
JI (BZZT)
JI
JI
WHAT!?
AH!
FUWA (LEAP)

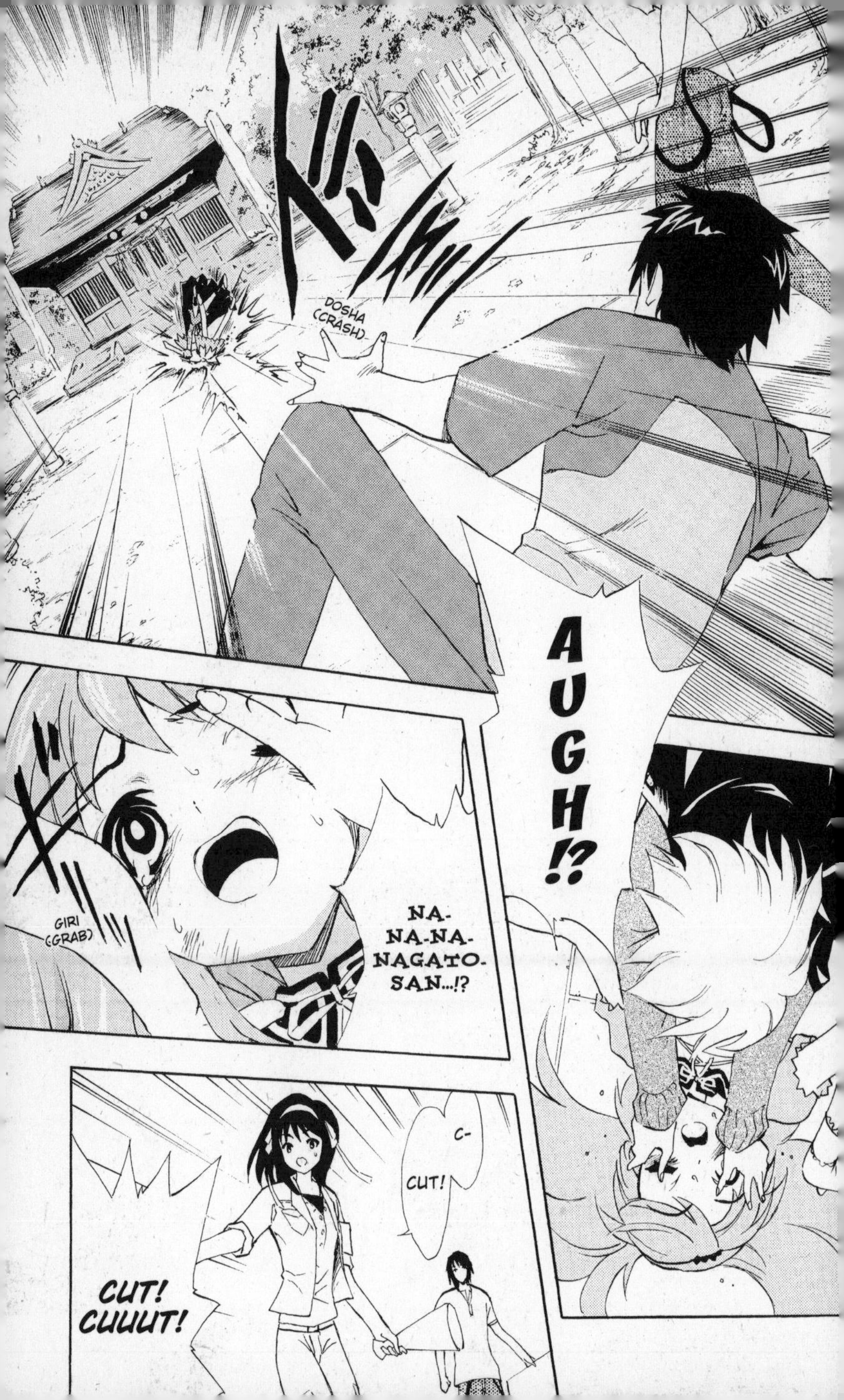
DOSHA (CRASH)
AUGH!?
NA-NA-NA-NAGATO-SAN...!?
GIRI (GRAB)
C-
CUT!
CUT! CUUUT!

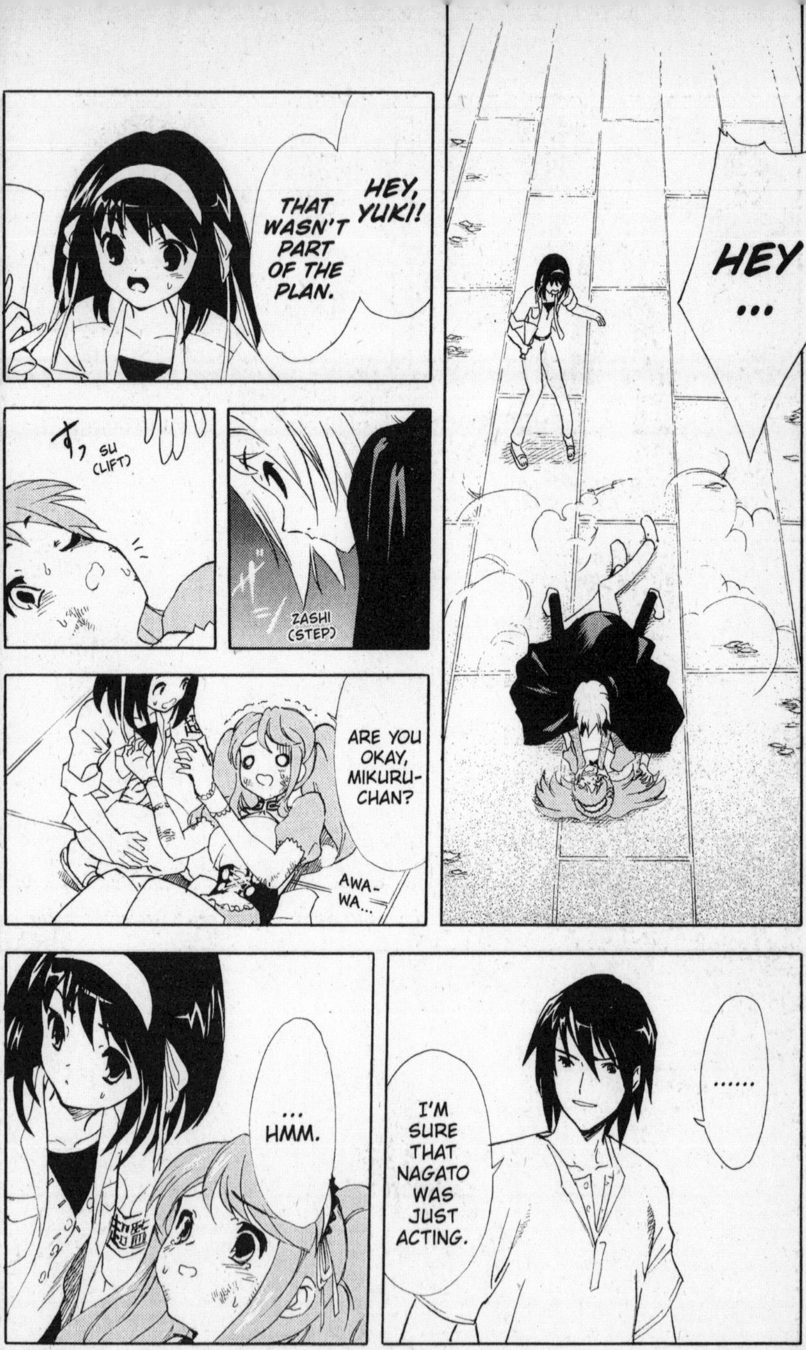
HEY ...
HEY, YUKI!
THAT WASN'T PART OF THE PLAN.
ZASHI (STEP)
すっ
SU (LIFT)
ARE YOU OKAY, MIKURU-CHAN?
AWAWA...
......
I'M SURE THAT NAGATO WAS JUST ACTING.
... HMM.

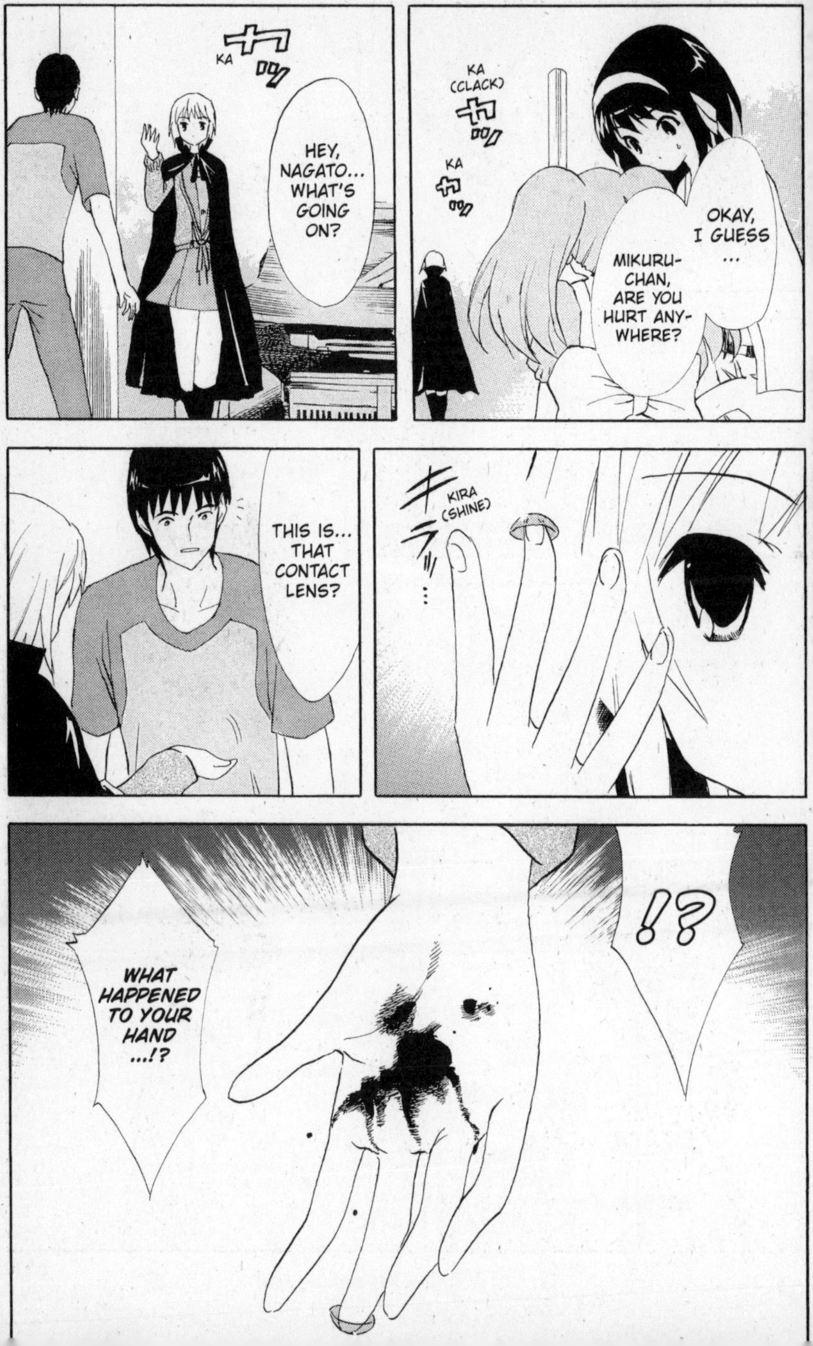
KA (CLACK)
KA
MIKURU-CHAN, ARE YOU HURT ANYWHERE?
OKAY, I GUESS ...
KA
HEY, NAGATO... WHAT'S GOING ON?
KIRA (SHINE)
...
THIS IS... THAT CONTACT LENS?
!?
WHAT HAPPENED TO YOUR HAND ...!?

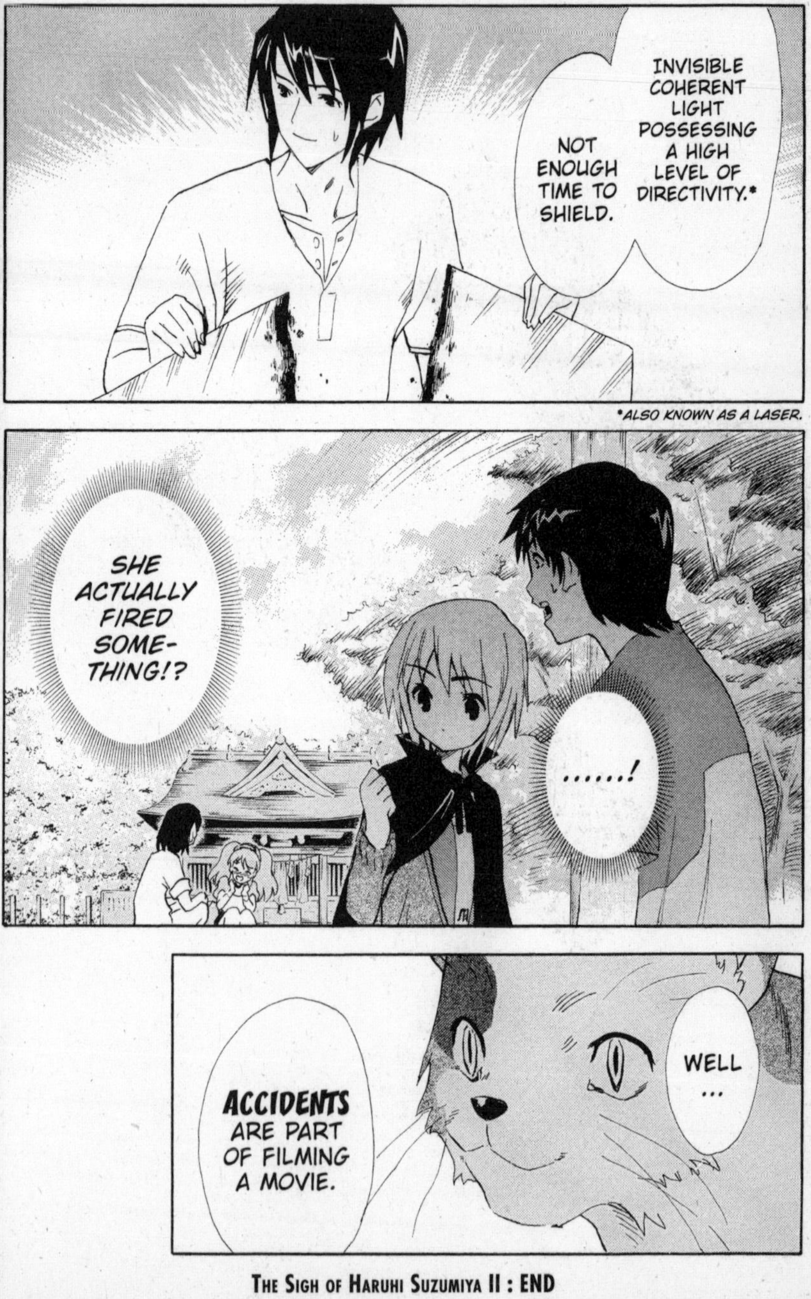
INVISIBLE COHERENT LIGHT POSSESSING A HIGH LEVEL OF DIRECTIVITY.*
NOT ENOUGH TIME TO SHIELD.
*ALSO KNOWN AS A LASER.
......!
SHE ACTUALLY FIRED SOME-THING!?
WELL ...
ACCIDENTS ARE PART OF FILMING A MOVIE.

THE SIGH OF HARUHI SUZUMIYA II : END

TO BE CONTINUED

The Melancholy of Haruhi Suzumiya
PREVIEW

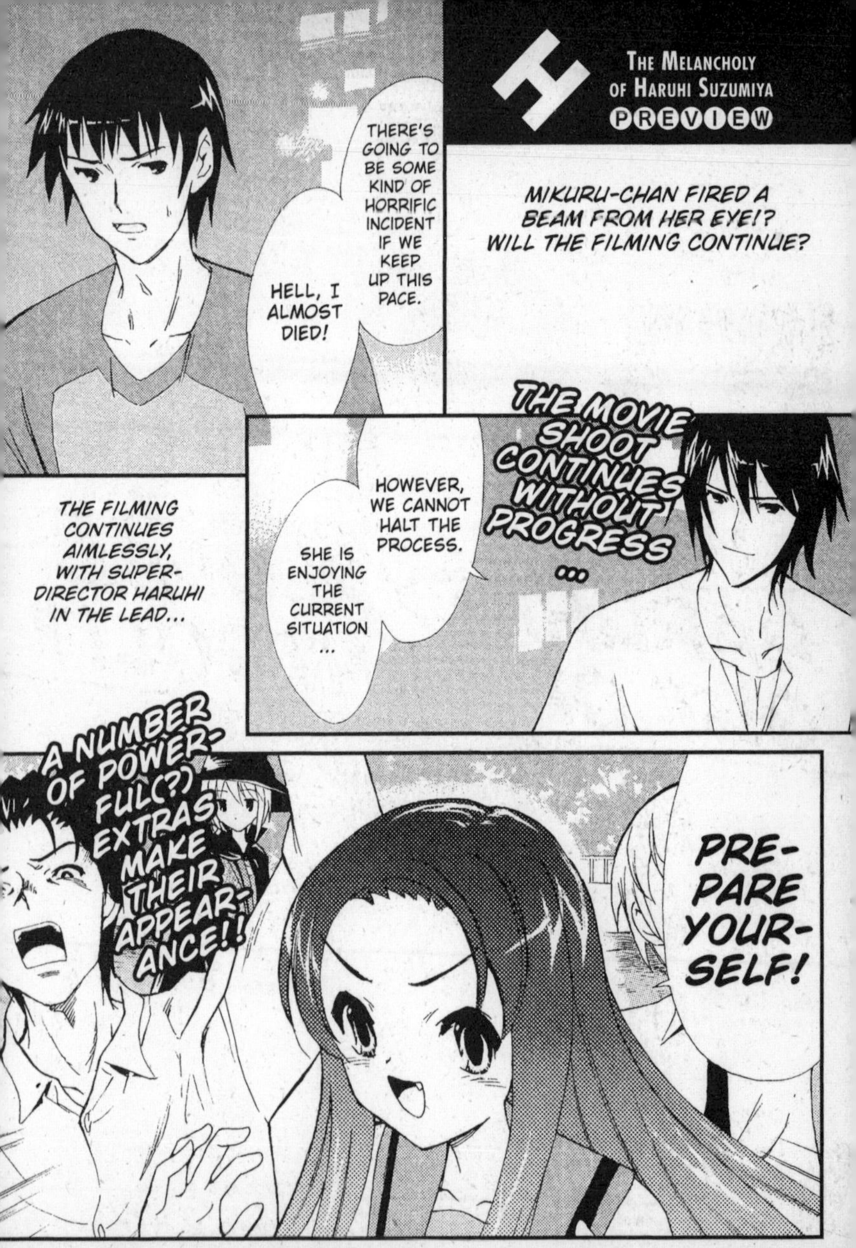
MIKURU-CHAN FIRED A BEAM FROM HER EYE!? WILL THE FILMING CONTINUE?
THERE'S GOING TO BE SOME KIND OF HORRIFIC INCIDENT IF WE KEEP UP THIS PACE.
HELL, I ALMOST DIED!
THE MOVIE SHOOT CONTINUES WITHOUT PROGRESS...
HOWEVER, WE CANNOT HALT THE PROCESS.
SHE IS ENJOYING THE CURRENT SITUATION...
THE FILMING CONTINUES AIMLESSLY, WITH SUPER-DIRECTOR HARUHI IN THE LEAD...
PRE-PARE YOUR-SELF!
A NUMBER OF POWER-FUL(?) EXTRAS MAKE THEIR APPEAR-ANCE!!

LOOK FORWARD TO THE GRAND CLIMAX OF THE BOREDOM ARC!!

VOLUME 6 ON SALE SOON!!

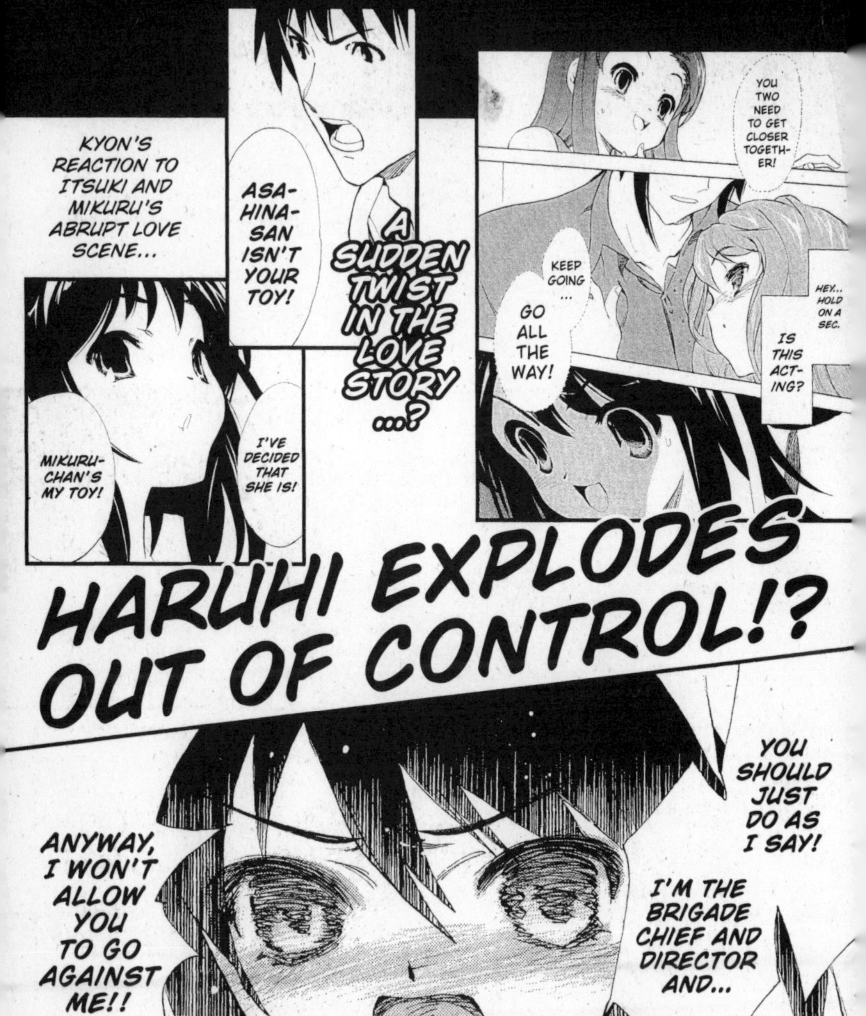
YOU TWO NEED TO GET CLOSER TOGETH-ER!
HEY... HOLD ON A SEC.
IS THIS ACT-ING?
KEEP GOING ...
GO ALL THE WAY!
ASA-HINA-SAN ISN'T YOUR TOY!
A SUDDEN TWIST IN THE LOVE STORY ...?
KYON'S REACTION TO ITSUKI AND MIKURU'S ABRUPT LOVE SCENE...
I'VE DECIDED THAT SHE IS!
MIKURU-CHAN'S MY TOY!
HARUHI EXPLODES OUT OF CONTROL!?
YOU SHOULD JUST DO AS I SAY!
I'M THE BRIGADE CHIEF AND DIRECTOR AND...
ANYWAY, I WON'T ALLOW YOU TO GO AGAINST ME!!
WILL THEY BE ABLE TO FINISH THE MOVIE...!!!?

THE MELANCHOLY OF HARUHI SUZUMIYA

THE MELANCHOLY OF HARUHI SUZUMIYA

Original Story: Nagaru Tanigawa
Manga: Gaku Tsugano
Character Design: Noizi Ito

Translation: Chris Pai for MX Media LLC
Lettering: Alexis Eckerman

SUZUMIYA HARUHI NO YUUTSU Volume 5 © Nagaru TANIGAWA • Noizi ITO
2007 © Gaku TSUGANO 2007. First published in Japan in 2007 by KADOKAWA
SHOTEN PUBLISHING CO., LTD., Tokyo. English translation rights arranged
with KADOKAWA SHOTEN PUBLISHING CO., LTD., Tokyo through TUTTLE-
MORI AGENCY, INC., Tokyo.

English translation © 2010 by Hachette Book Group, Inc.

Yen Press
Hachette Book Group
237 Park Avenue, New York, NY 10017

www.HachetteBookGroup.com
www.YenPress.com

Yen Press is an imprint of Hachette Book Group, Inc. The Yen Press name and
logo are trademarks of Hachette Book Group, Inc.

First Yen Press Edition: March 2010

ISBN: 978-0-316-08605-9

10 9 8 7 6 5 4 3 2 1

BVG

Printed in the United States of America